KANJI ICHI NI

ANDREW DYKSTRA
PROVOST
Kansai Gaidai Hawaii College

師

TEACHER, ARMY, EXPERT

KANJI PRESS

PACIFIC RIM CONNECTIONS

2

SHARK
(SPLIT REPRESENTATION)

SHARK
(SPLIT REPRESENTATION)

NORTHWEST COAST HAIDA INDIAN SPLIT REPRESENTATION OF A SHARK.
BULLETIN OF THE AMERICAN MUSEUM OF NATURAL HISTORY, VOL. IX, PP. 123-176.

背

THE BACK, BEHIND
(FACE THE EMPEROR)

燕

YEN STATE, PEKING

北

NORTH,

SHANG DYNASTY (1850-1100 B.C.) BRONZE VESSEL "MONSTER MASK".
NOTE HOW THE KANJI FOR NORTH IS SPLIT TO THE LEFT AND RIGHT.
RICHARD HUBER: TREASURY OF FANTASTIC AND MYTHOLOGICAL CREATURES: DOVER.

面

MASK,

龍

DRAGON, IMPERIAL
(SPLIT REPRESENTATION)

MAYAN TEMPLE SPLIT REPRESENTATION AT COPAN LIKE SHANG & HAIDA
R.A. FASQUELLE, W.L. FASH, JR.; PHOTOGRAPHS BY KENNETH GARRETT.
MAYAN ARTISTRY UNEARTHED. COURTESY OF THE NATIONAL GEOGRAPHIC SOCIETY. (9/91).

KANJI PRESS
2440 KUHIO AV. SUITE 1512
HONOLULU, HAWAII 96815

ISBN: 0-917880-02-1

CIRCUMPOLAR BRONZE MIRROR (HAN DYNASTY)

THE WHEEL OF THE LAW

TABLE OF CONTENTS

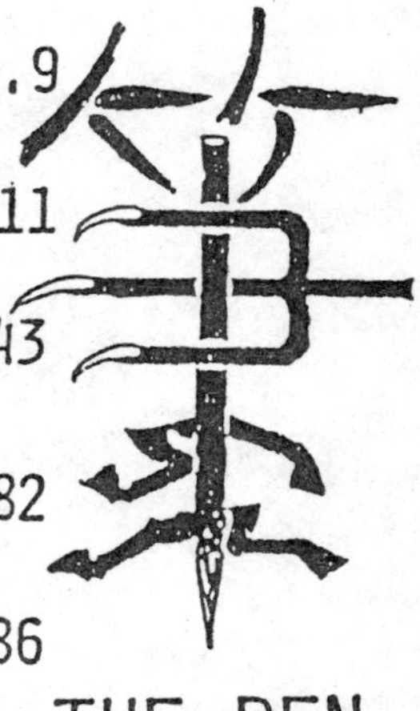

THE PEN 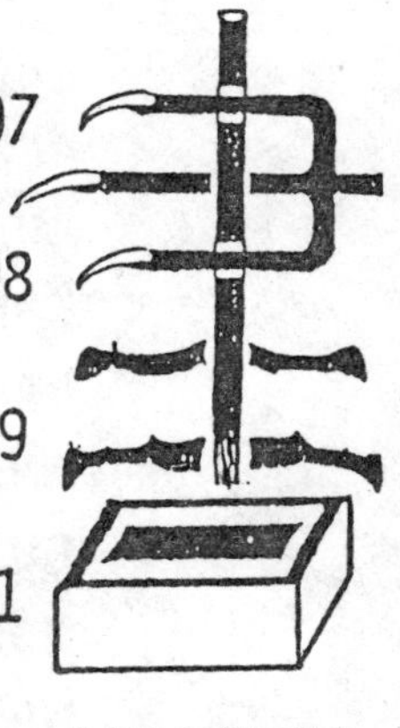 WRITES

***

NOTES: JME OR J IS THE ABBREVIATION FOR THE JAPANESE MINISTRY OF EDUCATION WHICH HAS ASSIGNED NUMBERS TO THE BASIC KANJI. R IS FOR RADICALS. SEE PP. 882-5.

KATAKANA ARE THE SYLLABARY SYMBOLS USED IN JAPANESE WRITING FOR FOREIGN NAMES AND WORDS.

HIRAGANA ARE THE SYLLABARY SYMBOLS USED IN JAPANESE WRITING AS CONVENIENT SUBSTITUTES FOR KANJI AS IN VERB ENDINGS AND POSTPOSITIONS.

INTRODUCTION

The KANJI are the written language of China and Japan also adopted more than a thousand years ago by Korea and Vietnam. KANJI are necessary to understand Chinese and Japanese thinking and culture. In many ways, the Japanese and Chinese people think in written KANJI as well as by sounds and concepts. Thus the Orient has a wealth of symbols and symbolism particularly its own that the alphabet-using countries lack.

Of course the alphabet is easier for reading and for writing, but literacy in KANJI has a far higher standard. The ability to visualize thousands of KANJI is to have a reservoir of mentally pictured symbols for objects, for actions, for ideas, and for combinations. An Oriental student of Chemistry simply adds the formulas for organic compounds to a multitude of learned KANJI compounds. KANJI archetypes flood the conscious and subconscious mind, providing awareness and subliminal perception. In poetry, the KANJI furbish the imagination and condition the similes and metaphors. To write the KANJI demanded artistic skill with the brush. The beauty, balance, and structure of the KANJI enrich architecture and provide an Esthetics that is not passively visual, but is frozen motion instantly unleashed by the empathetic muscles of the hand and the entire body. The KANJI on wall scrolls have the authority of canons of law.

The KANJI have Beauty's bared bones as strokes and their white spaces represent flesh in an analogy to the human body and to Physiology and to Anatomy. The use of the Chinese literati to govern the nation and of the KANJI to discipline and train the literati produced a "Rule of the KANJI" much like the "Rule of the Dead" related to worship of or reverence for ancestral spirits. This combination of Confucian principles and immersion in KANJI

WAS INTEGRAL IN FEUDAL JAPAN AND UNDER IMPERIAL GUIDANCE.

THAT WRITING IS MAGICAL IS A BELIEF IN MANY CULTURES. KANJI ARE REVERED AS SACRED. IN DYNASTIC CHINA, WASTE PAPER WITH KANJI WAS BURNED TO AVOID SACRILEGE. TAOIST MAGICIANS AND STREETSIDE FORTUNE TELLERS UTILIZED KANJI. WRITING THE CHINESE EMPEROR'S NAME IN FULL WAS TABOO.

THE VITALITY AND LIFE-FORCE OF THE KANJI INFUSE THEM WITH A POWER WHICH IS READILY TRANSMITTED. THE ORAL LEARNING IN THE CHINESE TRADITIONAL SCHOOLS REQUIRED EACH STUDENT TO MEMORIZE AND TO READ ALOUD AT HIS OWN PACE SO THAT A CACOPHONY OF SOUND ENTERED HIS EARS AS HE STUDIED. HE HEARD THE SAME LESSON INNUMERABLE TIMES. THIS IS RELATED TO MODERN AURAL-ORAL PEDAGOGY AND TO THE TALENT DEVELOPED IN THE ONE-ROOM SCHOOLHOUSE.

WHILE KANJI ARE STANDARDIZED IN A VARIETY OF STYLES, THEIR FORM AND FLOW ARE INDIVIDUALIZED BY THE WRITER IN A CREATIVITY THAT IS CONTROLLED BUT NOT CONSTRICTED. THESE SUPERIOR WRITTEN QUALITIES OF THE KANJI HAVE REDUCED THE SIGNIFICANCE OF SPEECH AND SPEECHES IN CHINESE HISTORY. NOT ORATORY BUT DOCUMENTARY RECORDS, ESSAYS, AND MEMORIALS TO THE THRONE ARE REMEMBERED. IN ARCHAEOLOGY, CONTEMPORARY CHINESE KANJI HAVE RECOGNIZABLE PREDECESSORS SCRATCHED ON DEER SHOULDER-BONES AND TORTOISE UNDER-SHELLS USED IN DIVINATION DURING THE SHANG DYNASTY (1766-1122 B.C.).

IN CONTRAST TO THE PICTORIAL WRITING OF GREAT NEAR EASTERN AND CENTRAL AMERICAN CIVILIZATIONS, THE CHINESE AND THE JAPANESE KANJI HAVE PERSISTED AND PERPETUATED THEMSELVES IN OUR MODERN WORLD. WITH THE ADVENT OF ELECTRONIC COMPUTERS, WORD PROCESSING, AND AUTOMATIC TRANSLATION DEVICES, THEY SEEM TO BE AN ETERNAL PART OF THE ORIENT. A FINAL ADVANTAGE OF THE KANJI IS THEIR POTENTIAL UNIVERSALITY. THESE WRITTEN SYMBOLS, DERIVED FROM THE SHANG AND STANDARDIZED IN THE

CH'IN DYNASTY (221-206 B.C.), CAN BE APPLIED SUCCESSFULLY TO ANY LANGUAGE JUST AS THEY HAVE BEEN TO VIETNAMESE, TO KOREAN, AND TO JAPANESE. THE GREATNESS AND GRANDEUR OF A KANJI-UNITED CHINESE EMPIRE CAN BE MEASURED BY THE CULTURAL ACCEPTANCE OF HER WRITTEN KANJI. WITHIN THAT EMPIRE, THE KANJI MAINTAINED A SOVEREIGNTY OVER PROVINCES WITH MUTUALLY UNINTELLIGIBLE DIALECTS, AND HELD A PLACE LIKE THAT OF LATIN IN FRAGMENTED MEDIEVAL CHRISTENDOM. EVEN TODAY, THE STRONGEST FORCE FOR CULTURAL AND RACIAL IDENTITY BETWEEN MOTHERLAND AND OVERSEAS CHINESE, BETWEEN TAIWAN AND MAINLAND CHINESE, AND EVEN BETWEEN THE DISSIMILAR CHINESE AND JAPANESE IS THE EVERYWHERE PRESENT AND THE UBIQUITOUS KANJI.

上

TO GO UP, TO RAISE, TO RISE, TOP, ON, ABOVE

KANJI ICHI NI

OUR TITLE, KANJI ICHI NI, IS FROM THE MARCHING CADENCE OF TROOPS IN JAPANESE, ICHI, NI, SAN, SHI. IT IS FOR YOUR PROGRESS AND RELATES TO THE COVER WITH FOUR CONVENTIONALIZED KANJI OF SOLDIERS WHO ARE PARADING TOWARDS THE CORNER KANJI SOLDIER. IN CHINESE, THE CADENCE IS I, ERH, SAN, SHIH ON TAIWAN OR YI, ER, SAN, SI IN THE PEOPLES' REPUBLIC, ACCORDING TO THE WADE-GILES OR PIN YIN ROMANIZATION. NOTE THE SIMILARITY BETWEEN THE CHINESE AND JAPANESE. 兵

SOLDIER

FOOT-IN-MOTION

是

RIGHT, JUST, NOW

KANJI ITCHY KNEE. BY NOW EVEN OUR GENTLEST READER, ALTHOUGH UNAWARE OF THE VIKING PETRO- OR PETER-GLYPHS AND THE EGYPTIAN FERTILITY GOD MIN, MUST HAVE OBSERVED THAT THE TITLED ITCHY KNEE IS THE PHALLIC PATELLA OR THE PATELLAR PHALLUS WHICH IS ON THE COVER OF THE KANJI ABC. NOTE SHAKESPEAR'S COMMENT IN ROMEO AND JULIET THAT "THE BAWDY HAND OF THE SUN-DIAL IS NOW UPON THE PRICK OF NOON." THIS RELATES PUNNINGLY TO ALL ITCHY KNEES, BUT ESPECIALLY TO JME 822 是 RIGHT, JUST, FROM NOW, (SUN-DIAL), AND JME 845 提 TO CARRY IN ONE'S HAND.

MIN

足 FOOT, LEG

VIKING PETRO-GLYPH

正 CORRECT, RIGHT

FERTILITY GOD MIN OF EGYPT

GUIDE TO USE OF THE KANJI ICHI NI

Japan's Ministry of Education has helped all students of kanji by assigning kanji numbers in the order of their importance. In general, these kanji are also important in learning Chinese, and have much the same meaning in both languages.

Above each large kanji in the main body of this book are the JME number, the number of strokes to write the kanji, and the radical number for finding the kanji in dictionaries. The little numbers by the strokes of the large kanji tell the order and direction of the strokes in writing. The number is at the beginning of the stroke. In general, one begins writing from the upper left and the strokes are drawn down and or to the right.

The Japanese words or sounds in large letters are of Chinese origin, but from various parts of China at various times. The Japanese words in small letters are of native Japanese origin. They are each followed by English meanings. The parentheses mean that the kanji are only used in compounds.

In the margins of the pages are the N numbers from Nelson's Japanese-English Character Dictionary, the Wade-Giles Chinese romanization with tone number, the M numbers from Mathews' Chinese-English Dictionary, the PRC (Peoples' Republic of China) romanization with an accent for the tone (the same tone as the Wade-Giles but indicated differently), and the English meanings for the Chinese.

In the appendix are the 214 radicals with meanings. The radical is the part of the kanji used to find the kanji in a kanji dictionary. Next is a list of kanji by the total number of strokes in each. An alphabetical list of Japanese vocabulary words follows. After this is a list

OF KATAKANA AND HIRAGANA SOMETIMES USED IN PLACE OF KANJI.

WITH EACH JME KANJI ARE USUALLY ILLUSTRATIONS OF THE PARTS THAT ARE COMBINED FOR THE COMPOSITE. THE DRAWINGS AND MEANINGS FOR THE PARTS USUALLY EXPLAIN THE JME KANJI AS AN ENTITY.

GENERALLY, YOU WILL HAVE LEARNED THE RELATED PARTS PREVIOUSLY. IF NOT, THEY CAN BE REVIEWED AS NECESSARY. GRADUALLY, ALL THE MEANINGS AND PARTS WILL MAKE SENSE TO YOU AND YOU WILL SUBCONSCIOUSLY BECOME AWARE OF THEIR SIGNIFICANCE.

INCLUDED IN UNOBTRUSIVE SMALL PRINT ARE QUOTATIONS, SOMETIMES CONNECTED WITH CHINA OR JAPAN BUT OFTEN WIDELY INTERNATIONAL IN SCOPE AND RELEVANCE. THEY ARE FOR YOUR ENJOYMENT AS WELL AS TO FACILITATE LEARNING.

PARTICULARLY FOR THOSE WHO HAVE BEEN LARGELY RESTRICTED TO THE LANGUAGES WITH ALPHABETS, THE WORLD OF THE KANJI CAN BECOME MOST EXCITING. AN UNEQUALLED INSIGHT CAN BE GOTTEN INTO THE THINKING PROCESSES OF THE JAPANESE AND CHINESE, THEIR CAPACITY FOR MEMORIZATION, ASSOCIATION, FLEXIBILITY, AND VISUALIZATION.

FOR RAPPORT WITH JAPANESE AND CHINESE, THE KANJI ARE INVALUABLE. BEGINNING WITH THE FORMALLY EXCHANGED NAME CARDS OR MEISHI, YOU WILL FIND THAT ANY ACCOMPLISHMENTS ON YOUR PART ARE RECOGNIZED AND MEET APPROVAL. EVEN A LIMITED KNOWLEDGE OF KANJI PROVIDES A COMMON BOND AND A SHARED BACKGROUND.

DO NOT BECOME DISCOURAGED AS YOU ACCUMULATE FAMILIAR KANJI. ALWAYS REMEMBER THAT YOU HAVE A GREAT HANDICAP IF YOU HAVE BEGUN TO STUDY KANJI LATER IN LIFE. REALIZE THAT ANY PROGRESS IS FOR YOU A GREAT ACHIEVEMENT. KEEP AT IT!!

I, (EASINESS); EKI, DIVINATION.

RAD 72 STROKE 8 JME 545

EASINESS, DIVINATION 易 IS A PICTOGRAPH OF THE CHAMELEON WHO EASILY 易 CHANGES COLOR. THESE COLOR CHANGES WERE USED IN DIVINATION 易

As the bright salamander in fire of the noonshine
  exults and is glad of his day,
The spirit that quickens my body rejoices to pass
  from the sunshine away.

Swinburne

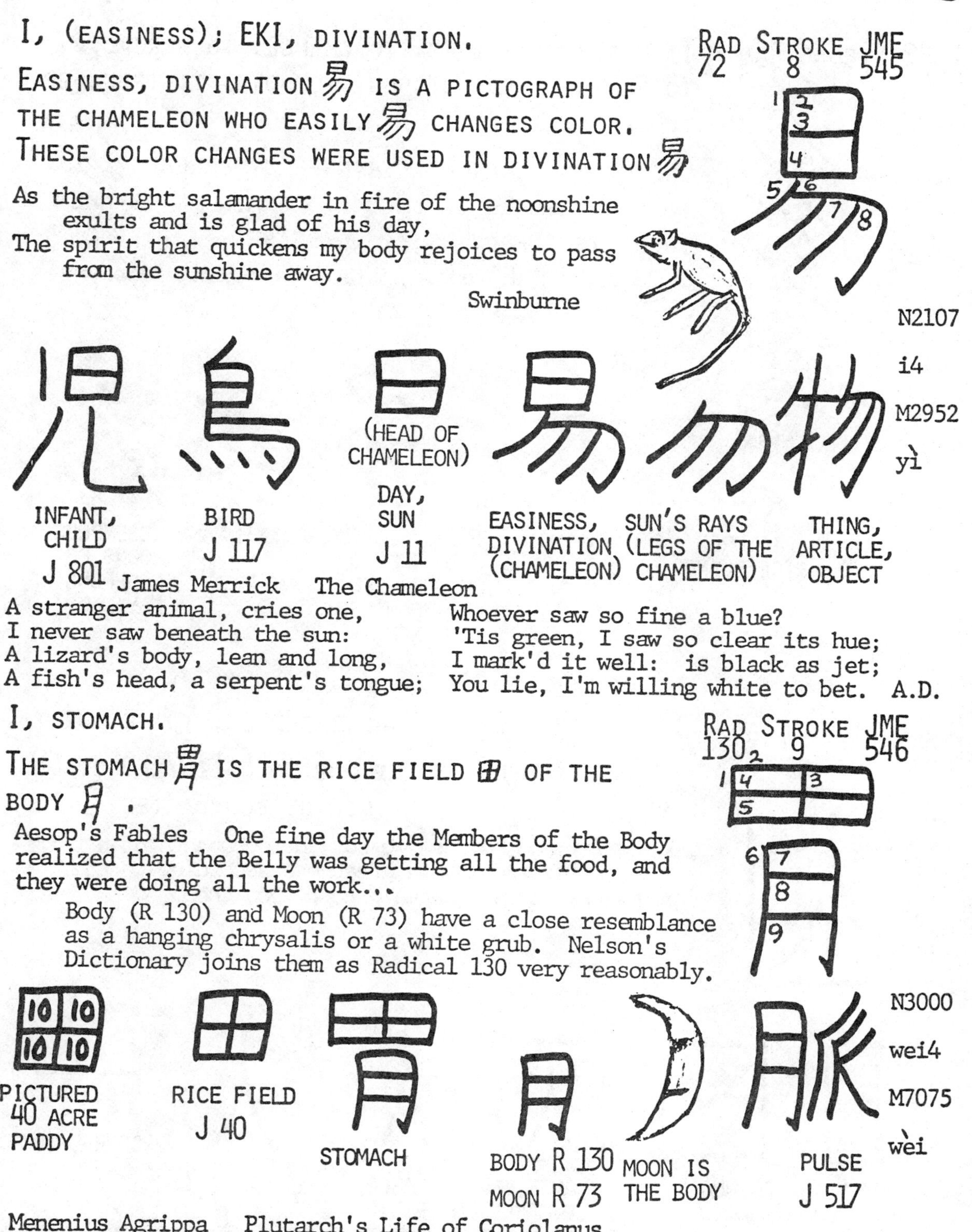

N2107 i4 M2952 yì

児 INFANT, CHILD J 801 — 鳥 BIRD J 117 — 日 (HEAD OF CHAMELEON) DAY, SUN J 11 — 易 EASINESS, DIVINATION (CHAMELEON) — 勿 SUN'S RAYS (LEGS OF THE CHAMELEON) — 物 THING, ARTICLE, OBJECT

James Merrick The Chameleon

A stranger animal, cries one,
I never saw beneath the sun:
A lizard's body, lean and long,
A fish's head, a serpent's tongue;
Whoever saw so fine a blue?
'Tis green, I saw so clear its hue;
I mark'd it well: is black as jet;
You lie, I'm willing white to bet. A.D.

I, STOMACH.

RAD 130 STROKE 9 JME 546

THE STOMACH 胃 IS THE RICE FIELD 田 OF THE BODY 月.

Aesop's Fables One fine day the Members of the Body realized that the Belly was getting all the food, and they were doing all the work...

Body (R 130) and Moon (R 73) have a close resemblance as a hanging chrysalis or a white grub. Nelson's Dictionary joins them as Radical 130 very reasonably.

N3000 wei4 M7075 wèi

PICTURED 40 ACRE PADDY — 田 RICE FIELD J 40 — 胃 STOMACH — 月 BODY R 130 MOON R 73 — MOON IS THE BODY — 脈 PULSE J 517

Menenius Agrippa Plutarch's Life of Coriolanus
...the stomach certainly does receive the general nourishment, but only to restore it again, and redistribute it among the rest.

JME 547 · STROKE 11 · RAD 115

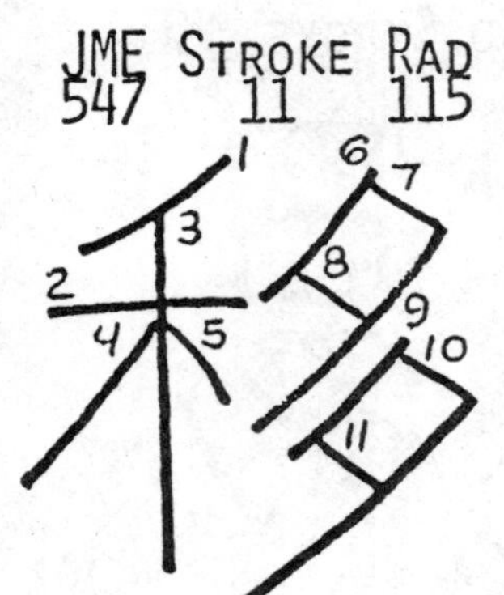

I; UTSURU, TO MOVE, TO CHANGE, TO SPREAD, TO BE INFECTED; UTSUSU, TO MOVE, TO TRANSFER, TO INFECT.

ONE MOVES, CHANGES, TRANSFERS, SPREADS 移 TO (THE LOCALE OF) MUCH 多 GRAIN 禾 AS WHEN THERE IS INFECTION 移 (DISEASE).

And Jacob said, Behold, I have heard that there is corn in Egypt: get you down thither... Genesis

N3282
i2
M2980
yí
move
shift
convey

PICTURED RICE PLANT

RICE, GRAIN
R 115

TO MOVE, CHANGE, TO SPREAD, BE INFECTED, TO TRANSFER, INFECT

MUCH, MANY
J 108

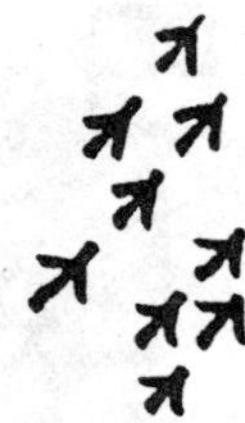
RESEMBLES MOONS OR ECHELONS OF FLYING BIRDS

JME 548 · STROKE 6 · RAD 31

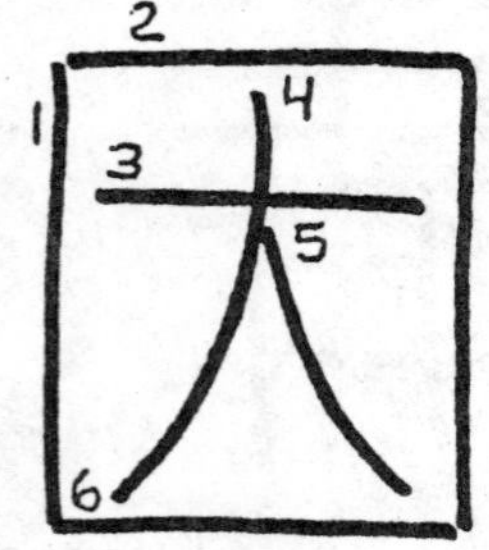

IN, CAUSE; YORU, TO BE BASED ON, TO BE DUE TO.

TO BE BASED ON, TO BE DUE TO 因 IS CAUSED 因 BY GREATNESS 大 CONFINED BY BOUNDARIES 囗 .

As Huxley and Toynbee noted, the occupants of a territory will respond with greatness according to the pressures or challenges placed upon them.

N1026
yin 1
M7407
yīn
because
reason
cause
then

国
COUNTRY
J 79
(JADE SEAL ENCLOSED BY BOUNDARIES)

BOUNDARY, BOX
R 31

因
CAUSE, TO BE BASED ON, TO BE DUE TO
(GREATNESS CONFINED BY BOUNDARIES)

大
LARGE, BIG, GREAT
J 22
(PERSON'S ARMS ARE SPREAD)

PERSON, MAN
J 30
(PERSON IS A FEATHERLESS BIPED)

一
ONE J 1
(SPREAD ARMS)

EI, PROSPERITY, SPLENDOR, HONOR, GLORY.
SAKAERU, TO PROSPER, TO FLOURISH.

RAD 75 STROKE 9 JME 549

A TREE 木 WITH ITS CROWN 冖 AND ADDED GROWTH ツ PROSPERS, FLOURISHES 栄 IN PROSPERITY, HONOR, SPLENDOR, GLORY 栄 (LIKE A PERSON).

And he shall be like a tree...and whatsoever he doeth shall prosper. Psalms

The righteous shall flourish like the palm tree; he shall grow like a cedar in Lebanon. Psalms

栄

N2239
jung2
M7582
róng
glory
splendor
honor
prosperity

学 LEARNING, SCIENCE, TO LEARN J 57

労 LABOR, SERVICE, TROUBLE J 542

栄 PROSPERITY, SPLENDOR, HONOR, GLORY, TO PROSPER, TO FLOURISH

木 TREE J 15

冖 CROWN

EMP. CH'ENG T'ANG

ツ (ADDED GROWTH)

Those that are planted in the house of the Lord shall flourish in the courts of our God. They shall bring forth fruit in old age; Psalms

EI, LONG, LENGTHY, ETERNAL, PERPETUAL.

RAD 3 STROKE 5 JME 550

EXTENDED IN TIME AND SPACE 丶
LIKE DIRECTIONAL POLARIS 亠
THE ARCTIC ICE 氷
IS LONG, LENGTHY, ETERNAL, PERPETUAL 永

永

Childe Harold's Pilgrimage Lord Byron
Dark-heaving...boundless, endless, and sublime...
The image of eternity
And I have loved thee, Ocean! and my joy

N130
yung3
M7589
yǒng
perpetual
eternal
long

(PICTURED STREAM EDDIES)

水 WATER J 14

氷 ICE J 498

永 LONG, LENGTHY, ETERNAL, PERPETUAL

丶 DOT R 4

亠 DIRECTION R 8

EXTENSION IN TIME & SPACE

Of youthful sports was on thy breast to be
Borne, like thy bubbles, onward: from a boy
I wanton'd with thy breakers,...

泳 TO SWIM J 352

551

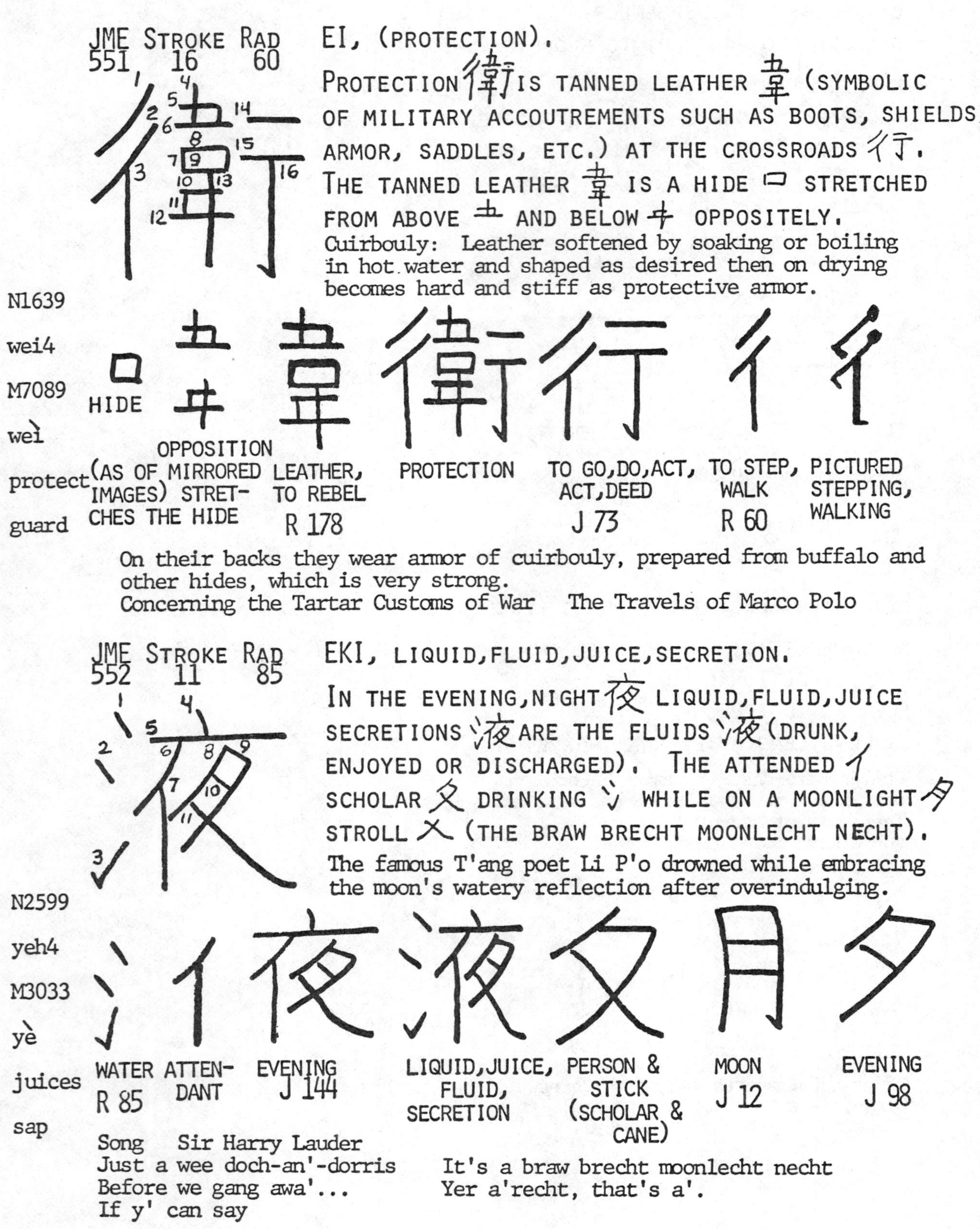

JME 551, STROKE 16, RAD 60

EI, (PROTECTION).

PROTECTION 衛 IS TANNED LEATHER 韋 (SYMBOLIC OF MILITARY ACCOUTREMENTS SUCH AS BOOTS, SHIELDS, ARMOR, SADDLES, ETC.) AT THE CROSSROADS 行. THE TANNED LEATHER 韋 IS A HIDE 口 STRETCHED FROM ABOVE 五 AND BELOW 㐄 OPPOSITELY.

Cuirbouly: Leather softened by soaking or boiling in hot water and shaped as desired then on drying becomes hard and stiff as protective armor.

N1639

wei4

M7089

weì

protect

guard

口 HIDE

五 㐄 OPPOSITION (AS OF MIRRORED IMAGES) STRETCHES THE HIDE

韋 LEATHER, TO REBEL R 178

衛 PROTECTION

行 TO GO, DO, ACT, ACT, DEED J 73

彳 TO STEP, WALK R 60

彳 PICTURED STEPPING, WALKING

On their backs they wear armor of cuirbouly, prepared from buffalo and other hides, which is very strong.
Concerning the Tartar Customs of War   The Travels of Marco Polo

JME 552, STROKE 11, RAD 85

EKI, LIQUID, FLUID, JUICE, SECRETION.

IN THE EVENING, NIGHT 夜 LIQUID, FLUID, JUICE SECRETIONS 液 ARE THE FLUIDS 液 (DRUNK, ENJOYED OR DISCHARGED). THE ATTENDED 亻 SCHOLAR 夂 DRINKING 氵 WHILE ON A MOONLIGHT 月 STROLL 夂 (THE BRAW BRECHT MOONLECHT NECHT).

The famous T'ang poet Li P'o drowned while embracing the moon's watery reflection after overindulging.

N2599

yeh4

M3033

yè

juices

sap

氵 WATER R 85

亻 ATTENDANT

夜 EVENING J 144

液 LIQUID, JUICE, FLUID, SECRETION

夂 PERSON & STICK (SCHOLAR & CANE)

月 MOON J 12

夕 EVENING J 98

Song   Sir Harry Lauder
Just a wee doch-an'-dorris
Before we gang awa'...
If y' can say
It's a braw brecht moonlecht necht
Yer a'recht, that's a'.

I am weary with my groaning (rutting sounds), all the night make I my bed to swim; I water my couch with my tears (fluids).   Psalms

EN; ENZURU, TO PERFORM, TO ACT, TO ENACT, TO STAGE, TO PUT ON.

RAD 85 STROKE 14 JME 553

演

TO PERFORM, TO ACT, TO ENACT, TO STAGE, TO PUT ON 演 (IS THE COMIC SCENE OF) THE ZODIAC TIGER 寅 AND WATER 氵 (WHICH CATS GENERALLY DISLIKE ALTHO THE MANCHURIAN AND FUKIENNESE TIGERS CAN SWIM IF NECESSARY).

Greenes, groats-worth of witte... Robert Greene
with his Tygers heart wrapt in a Players hide (ref. to Shakespear)

N2685
yen3
M7403
yǎn
extended
wide
practice
to drill

PICTURED TIGER BY WATER — DROPS — 氵 WATER — 演 TO PERFORM, ACT, ENACT, TO STAGE, TO PUT ON — 寅 ZODIAC TIGER — 宀 ROOF (OF DEN) R 40 — 黄 YELLOW J 214

There was a young lady of Niger
Who went for a ride on a tiger;
They came back from the ride
With the lady inside
And a smile on the face of the tiger.

Ō, (MIDDLE).

RAD 1 STROKE 5 JME 554

央

A PERSON 人 IN A GREAT 大 SPACE 冂.

Also Sprach Zarathustra Friedrich Nietzsche
In the meantime the tightrope walker began his act. He had stepped from a little door and walked on the rope stretched between two towers and over the marketplace. When he was exactly in the middle of his walk...

N86
yang 1
M7239
yāng
center
finish
conclude

一 ONE J 1 (LEVEL BALANCING STICK) — 人 PERSON, MAN, MANKIND R 9 — 央 MIDDLE — 冂 SPACE — 英 ENGLAND, EXCELLENT J 353 (GRASS, NOMAD'S NECESSITY AND A MIDDLE LOCATION) — 中 MIDDLE, INSIDE J 23

555

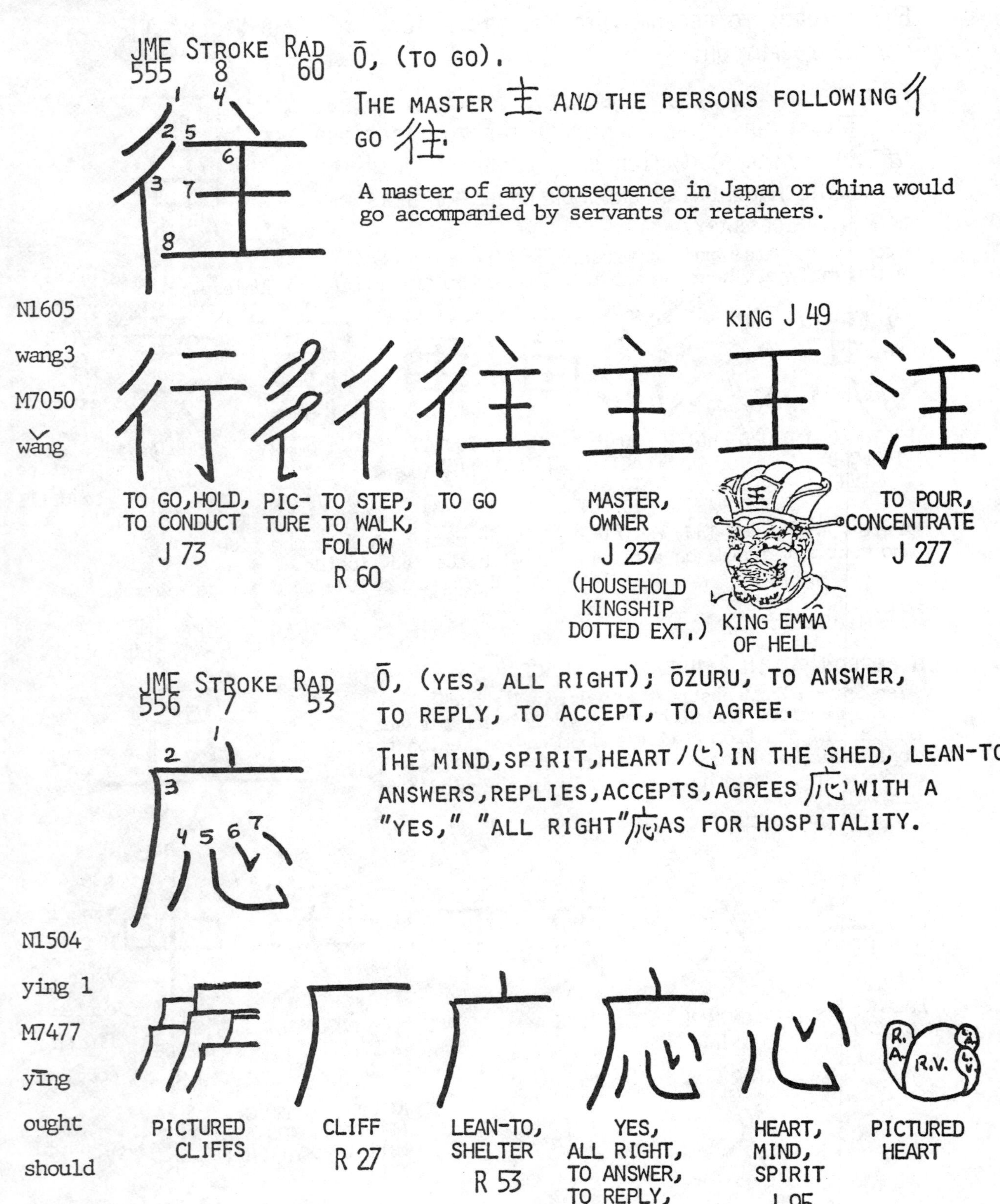

N1605

wang3

M7050

wǎng

N1504

ying 1

M7477

yīng

ought

should

must

right

proper

fitting

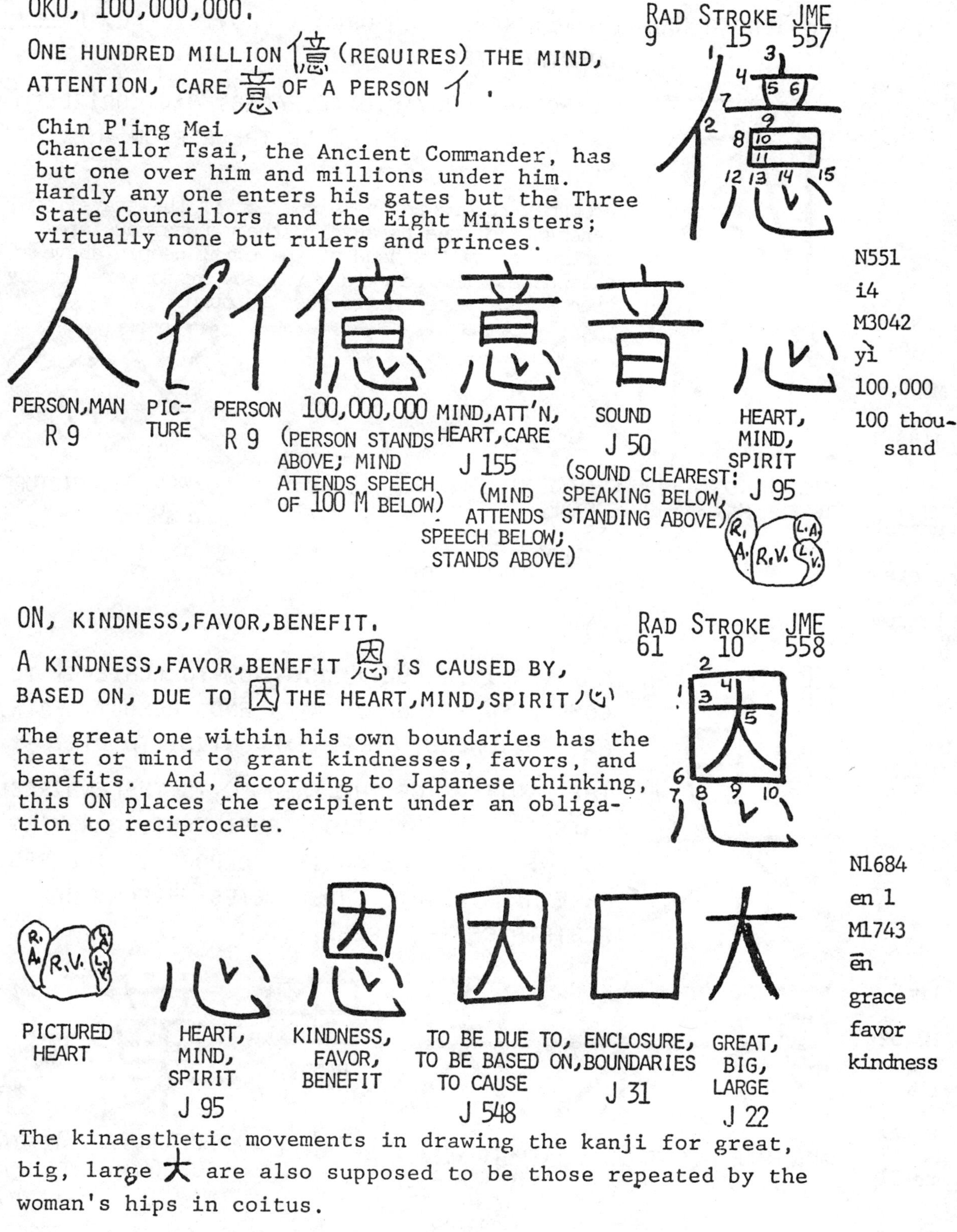

OKU, 100,000,000.

RAD 9 STROKE 15 JME 557

ONE HUNDRED MILLION 億 (REQUIRES) THE MIND, ATTENTION, CARE 意 OF A PERSON 亻.

Chin P'ing Mei
Chancellor Tsai, the Ancient Commander, has but one over him and millions under him. Hardly any one enters his gates but the Three State Councillors and the Eight Ministers; virtually none but rulers and princes.

N551
i4
M3042
yì
100,000
100 thousand

ON, KINDNESS, FAVOR, BENEFIT.

RAD 61 STROKE 10 JME 558

A KINDNESS, FAVOR, BENEFIT 恩 IS CAUSED BY, BASED ON, DUE TO 因 THE HEART, MIND, SPIRIT 心

The great one within his own boundaries has the heart or mind to grant kindnesses, favors, and benefits. And, according to Japanese thinking, this ON places the recipient under an obligation to reciprocate.

N1684
en 1
M1743
ēn
grace
favor
kindness

The kinaesthetic movements in drawing the kanji for great, big, large 大 are also supposed to be those repeated by the woman's hips in coitus.

JME 559 | STROKE 6 | RAD 9

KA, KE; KARI, TEMPORARY, PROVISIONAL, FALSE, UNAUTHORIZED.

TEMPORARY, PROVISIONAL, FALSE, UNAUTHORIZED 仮 IS THE ANTITHESIS 反 OF THE PERSON 亻 (WHO IS GENUINE AND LASTING).

Probably refers to the situation of the traveling merchant of the caravan in the mountainous area controlled by the hand of the cliff people above the passes, the temporary quality or dangers in any truce or arrangement to pass through.

N382

chia3

M599

jiǎ

false

unreal

pretend

borrow

亻 仮 反 厂 又

PICTURE

亻 PERSON, MAN R 9

仮 TEMPORARY, PROVISIONAL, FALSE, UNAUTHORIZED (HAND OF CLIFF DWELLER)

反 ANTITHESIS, ANTI- J 492 (HAND FROM THE CLIFF)

厂 CLIFF R 27

又 HAND J 29

PICTURED HAND

JME 560 | STROKE 8 | RAD 75

KA, (FRUIT, RESULT); HATASU, TO ACHIEVE, TO COMPLETE, PERFORM; HATE, END, RESULT, FATE; HATERU, TO END, TO BE EXHAUSTED, TO DIE.

THE FRUIT 果 OF THE TREE 木 IS THE END, RESULT, FATE, THE REALIZATION, FUFILMENT, CARRYING OUT 果 (THE TREE'S LIFE-PURPOSE). THE FRUIT IS EXHAUSTED, IS ENDED, DIES 果 (FOR THE REBIRTH OF THE TREE).

N107

kuo3

M3732

guǒ

surely

really

results

男 MAN, MALE J 109

木 TREE, WOOD J 15

果 (FRUIT, RESULT) TO ACHIEVE, TO COMPLETE, TO PERFORM, END, RESULT, FATE, TO END, BE EXHAUSTED

田 PADDY, RICE FIELD J 40

菓 FRUIT, NUT, BERRY N 3980

MOMOTARŌ PEACH-BOY

As round as appil
was his face.
Romance of the Rose

The ripest peach is highest
on the tree.
James Whitcomb Riley

KA; KAWA, RIVER, STREAM.

RAD 85 STROKE 8 JME 561

RIVER, STREAM 河 IS WATER 氵 (JETTING) LIKE SPIKES, NAILS 丁 FROM AN APERTURE, MOUTH 口.

The Book of Poetry James Legge
Along the Ho we watch the flow
Of its embankèd stream.

Ho is the Huang Ho or Yellow River, which is the river of north China (written with this kanji)

N2350
ho2
M2111
hé
stream
river
Yellow R.

歌 SONG, TO SING J 166
何 WHAT, HOW MANY J 51
DROPS
氵 WATER R 85
河 RIVER, STREAM
口 MOUTH J 27
丁 "D" GRADE, 120 YDS., DIVISION OF WARD, TOWN, NAIL

The Yellow River has changed its course more than a dozen times in 2500 years. The flood waters have often penetrated the dyked banks. The Yellow River's bed is above the surrounding land in many areas. Its outlet to the sea has changed by hundreds of miles.

KA; SUGIRU, TO PASS, TO EXCEED, TO ELAPSE; SUGOSU, TO PASS, TO SPEND;

RAD 162 STROKE 12 JME 562

TO PASS, TO EXCEED, TO ELAPSE, TO SPEND 過 BY STOPPING AND GOING 辶 UNTIL A BONE 骨 (SKELETON). (ALSO OVEREATING, PERHAPS IRONIC)

(from) Staccato Obligato A.D.
Cobblestones and tiled roofs;
Knucklebones and horses' hoofs;

N4723
kuo4
M3730
guò
to pass
cross over
past or perfect tense sign

辶 STOP & GO R 162
過 TO PASS, TO EXCEED, TO ELAPSE, TO SPEND
週 A WEEK J 242
回 A TURN, TO TURN J 168
骨 BONE, SKELETON R 188
SKULL & BONES, TO BONE, DISARTICULATE

The Pauper's Drive Rhymes and Roundelays Thomas Noel
Rattle his bones over the stones;
He's only a pauper whom nobody owns!

563

JME 563 · STROKE 8 · RAD 9

KA; ATAI, PRICE,VALUE; ATAI SURU, TO BE WORTH.

THE PERSON 亻 FROM THE WEST 西 IS OF VALUE PRICE, WORTH 価 (AS A SPECIALIST WITH HORSES FROM TURKESTAN).

We were young, we were merry, we were very, very wise,
And the door stood open at our feast,
When there passed us a woman with the West in her eyes,
And a man with his back to the East.
Mary Coleridge Unwelcome

N422

chia4

M603

jià

price

value

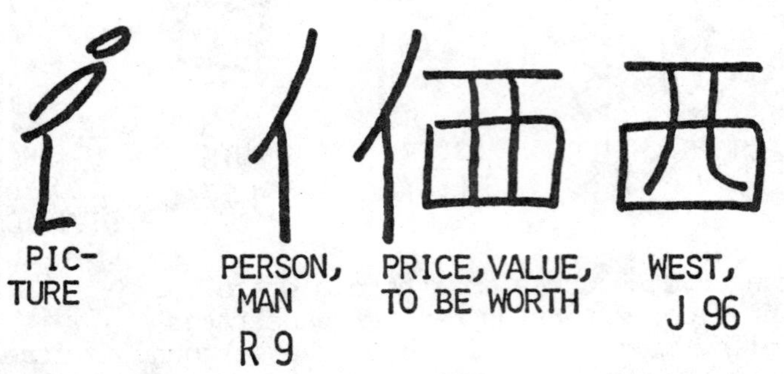

Oh, young Lochinvar is come
out of the West,
Through all the wide Border
his steed was the best.
So faithful in love, and so
dauntless in war,
There never was knight like
the young Lochinvar.
Sir Walter Scott Marmion

The Fair Maid of the West OR A Girle Worth Gold is a two-part comedy by Heyward printed in 1631.

JME 564 · STROKE 15 · RAD 149

KA, LESSON,SECTION,DEPARTMENT.

THE LESSON,SECTION,DEPARTMENT 課 IS THE FRUIT, RESULT 果 OF WORDS 言 .

Inaugural Address at the University of St. Andrews
To question all things; ---never to turn away from any difficulty; to accept no doctrine either from ourselves or from other people without a rigid scrutiny by negative criticism; letting no fallacy, or incoherence, or confusion of thought, step by unpercieved; above all, to insist upon having the meaning of a word clearly understood before using it,

N4389

k'e4

k'o4

M3394

kè

task

lesson

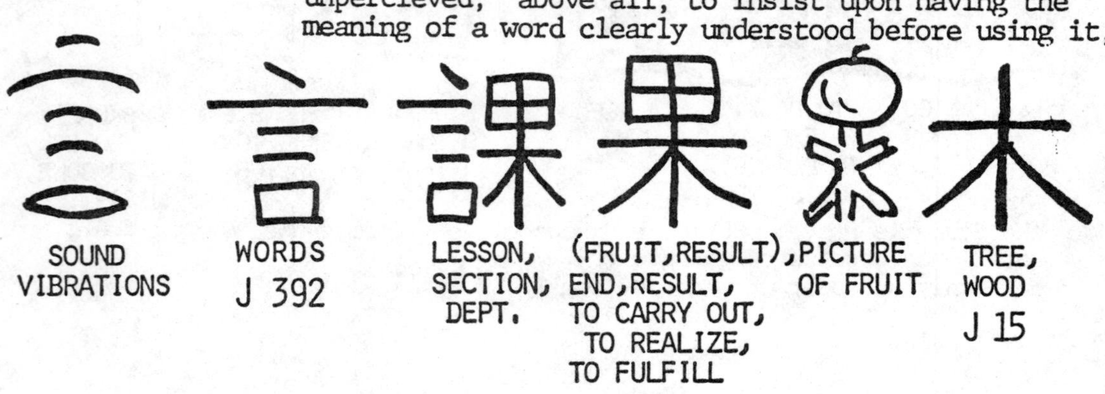

and the meaning of a proposition before assenting to it; ---these are the lessons we learn from ancient dialecticians. John Stuart Mill

GA, (CONGRATULATIONS).

RAD 154 STROKE 12 JME 565

CONGRATULATIONS 賀 ON THE ADDING, INCREASING 加 SEA SHELLS 貝 (COWRIES OF WEALTH).

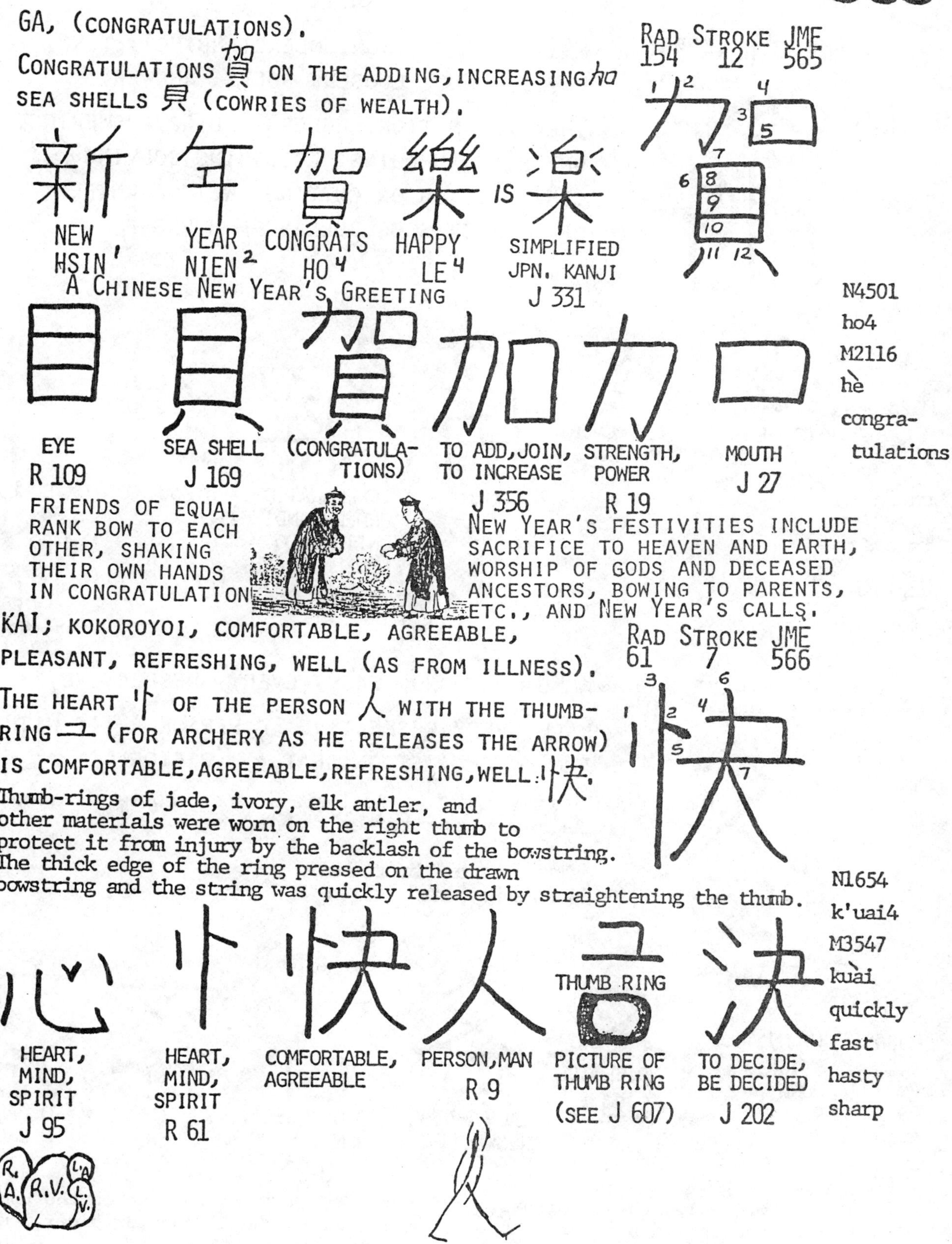

N4501 ho4 M2116 hè congratulations

FRIENDS OF EQUAL RANK BOW TO EACH OTHER, SHAKING THEIR OWN HANDS IN CONGRATULATION

NEW YEAR'S FESTIVITIES INCLUDE SACRIFICE TO HEAVEN AND EARTH, WORSHIP OF GODS AND DECEASED ANCESTORS, BOWING TO PARENTS, ETC., AND NEW YEAR'S CALLS.

KAI; KOKOROYOI, COMFORTABLE, AGREEABLE, PLEASANT, REFRESHING, WELL (AS FROM ILLNESS).

RAD 61 STROKE 7 JME 566

THE HEART 忄 OF THE PERSON 人 WITH THE THUMB-RING コ (FOR ARCHERY AS HE RELEASES THE ARROW) IS COMFORTABLE, AGREEABLE, REFRESHING, WELL 快.

Thumb-rings of jade, ivory, elk antler, and other materials were worn on the right thumb to protect it from injury by the backlash of the bowstring. The thick edge of the ring pressed on the drawn bowstring and the string was quickly released by straightening the thumb.

N1654 k'uai4 M3547 kuài quickly fast hasty sharp

567

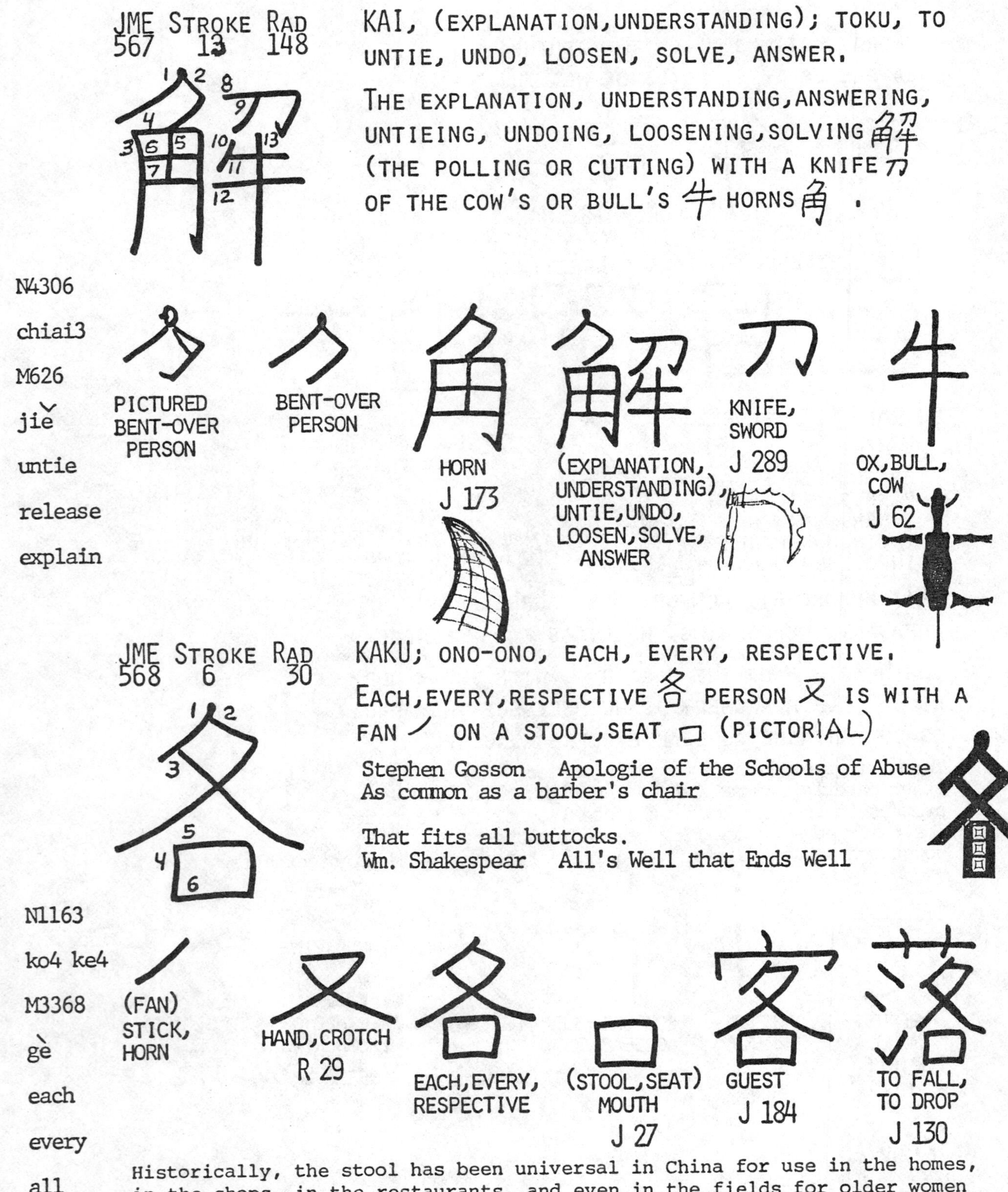

JME 567 STROKE 13 RAD 148

KAI, (EXPLANATION, UNDERSTANDING); TOKU, TO UNTIE, UNDO, LOOSEN, SOLVE, ANSWER.

THE EXPLANATION, UNDERSTANDING, ANSWERING, UNTIEING, UNDOING, LOOSENING, SOLVING 解 (THE POLLING OR CUTTING) WITH A KNIFE 刀 OF THE COW'S OR BULL'S 牛 HORNS 角.

N4306

chiai3

M626

jiě

untie

release

explain

PICTURED BENT-OVER PERSON

BENT-OVER PERSON

角 HORN J 173

解 (EXPLANATION, UNDERSTANDING), UNTIE, UNDO, LOOSEN, SOLVE, ANSWER

刀 KNIFE, SWORD J 289

牛 OX, BULL, COW J 62

JME 568 STROKE 6 RAD 30

KAKU; ONO-ONO, EACH, EVERY, RESPECTIVE.

EACH, EVERY, RESPECTIVE 各 PERSON 夂 IS WITH A FAN ノ ON A STOOL, SEAT 口 (PICTORIAL)

Stephen Gosson Apologie of the Schools of Abuse
As common as a barber's chair

That fits all buttocks.
Wm. Shakespear All's Well that Ends Well

N1163

ko4 ke4

M3368

gè

each

every

all

ノ (FAN) STICK, HORN

夂 HAND, CROTCH R 29

各 EACH, EVERY, RESPECTIVE

口 (STOOL, SEAT) MOUTH J 27

客 GUEST J 184

落 TO FALL, TO DROP J 130

Historically, the stool has been universal in China for use in the homes, in the shops, in the restaurants, and even in the fields for older women weeding or removing insects by hand. The low height of the stool is modest even as a younger woman's figure was displayed to advantage. Constant use of the stool has made Chinese and Japanese comfortable in positions that are cramped and awkward for most Westerners.

KAKU, STATUS, RANK, CASE (LAW OR GRAMMAR).

RAD 75 STROKE 10 JME 569

EACH, EVERY, RESPECTIVE 各 PERSON 夂 SITS ON A STOOL 口 OF (A KIND OF) WOOD 木 ACCORDING TO STATUS, RANK, CASE 格 (EN BANC OR DUCKING STOOL).

格

Socially and historically, human positional elevation from the floor or platform to the intermediate stool and to the chair conveyed status as the case might be. The stool was generally of wood.

HECTOR & ACHILLES

木 TREE, WOOD J 15

格 STATUS, RANK, CASE

各 EACH, EVERY, RESPECTIVE J 568

GRAPHIC: (PORCELAIN STOOL)

N2259
ke2
M3309
gé
to reach
come
go
correct
rule
limit

Grongar Hill John Dyer

Below me Trees unnumber'd rise,
Beautiful in various Dies:
The gloomy Pine, the Poplar blue,
The yellow Beech, the sable Yew,
The slender Fir that taper grows,
The sturdy Oak with broad-spread Boughs.

Who climbs the grammar-tree, distinctly knows
Where noun and verb and participle grows. Dryden

KAKU; TASHIKA, SURE, RELIABLE, ACCURATE; TASHIKAMERU, TO ASCERTAIN, TO CONFIRM.

RAD 112 STROKE 15 JME 570

THE CRESTED 冖 SHORT-TAILED BIRD 隹 ON THE ROCK 石 CLIFF 厂 IS SURE, RELIABLE, ACCURATE ASCERTAINS, CONFIRMS 確 (IN DIVING ON HIS PREY)

確

Ramses II at the Battle of Kadesh: I shall attack the Hittites like a striking falcon, killing, butchering, and felling them to earth.

厂 CLIFF R 27

石 STONE J 44

確 SURE, RELIABLE, ACCURATE, TO ASCERTAIN, TO CONFIRM

隹 SHORT-TAILED BIRD R 172

ARCHAIC KANJI OF SHORT-TAILED BIRD

冖 CROWN, CAP, CREST R 14

N3217
ch'ueh4
M1181
què
really
actual
firm

PICTURE OF CLIFFS

Colloquy in Black Rock Robert Traill Spence Lowell

Over the drum-beat of St. Stephen's choir
I hear him, Stupor Mundi, and the mud
Flies from his hunching wings and beak --- my heart,
The blue kingfisher dives on you in fire.

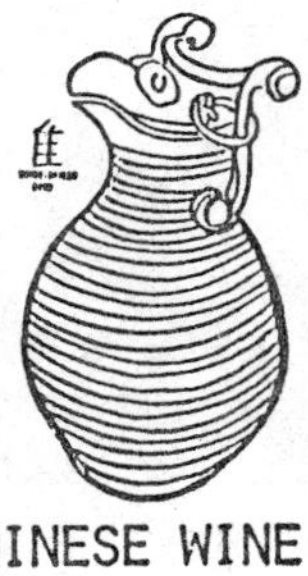

CHINESE WINE JUG

571

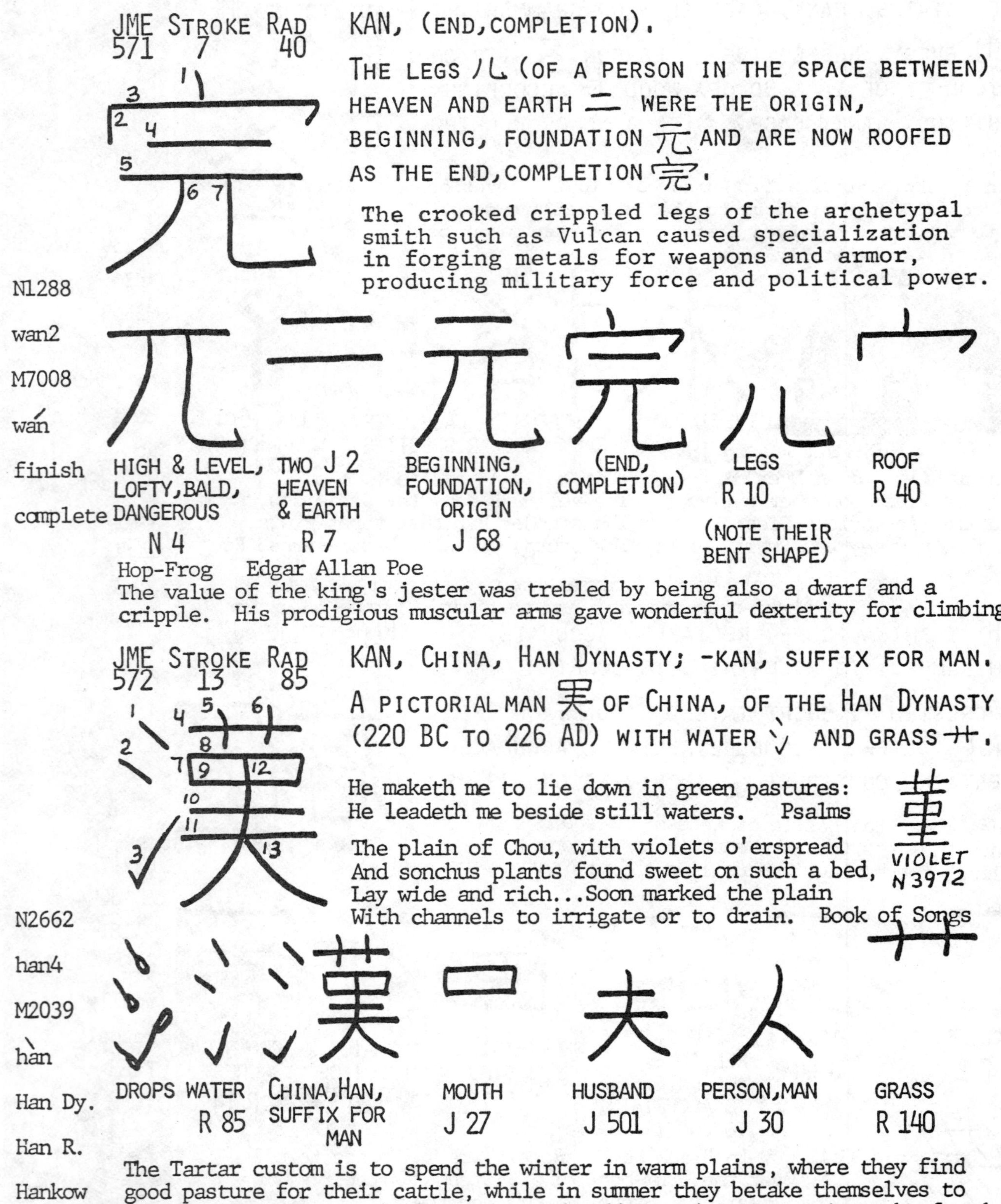

JME STROKE RAD
571 7 40

KAN, (END, COMPLETION).

THE LEGS 儿 (OF A PERSON IN THE SPACE BETWEEN) HEAVEN AND EARTH 二 WERE THE ORIGIN, BEGINNING, FOUNDATION 元 AND ARE NOW ROOFED AS THE END, COMPLETION 完.

The crooked crippled legs of the archetypal smith such as Vulcan caused specialization in forging metals for weapons and armor, producing military force and political power.

N1288
wan2
M7008
wán
finish
complete

兀 HIGH & LEVEL, LOFTY, BALD, DANGEROUS N 4

二 TWO J 2 HEAVEN & EARTH R 7

元 BEGINNING, FOUNDATION, ORIGIN J 68

完 (END, COMPLETION)

儿 LEGS R 10 (NOTE THEIR BENT SHAPE)

宀 ROOF R 40

Hop-Frog Edgar Allan Poe
The value of the king's jester was trebled by being also a dwarf and a cripple. His prodigious muscular arms gave wonderful dexterity for climbing.

JME STROKE RAD
572 13 85

KAN, CHINA, HAN DYNASTY; -KAN, SUFFIX FOR MAN.

A PICTORIAL MAN 𦰩 OF CHINA, OF THE HAN DYNASTY (220 BC TO 226 AD) WITH WATER 氵 AND GRASS 艹.

He maketh me to lie down in green pastures:
He leadeth me beside still waters. Psalms

The plain of Chou, with violets o'erspread
And sonchus plants found sweet on such a bed,
Lay wide and rich...Soon marked the plain
With channels to irrigate or to drain. Book of Songs

堇 VIOLET N3972

N2662
han4
M2039
hàn
Han Dy.
Han R.
Hankow

氵 DROPS WATER R 85

漢 CHINA, HAN, SUFFIX FOR MAN

口 MOUTH J 27

夫 HUSBAND J 501

人 PERSON, MAN J 30

艹 GRASS R 140

The Tartar custom is to spend the winter in warm plains, where they find good pasture for their cattle, while in summer they betake themselves to a cool climate among the mountains and valleys, where water is to be found as well as woods and pastures.
Concerning the Customs of the Tartars: The Travels of Marco Polo

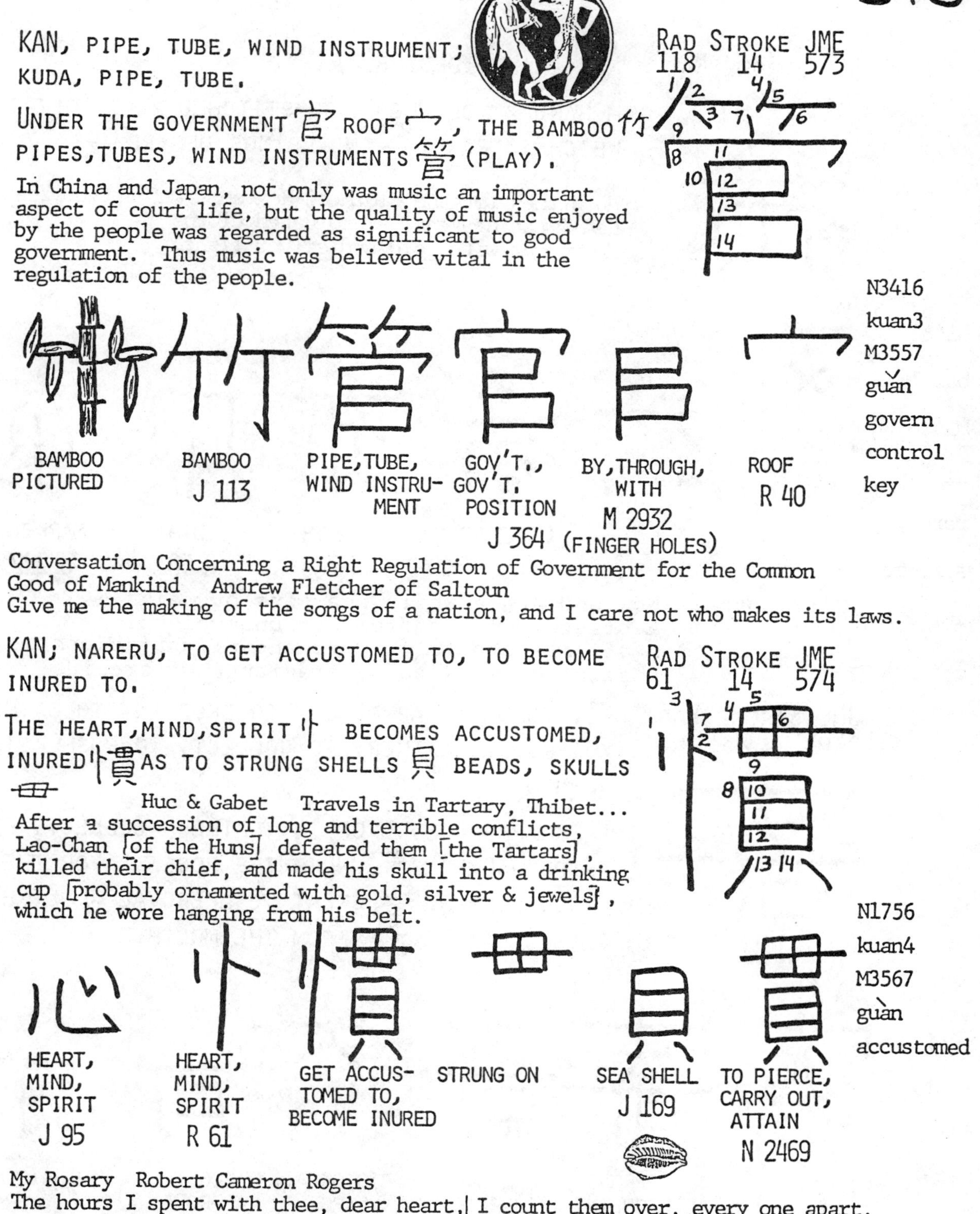

KAN, PIPE, TUBE, WIND INSTRUMENT; KUDA, PIPE, TUBE.

RAD 118 STROKE 14 JME 573

UNDER THE GOVERNMENT 官 ROOF 宀, THE BAMBOO 竹 PIPES, TUBES, WIND INSTRUMENTS 管 (PLAY).

In China and Japan, not only was music an important aspect of court life, but the quality of music enjoyed by the people was regarded as significant to good government. Thus music was believed vital in the regulation of the people.

N3416
kuan3
M3557
guǎn
govern
control
key

BAMBOO PICTURED — BAMBOO J 113 — PIPE, TUBE, WIND INSTRUMENT — GOV'T., GOV'T. POSITION J 364 — BY, THROUGH, WITH M 2932 (FINGER HOLES) — ROOF R 40

Conversation Concerning a Right Regulation of Government for the Common Good of Mankind   Andrew Fletcher of Saltoun
Give me the making of the songs of a nation, and I care not who makes its laws.

KAN; NARERU, TO GET ACCUSTOMED TO, TO BECOME INURED TO.

RAD 61 STROKE 14 JME 574

THE HEART, MIND, SPIRIT 忄 BECOMES ACCUSTOMED, INURED 慣 AS TO STRUNG SHELLS 貝 BEADS, SKULLS 毌

Huc & Gabet   Travels in Tartary, Thibet...
After a succession of long and terrible conflicts, Lao-Chan [of the Huns] defeated them [the Tartars], killed their chief, and made his skull into a drinking cup [probably ornamented with gold, silver & jewels], which he wore hanging from his belt.

N1756
kuan4
M3567
guàn
accustomed

HEART, MIND, SPIRIT J 95 — HEART, MIND, SPIRIT R 61 — GET ACCUSTOMED TO, BECOME INURED — STRUNG ON — SEA SHELL J 169 — TO PIERCE, CARRY OUT, ATTAIN N 2469

My Rosary   Robert Cameron Rogers
The hours I spent with thee, dear heart,
Are a string of pearls to me;
I count them over, every one apart,
My rosary, my rosary.

Marquesans' prize skulls strung through nose and mouth hung from their sides.

575

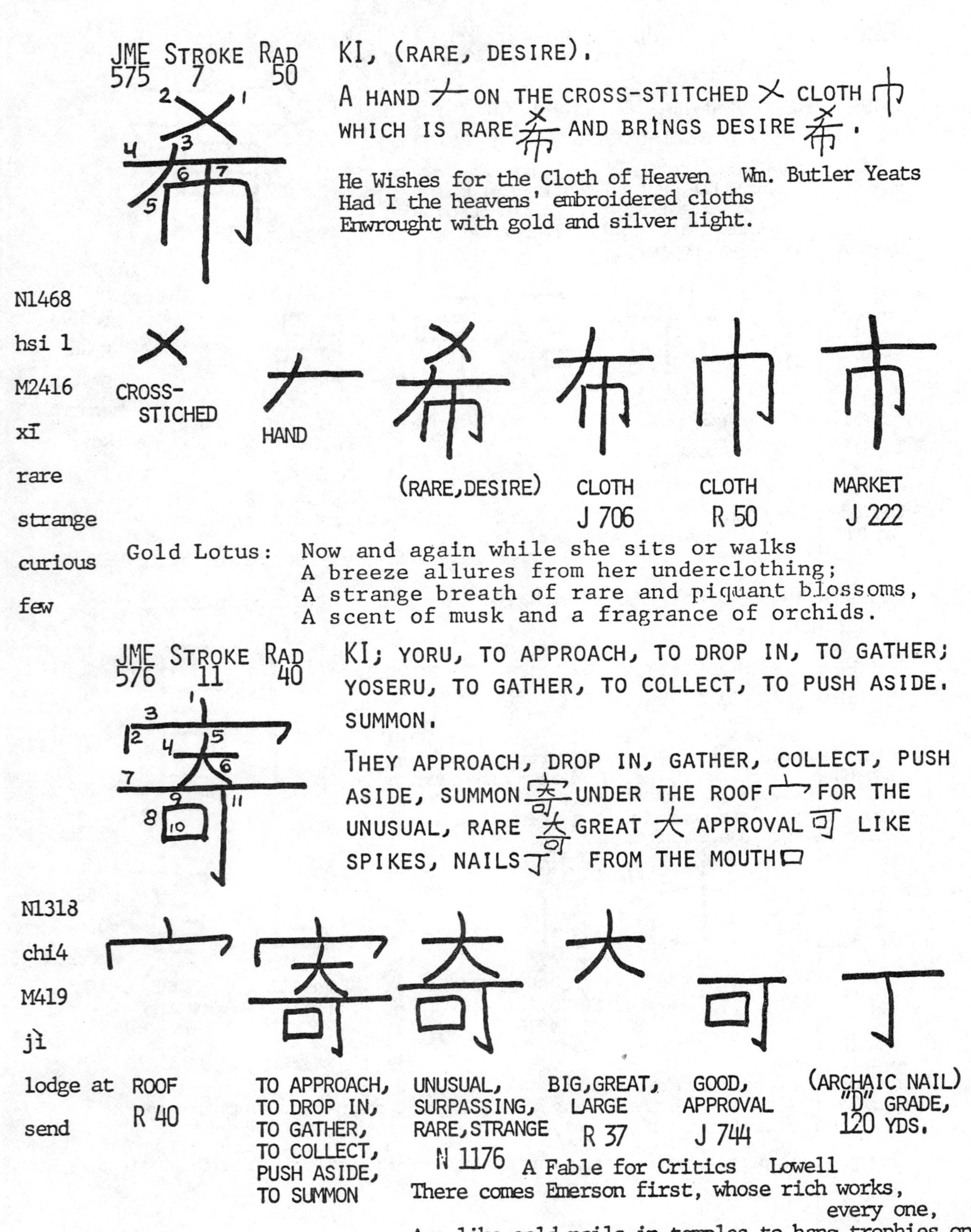

JME 575 | STROKE 7 | RAD 50

KI, (RARE, DESIRE).

A HAND 𠂇 ON THE CROSS-STITCHED 㐅 CLOTH 巾 WHICH IS RARE 希 AND BRINGS DESIRE 希.

He Wishes for the Cloth of Heaven Wm. Butler Yeats
Had I the heavens' embroidered cloths
Enwrought with gold and silver light.

N1468
hsi 1
M2416
xī
rare
strange
curious
few

Gold Lotus: Now and again while she sits or walks
A breeze allures from her underclothing;
A strange breath of rare and piquant blossoms,
A scent of musk and a fragrance of orchids.

JME 576 | STROKE 11 | RAD 40

KI; YORU, TO APPROACH, TO DROP IN, TO GATHER; YOSERU, TO GATHER, TO COLLECT, TO PUSH ASIDE. SUMMON.

THEY APPROACH, DROP IN, GATHER, COLLECT, PUSH ASIDE, SUMMON 寄 UNDER THE ROOF 宀 FOR THE UNUSUAL, RARE 奇 GREAT 大 APPROVAL 可 LIKE SPIKES, NAILS 丁 FROM THE MOUTH 口

N1318
chi4
M419
jì
lodge at
send

A Fable for Critics Lowell
There comes Emerson first, whose rich works, every one,
Are like gold nails in temples to hang trophies on;

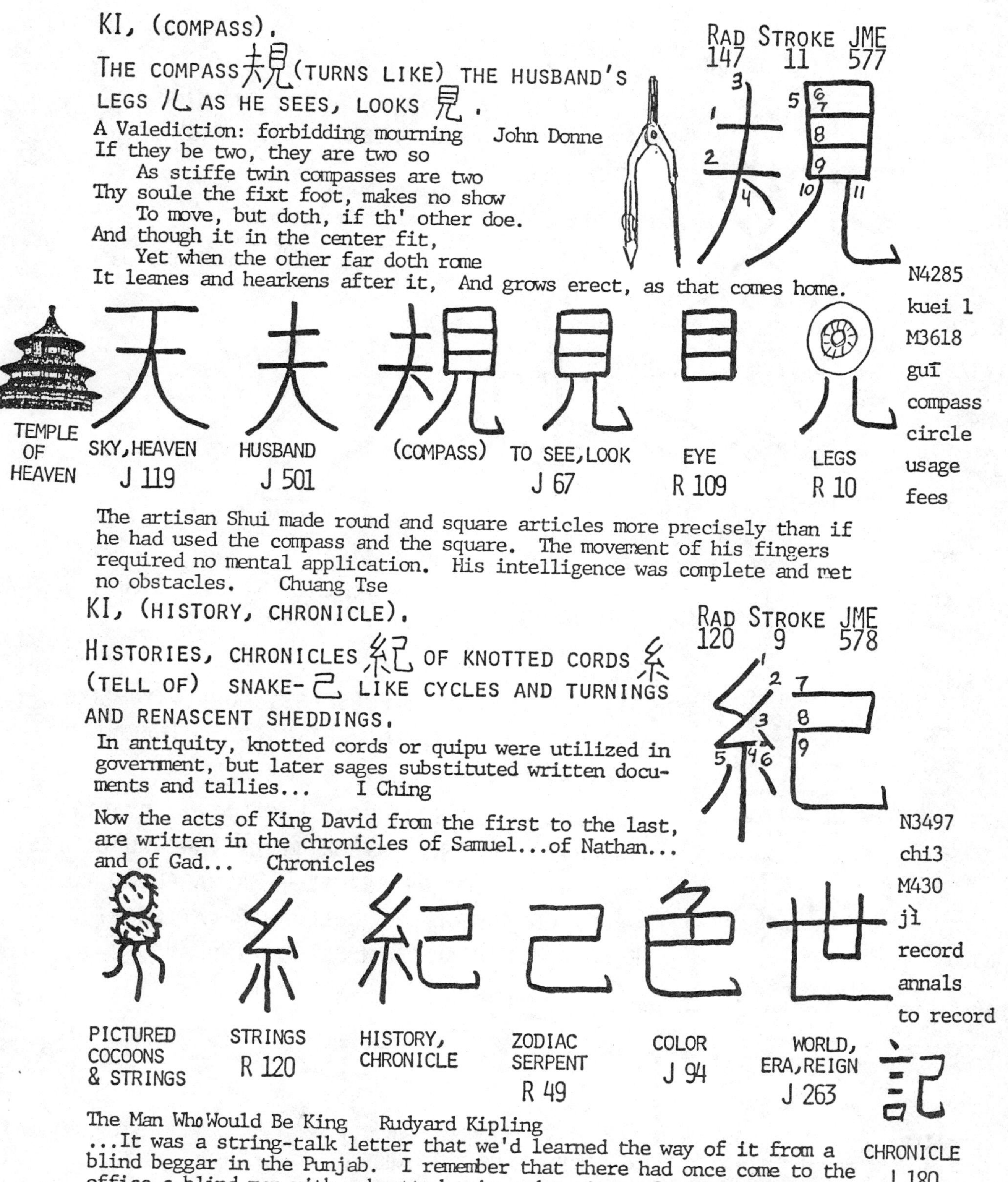

KI, (COMPASS).

THE COMPASS 規 (TURNS LIKE) THE HUSBAND'S LEGS 儿 AS HE SEES, LOOKS 見.

RAD 147 STROKE 11 JME 577

A Valediction: forbidding mourning   John Donne
If they be two, they are two so
    As stiffe twin compasses are two
Thy soule the fixt foot, makes no show
    To move, but doth, if th' other doe.
And though it in the center fit,
    Yet when the other far doth rome
It leanes and hearkens after it, And grows erect, as that comes home.

N4285
kuei 1
M3618
guī
compass
circle
usage
fees

The artisan Shui made round and square articles more precisely than if he had used the compass and the square. The movement of his fingers required no mental application. His intelligence was complete and met no obstacles.   Chuang Tse

KI, (HISTORY, CHRONICLE).

HISTORIES, CHRONICLES 紀 OF KNOTTED CORDS 糸 (TELL OF) SNAKE-己 LIKE CYCLES AND TURNINGS AND RENASCENT SHEDDINGS.

RAD 120 STROKE 9 JME 578

In antiquity, knotted cords or quipu were utilized in government, but later sages substituted written documents and tallies...   I Ching

Now the acts of King David from the first to the last, are written in the chronicles of Samuel...of Nathan... and of Gad...   Chronicles

N3497
chi3
M430
jì
record
annals
to record

記
CHRONICLE
J 180

The Man Who Would Be King   Rudyard Kipling
...It was a string-talk letter that we'd learned the way of it from a blind beggar in the Punjab. I remember that there had once come to the office a blind man with a knotted twig and a piece of string which he wound around the twig according to some cipher of his own. He could, after the lapse of days or hours, repeat the sentence which he had reeled.

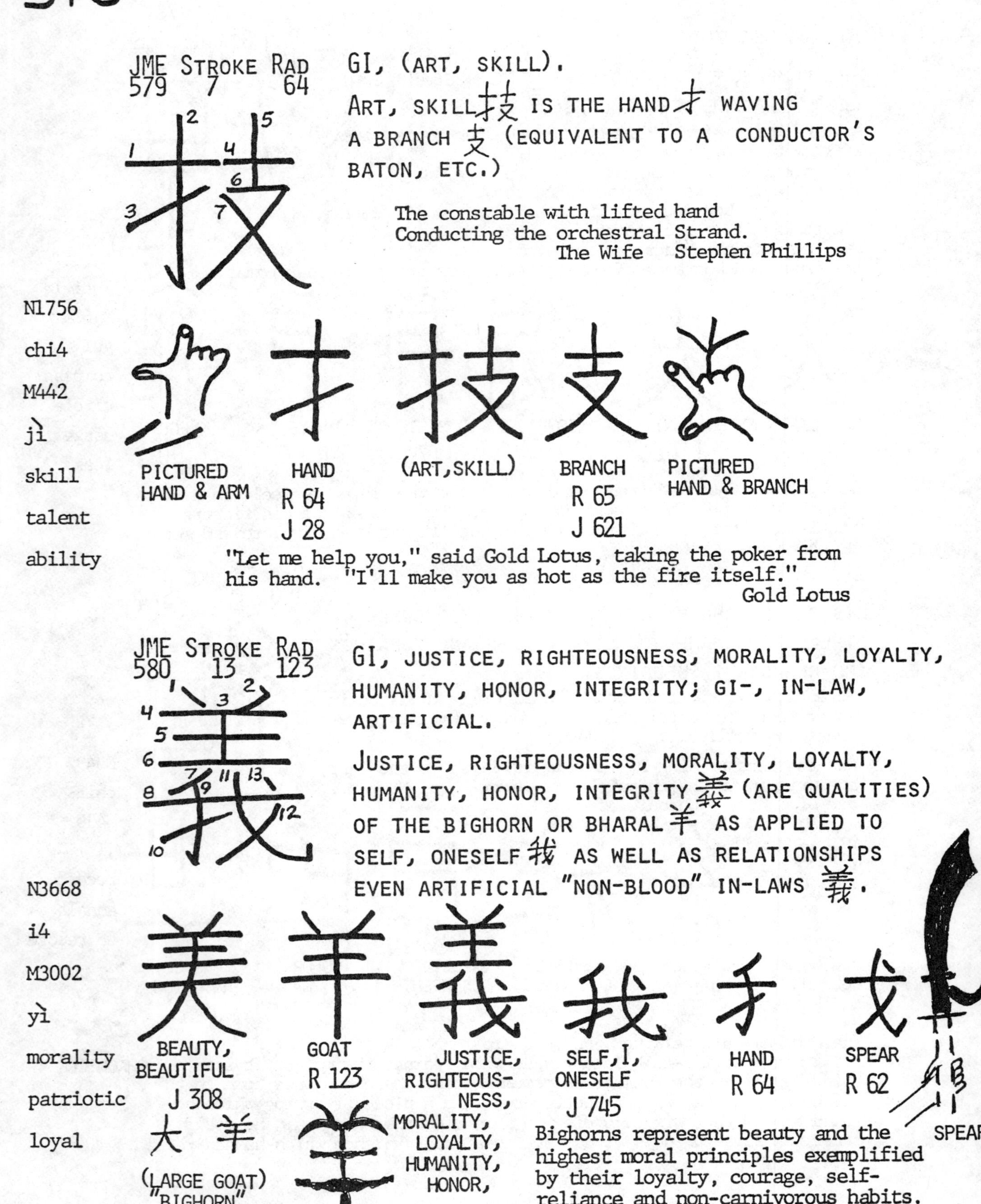

GI, (ART, SKILL).

ART, SKILL 技 IS THE HAND 扌 WAVING A BRANCH 支 (EQUIVALENT TO A CONDUCTOR'S BATON, ETC.)

> The constable with lifted hand
> Conducting the orchestral Strand.
>
> The Wife Stephen Phillips

"Let me help you," said Gold Lotus, taking the poker from his hand. "I'll make you as hot as the fire itself."

Gold Lotus

GI, JUSTICE, RIGHTEOUSNESS, MORALITY, LOYALTY, HUMANITY, HONOR, INTEGRITY; GI-, IN-LAW, ARTIFICIAL.

JUSTICE, RIGHTEOUSNESS, MORALITY, LOYALTY, HUMANITY, HONOR, INTEGRITY 義 (ARE QUALITIES) OF THE BIGHORN OR BHARAL 羊 AS APPLIED TO SELF, ONESELF 我 AS WELL AS RELATIONSHIPS EVEN ARTIFICIAL "NON-BLOOD" IN-LAWS 義.

Bighorns represent beauty and the highest moral principles exemplified by their loyalty, courage, self-reliance and non-carnivorous habits.

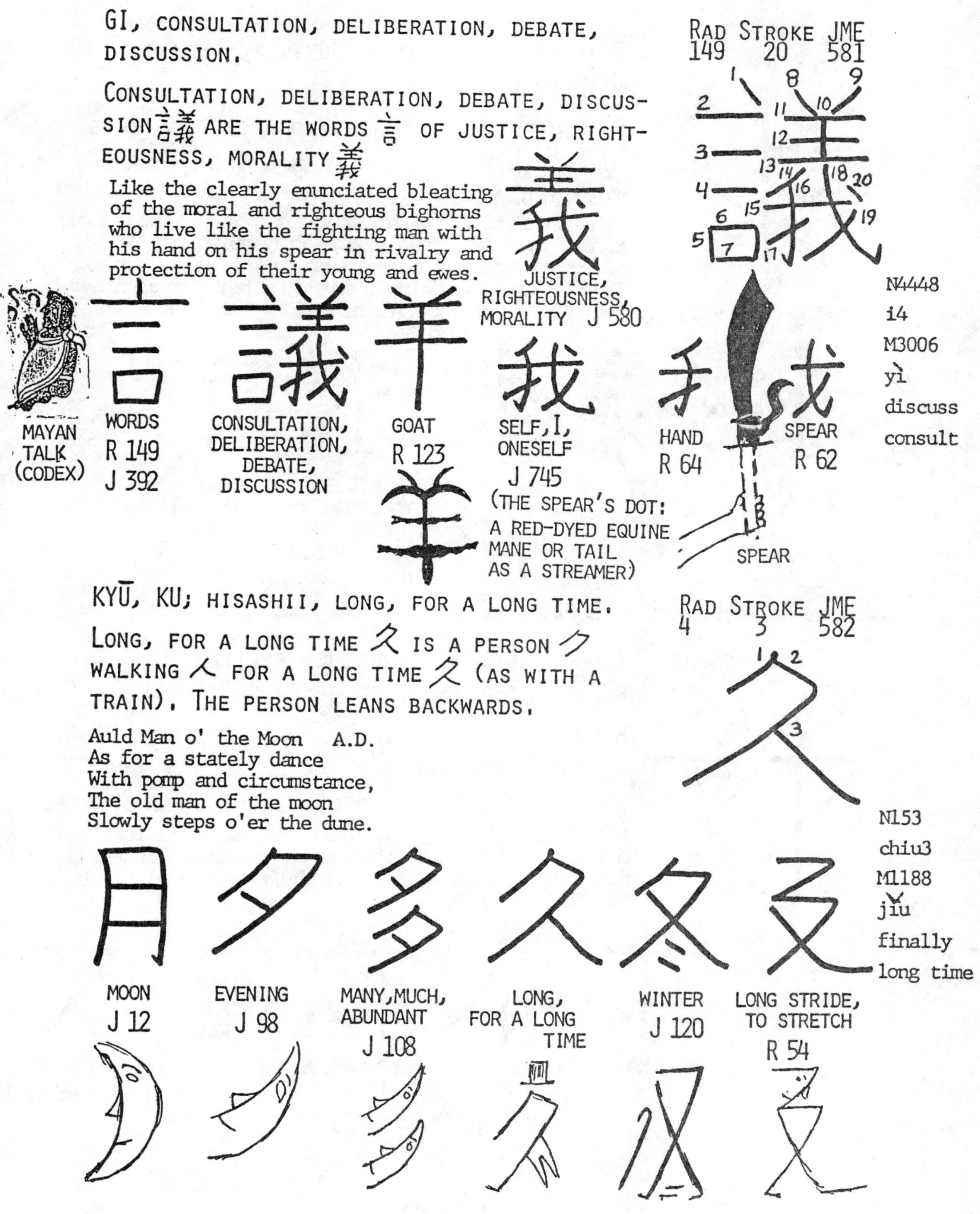

GI, CONSULTATION, DELIBERATION, DEBATE, DISCUSSION.

RAD 149 STROKE 20 JME 581

CONSULTATION, DELIBERATION, DEBATE, DISCUSSION 議 ARE THE WORDS 言 OF JUSTICE, RIGHTEOUSNESS, MORALITY 義

Like the clearly enunciated bleating of the moral and righteous bighorns who live like the fighting man with his hand on his spear in rivalry and protection of their young and ewes.

N4448
i4
M3006
yì
discuss
consult

KYŪ, KU; HISASHII, LONG, FOR A LONG TIME.

RAD 4 STROKE 3 JME 582

LONG, FOR A LONG TIME 久 IS A PERSON ク WALKING 人 FOR A LONG TIME 久 (AS WITH A TRAIN). THE PERSON LEANS BACKWARDS.

Auld Man o' the Moon A.D.
As for a stately dance
With pomp and circumstance,
The old man of the moon
Slowly steps o'er the dune.

N153
chiu3
M1188
jiǔ
finally
long time

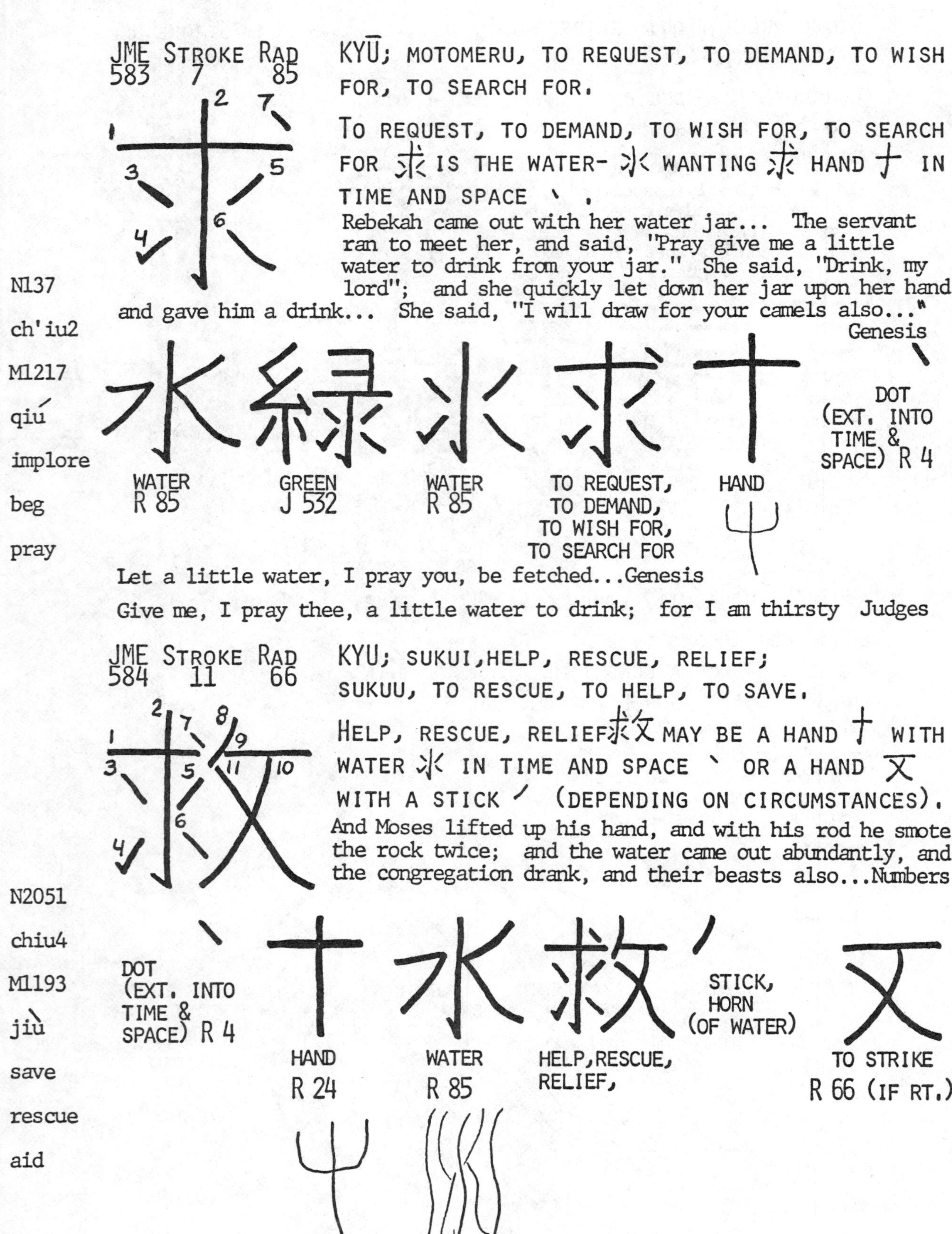
JME STROKE RAD
583 7 85
KYŪ; MOTOMERU, TO REQUEST, TO DEMAND, TO WISH FOR, TO SEARCH FOR.
TO REQUEST, TO DEMAND, TO WISH FOR, TO SEARCH FOR 求 IS THE WATER- 氺 WANTING 求 HAND 扌 IN TIME AND SPACE 丶 .
Rebekah came out with her water jar... The servant ran to meet her, and said, "Pray give me a little water to drink from your jar." She said, "Drink, my lord"; and she quickly let down her jar upon her hand, and gave him a drink... She said, "I will draw for your camels also..." Genesis
N137
ch'iu2
M1217
qiú
implore
beg
pray
水 WATER R 85
緑 GREEN J 532
氺 WATER R 85
求 TO REQUEST, TO DEMAND, TO WISH FOR, TO SEARCH FOR
十 HAND
DOT (EXT. INTO TIME & SPACE) R 4
Let a little water, I pray you, be fetched...Genesis
Give me, I pray thee, a little water to drink; for I am thirsty Judges
JME STROKE RAD
584 11 66
KYU; SUKUI, HELP, RESCUE, RELIEF;
SUKUU, TO RESCUE, TO HELP, TO SAVE.
HELP, RESCUE, RELIEF 救 MAY BE A HAND 扌 WITH WATER 氺 IN TIME AND SPACE 丶 OR A HAND 攵 WITH A STICK ノ (DEPENDING ON CIRCUMSTANCES).
And Moses lifted up his hand, and with his rod he smote the rock twice; and the water came out abundantly, and the congregation drank, and their beasts also...Numbers
N2051
chiu4
M1193
jiù
save
rescue
aid
DOT (EXT. INTO TIME & SPACE) R 4
十 HAND R 24
水 WATER R 85
救 HELP, RESCUE, RELIEF,
STICK, HORN (OF WATER)
攵 TO STRIKE R 66 (IF RT.)

KYŪ, WAGE, GIFT; KYUSURU, TO GRANT, TO SUPPLY. RAD 120 STROKE 12 JME 585

GIFT, TO GRANT, TO SUPPLY 給 IS TO FIT 合 TOGETHER 合 IN UNION 合 THE STRINGS 糸 (OF CASH).

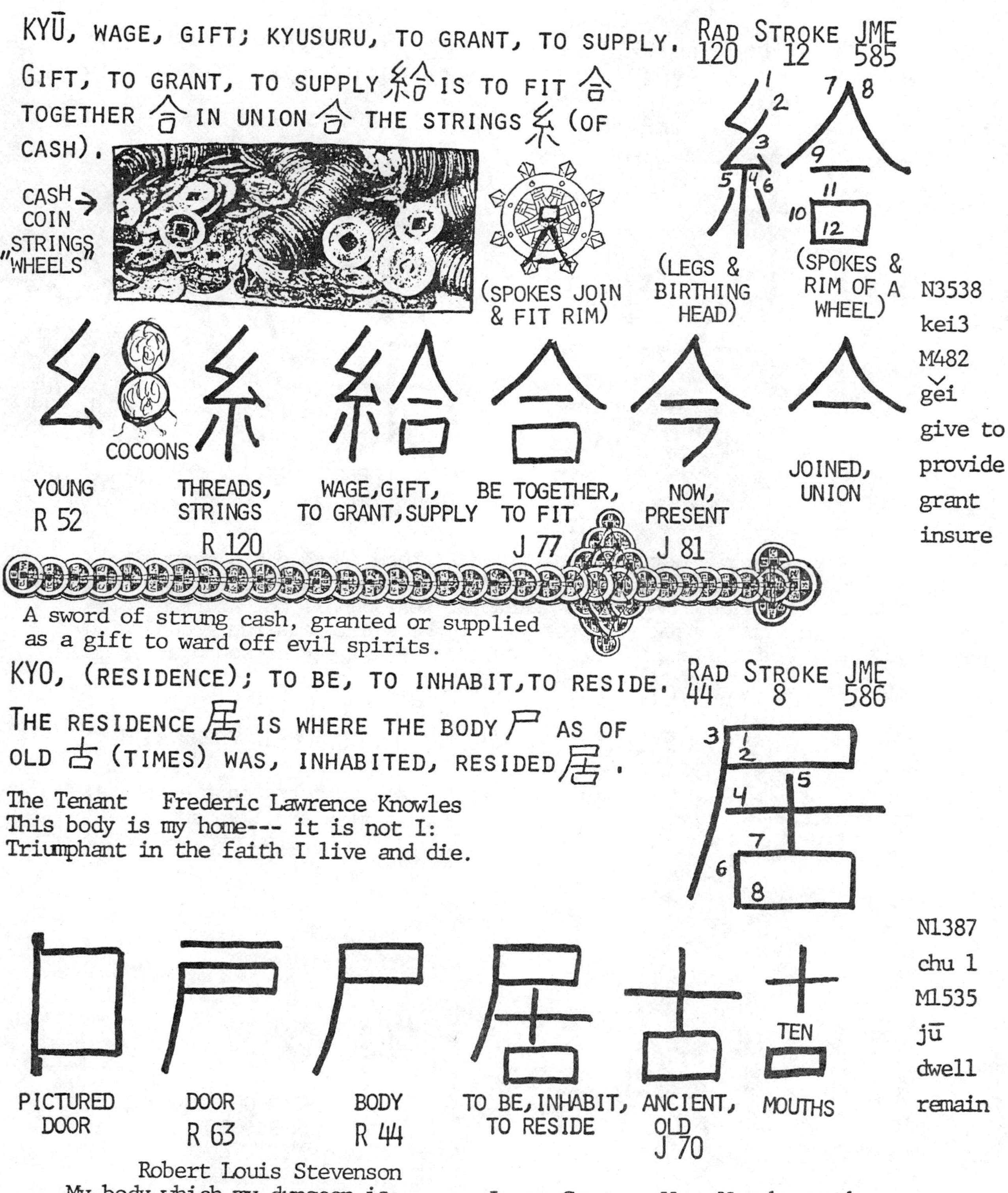

A sword of strung cash, granted or supplied as a gift to ward off evil spirits.

KYO, (RESIDENCE); TO BE, TO INHABIT, TO RESIDE. RAD 44 STROKE 8 JME 586

THE RESIDENCE 居 IS WHERE THE BODY 尸 AS OF OLD 古 (TIMES) WAS, INHABITED, RESIDED 居.

The Tenant Frederic Lawrence Knowles
This body is my home--- it is not I:
Triumphant in the faith I live and die.

Robert Louis Stevenson
My body which my dungeon is,
And yet my parks and palaces:
Which is so great that there I go
All the day long to and fro.

Lucy Gray Wm. Wordsworth
The sweetest thing that ever grew
Beside a human door.

587

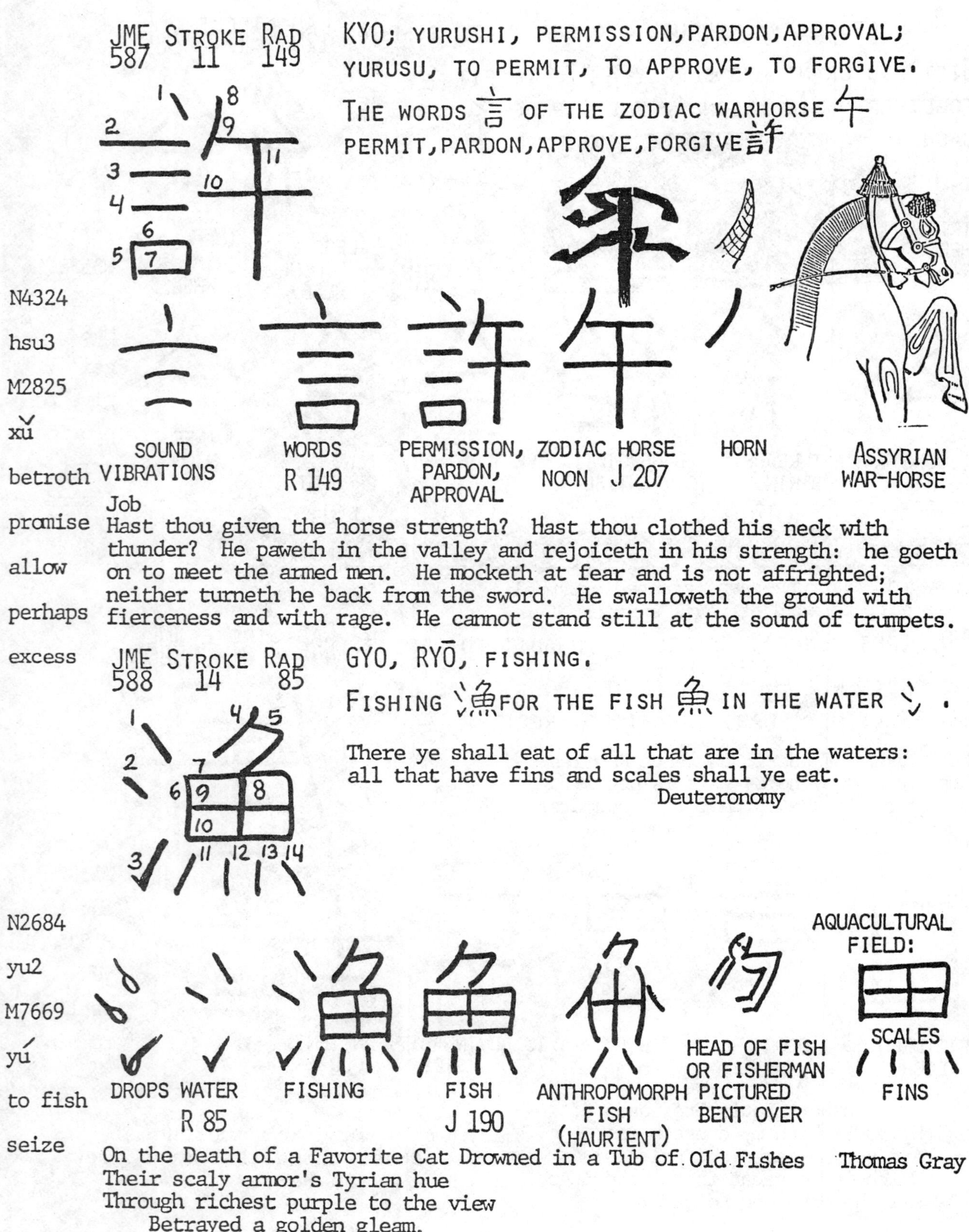

JME 587 STROKE 11 RAD 149

KYO; YURUSHI, PERMISSION, PARDON, APPROVAL; YURUSU, TO PERMIT, TO APPROVE, TO FORGIVE.

THE WORDS 言 OF THE ZODIAC WARHORSE 午 PERMIT, PARDON, APPROVE, FORGIVE 許

N4324

hsu3

M2825

xǔ

betroth

promise

allow

perhaps

excess

Job

Hast thou given the horse strength? Hast thou clothed his neck with thunder? He paweth in the valley and rejoiceth in his strength: he goeth on to meet the armed men. He mocketh at fear and is not affrighted; neither turneth he back from the sword. He swalloweth the ground with fierceness and with rage. He cannot stand still at the sound of trumpets.

JME 588 STROKE 14 RAD 85

GYO, RYŌ, FISHING.

FISHING 漁 FOR THE FISH 魚 IN THE WATER 氵.

There ye shall eat of all that are in the waters:
all that have fins and scales shall ye eat.
Deuteronomy

N2684

yu2

M7669

yú

to fish

seize

On the Death of a Favorite Cat Drowned in a Tub of Old Fishes — Thomas Gray

Their scaly armor's Tyrian hue
Through richest purple to the view
Betrayed a golden gleam.

KYŌ, INTEREST, ENTERTAINMENT, PLEASURE; KO; OKORU, TO RISE, TO PROSPER; OKOSU, TO REVIVE, TO RAISE UP, TO RESTORE (FORTUNES).

RAD 12 STROKE 16 JME 589

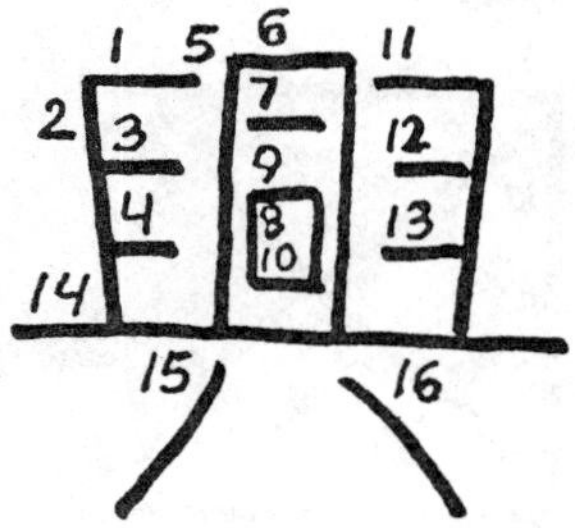

THE HANDS 𦥑 (PLACE) THE SAME 同 INTERESTS, ENTERTAINMENT, PLEASURES 興 ON THE TABLE 六 WITH LEGS ノ ＼. THE (LOADED) TABLE 興 MEANS RISE, PROSPER, REVIVE, RAISE UP, RESTORE 興.

N615
hsing 1
M2753
xīn
prosper
begin
increase
rise
raise
flourish

共	六	興	同	𦥑	 𦥑
BOTH, TOGETHER J 376	(TABLE WITH LEGS)	INTEREST, ENTERTAINMENT, PLEASURE, TO RISE, PROSPER, REVIVE, RESTORE	SAME J 295	HANDS (ON LEFT & RT.)	ARCHAIC HANDS

Thomas Stearns Eliot   The Love Song of Alfred Prufrock
I should have been a pair of ragged claws
Scuttling across the floor of silent seas.

KIN, (LEVEL, EQUALITY).

RAD 32 STROKE 7 JME 590

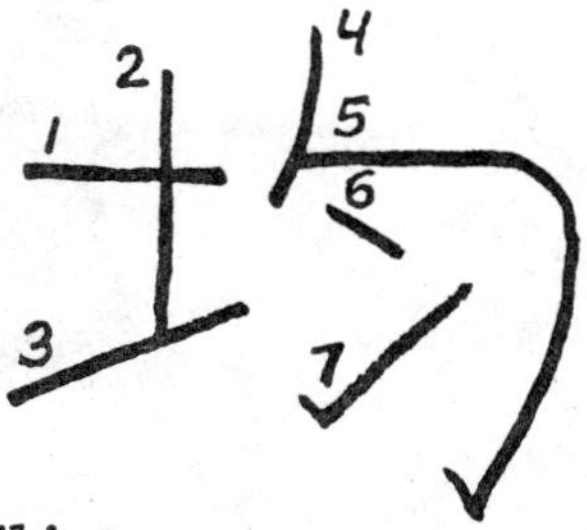

THE BENDING OVER SHADOOF 勹 (DIPS) EQUAL 均 (BUCKETS OF WATER) REPEATEDLY ⺀ FOR LEVEL, EQUALITY 均 (IN THE FIELDS). THE SHADOOF IS POSITIONED ON THE EARTH 土 AS IT REACHES AND CARRIES THE WATER FROM CANAL, RIVER, OR WELL TO THE LAND.

I have measured out my life with coffee spoons. T.S. Eliot

N1065
chun 1
M1724
jūn
equal
equality
fairly

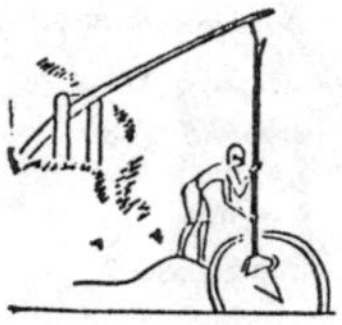	土	均	勻	勹	次
EGYPT SHADOOF	SOIL, EARTH J 17	LEVEL, EQUALITY	DIP, LADLE, MEASURE OF AREA OR CAPACITY N 740	WRAPPING R 20	ORDER, NEXT, SEQUENCE J 227

The Histories   Herodotus
A well five miles distance from Ardericca yields three different products, bitumen, salt, and oil. The contrivance used to raise the fluid is a shadoof. The long pole is balanced on a fulcrum. At one end of the pole, half a wineskin is attached to a rope. The wineskin is dipped to draw up the liquid which is poured into a tank, and then drained into another container where the three products become separated, the bitumen and salt hardening promptly.

JME 591 STROKE 4 RAD 22

KU, WARD, DISTRICT, SECTION.

WARD, DISTRICT, SECTION 区 IS A SUBDIVIDED ㄨ SPACE ⼕ (OF THE CITY).

A ward is a division of the city for administrative, representative, or electoral purposes.

Ward is related to warden meaning to watch over, guard.

N757

ch'u 1

M1599

qū

place

district

RESET STARS OF DIPPER

DRAWING, PLAN J 261

ENCLOSURE, BOX ON SIDE R 22

WARD, DISTRICT, SECTION

CROSS-STITCH BLADES, SHEARS, FIVE

TO BE MIXED J 212

MAYAN DIPPER OF STARS

(MAP OF THE GREAT BEAR, BIG DIPPER, SEVEN STARS)

JME 592 STROKE 5 RAD 30

KU, PHRASE, CLAUSE, SENTENCE, VERSE, STANZA.

THE MOUTH 口 (LIKE THE SHADOOF 勹 DIPS AGAIN) FOR A PHRASE, CLAUSE, SENTENCE, VERSE, STANZA 句

O let us howle, some heavy note,
    some deadly-dogged howle,
Sounding, as from the threatning throat,
    of beastes, and fatall fowle.
John Webster The Dutchesse of Malfy

N745

chu4

M1541

jù

sentence

phrase

PUP, DOG N 2875

MOUTH J 27

PHRASE, CLAUSE, VERSE, STANZA, SENTENCE

DIP, LADLE, UNIT OF AREA OR CAPACITY

WRAPPING R 20

TO WRAP, COVER J 511

A Connecticut Yankee at King Arthur's Court Mark Twain
Whenever the literary German dives into a sentence, that is the last you are going to see of him till he emerges on the other side of the Atlantic with his verb in his mouth.

He mouths a sentence as a cur mouths a bone. Charles Churchill

GUN, ARMY, TROOPS, MILITARY AUTHORITIES.

RAD 14 STROKE 9 JME 593

THE ARMY, TROOPS, MILITARY AUTHORITIES 軍 HAD A CHARIOT 車 WITH A COVER 冖.

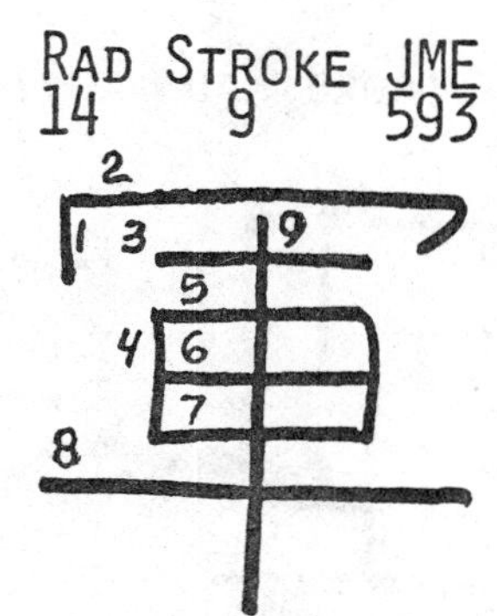

The ancient Chinese concept was that the earth and sky formed a great chariot, the earth was the flat chariot bed, and the sky was the umbrella on a tilted pole. The umbrella, whether the nine-tiered article of the Siamese emperor or that of Little Black Sambo and the tiger, denoted authority.

N628
chun 1
M1722
jūn
military
army

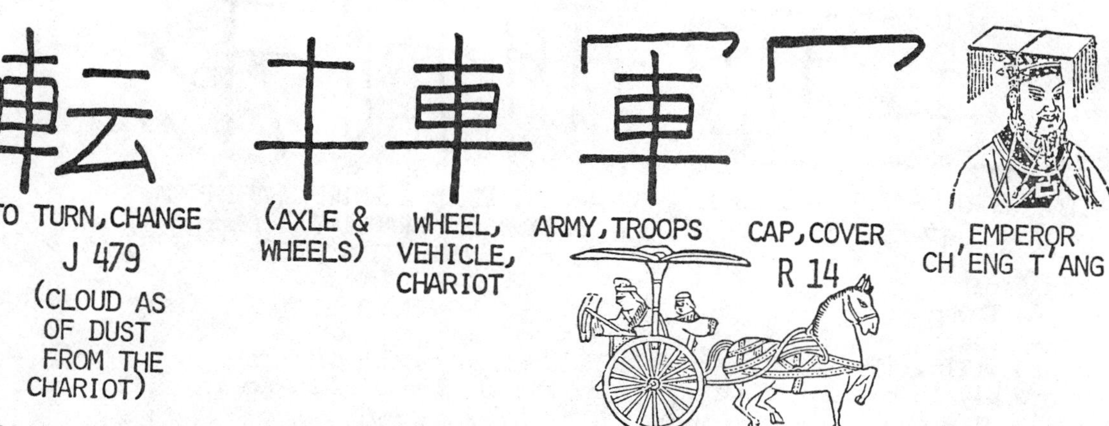

GUN; MURE, GROUP, CROWD, FLOCK, HERD, SWARM, COMMON RUN; MURERU, MURAGARU, TO CROWD, FLOCK, SWARM IV.

RAD 123 STROKE 13 JME 594

A GROUP, FLOCK, HERD, SWARM, COMMON RUN 群 OF YOU, MISTERS, MASTERS 君 CROWDS, FLOCKS LIKE A FLOCK, HERD 群 OF GOATS 羊.

Trotter: Instincts of the Herd in Peace and War

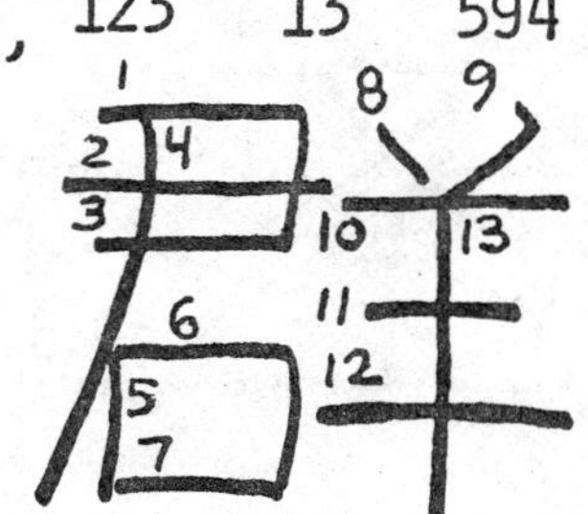

N3667
ch'un2
M1737
qún
flock
herd
class
social

郡 君 群 羊

HORNS
HEAD
FORELEGS
BODY
HIND LEGS
TAIL

COUNTRY, DISTRICT
J 384

GENTLEMAN, MR.
J 198

GROUP, CROWD, FLOCK, HERD, TO CROWD, FLOCK,

GOAT
R 123

A.D.
STICK IN HAND, MOUTHS COMMAND SHEEP AND LAND.

Idylls of the King The Passing of Arthur Lord Tennyson
For what are men better than sheep or goats
That nourish a blind life within the brain.

IBEX

The Mysterious Stranger Mark Twain
"Still, it is true, lamb, said Satan. "Look at you in war, what mutton you are, and how rediculous!"

JME 595 STROKE 9 RAD 32

KEI; KATA (GATA), MODEL, MOLD, TYPE, PATTERN.

MODEL, MOLD, TYPE, PATTERN 型 ON EARTH 土 IS PUNISHMENT, PENALTY 刑.

Patterns Amy Lowell
I walk down the garden-paths,
And all the daffodils
Are blowing, and the bright blue squills
I walk down the patterned garden-paths
In my stiff brocaded gown
With my powdered hair and jeweled fan,

N1077

hsing2

M2756

xíng

statute

law

mold

土 型 刑 形

EARTH ALTAR | EARTH, SOIL J 17 | MODEL, MOLD, TYPE, PATTERN | PUNISHMENT, PENALTY N 670 | (BODY & KNIFE) FOR BRANDING, AMPUTATION, & CASTRATION AS PENALTIES | SHAPE, FORM J 200

I too am a rare
Pattern. As I wander down
The garden-paths.
The blue and yellow flowers
stood up proudly in the sun, Each one

I stood upright too,
Held rigid to the pattern
By the stiffness of my gown;

JME 596 STROKE 11 RAD 120

KEI, LONGITUDE; KYO, SUTRA; HERU, TO PASS, TO ELAPSE, TO PASS THROUGH.

THE HAND 又 ON THE EARTH 土 MAKES LIGHT, EASY, SLIGHT 軽 THREAD- 糸 (LIKE LINES SUCH AS OF) LONGITUDE 経 OR THE SUTRAS 経.

The Deformed Transformed Lord Byron
CAESAR It answers better to resolve the alphabet
Back into hieroglyphics. Like your statesman,
And prophet, pontiff, doctor, alchymist,
Philosopher, and what not, they have built

N3523

ching 1

M1123

jīng

classics

to plan

to pass

manage

meridians

warp

糸 経 又 土 軽

COCOONS & THREADS | THREADS, STRINGS R 120 | LONGITUDE, TO PASS, ELAPSE, PASS THROUGH | HAND R 29 | EARTH, SOIL J 17 | LIGHT (IN WT.), SLIGHT, EASY J 387

More Babels, without new dispersion, ---
They are wiser now, and will not separate
For nonsense. Nay, it is their brotherhood,
Their Shibboleth, their Koran, Talmud, their
Cabala; their best brick-work, wherewithal
They build more---

KETSU, LACK, GAP; KAKERU, BE BROKEN OFF, LACK, TO BE CHIPPED IV; KAKU, TO LACK, TO BREAK.

RAD	STROKE	JME
76	4	597

(THE LUNGS) IN THE COVER ⺈ (OF THE BODY) WANT, LACK 欠 THE ENTRY 入 (OF AIR).
LACKING, WANTING THE AIR, THE BODY IS BROKEN.

欠

The Nightingale Gerard Manley Hopkins
I thought the air must cut and strain
The windpipe when he sucked his breath
And when he turned it back again

歌 入 人 欠 ⺈ 次

SONG,TO SING J 166 | TO ENTER, PUT IN J 125 | TO ENTER, PUT IN J 125 | LACK,GAP, BE BROKEN OFF, BE CHIPPED, R 76 | BEND OVER, COVER | NEXT J 227

N2412
ch'ien4
M904
qiàn
owe
deficient

The music must be death.
With not a thing to make me fear,
A singing bird in morning clear
To me was terrible to hear.

KEN, MATTER, CASE.
THE PERSON 亻 HAS A MATTER, CASE 件 ABOUT A COW, BULL 牛.

RAD	STROKE	JME
9	6	598

Robert Louis Stevenson The Cow
The friendly cow all red and white,
I love with all my heart
She gives me cream with all her might
To eat with apple tart.

件

亻 件 牛 告

PICTURE PERSON, MAN | MATTER,CASE | BULL,OX,COW J 62 | PICTURED BULL,OX,COW | TO TELL, INFORM J 398

N368
chien4
M862
jiàn
article
to divide

Like "Having to see a man about a horse (cow)."

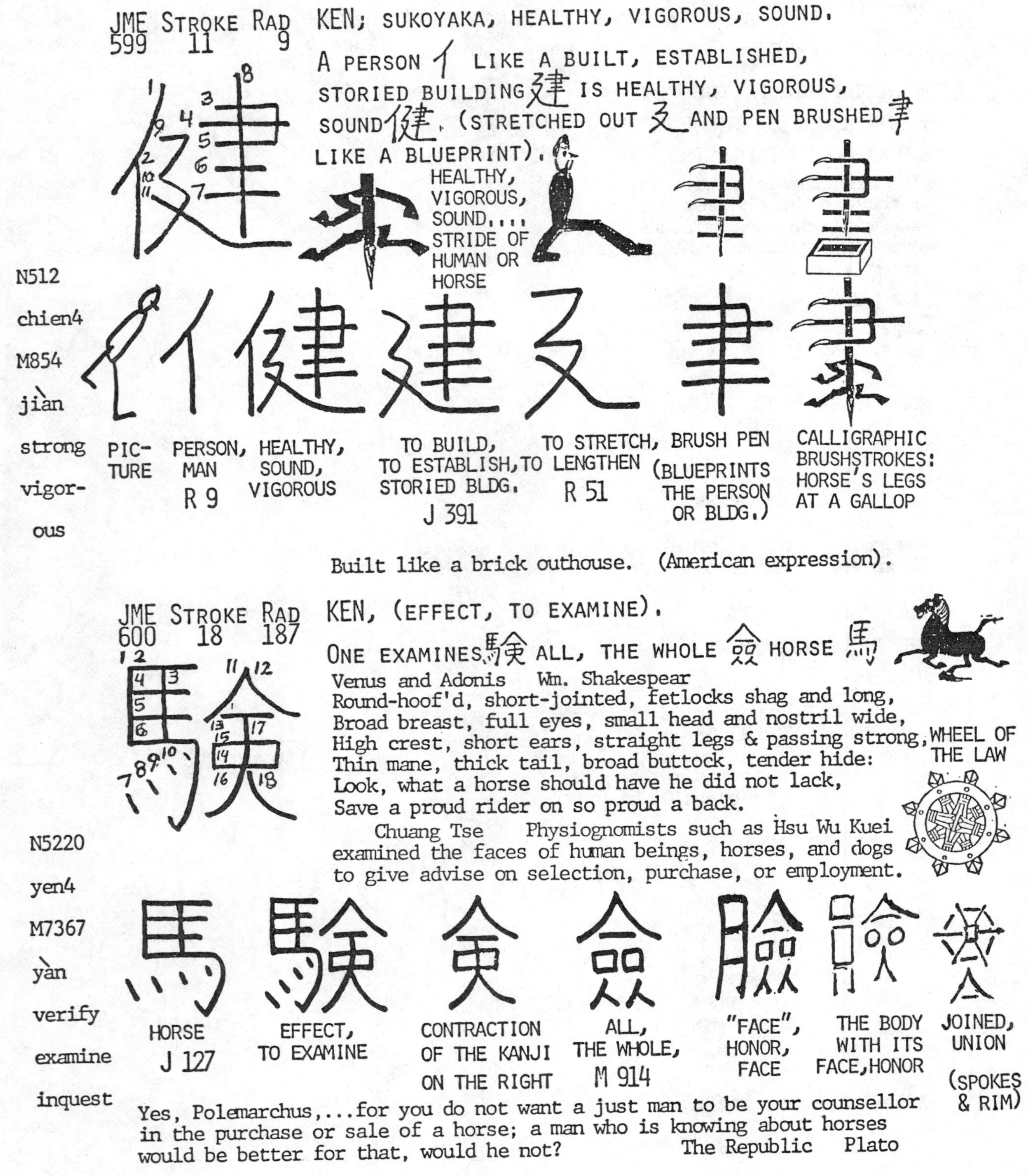

JME 599 Stroke 11 Rad 9

KEN; SUKOYAKA, HEALTHY, VIGOROUS, SOUND.

A PERSON 亻 LIKE A BUILT, ESTABLISHED, STORIED BUILDING 建 IS HEALTHY, VIGOROUS, SOUND 健. (STRETCHED OUT 廴 AND PEN BRUSHED 聿 LIKE A BLUEPRINT).

HEALTHY, VIGOROUS, SOUND,... STRIDE OF HUMAN OR HORSE

N512
chien4
M854
jiàn
strong
vigor-ous

PICTURE — PERSON, MAN R 9 — HEALTHY, SOUND, VIGOROUS — TO BUILD, TO ESTABLISH, STORIED BLDG. J 391 — TO STRETCH, TO LENGTHEN R 51 — BRUSH PEN (BLUEPRINTS THE PERSON OR BLDG.) — CALLIGRAPHIC BRUSHSTROKES: HORSE'S LEGS AT A GALLOP

Built like a brick outhouse. (American expression).

JME 600 Stroke 18 Rad 187

KEN, (EFFECT, TO EXAMINE).

ONE EXAMINES 験 ALL, THE WHOLE 僉 HORSE 馬

Venus and Adonis Wm. Shakespear
Round-hoof'd, short-jointed, fetlocks shag and long,
Broad breast, full eyes, small head and nostril wide,
High crest, short ears, straight legs & passing strong,
Thin mane, thick tail, broad buttock, tender hide:
Look, what a horse should have he did not lack,
Save a proud rider on so proud a back.

WHEEL OF THE LAW

Chuang Tse Physiognomists such as Hsu Wu Kuei examined the faces of human beings, horses, and dogs to give advise on selection, purchase, or employment.

N5220
yen4
M7367
yàn
verify
examine
inquest

HORSE J 127 — EFFECT, TO EXAMINE — CONTRACTION OF THE KANJI ON THE RIGHT — ALL, THE WHOLE, M 914 — "FACE", HONOR, FACE — THE BODY WITH ITS FACE, HONOR — JOINED, UNION (SPOKES & RIM)

Yes, Polemarchus,...for you do not want a just man to be your counsellor in the purchase or sale of a horse; a man who is knowing about horses would be better for that, would he not? The Republic Plato

GEN; KAGIRI, LIMIT, AS FAR AS POSSIBLE; KAGIRU, TO LIMIT, TO RESTRICT.

FROM THE MOUND 阝 TO THE ROOTS 艮 IS THE LIMIT, AS FAR AS POSSIBLE 限.

RAD 170 STROKE 9 JME 601

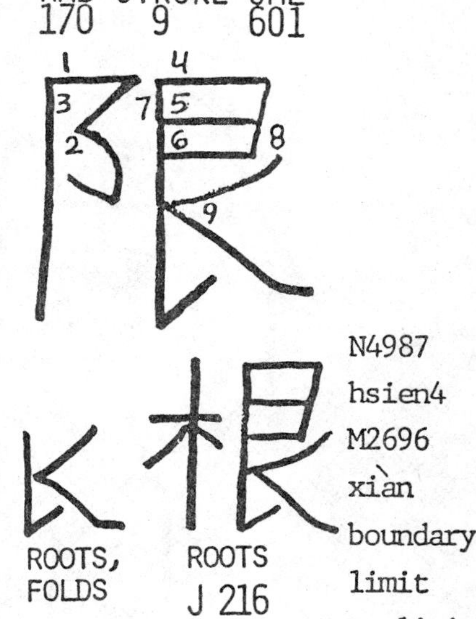

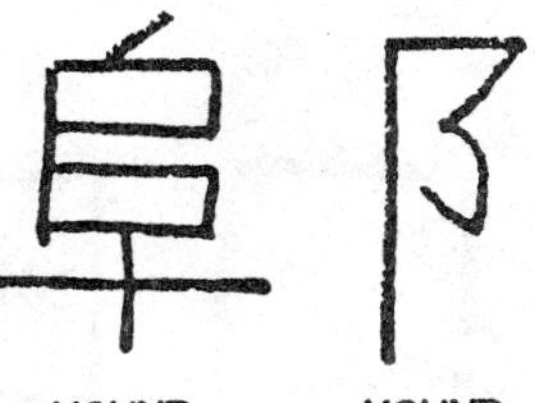

MOUND R 170 — MOUND R 170

LIMIT, AS FAR AS POSSIBLE, TO LIMIT

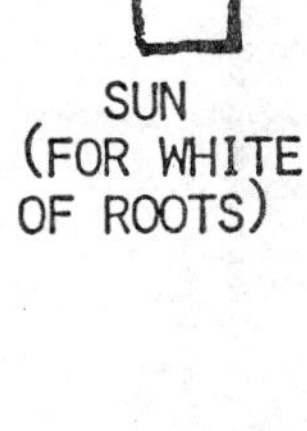

SUN (FOR WHITE OF ROOTS)

ROOTS, FOLDS — ROOTS J 216

N4987
hsien4
M2696
xiàn
boundary
limit
to limit

GEN, (PRESENT, EXISTING, ACTUAL); ARAWARERU, TO APPEAR, COME IN SIGHT, BE REVEALED; ARAWASU, TO SHOW, TO DISPLAY, TO REPRESENT.

THE PRESENT, EXISTING, ACTUAL 現 KING 王 APPEARS, COMES INTO SIGHT, IS REVEALED, SHOWS, DISPLAYS, IS REPRESENTED 現 AS HE SEES, LOOKS 見 ON INSPECTION TOURS.

RAD 96 STROKE 11 JME 602

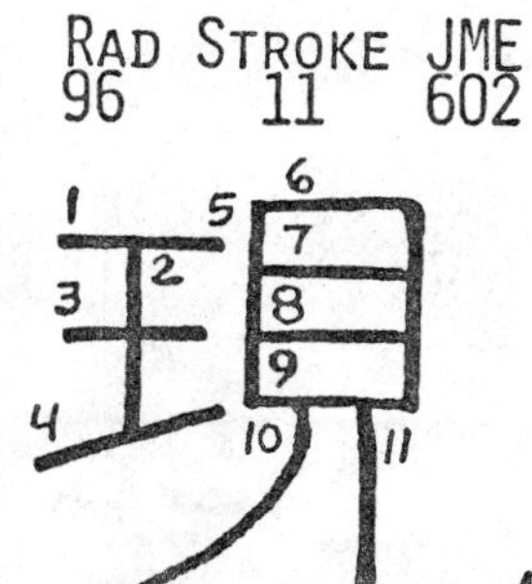

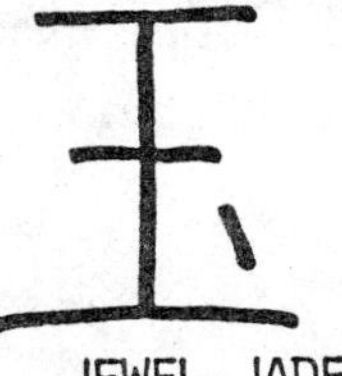

JEWEL, JADE J 64

(THE ROYAL JADE SEAL EXTENDS KINGLY AUTHORITY)

KING J 49

(VERTICAL KING LINE MEDIATES AMONG THE HORIZONTAL HEAVEN, MAN, EARTH LINES)

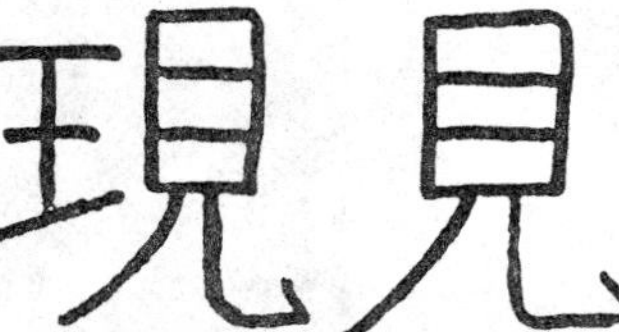

PRESENT, EXISTING, ACTUAL, TO APPEAR, COME IN SIGHT, BE REVEALED

TO SEE, TO LOOK J 67

PICTURE OF WALKING EYE

PICTURE OF KING'S JADE BEADS ON A STRING

N2943
hsien4
M2684
xiàn
now
at present
to appear
to see

("KING" KANJI IS ON THE FOREHEADS OF THE KING OF HELL AND TIGER KING OF BEASTS)

JME 603 STROKE 10 RAD 9

KO, KA, (INDIVIDUAL), COUNTER FOR ARTICLES.
A PERSON 亻 WHO IS OLD 古 AND HARD 固 AND AN INDIVIDUAL 個 CAN BE ENUMERATED 個.

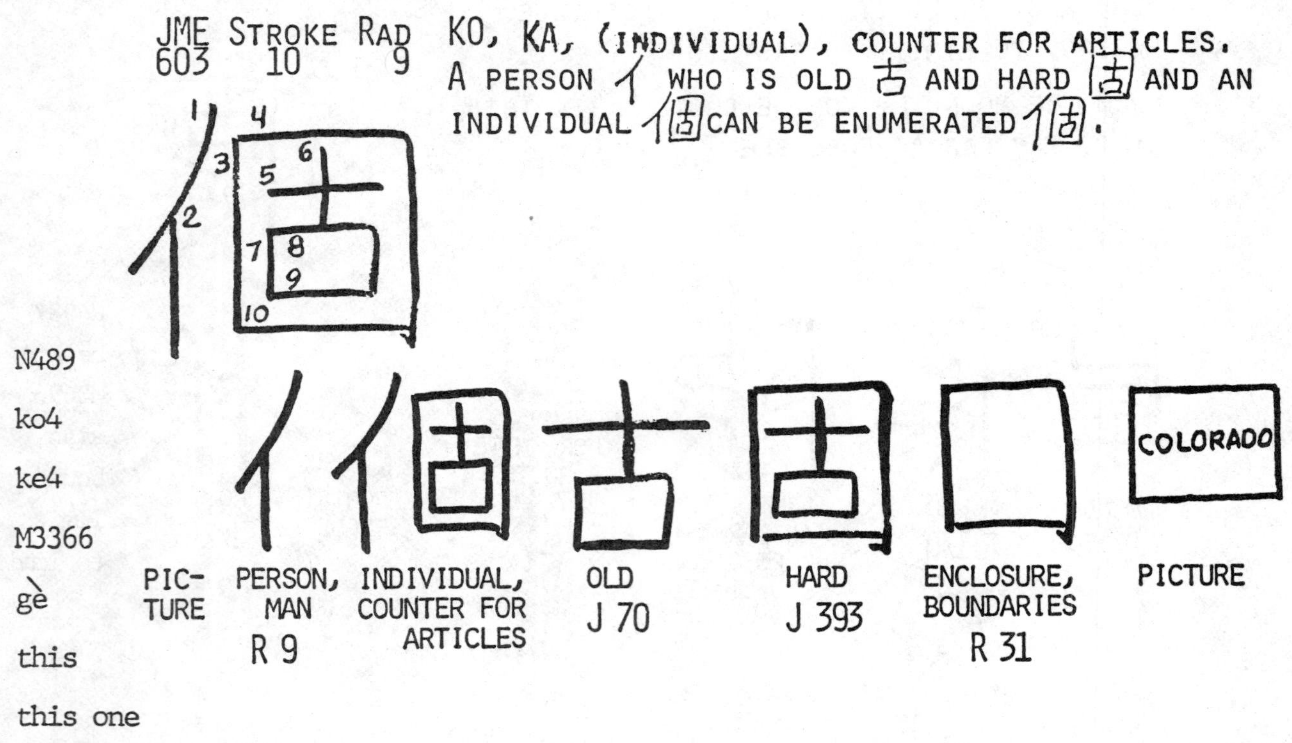

N489
ko4
ke4
M3366
gè
this
this one
enumerator

JME 604. STROKE 20 RAD 149

GO, (TO PROTECT, TO DEFEND).
THE WORDS 言 OF THE SHORT-TAILED BIRD 隹 IN ITS GRASS 艹 (NEST) PROTECT, DEFEND 護. AGAINST OR LIKE A HAND 又.

THE FALCONS AS ON THE RIGHT SHIELD ARE USUALLY BORNE WITH CLOSE WINGS SO AS TO BE DISTINGUISHED FROM THE EAGLE OF HERALDRY. THE LEFT SHIELD HAS TWO CROWS OR CORBIES.

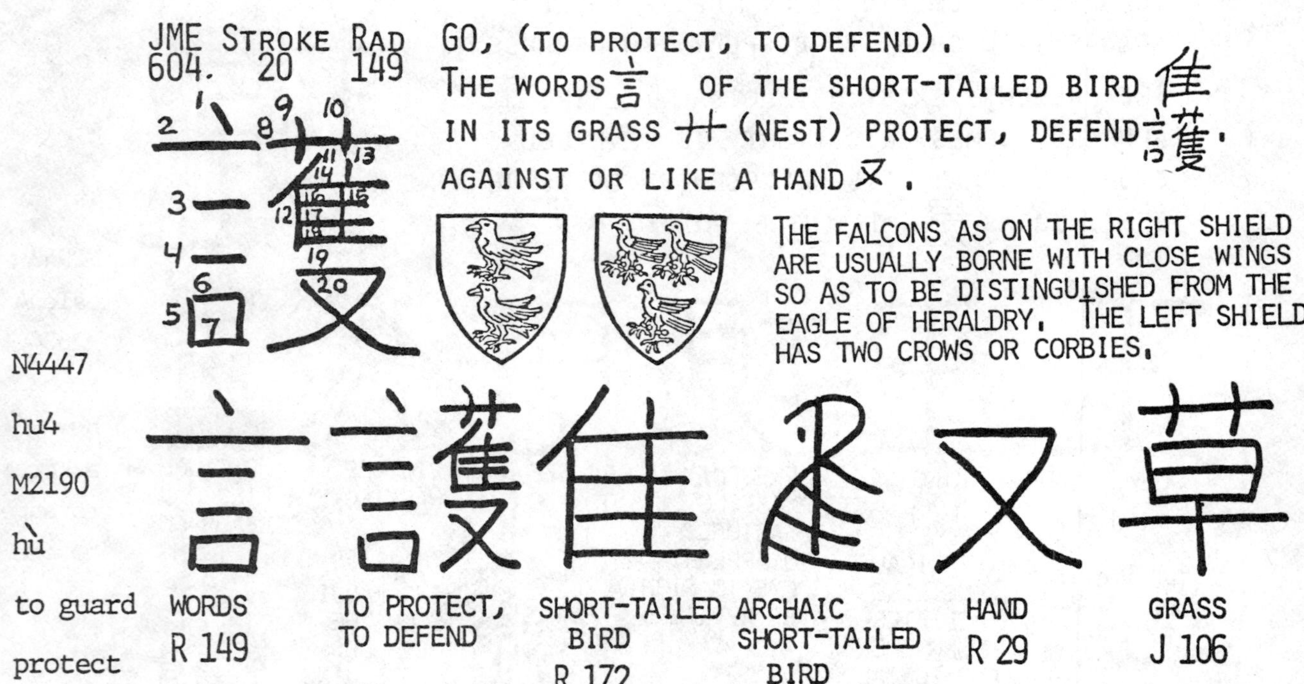

N4447
hu4
M2190
hù
to guard
protect

The short-tailed birds have been protecting and defending their nests for centuries against egg collectors and those who steal the nestlings, especially for hawking. In Japan, the Hawk Office arranged the presentation of hawks from the provinces to the Imperial court. Yamato monogatari.

KŌ, MERITS, SUCCESS, CREDIT, HONOR;
KU, MERITS.

RAD 48 STROKE 5 JME 605

THE STRENGTH, POWER 功 OF THE WORKER 工 IN CONSTRUCTION 工 HAS MERITS, SUCCESS, CREDIT, HONOR 功.

功

N1454 kung 1 M3698 gōng merit

左	工	功	力	男	労
LEFT J 18 (WORKMAN ALSO USES LEFT HAND)	WORKMAN, CONSTRUCTION J 71 (VERTICAL PLUMBLINE CEILING TO FLOOR)	MERITS, SUCCESS, CREDIT, HONOR (STRENGTH AND WORKMANSHIP)	STRENGTH, POWER J 148	MAN, MALE J 109	LABOR, SERVICE, TROUBLE J 542

KO, ATSUI, THICK, CORDIAL, KIND, IMPUDENT.

RAD 27 STROKE 9 JME 606

THE MOUTH SPEAKING 曰 FROM THE CLIFF 厂 OF THE CHILD 子 IS THICK, CORDIAL, KIND, IMPUDENT 厚. (THIS IS THE CLIFF 厂 THAT PRESSURES 圧 THE EARTH 土 BY ITS HILLSMEN).

厚

N824 hou4 M2147 hòu thick generous

	厂	厚	曰	子	音
PICTURE OF CLIFFS	CLIFF R 27	THICK, CORDIAL, KIND, IMPUDENT (IS THE SPEECH OF CLIFF CHILD)	SAY, SPEAK J 72	CHILD J 31	SOUND J 50 (VOICE BELOW CLEAR TO STANDEE ABOVE)

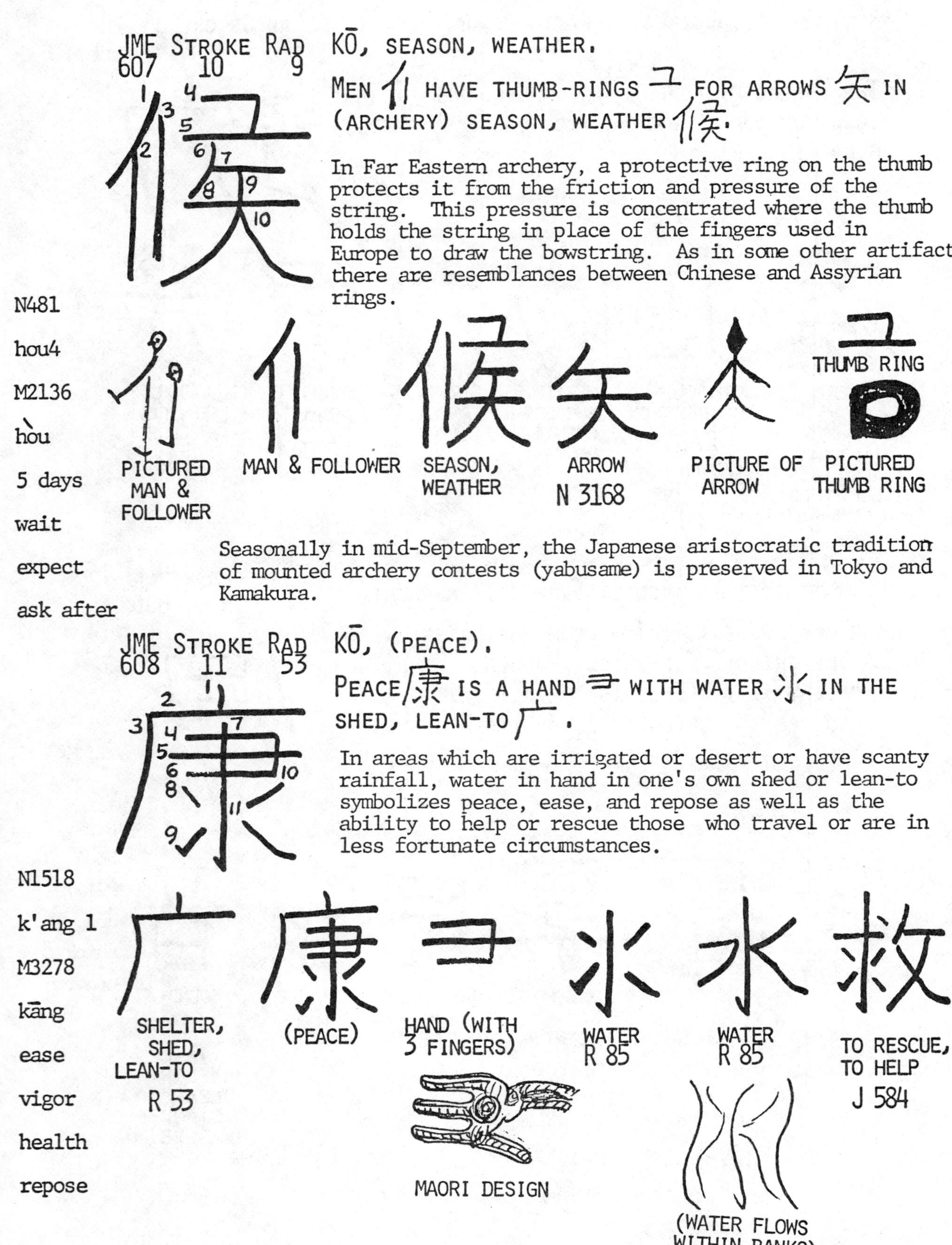

JME 607 · Stroke 10 · Rad 9

KŌ, SEASON, WEATHER.

MEN 亻 HAVE THUMB-RINGS コ FOR ARROWS 矢 IN (ARCHERY) SEASON, WEATHER 候.

In Far Eastern archery, a protective ring on the thumb protects it from the friction and pressure of the string. This pressure is concentrated where the thumb holds the string in place of the fingers used in Europe to draw the bowstring. As in some other artifacts, there are resemblances between Chinese and Assyrian rings.

N481

hou4

M2136

hòu

5 days

wait

expect

ask after

PICTURED MAN & FOLLOWER · MAN & FOLLOWER · SEASON, WEATHER · ARROW N 3168 · PICTURE OF ARROW · THUMB RING · PICTURED THUMB RING

Seasonally in mid-September, the Japanese aristocratic tradition of mounted archery contests (yabusame) is preserved in Tokyo and Kamakura.

JME 608 · Stroke 11 · Rad 53

KŌ, (PEACE).

PEACE 康 IS A HAND ヨ WITH WATER 氺 IN THE SHED, LEAN-TO 广.

In areas which are irrigated or desert or have scanty rainfall, water in hand in one's own shed or lean-to symbolizes peace, ease, and repose as well as the ability to help or rescue those who travel or are in less fortunate circumstances.

N1518

k'ang 1

M3278

kāng

ease

vigor

health

repose

广 SHELTER, SHED, LEAN-TO R 53 · 康 (PEACE) · ヨ HAND (WITH 3 FINGERS) · 氺 WATER R 85 · 水 WATER R 85 · 救 TO RESCUE, TO HELP J 584

MAORI DESIGN

(WATER FLOWS WITHIN BANKS)

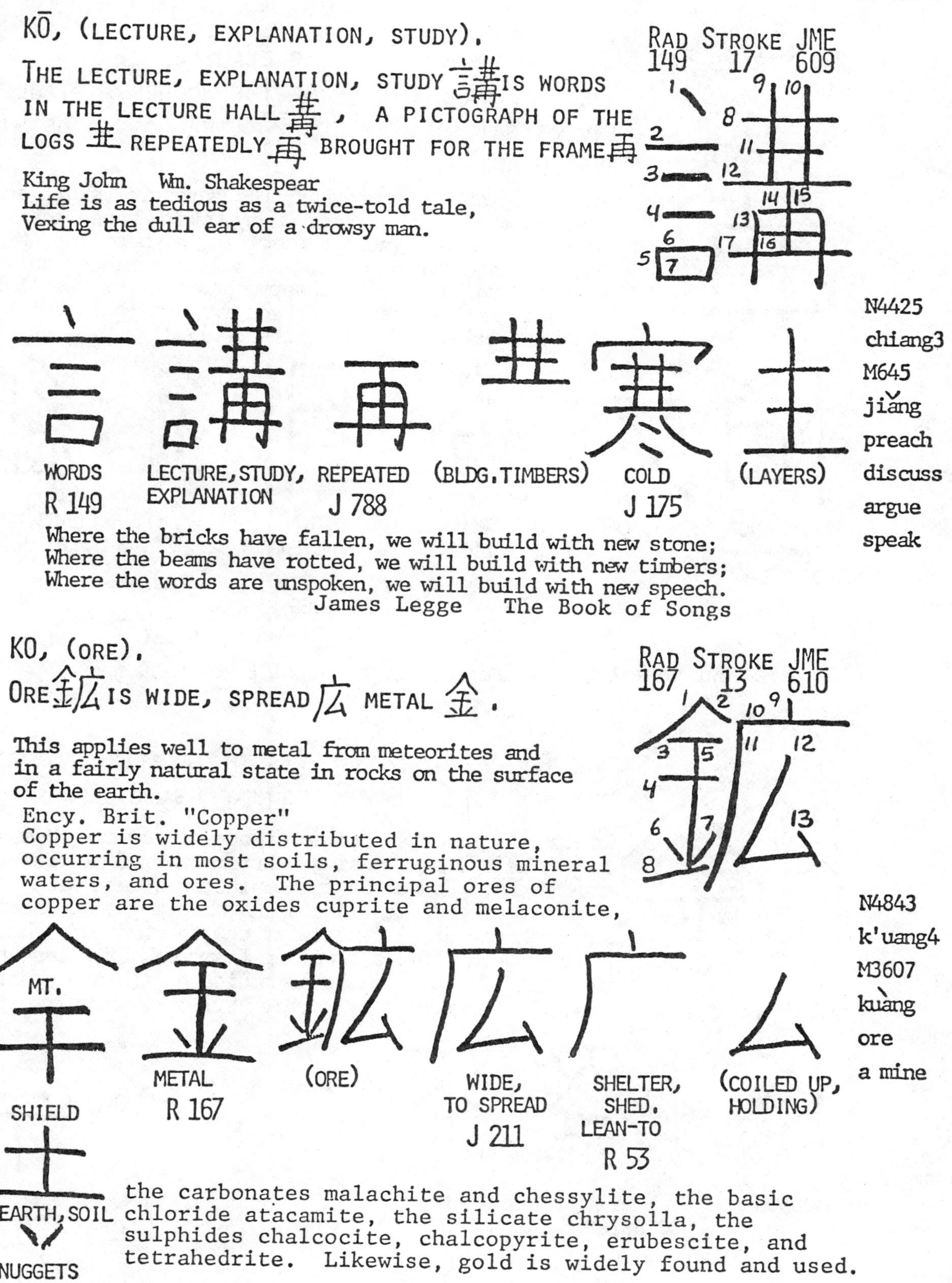

KŌ, (LECTURE, EXPLANATION, STUDY).

RAD 149 STROKE 17 JME 609

THE LECTURE, EXPLANATION, STUDY 講 IS WORDS IN THE LECTURE HALL 冓, A PICTOGRAPH OF THE LOGS 井 REPEATEDLY 再 BROUGHT FOR THE FRAME 再

King John Wm. Shakespear
Life is as tedious as a twice-told tale,
Vexing the dull ear of a drowsy man.

N4425
chiang3
M645
jiǎng
preach
discuss
argue
speak

Where the bricks have fallen, we will build with new stone;
Where the beams have rotted, we will build with new timbers;
Where the words are unspoken, we will build with new speech.
James Legge The Book of Songs

KO, (ORE).

RAD 167 STROKE 13 JME 610

ORE 鉱 IS WIDE, SPREAD 広 METAL 金.

This applies well to metal from meteorites and in a fairly natural state in rocks on the surface of the earth.

Ency. Brit. "Copper"
Copper is widely distributed in nature, occurring in most soils, ferruginous mineral waters, and ores. The principal ores of copper are the oxides cuprite and melaconite,

N4843
k'uang4
M3607
kuàng
ore
a mine

the carbonates malachite and chessylite, the basic chloride atacamite, the silicate chrysolla, the sulphides chalcocite, chalcopyrite, erubescite, and tetrahedrite. Likewise, gold is widely found and used.

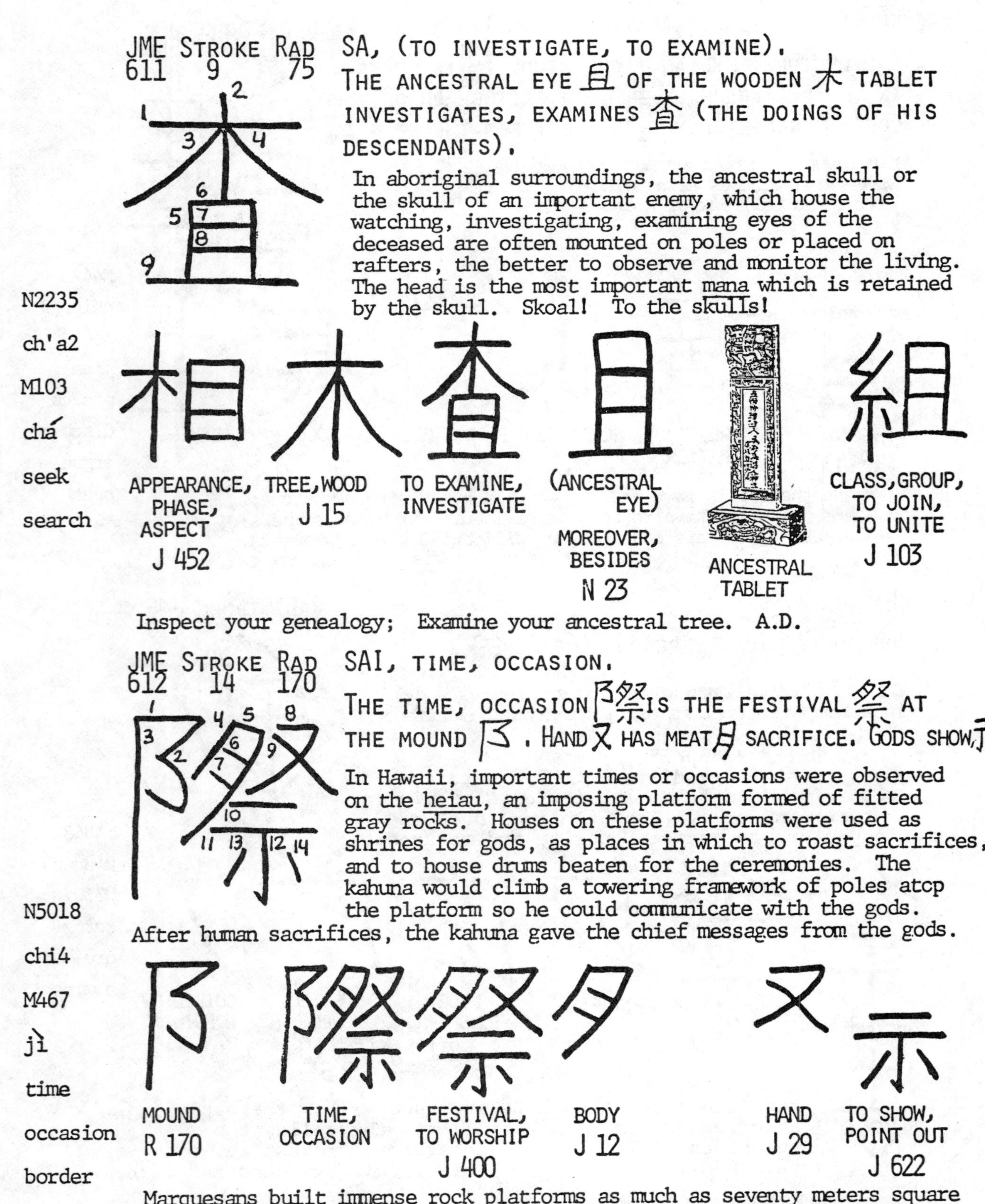

JME 611 STROKE 9 RAD 75

SA, (TO INVESTIGATE, TO EXAMINE).

THE ANCESTRAL EYE 且 OF THE WOODEN 木 TABLET INVESTIGATES, EXAMINES 査 (THE DOINGS OF HIS DESCENDANTS).

In aboriginal surroundings, the ancestral skull or the skull of an important enemy, which house the watching, investigating, examining eyes of the deceased are often mounted on poles or placed on rafters, the better to observe and monitor the living. The head is the most important mana which is retained by the skull. Skoal! To the skulls!

N2235

ch'a2

M103

chá

seek

search

相 APPEARANCE, PHASE, ASPECT J 452

木 TREE, WOOD J 15

査 TO EXAMINE, INVESTIGATE

且 (ANCESTRAL EYE) MOREOVER, BESIDES N 23

ANCESTRAL TABLET

組 CLASS, GROUP, TO JOIN, TO UNITE J 103

Inspect your genealogy; Examine your ancestral tree. A.D.

JME 612 STROKE 14 RAD 170

SAI, TIME, OCCASION.

THE TIME, OCCASION 際 IS THE FESTIVAL 祭 AT THE MOUND 阝. HAND 又 HAS MEAT 月 SACRIFICE. GODS SHOW 示.

In Hawaii, important times or occasions were observed on the heiau, an imposing platform formed of fitted gray rocks. Houses on these platforms were used as shrines for gods, as places in which to roast sacrifices, and to house drums beaten for the ceremonies. The kahuna would climb a towering framework of poles atcp the platform so he could communicate with the gods. After human sacrifices, the kahuna gave the chief messages from the gods.

N5018

chi4

M467

jì

time

occasion

border

阝 MOUND R 170

際 TIME, OCCASION

祭 FESTIVAL, TO WORSHIP J 400

夕 BODY J 12

又 HAND J 29

示 TO SHOW, POINT OUT J 622

Marquesans built immense rock platforms as much as seventy meters square where their carved idols were grouped and their ceremonies were held.

ZAI, OUTSKIRTS, SUBURBS, COUNTRY; -ZAI, TO BE LOCATED IN; ARU, TO HAVE.

THE PERSON'S 亻 RIGHT HAND 𠂇 ON THE EARTH 土 HAVING 在 (PROPERTY) LOCATED IN 在 THE OUTSKIRTS, SUBURBS, COUNTRY 在.

RAD 32 STROKE 6 JME 613

在

有 TO HAVE, TO EXIST J 523

ARCHAIC HAND

HAND

PICTURE

亻 PERSON J 9

在 OUTSKIRTS, SUBURBS, COUNTRY, BE LOCATED IN, TO HAVE

土 SOIL, EARTH J 17

陸 LAND J 529

N1055
tsai4
M6657
zài
be present
be alive
at
in
on

To have and to hold. Landholder. Landowner.

SATSU, SAI, KOROSU, TO KILL, TO MURDER.

THE TREE 木 (CLUB) STRIKES 殳 AS A WING 几 OR A LEFT HAND 又 WITH CUTTING BLADES 㐅 KILLS, MURDERS 殺.

RAD 79 STROKE 10 JME 614

殺

The crossed lines which are the crest of onetime Lords of Nihonmatsu are said to have been accidentally designed as a broad X by an ancestor wiping his bloody sword on the cloth over his thigh as he killed opponent after opponent in a single battle.

㐅 BLADE, SHEARS

木 TREE, WOOD J 15

殺 TO KILL, TO MURDER

殳 TO STRIKE, R 79

几 WING, TABLE, STOOL R 16

又 HAND R 29

N2454
sha 1
M5615
shā
kill
destroy
murder

The way they administer justice is this. When any one has committed a petty theft, they give him, under the orders of authority, seven blows of a stick, or seventeen, or twenty-seven, or thirty-seven, or forty-seven, and so forth, ... Of these beatings, sometimes they die.

The Travels of Marco Polo

JME 615 Stroke 1 Rad 172

雑

ZATSU, ZŌ, MISCELLANEOUS;
ZATSU NA, ROUGH, COARSE, RUDE.

NINE 九 IS A ROUGH MISCELLANEOUS 雑 (ODD NUMBER) LIKE THE SHORT-TAILED BIRDS 隹 IN THE TREE 木 WHO ARE ROUGH, COARSE, RUDE 雑.

N5032
tsa2
M6646
zá
mixed
confused
misc.

集 TO COLLECT, TO GATHER J 243
木 TREE, WOOD J 15
九 NINE R 9
雑 ROUGH, RUDE, COARSE
隹 SHORT-TAILED BIRD R 172
ARCHAIC SHORT-TAILED BIRD

"The Normans," said King Harold, "are good vassals, ...They have brought long lances and swords, but ye have pointed lances and keen-edged bills; and I do not expect that their arms can stand against yours."
Norman Conquest of England. Sir Edw. Creasy

JME 616 Stroke 8 Rad 28

参

SAN, THREE (FOR LEGAL USE);
MAIRU, TO GO, TO COME, TO VISIT, TO VISIT A SHRINE, TO BE DEFEATED, TO DIE.

THE STARS 厶 OF ORION'S BELT — GO, COME, VISIT 参 AS THREE SHADOWS, SHAPES 彡 ON THE CLOUD-GIRDED MOUNTAIN-人 SIDE. THEY ARE THE THREE KINGS VISITED IN A SHRINE AND BEFORE WHOM THERE IS DEFEAT OR DEATH.

N850
ts'an 1
M6685
cān
to counsel
to consult
1 of 3
to visit

厶 COILED, HELD
Note star-shapes of Van Gogh
PICTURED
大 GREAT R 37 (GIRDED MT.)
参 TO GO, COME, TO VISIT, BE DEFEATED, TO DIE
彡 HAIR, SHAPE, SHADOWS R 59
形 SHAPE, FORM J 200

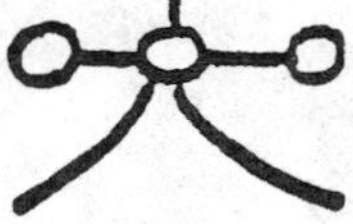

Hoshikage A.D.
Three lighted star-shadows come nightly to me
As slanted shades striping the mountainside lee;
As the Belt of Orion they come and they go,
Three kings are three stars are three shadows I know.

Die heil'gen
drei Könige
aus Morgenland.
Heine

SAN; KAIKO, SILKWORM.

RAD 1 | STROKE 10 | JME 617

THE SILKWORM 蚕 IS THE HEAVENLY 天 INSECT 虫.

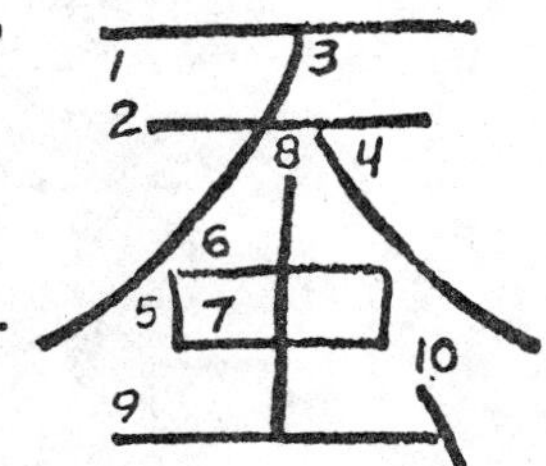

The silkworm represents industry. Yellow silk is spun by the Bombyx Mori which is fed mulberry leaves. The caterpillar was domesticated by the consort of the Yellow Emperor, who was deified as the Goddess of Silk. In some areas, women hatch the eggs by the warmth of their bodies or under their blankets. Note the symbolism of the kanji which shows the silkworm

N57
ts'an2
M6698
cán
silkworm

一 ONE J 1 / 大 GREAT R 37 — 天 HEAVEN, SKY J 119 — 蚕 SILKWORM — 虫 WORM, INSECT J 114 — 中 MIDDLE J 23

INSECT

sheltered or protected under the legs of heaven. The silkworms shed their skins a number of times and eat several times their weight in leaves between moultings. The silkworms are very sensitive to noise and diet and must be treated with great care.

SAN, ACID.

RAD 164 | STROKE 14 | JME 618

ACIDS 酸 OXIDIZED FROM COILED ム STORED SAKE 酒 (STIRRED) DIVIDED 儿 BY THE STICK ／ IN HAND 夂.

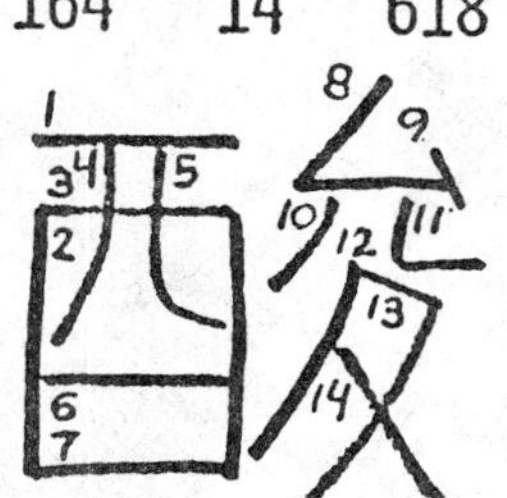

On standing too long, apple cider becomes vinegar or acetic acid, showing the close relationship as in the kanji between the alcoholic beverage and acid.

N4789
suan 1
M5514
suān
sour
acid

酒 SAKE J 422 — 酉 ZODIAC COCK (COCK'S RED-AS-WINE BLOOD USED IN SACRIFICE LIKE LIQUOR) — 酸 ACID — ム COILED — 儿 DIVIDED (LEGS) — 夂 ROD IN HAND R 34

There is an analogy portrayed here between the hatching of eggs and the fermenting of liquor.

JME 619 Stroke 15 Rad 154

SAN, (TO ASSIST, TO AGREE WITH, TO PRAISE).
HUSBANDS 夫夫 ASSISTING, AGREEING WITH, PRAISING 賛 WITH SEA SHELLS 貝 (COWRIE MONEY).

N4516
tsan4
M6676
zàn
assist
praise

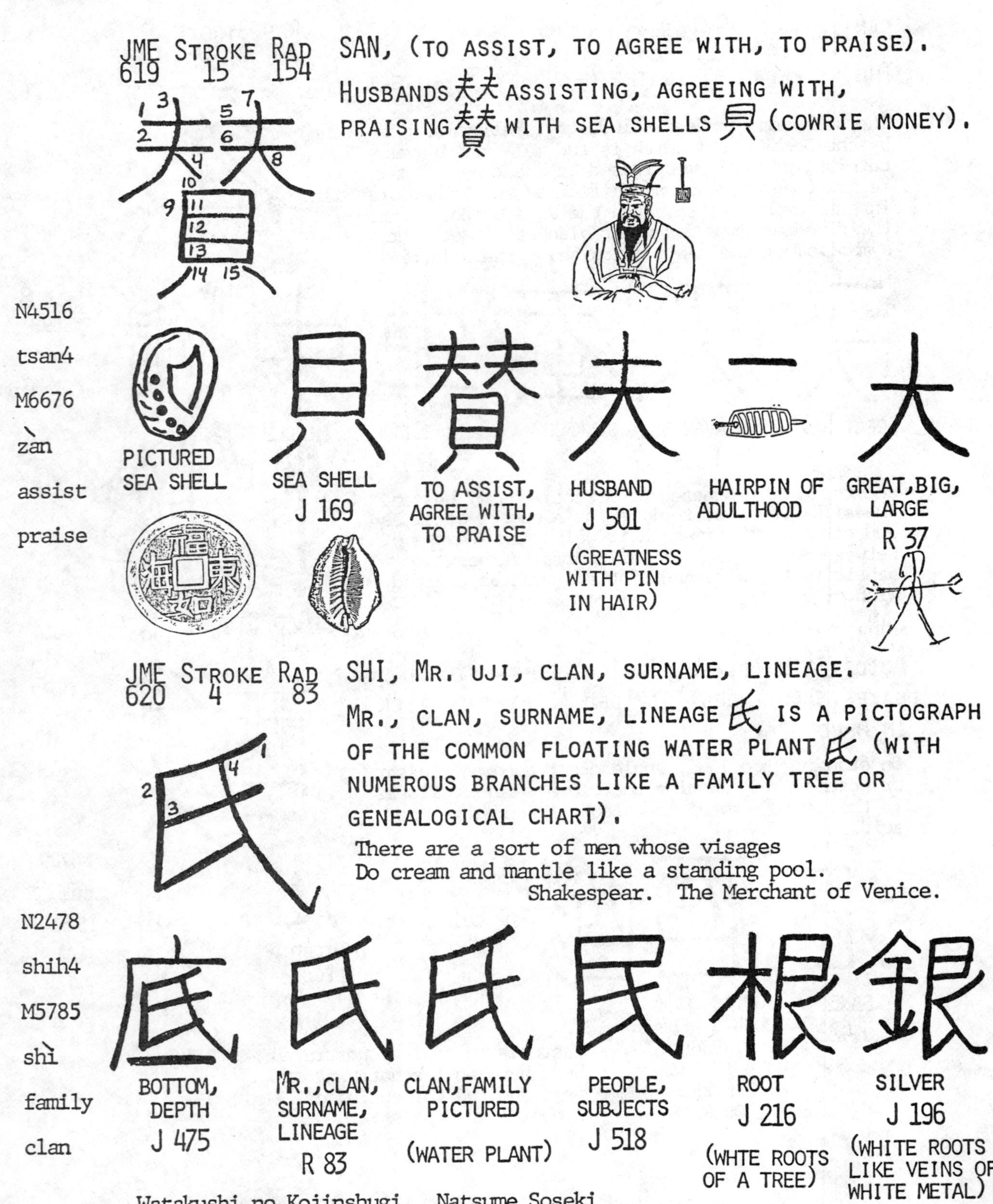

JME 620 Stroke 4 Rad 83

SHI, MR. UJI, CLAN, SURNAME, LINEAGE.
MR., CLAN, SURNAME, LINEAGE 氏 IS A PICTOGRAPH OF THE COMMON FLOATING WATER PLANT 氏 (WITH NUMEROUS BRANCHES LIKE A FAMILY TREE OR GENEALOGICAL CHART).

There are a sort of men whose visages
Do cream and mantle like a standing pool.
Shakespear. The Merchant of Venice.

N2478
shih4
M5785
shì
family
clan

Watakushi no Kojinshugi Natsume Soseki
Finally I realized that I was no better than an unattached floating weed.

SHI, BRANCH; SASAERU, TO SUPPORT, TO MAINTAIN. RAD 65 STROKE 4 JME 621

THE HAND 又 WITH THE MOVING 一 BRANCH 丨 SUPPORTS MAINTAINS 支.

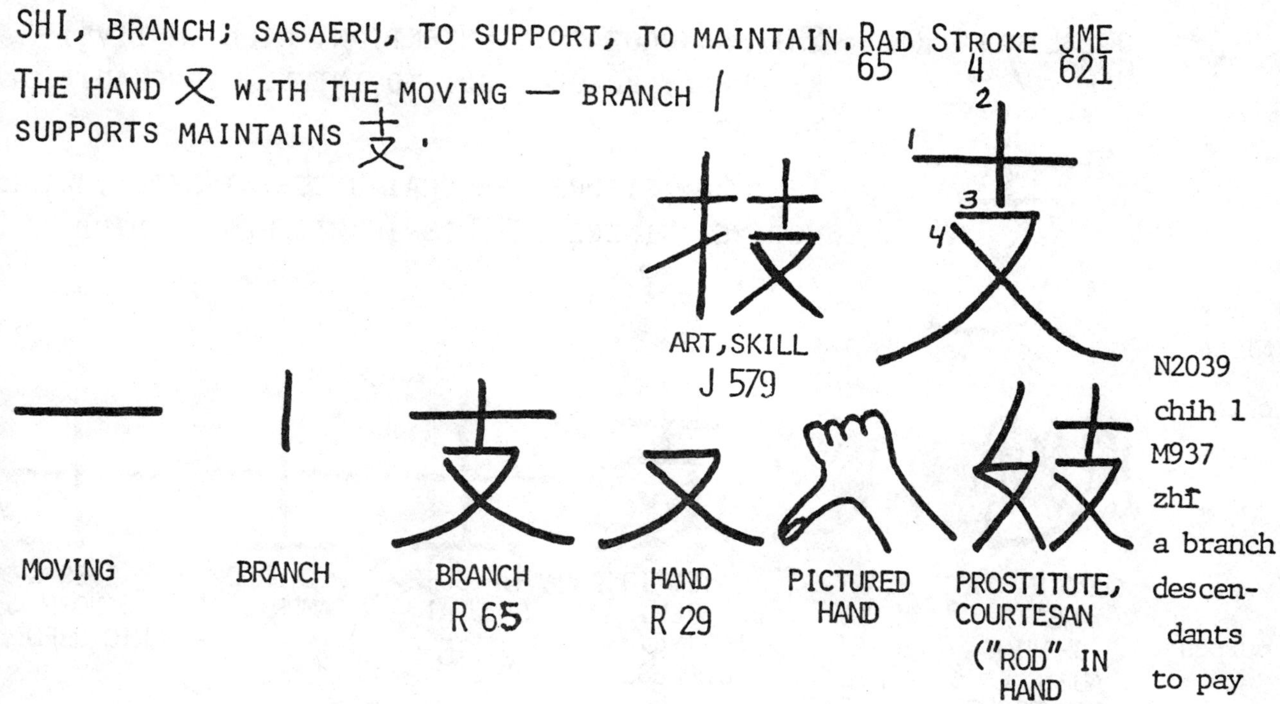

N2039
chih 1
M937
zhī
a branch
descendants
to pay

JI, SHI; SHIMESU, TO SHOW, TO INDICATE, TO POINT OUT.

RAD 113 STROKE 5 JME 622

THE RAYS 小 OF THE CHINESE "THREE LIGHTS", (OR SUN, MOON, AND STARS) SHOW, INDICATE, POINT OUT 示 FROM HEAVEN 一 TO EARTH 一.

Let there be lights in the firmament of the heavens to divide the day from the night, and let them be for signs and seasons, and for days and years. Genesis

1 2 3 4 5 示

二 示 小 光

PICTURED

HEAVEN & EARTH R 7

TO SHOW, TO INDICATE, POINT OUT

THREE LIGHTS

TO SHINE J 72 (HERE RAYS ARE ABOVE)

N3228
shih4
M5788
shì
omen
manifest
proclaim
exhibit

Ssu-ma Ch'ien Shih Chi
(Emperor) Huang Ti ordered Hsi Ho to supervise the observation of the sun, I Chang the observation of the moon, and Yu Chu the observation of the stars.

JME 623 | STROKE 7 | RAD 32

志

SHI; KOKOROZASHI, INTENTION, WILL, MOTIVE, KINDNESS; KOKOROZASU, TO INTEND, TO PLAN, TO AIM AT.

THE MAN, FIGURE, SAMURAI'S 士 INTENTION, WILL, MOTIVE, KINDNESS 志 IS IN HIS HEART, MIND, SPIRIT 心.

N1064

chih4

M971

zhì

will

purpose

SUPERIMPOSED HEART SHOWING AURICLES & VENTRICLES — HEART, MIND, SPIRIT J 95 — INTENTION, WILL, MOTIVE, KINDNESS — MAN, FIGURE, SAMURAI J 410 — PICTURED SAMURAI — EYES & NOSE PICTURED

JME 624 | STROKE 10 | RAD 2

師

SHI, TEACHER, MASTER, ARMY, EXPERT.

THE TEACHER, MASTER, ARMY, EXPERT 師 HAS THE FIRST 一 CLOTH, BANNER 巾 ON THE CITY BUILDINGS 𠂤.

Observations by Mr. Dooley. The Philippine Peace. The flag floats free an' well guarded over the govermint offices, an' th' cheery people come an' go on their errands-- go out alone an' come back with th' throops. Finley Peter Dunne

GEN. YO FEI

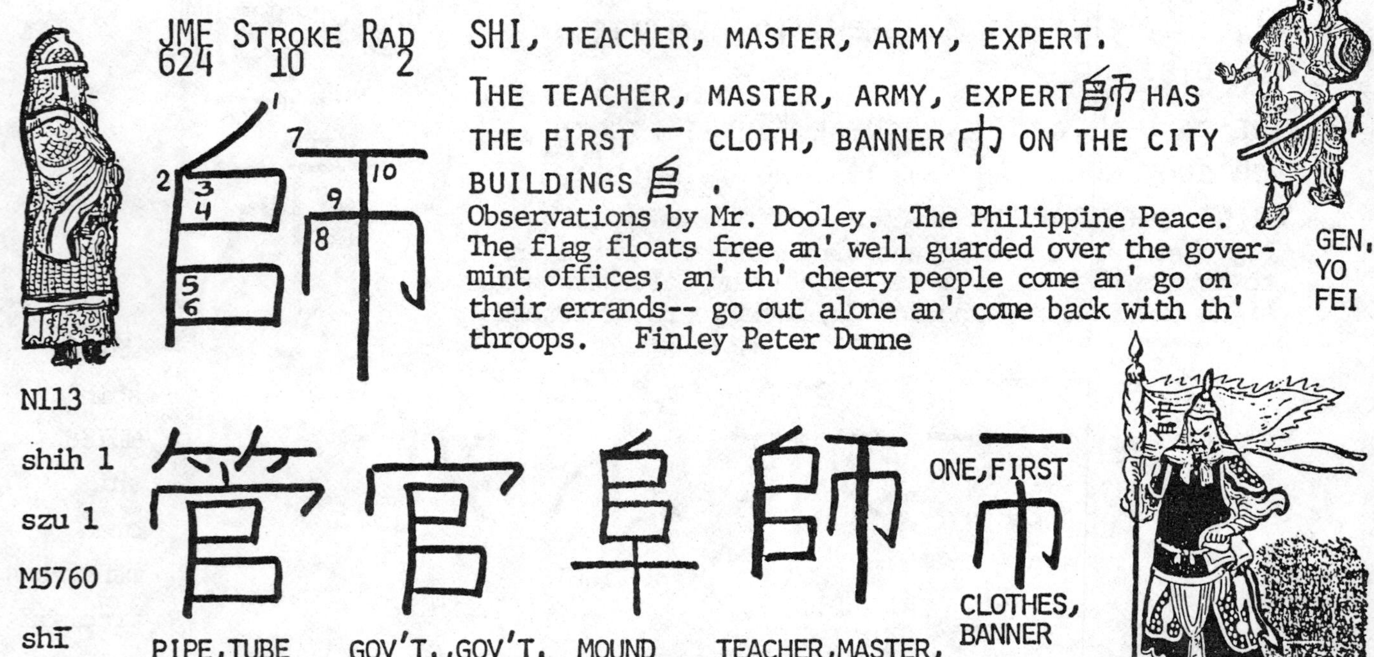

N113

shih 1

szu 1

M5760

shī

teacher

instructor

army

PIPE, TUBE J 573 — GOV'T., GOV'T. POSITION J 364 — MOUND J 170 — TEACHER, MASTER, ARMY, EXPERT — ONE, FIRST CLOTHES, BANNER R 50

GOD OF THE FLAG (WORSHIPPED BY MILITARY

Tao Te Ching

The teachers, experts, tacticians, and strategists who commanded ancient armies had impenetrable and unfathomable minds which were piercing, flexible, profound, and subtle.

JI; NIRU, TO RESEMBLE.

RAD 9 STROKE 7 JME 625

A PERSON 亻 RESEMBLES 似 THE BREATH ㄥ OF A PERSON 人.

We are shadow and dust or form and breath. The person coiled like a puff of frosty breath or like a snake is yet like the person standing or walking, and still resembles that person dying. The Mayan hieroglyphs of a person speaking include the breath, proceeding from the mouth for likeness.

似

亻 似 ㄥ 人 去

PICTURED MAN — 亻 PERSON, MAN R 9 — 似 TO RESEMBLE — ㄥ (BREATH, COILED, HELD) — 人 PERSON, MAN R 9 — 去 TO LEAVE J 189 (PERSON COILED)

N376
szu4
M5593
shì
sì
resemble
like

Fables: L'Homme et la Couleuvre   Jean de la Fontaine
A ces mots, l'animal pervers
C'est le serpent que je veux dire
Et non l'homme: on pourrait aisement s'y tromper.

And He breathed in man the breath of life.   Genesis

死 DEATH, TO DIE J 223 (INVERTED MAN ON RT.)

JI, WORD, SPEECH, EXPRESSION, SENTENCE;
JI SURU, TO RESIGN, TO LEAVE, TO DECLINE.

RAD 135 STROKE 13 JME 626

THE BITTER, HARD, SEVERE 辛 WORDS, EXPRESSION, SENTENCE 辞 IS TO RESIGN, TO LEAVE, TO DECLINE 辞.

...sage Milton's wormwood words...
Thomas Hardy   Lausanne

辞

話 舌 辞 辛 苦 苦

話 STORY, TO SPEAK J 151 — 舌 TONGUE R 135 J 827 — 辞 WORD, SPEECH, EXPRESSION, SENTENCE, TO RESIGN, TO LEAVE, DECLINE — 辛 BITTER, HARD, PUNGENT, HOT — 苦 ANXIETY, PAINFUL, BITTER J 197 — 苦 PICTURED ANXIETY, PAIN, BITTERNESS

N3860
tz'u2
M6984
cí
words
speech
resign
decline

莘 MEDICINAL PLANT: BITTER DRIED LEAVES FOR ARTHRITIS

JME 627 Stroke 19 Rad 149

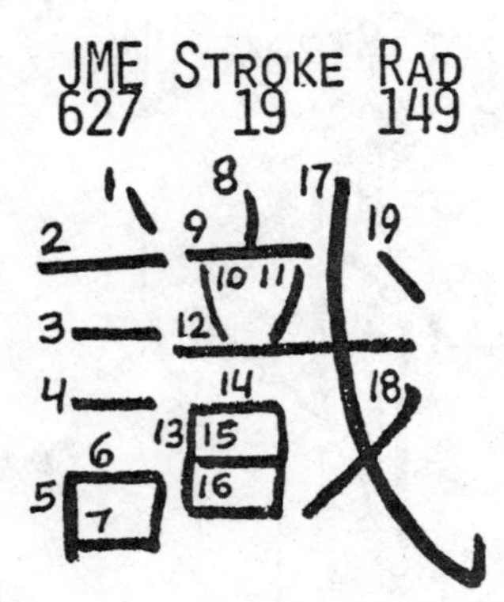

SHIKI, TO KNOW, TO DISCRIMINATE, TO WRITE.

THE SOUND 音 OF THE WORDS 言 (OF THE ONE WHO) KNOWS, DISCRIMINATES, HAS WRITTEN 言戠 THE WEAVING 織 (WORK, DUTIES).

I broider the world upon a loom,
I broider with dreams my tapestry;
Here in a little lonely room
I am master of earth and sea,
And the planets come to me.

The Loom of Dreams
Arthur Symons

N4438
shih4
M5825
shì
know
recog-
nize
distinguish

言	言	識	音	戈	戈
SOUND VIBRATIONS	WORDS, SPEECH R 149 J392	TO KNOW, WRITE, DISCRIMINATE	SOUND J 50	SPEAR R 62	PICTURED SPEAR & HAND

A Coat William Butler Yeats
I made my song a coat
Covered with embroideries
Out of old mythologies
From heel to throat;

JME 628 Stroke 15 Rad 154

質

SHITSU, QUALITY, SUBSTANCE, MATTER;
SHICHI, HOSTAGE, PAWN, PLEDGE.

AS HOSTAGES, PAWNS, PLEDGES, 質 AXES 斤斤 AND SEA SHELLS 貝 (COWRIES) DO HAVE QUALITY SUBSTANCE, MATTER 質 (OBVIOUS WORTH).

N4518
chih2
M1009
zhì
matter
substance
confront
pledge
pawn

賛	貝	質	斤斤	斤	
TO PRAISE, TO ASSIST, TO AGREE J 619	SEA SHELL J 169	QUALITY, SUBSTANCE, HOSTAGE, PLEDGE, PAWN	AXES	AXE R 69	PICTURED HAN AXE

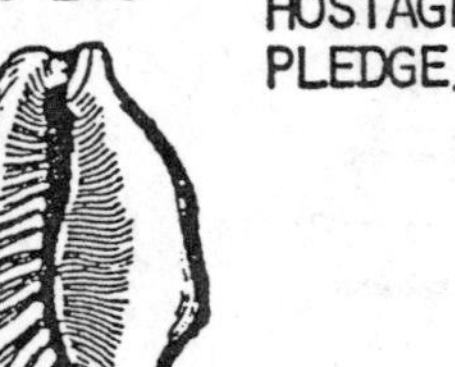

PICTURED BRONZE HAN SPADE

629

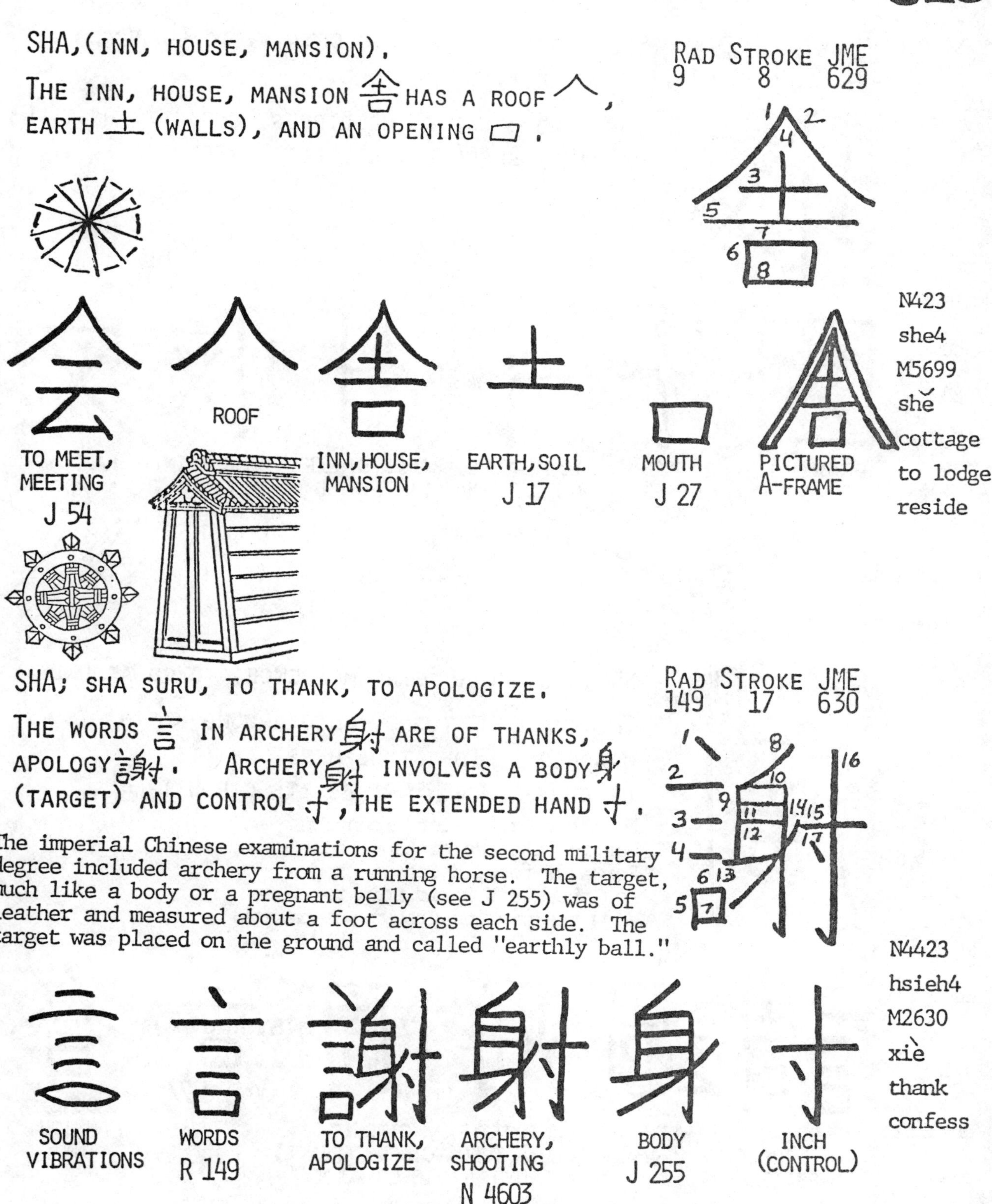

SHA, (INN, HOUSE, MANSION).

THE INN, HOUSE, MANSION 舍 HAS A ROOF 人, EARTH 土 (WALLS), AND AN OPENING 口.

RAD 9 STROKE 8 JME 629

会 TO MEET, MEETING J 54

人 ROOF

舍 INN, HOUSE, MANSION

土 EARTH, SOIL J 17

口 MOUTH J 27

PICTURED A-FRAME

N423
she4
M5699
shě
cottage
to lodge
reside

SHA; SHA SURU, TO THANK, TO APOLOGIZE.

THE WORDS 言 IN ARCHERY 射 ARE OF THANKS, APOLOGY 謝. ARCHERY 射 INVOLVES A BODY 身 (TARGET) AND CONTROL 寸, THE EXTENDED HAND 寸.

RAD 149 STROKE 17 JME 630

The imperial Chinese examinations for the second military degree included archery from a running horse. The target, much like a body or a pregnant belly (see J 255) was of leather and measured about a foot across each side. The target was placed on the ground and called "earthly ball."

SOUND VIBRATIONS

言 WORDS R 149

謝 TO THANK, APOLOGIZE

射 ARCHERY, SHOOTING N 4603

身 BODY J 255

寸 INCH (CONTROL)

N4423
hsieh4
M2630
xiè
thank
confess

The successful competitors paid respectful formal visits to the higher mandarins and then visited friends with great show and pomp, accompanied by banners and music, to be honored and receive congratulations.

631

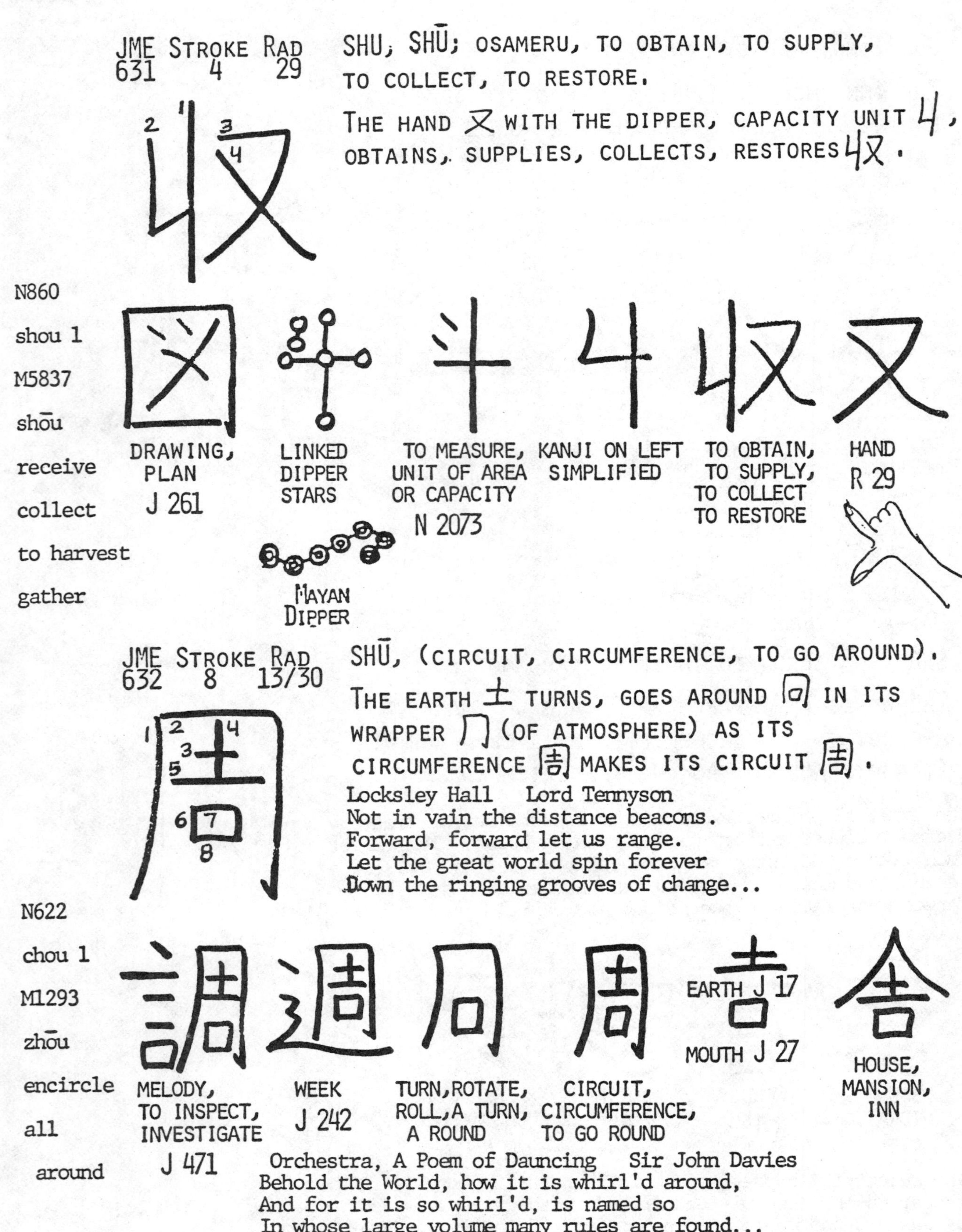

JME 631 Stroke 4 Rad 29

SHU; SHŪ; OSAMERU, TO OBTAIN, TO SUPPLY, TO COLLECT, TO RESTORE.

THE HAND 又 WITH THE DIPPER, CAPACITY UNIT 丩, OBTAINS, SUPPLIES, COLLECTS, RESTORES 収.

N860
shou 1
M5837
shōu
receive
collect
to harvest
gather

DRAWING, PLAN J 261 — LINKED DIPPER STARS — TO MEASURE, UNIT OF AREA OR CAPACITY N 2073 — KANJI ON LEFT SIMPLIFIED — TO OBTAIN, TO SUPPLY, TO COLLECT TO RESTORE — HAND R 29

MAYAN DIPPER

JME 632 Stroke 8 Rad 13/30

SHŪ, (CIRCUIT, CIRCUMFERENCE, TO GO AROUND).

THE EARTH 土 TURNS, GOES AROUND 回 IN ITS WRAPPER 冂 (OF ATMOSPHERE) AS ITS CIRCUMFERENCE 周 MAKES ITS CIRCUIT 周.

Locksley Hall Lord Tennyson
Not in vain the distance beacons.
Forward, forward let us range.
Let the great world spin forever
Down the ringing grooves of change...

N622
chou 1
M1293
zhōu
encircle
all
around

調 MELODY, TO INSPECT, INVESTIGATE J 471 — 週 WEEK J 242 — TURN, ROTATE, ROLL, A TURN, A ROUND — 周 CIRCUIT, CIRCUMFERENCE, TO GO ROUND — EARTH J 17, MOUTH J 27 — HOUSE, MANSION, INN

Orchestra, A Poem of Dauncing Sir John Davies
Behold the World, how it is whirl'd around,
And for it is so whirl'd, is named so
In whose large volume many rules are found...

SHŪ, SHU, TO STUDY, TO COMPLETE A COURSE.

RAD 9 STROKE 10 JME 633

TO STUDY, TO COMPLETE A COURSE 修 IS LIKE A PERSON 亻 WITH HIS ATTENDANT | WITH STICK / IN HAND 又 PROBING 攵 THE SHAPE, SHADOWS 彡 (OF A FORD ACROSS THE WATER).

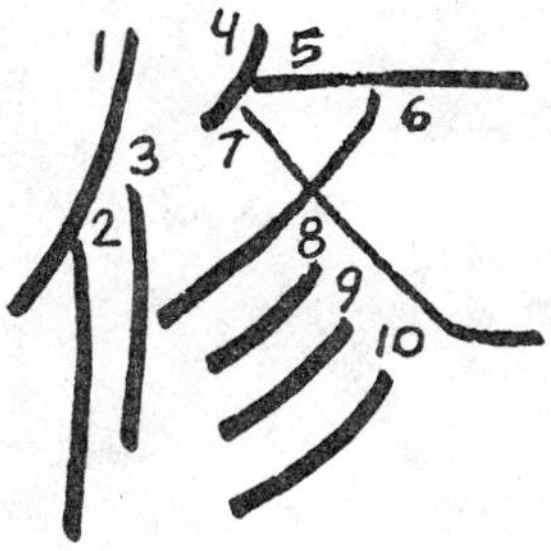

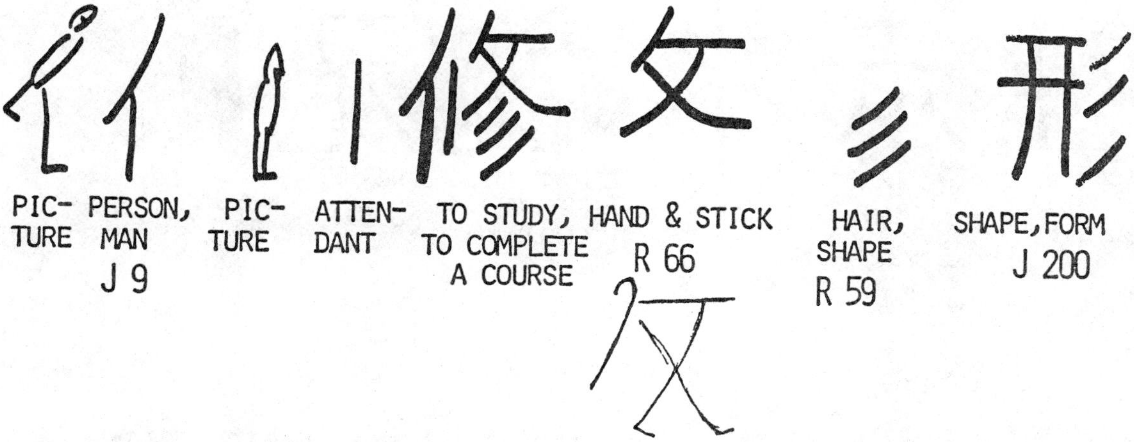

亻 PIC-TURE | 亻 PERSON, MAN J 9 | PIC-TURE | | ATTEN-DANT | 修 TO STUDY, TO COMPLETE A COURSE | 攵 HAND & STICK R 66 | 彡 HAIR, SHAPE R 59 | 形 SHAPE, FORM J 200

N491
hsiu 1
M2794
xiū
repair
regulate
cultivate
reform

SHUKU; YADO, INN; YADORU, TO LODGE.

RAD 40 STROKE 11 JME 634

THE INN, TO LODGE 宿 IS A ROOF 宀 OVER A HUNDRED 百 PERSONS 亻.

This kanji also means the twenty-eight lunar mansions or resting-places along the path of the moon in astrology and astronomy.

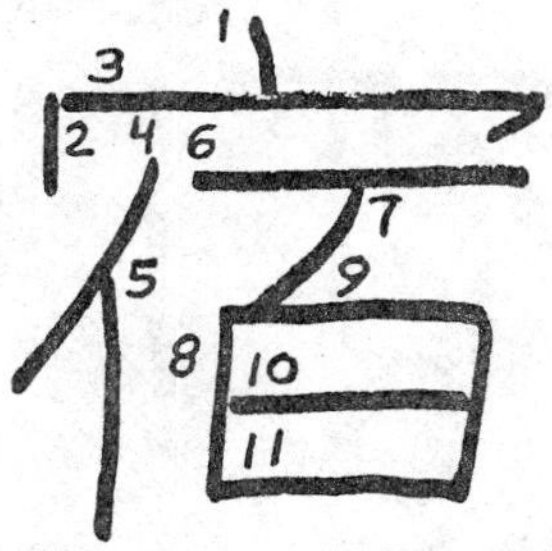

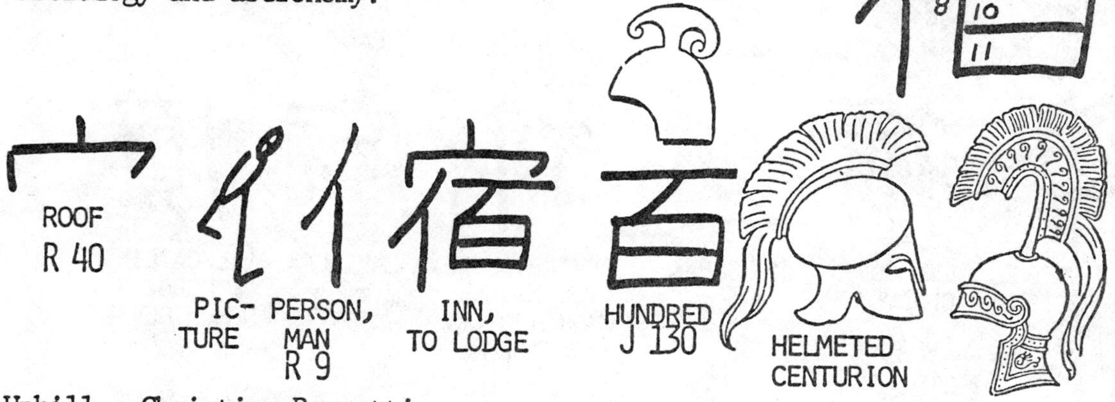

宀 ROOF R 40 | PIC-TURE | 亻 PERSON, MAN R 9 | 宿 INN, TO LODGE | 百 HUNDRED J 130 | HELMETED CENTURION

N1317
su4
M5498
sù
lodge
stay a night

Uphill Christina Rossetti
But is there for the night a resting-place? A roof for when the slow dark hours begin. May not the darkness hide it from my face? You cannot miss that inn. Shall I find comfort, travel-sore and weak? Of labour you shall find the sum. Will there be beds for all that seek? Yea, beds for all who come.

635

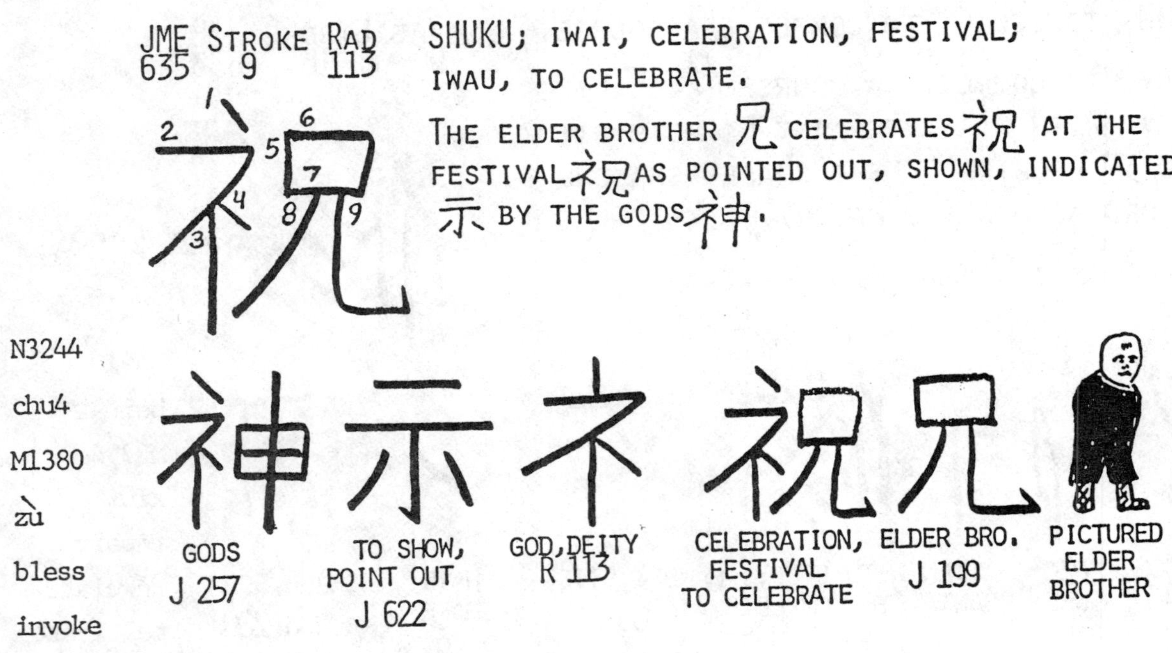

JME 635 STROKE 9 RAD 113

SHUKU; IWAI, CELEBRATION, FESTIVAL; IWAU, TO CELEBRATE.

THE ELDER BROTHER 兄 CELEBRATES 祝 AT THE FESTIVAL 祝 AS POINTED OUT, SHOWN, INDICATED 示 BY THE GODS 神.

祝

N3244

chu4

M1380

zù

bless

invoke

pray

JME 636 STROKE 11 RAD 60/144

JUTSU, ART, ARTIFICE, TECHNIQUE, MAGIC, TRICK, MEANS, STRATAGEM.

ART, ARTIFICE, TECHNIQUE, MAGIC, TRICK, MEANS, STRATAGEM 術 IS THE EXTENSION IN TIME AND IN SPACE 丶 OF THE MANDRAKE OR THE HEMP 麻 (STEAMED FOR A SCYTHIAN ORGY) AT THE MEETING PLACE OR MAGIC CROSSROADS 行 BY TEZCATLIPOCA, THE GOD OF WIZARDS AND MAGICIANS 魔

術

N1621

shu4

M5889

shù

device

artifice

trick

mystery

art

method

衛	行	述	術	麻	魔
TO DEFEND, PROTECT	TO GO, CONDUCT	TO SPEAK	ART, ARTIFICE, TECHNIQUE, MAGIC, TRICK, STRATAGEM	HEMP, FLAX	(TEZCATLIPOCA) DEMON, DEVIL
J 551	J 73	J 809		N 5390	N 5398

木 : 朮 :: 人 : 尤

TREE HASHISH PERSON SUPERB

Walter Melville
Dirty work at the crossroads.

Raising the Devil by taking a black cock to a crossroads at midnight & shouting thrice: "Poule noire à vendre!"

JUN, (WATER-LEVEL, RULE, TO CORRESPOND TO, TO IMITATE; JUN-, SEMI-, ASSOCIATE, RULE.)

THE RULE 準 IS THAT WATER 氵 CORRESPONDS TO, IMITATES, ("SEEKS") 準 ITS OWN LEVEL 準, (BALANCED AS) THAT SHORT-TAILED HAWK OR FALCON 隹 ON THE FALCONER'S HAND 十 OR WRIST, THE ASSOCIATE 準 OF THE FALCONER.

RAD 24 STROKE 13 JME 637

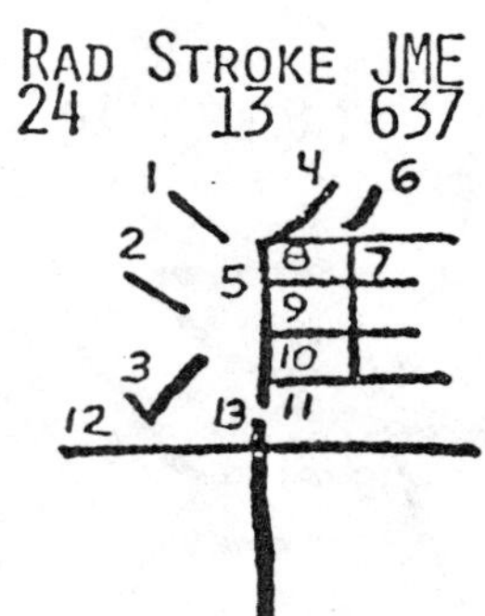

N791
chun3
M1488
zhǔn
water-level
regulate
admit
equalize
exact
true

DROPS WATER R 85 | ARCHAIC KANJI FOR SHORT-TAILED BIRD | SHORT-TAILED BIRD R 172 | WATER LEVEL, RULE, IMITATE, CORRESPOND TO, ASSOCIATE, RULE OF FALCON) | HAND (OR PERCH | ARCHAIC KANJI FOR HAND

CHINESE BRONZE WINE JUG

A thick glove or gauntlet is worn on the hand for the hawk. She is carried as much as possible and fed by hand. She is constantly caressed or stroked by a feather, and has a padded perch.

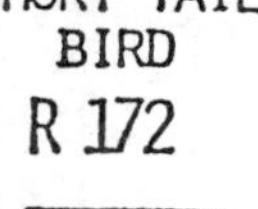

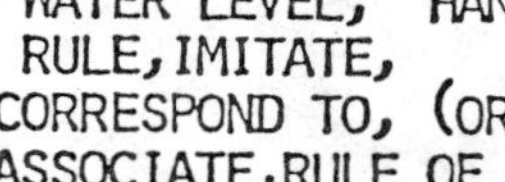

JO, PREFACE, BEGINNING.

THE PREFACE, BEGINNING 序 (TO WAR) IS THE STORAGE OF PREVIOUS 予 (PRE-HALBERD WEAPONS) IN SHEDS, LEAN-TOS 广 TO MAKE HALBERDS 矛.

There is, perhaps, an analogy to the nuclear warheads in silos on our more sophisticated and modern level.

RAD 53 STROKE 7 JME 638

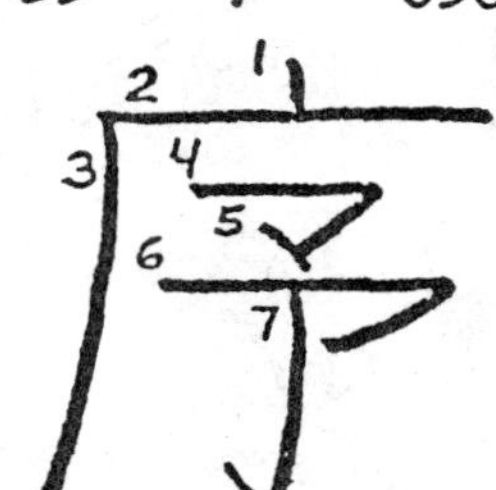

N1502
hsu4
M2851
xù
preface
order
orderly

SHELTER, SHED, LEAN-TO R 53 (PLACE FOR HALBERD SHAFT, HAFT STORAGE)

PREFACE, BEGINNING (OF WAR ACCUMULATION OF WEAPONRY)

PREVIOUS J 525 (HALBERD HAFT, SHAFT PREVIOUS TO HEADED COMPLETION)

HALBERD R 110

HALBERD

(ARCHAIC NAIL) 120 YDS., DEPT. OF TOWN OR WARD (NAIL HEAD AND BODY LIKE HALBERD)

TO SPILL (CRESCENT BLADE OR POINTED HEAD OF HALBERD)

JME 639 | STROKE 8 | RAD 4/64

SHŌ; UKETAMAWARU, TO HEAR.

THE CHILD 子 IS HEARD 承 ITS HANDS 手 ARE ACTIVE 三 LIKE (RUNNING) WATER 水.

承

N197
ch'eng2
M386
chéng
receive
inherit
contain
undertake

川 PICTURED STREAM — 水 WATER R 85 — 承 TO HEAR — 子 CHILD J 31 — 手 HAND J 28 — 三 THREE J 3 (MOVEMENT)

JME 640 | STROKE 9 | RAD 4/109

SEI, SHŌ, MINISTRY, DEPARTMENT; HABUKU, OMIT, CURTAIL, ECONOMIZE; KAERI(MIRU), TO EXAMINE ONESELF.

THE SMALL 少 (NARROWED, SCRUTINIZING) EYE 目 OF THE DEPARTMENT, GOVERNMENT 省 EXAMINES ITSELF 省, OMITTING, CURTAILING, ECONOMIZING 省. Censors were the eyes and ears of the throne. We have our watchful Big Brother.

省

N218
sheng3
M5744
shěng
province
examine
watch

丿 BAND (LIKE MUSCLES NARROWING EYE) — 小 SMALL J 24 — 少 FEW, LITTLE J 93 — 省 MINISTRY, DEPT., TO OMIT, TO CURTAIL, ECONOMIZE — 目 EYE R 109 — PICTURED OBLIQUE EYE

The other boys chose the cowherd's son to become their king. He gave them orders to hold his horse, to be his guards, one was to be the king's eye, and others were to carry his messages. Persian Wars Herodotus

SHO, PRIZE.

RAD 42 STROKE 15 JME 641

THE PRIZE 賞 IS RESPECTED, DESIRED 尚 LIKE A SHINING 光 ROOF 宀 RIDGEPOLE 尚 AND IS A PRIZE 賞 LIKE THE SEA SHELL 貝 (COWRIE).

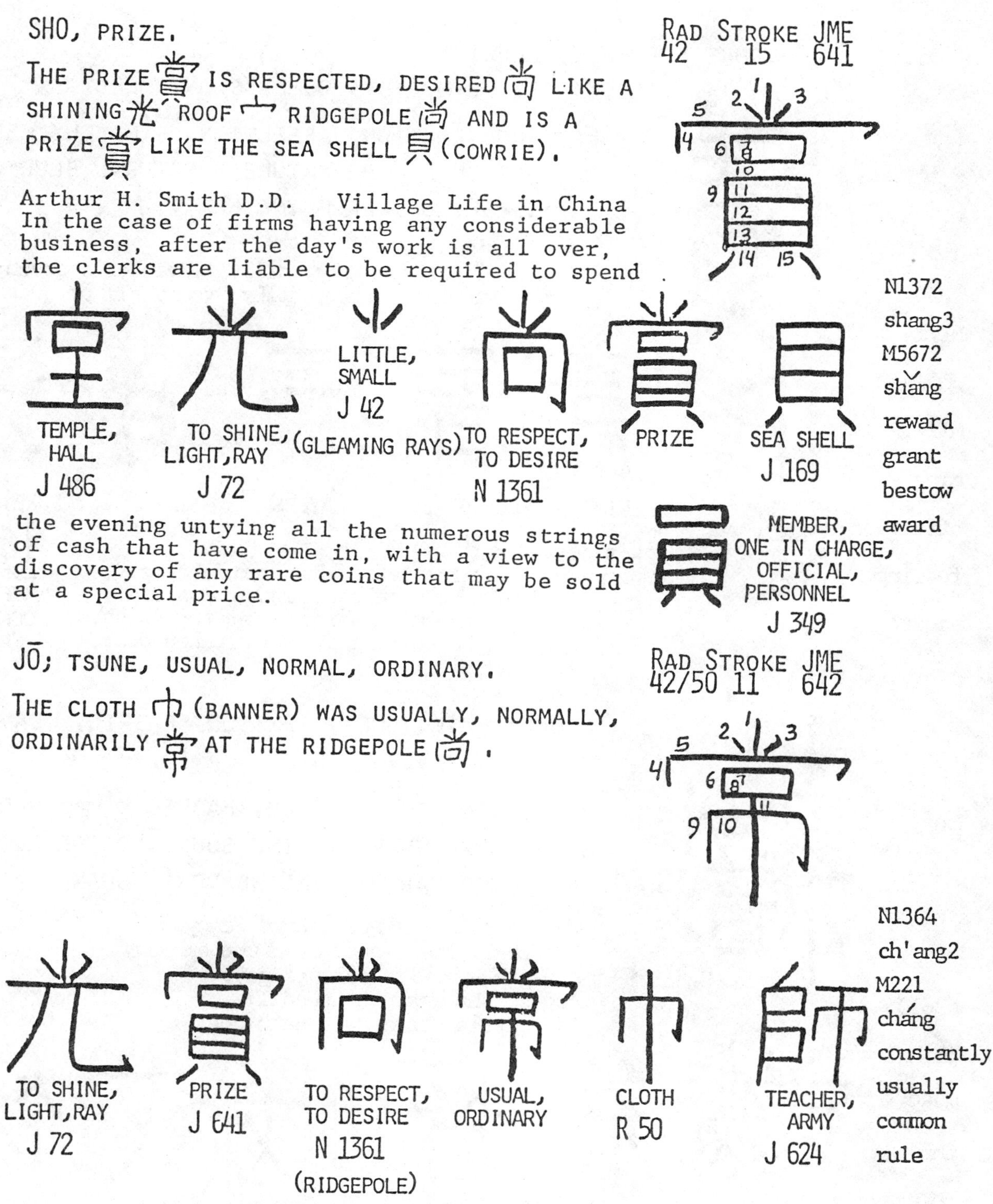

Arthur H. Smith D.D. Village Life in China
In the case of firms having any considerable business, after the day's work is all over, the clerks are liable to be required to spend the evening untying all the numerous strings of cash that have come in, with a view to the discovery of any rare coins that may be sold at a special price.

N1372
shang3
M5672
shǎng
reward
grant
bestow
award

JŌ; TSUNE, USUAL, NORMAL, ORDINARY.

RAD 42/50 STROKE 11 JME 642

THE CLOTH 巾 (BANNER) WAS USUALLY, NORMALLY, ORDINARILY 常 AT THE RIDGEPOLE 尚.

N1364
ch'ang2
M221
cháng
constantly
usually
common
rule

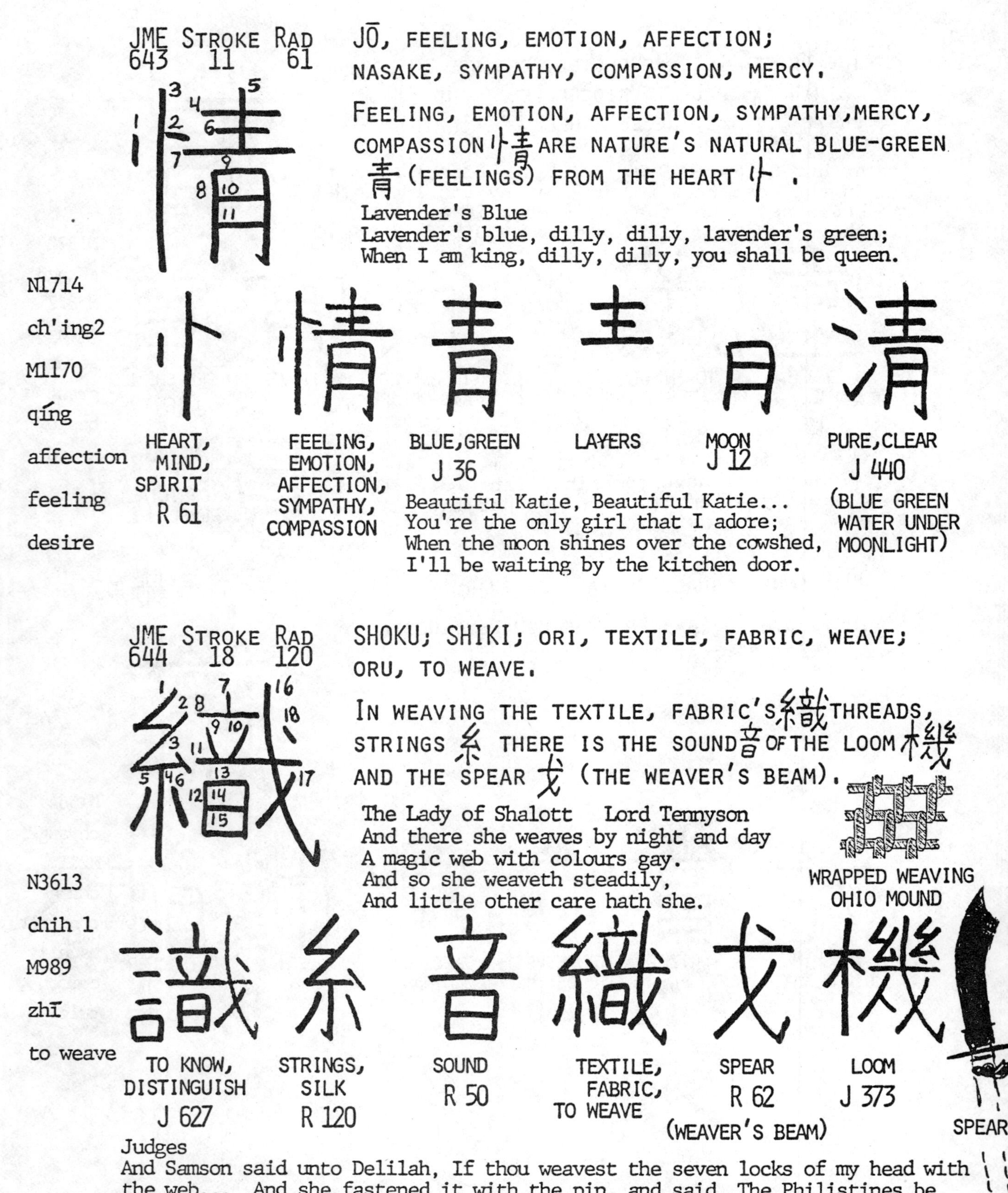

JME 643 STROKE 11 RAD 61

情

JŌ, FEELING, EMOTION, AFFECTION; NASAKE, SYMPATHY, COMPASSION, MERCY.

FEELING, EMOTION, AFFECTION, SYMPATHY, MERCY, COMPASSION 情 ARE NATURE'S NATURAL BLUE-GREEN 青 (FEELINGS) FROM THE HEART 忄.

Lavender's Blue
Lavender's blue, dilly, dilly, lavender's green;
When I am king, dilly, dilly, you shall be queen.

N1714
ch'ing2
M1170
qíng
affection
feeling
desire

忄	情	青	龶	月	清
HEART, MIND, SPIRIT R 61	FEELING, EMOTION, AFFECTION, SYMPATHY, COMPASSION	BLUE, GREEN J 36	LAYERS	MOON J 12	PURE, CLEAR J 440 (BLUE GREEN WATER UNDER MOONLIGHT)

Beautiful Katie, Beautiful Katie...
You're the only girl that I adore;
When the moon shines over the cowshed,
I'll be waiting by the kitchen door.

JME 644 STROKE 18 RAD 120

織

SHOKU; SHIKI; ORI, TEXTILE, FABRIC, WEAVE; ORU, TO WEAVE.

IN WEAVING THE TEXTILE, FABRIC'S 織 THREADS, STRINGS 糸 THERE IS THE SOUND 音 OF THE LOOM 機 AND THE SPEAR 戈 (THE WEAVER'S BEAM).

The Lady of Shalott Lord Tennyson
And there she weaves by night and day
A magic web with colours gay.
And so she weaveth steadily,
And little other care hath she.

WRAPPED WEAVING OHIO MOUND

N3613
chih 1
M989
zhī
to weave

識	糸	音	織	戈	機
TO KNOW, DISTINGUISH J 627	STRINGS, SILK R 120	SOUND R 50	TEXTILE, FABRIC, TO WEAVE	SPEAR R 62 (WEAVER'S BEAM)	LOOM J 373

SPEAR

Judges
And Samson said unto Delilah, If thou weavest the seven locks of my head with the web... And she fastened it with the pin, and said, The Philistines be upon thee, Samson. And he awoke and went away with the pin of the beam, and with the web.

SEI, SEX, NATURE, ATTRIBUTES;
SHŌ, NATURE, DISPOSITION.

RAD 61 STROKE 8 JME 645

SEX, NATURE, ATTRIBUTES, DISPOSITION 性 ARE IN THE HEART, MIND, SPIRIT 忄 FROM BIRTH 生.

Trimetrical Classic (primer of Chinese Edu.)
Men at their birth, are by nature radically good; in their nature they approximate, but in practice differ widely.
(The opening lines, once universally learned).

性

ARCHAIC KANJI HEART — 心 HEART J 95 — 忄 HEART, MIND, SPIRIT R 61 — 性 SEX, NATURE, ATTRIBUTES, DISPOSITION — 生 BIRTH, LIFE, TO LIVE J 34 — 青 BLUE, GREEN J 36

N1666
hsing4
M2771
xìng
nature
spirit
sex

Sex and Temperament Margaret Mead

SEI, SHŌ; MATSURIGOTO, GOVERNMENT, RULE.

RAD 66 STROKE 9 JME 646

GOVERNMENT, RULE 政 IS WHAT IS CORRECT, RIGHT 正 ACC. TO THE STICK ノ IN HAND 攵.

The Dunciad Alexander Pope
The right divine of kings to govern wrong.

Speak softly and carry a big stick. You will go far.
Theodore Roosevelt

政

PICTURED STANDING FOOT — 正 CORRECT, RIGHT J 46 — 政 GOV'T., RULE — 攵 STICK IN HAND R 66 — 又 HAND R 29 — ノ STICK

N2045
cheng4
M355
zhèng
to rule
gov't
adm
laws

正 攵

JME	STROKE	RAD
647	14	119

SEI, SPIRIT, GHOST, ENERGY, VITALITY, SEMEN, GRAIN; SHŌ.

THE SPIRIT, GHOST, ENERGY, VITALITY, SEMEN, GRAIN 精 IS THE NATURAL BLUE-GREEN 青 RICE 米.

精

N3480
ching 1
M1149
jīng
essence
refined
delicate

氣 OLD KANJI: SPIRIT, MIND, ENERGY

気 SPIRIT, MIND, ENERGY J 59

精 SPIRIT, GHOST, ENERGY, SEMEN, VITALITY, GRAIN

青 BLUE, GREEN J 36

情 FEELING, LOVE, SYMPATHY, MERCY J 643

晴 TO CLEAR, FINE WEATHER J 265

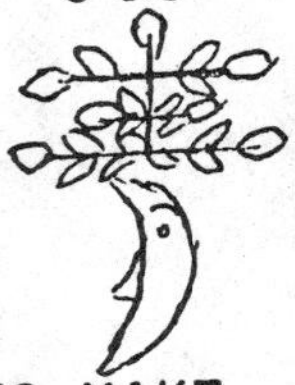

JME	STROKE	RAD
648	14	145

SEI; SEI SURU, TO MAKE, TO MANUFACTURE; -SEI, MAKE, MANUFACTURE.

To CUT 刂 (KNIFE) A COW-牛 HIDE, CLOTH 巾 FOR CLOTHES 衣.

製

PIECES FROM THE SKIN ARRANGED

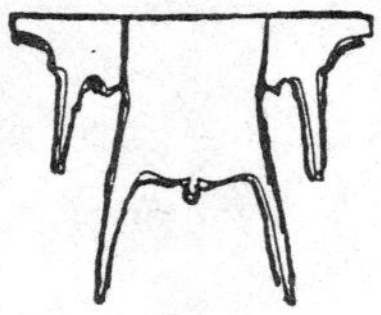

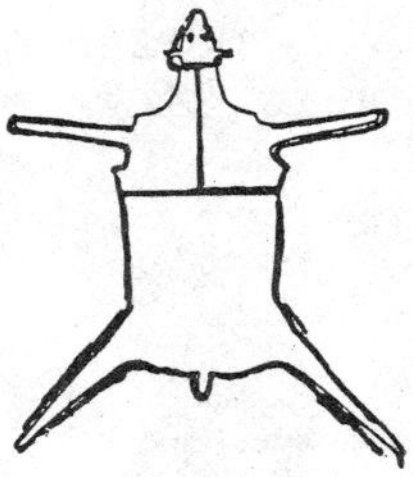

SKIN CUT & FOLDED TO MAKE A PONCHO TYPE SHIRT

N4249
chih4
M987
zhì
cut out
clothes
make
construct

牛 BULL, OX, COW J 62

巾 CLOTH R 50

製 TO MAKE, TO MANUFACTURE

刂 KNIFE, SWORD

衣 CLOTHES J 341

衣 PICTURED CLOTHES

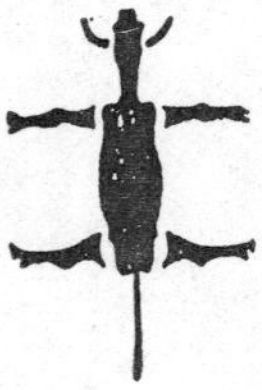

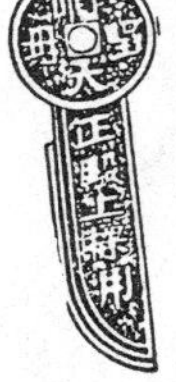

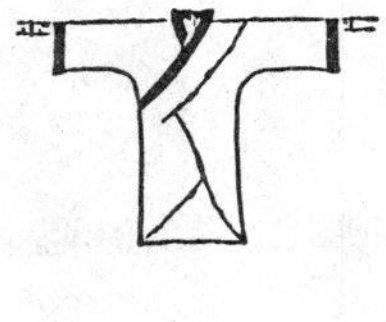

SEKI; SEMERU, TO BLAME, TO CONDEMN, TO URGE, TO TORTURE.

RAD	STROKE	JME
154	11	649

To BLAME, TO CONDEMN, TO URGE, TO TORTURE 責 (THE ONE WHO) PILED UP, STASHED, ACCUMULATED 積 LAYERS 圭 OF COWRIE 貝 (SO HE DISGORGES HIS WEALTH).

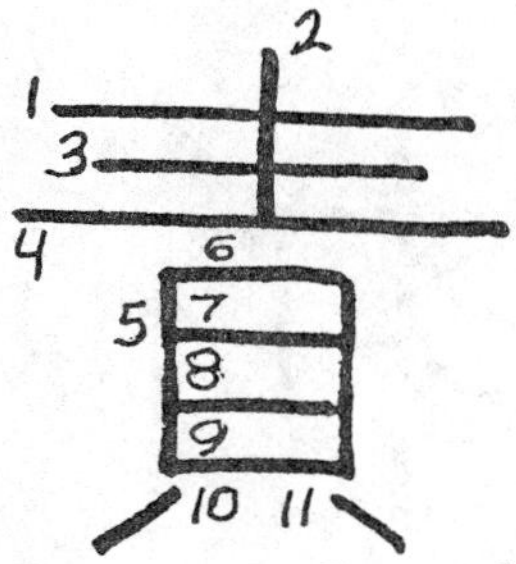

1 2 3 4 5 6 7 8 9 10 11

積 精 生 責 貝

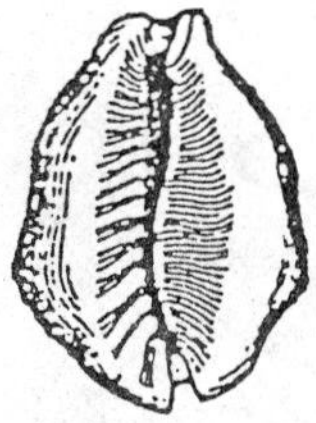

PILED UP, STASHED, ACCUMULATED J 445

SPIRIT, VITALITY J 647

BIRTH, LIFE, TO LIVE J 34

TO BLAME, CONDEMN, URGE, TORTURE

SEA SHELL J 169

PICTURED SHELL

N4492
tsai2
tse2
M6748
zé
blame
punish
duty

The cowrie is said to have a tantalizing resemblance to the vulva of an animal or human being. Perhaps its monetary value is also derived from this similarity, especially in cultures where women were also accumulated as indicators of affluence, as were animals.

SEKI, EXPLOITS, TO SPIN.

RAD	STROKE	JME
120	17	650

EXPLOITS, SPINNING 績 ARE LIKE PILING UP, ACCUMULATING 積 SILKEN STRANDS 糸 LIKE LAYERS 圭 OF COWRIE 貝.

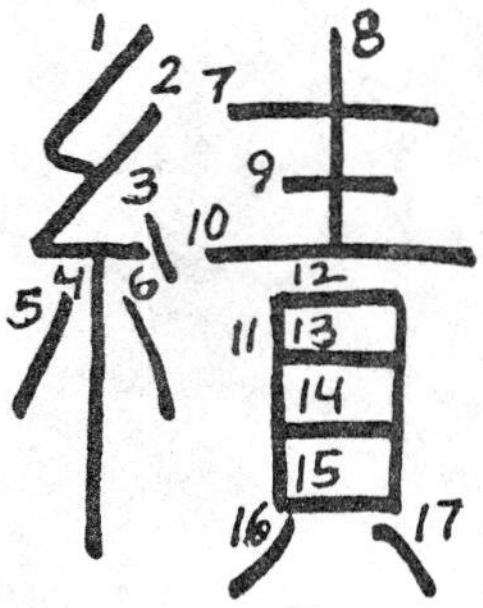

A miller said, "I have a daughter who can spin straw into gold."
The King said, "That is an art which pleases me well."

Rumpelstiltskin Wilhelm and Jakob Grimm

1 2 3 4 5 6 7 8 9 10 11 12 13 14 15 16 17

糸 績 責 生 貝

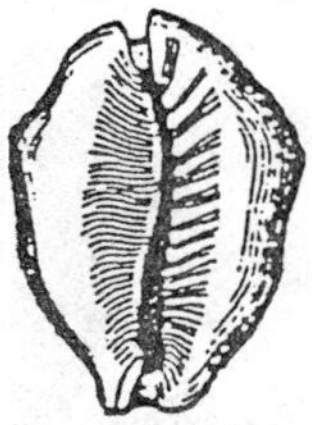

STRINGS, SILK R 120

EXPLOITS, TO SPIN

TO BLAME, CONDEMN, URGE, TORTURE J 649

BIRTH, LIFE, TO LIVE J 34

SEA SHELL J 169

PICTURED SHELL

N3602
chi 1
M501
jī
spin
twist
complete
merit

Make me, O Lord, Thy spinning-Wheel complete.
Thy holy Word my distaff make for me;
Make mine affections Thy swift flyers neat;
And make my soul Thy holy spool to be;

Housewifery
Edward Taylor

JME STROKE RAD
651 7 64

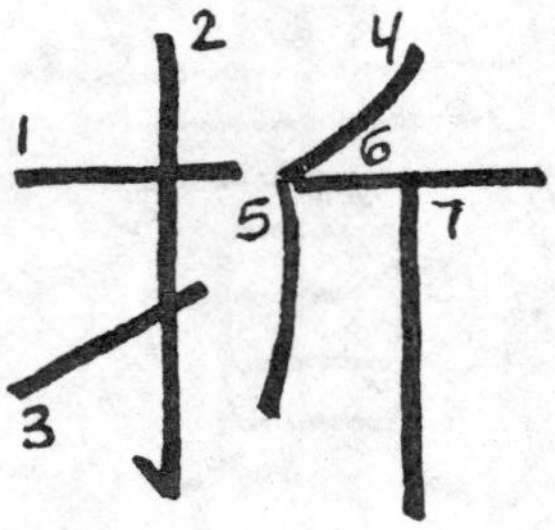

SETSU, ORU, TO BREAK, TO SNAP, TO FRACTURE, TO FOLD, TO BEND.

折

1 2 3 4 5 6 7

THE AXE 斤 IN HAND 扌 BREAKS, SNAPS, FRACTURES, FOLDS, BENDS 折.

Abimelech took an axe in his hand, and cut down a bough from the trees, ... And all the people likewise cut down every man his bough...
Judges 9:48-49

N1855

che2

M267

zhé

snap

break

reduce

deduct

扌 折 斤

PICTURED HAND & ARM

HAND R 64

TO BREAK, SNAP, TO FRACTURE, TO FOLD, BEND

AXE R 69

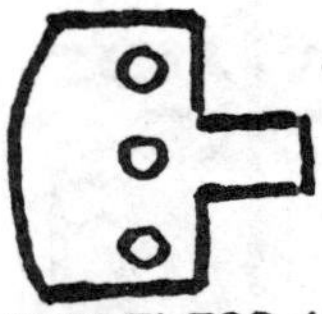

HANDLELESS PICTURED AXE (BRONZE HAN)

HANDLELESS PICTURED HAN SPADE OF BRONZE

Norman Conquest of England: Battle of Hastings Sir Edward Creasy
Another Norman sprang forward...but...an Englishman with his long-handled axe struck him over the back, breaking all his bones, so that his entrails and lungs gushed forth.

JME STROKE RAD
652 11 64

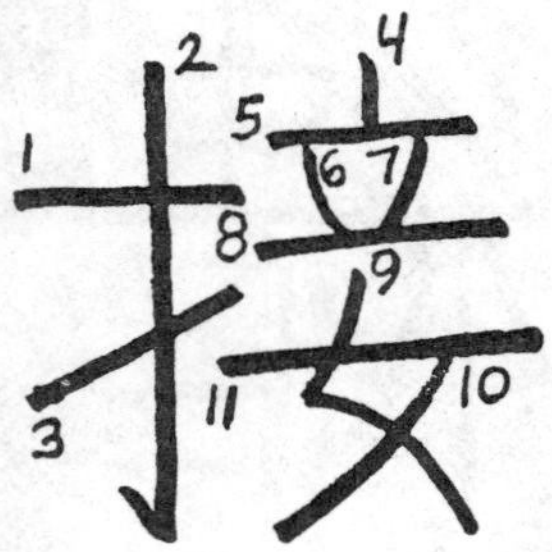

SETSU; SESSURU, TO TOUCH, TO CONTACT, TO ENCOUNTER, TO EXPERIENCE.

接

1 2 3 4 5 6 7 8 9 10 11

ONE'S HAND 扌 TOUCHES, CONTACTS, ENCOUNTERS, EXPERIENCES 接 THE CONCUBINE 妾 (THE STANDING 立 WOMAN 女 IN ATTENDANCE).

Plum Blossoms in a Golden Vase
Hsi Men's hands caressed the silk up the back of her thighs and along the cleft between her firm buttocks.

N1951

chieh 1

M800

jiē

receive

welcome

meet, accept

join, connect

扌 接 妾 立 女

PICTURED HAND & ARM

HAND R 64

TO TOUCH, TO CONTACT, TO ENCOUNTER, TO EXPERIENCE

CONCUBINE N 3346

TO STAND, STANDING R 117

WOMAN, GIRL, FEMALE R 38

Plum Blossoms in a Golden Vase (Chin P'ing Mei)
As they were alone in the chamber, Hsi Men took advantage of the opportunity to draw her close and handle her voluptuous breasts.

SETSU; MOKERU, TO PREPARE, TO PROVIDE, TO ESTABLISH, TO ORGANIZE.

THE WORDS 言 THAT STRIKE 殳 LIKE A WING 几 OR A HAND 又 PREPARE, PROVIDE, ESTABLISH, ORGANIZE 設.

Hudibras Samuel Butler
And prove their doctrine orthodox
By apostolic blows and knocks.

RAD 149 STROKE 11 JME 653

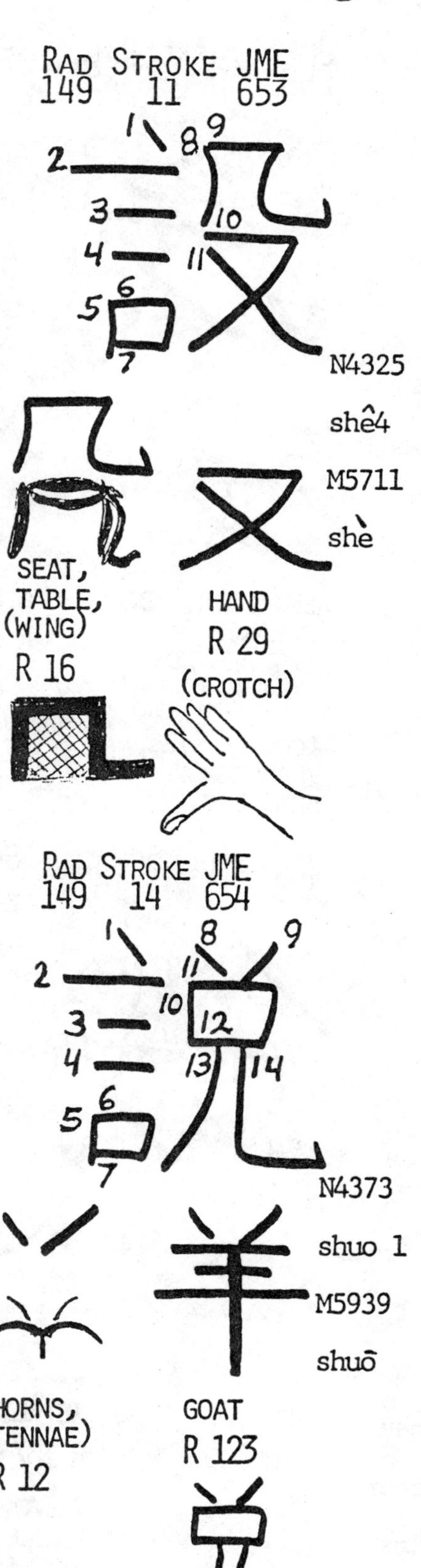

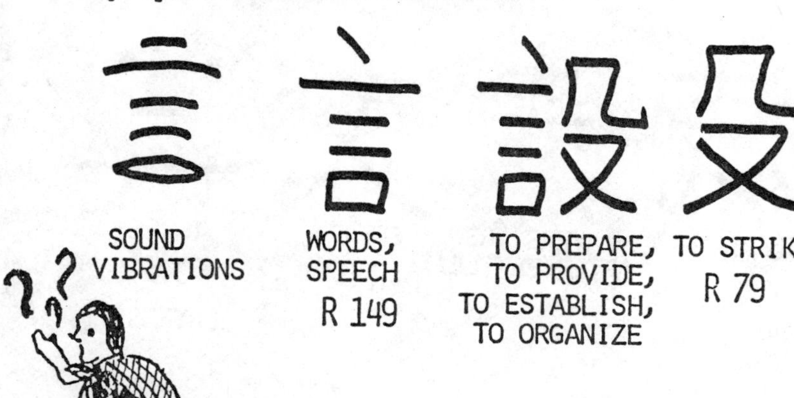

SETSU, OPINION, THEORY; ZEI, TOKU, TO EXPLAIN, TO ADVOCATE, TO PREACH.

THE WORDS 言 OF ELDER BROTHER 兄 WITH HIS ANTENNAE OR HORNS 丷 (OUT) EXCHANGING 兑 OPINIONS, THEORIES 説 AS HE EXPLAINS, ADVOCATES, PREACHES 説.

RAD 149 STROKE 14 JME 654

Hudibras Samuel Butler
He could distinguish and divide
A hair 'twixt south and southwest side,
On either which he would dispute,
Confute, change hands, and still confute.

655

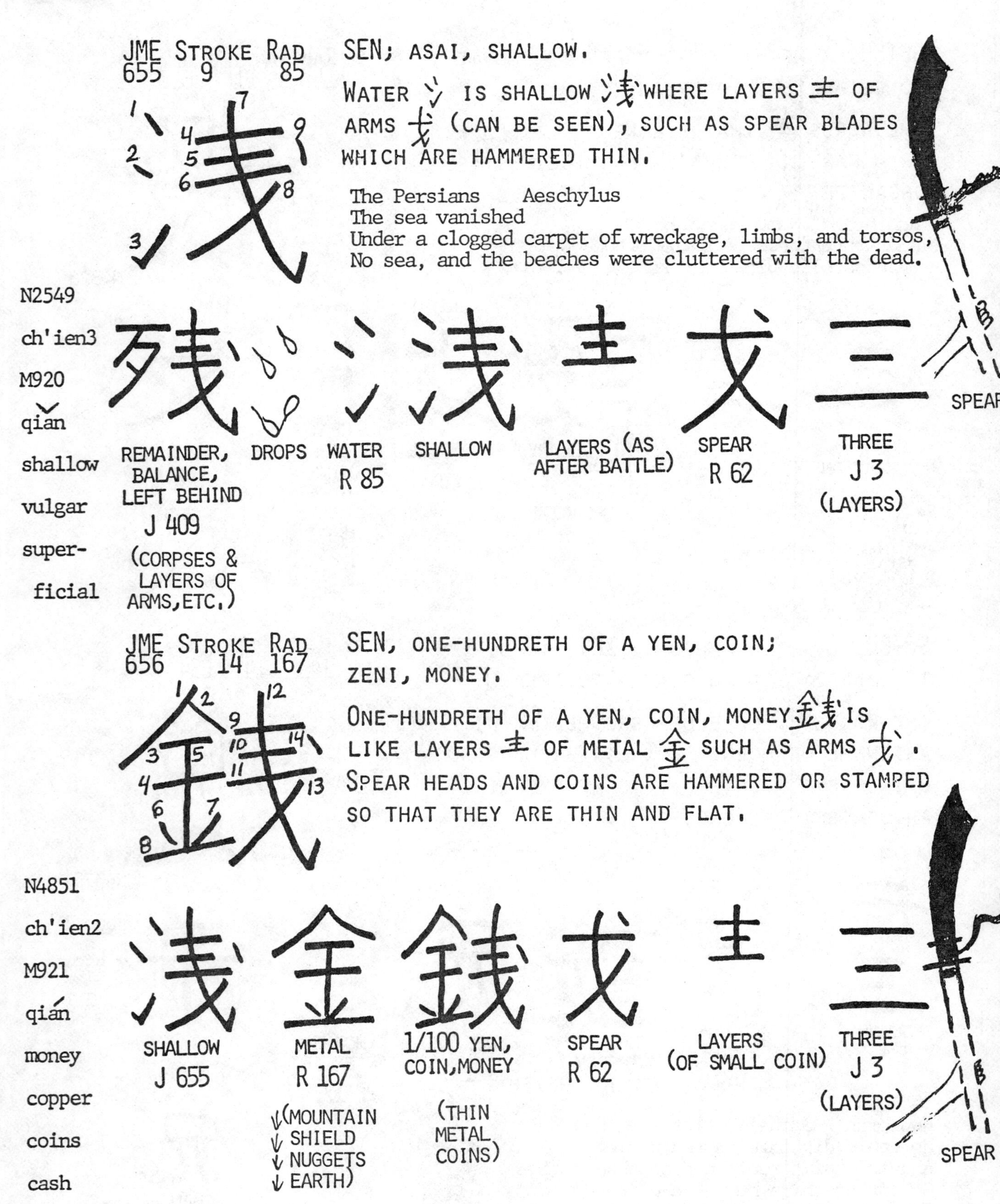

JME 655 · Stroke 9 · Rad 85

浅

SEN; ASAI, SHALLOW.

WATER 氵 IS SHALLOW 浅 WHERE LAYERS 圭 OF ARMS 戈 (CAN BE SEEN), SUCH AS SPEAR BLADES WHICH ARE HAMMERED THIN.

The Persians Aeschylus
The sea vanished
Under a clogged carpet of wreckage, limbs, and torsos,
No sea, and the beaches were cluttered with the dead.

N2549
ch'ien3
M920
qiǎn
shallow
vulgar
super-
ficial

残 — REMAINDER, BALANCE, LEFT BEHIND J 409 (CORPSES & LAYERS OF ARMS, ETC.)
DROPS
氵 — WATER R 85
浅 — SHALLOW
圭 — LAYERS (AS AFTER BATTLE)
戈 — SPEAR R 62
三 — THREE J 3 (LAYERS)
SPEAR

JME 656 · Stroke 14 · Rad 167

銭

SEN, ONE-HUNDRETH OF A YEN, COIN; ZENI, MONEY.

ONE-HUNDRETH OF A YEN, COIN, MONEY 銭 IS LIKE LAYERS 圭 OF METAL 金 SUCH AS ARMS 戈. SPEAR HEADS AND COINS ARE HAMMERED OR STAMPED SO THAT THEY ARE THIN AND FLAT.

N4851
ch'ien2
M921
qián
money
copper
coins
cash
wealth

浅 — SHALLOW J 655
金 — METAL R 167 (MOUNTAIN ↓ SHIELD ↓ NUGGETS ↓ EARTH)
銭 — 1/100 YEN, COIN, MONEY (THIN METAL COINS)
戈 — SPEAR R 62
圭 — LAYERS (OF SMALL COIN)
三 — THREE J 3 (LAYERS)
SPEAR

SO, ANCESTOR, FOUNDER.

RAD 113 STROKE 9 JME 657

THE ANCESTOR, FOUNDER'S 祖 EYE 且 (TABLET, TOMBSTONE, FUNERARY FURNITURE, URN) SHOWS, INDICATES, POINTS OUT 示 (IN PROTECTING THE DESCENDANTS' INTERESTS).

祖

Soldiers, from the summits of these pyramids
forty centuries stare down at you. Napoleon

The old Ancestral Spirits knew and felt
The House's malediction The Haunted House Thomas Hood

N3243 tsu3 M6815 zǔ ancestor grand-father founder origin

組	查	神	衤	祖	且
CLASS, GROUP, JOIN, UNITE J 103	TO EXAMINE, INVESTIGATE J 611	GOD, DEITY J 257	GOD R 113	ANCESTOR, FOUNDER	BESIDES, MOREOVER N 23 (ANCESTRAL TABLET, EYE)

Roughing It Mark Twain
Chinamen....worship their departed ancestors, in fact.

Lays of Ancient Rome Macaulay
And how can man die better
Than facing fearful odds
For the ashes of his fathers
And the temples of his gods?

SO, PRINCIPLE, ELEMENT;
SU, NAKED, UNCOVERED, SIMPLE.

RAD 120 STROKE 10 JME 658

WHEN THE LAYERS 𡗗 OF STRINGS, SILK 糸 ARE UNREELED 丨 FROM THE COCOONS 幺, THE PRINCIPLE, ELEMENT 素 IS NAKED, UNCOVERED, SIMPLE 素.

素

The silkworm dies and is exposed in the reeling of the silk from its cocoon. The silkworms may be killed by steam.

N3511 su4 M5490 sù plain white simple

丨	三	素	糸	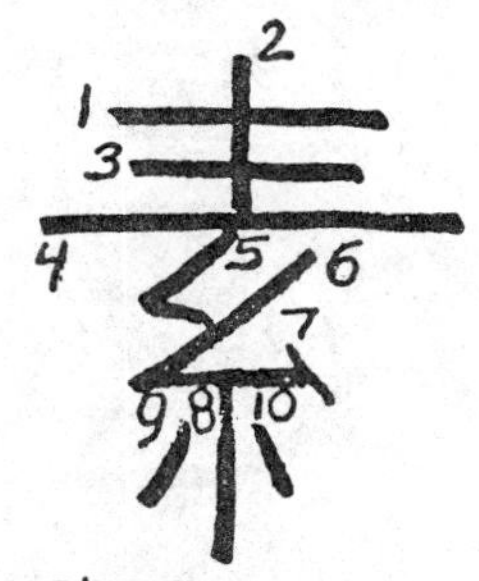	小
(UNREELED)	THREE J 3 (LAYERS) HEAVEN MAN EARTH	PRINCIPLE, ELEMENT, NAKED, UNCOVERED, SIMPLE	STRINGS, SILK R 120	PICTURED COCOONS & THREADS	LITTLE, SMALL R 42

659

JME 659 Stroke 10 Rad 9

SŌ; KURA, WAREHOUSE, STOREHOUSE.

A WAREHOUSE, STOREHOUSE 倉 IS FOR FOOD 食 AND HAS A MOUTH 口 (OPENING). NOTE THE PICTOGRAPH EFFECT WITH ROOF & DOOR PANEL.

倉

The nomadic custom of caching food, and of a grain pit dug into the earthen floor of an abode, persisted in Japan with storehouses and warehouses which hold grain, soybeans, and merchandise. These warehouses and storehouses with tiled roofs and thick clay walls are very common in the countryside and city where they provide protection against losses which are of course natural to the flammable Japanese houses. The word kura is derived from a seat or position such as that of the grain deities who protected the vital seed rice for the next planting season. These storehouses which dot the Japanese landscape are of great importance to protect capital.

N486

ts'ang 1

M6707

cāng

granary

bin

食 FOOD J 253 | 門 GATE J 143 | 戸 DOOR J 27 | 亼 JOINED, CLOSE | 倉 WAREHOUSE, STOREHOUSE | 口 MOUTH J 27

JME 660 Stroke 13 Rad 61

SŌ, IDEA, THOUGHT.

THE HEART, MIND, SPIRIT 心 HAS AN IDEA, THOUGHT 想 WHEN THE TREE 木 IS EYED 目. APPEARANCE, ASPECT 相 OF EYE 目 AND OF TREE 木 (GIVE) HEART, MIND, SPIRIT 心 IDEA, THOUGHT 想.

想

N1728

hsiang3

M2564

xiǎng

think

hope

PICTURED ANATOMICAL HEART (RA, LA, RV, LV) | 心 MIND, SPIRIT, HEART J 95 | 木 TREE, WOOD J 15 | 想 IDEA, THOUGHT | 相 APPEARANCE, ASPECT, MUTUAL J 452 | 目 EYE J 25

SŌ, (WHOLE, ALL, GENERAL, TOTAL).

THE WHOLE, ALL, GENERAL, TOTAL 総 OF THE PUBLIC 公 HEART, MIND, SPIRIT 心 IS STRUNG BY STRINGS, THREADS 糸.

RAD	STROKE	JME
120	14	661

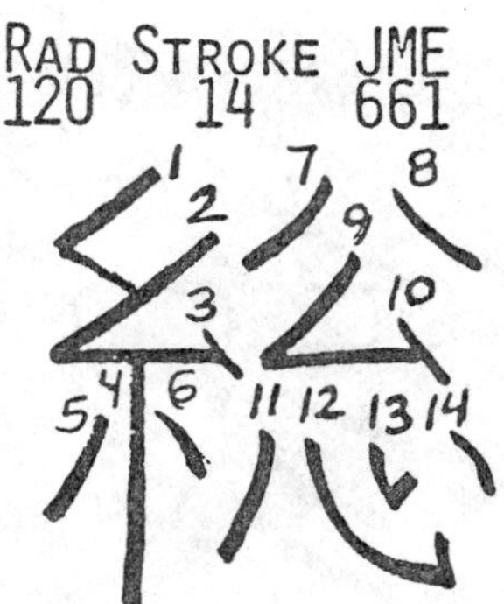

N3567
tsung3
M6912
zǒng
all
general

COCOONS & THREADS

THREADS, STRINGS, SILK
R 120

WHOLE, ALL, GENERAL, TOTAL

公
PUBLIC
J 210

心
HEART, MIND, SPIRIT
J 95

PICTURED ANATOMICAL HEART

ZŌ; TSUKURI, STRUCTURE, PHYSIQUE;
TSUKURU, TO MAKE, TO CREATE, TO BUILD;
-ZUKURI, MADE OF, WORK, ARCHITECTURAL STYLE.

ONE STOPS & GOES ⻌ AND TELLS, INFORMS 告 WITH THE MOUTH 口 OF A BULL 牛 ABOUT THE STRUCTURE, PHYSIQUE 造 BEING MADE, CREATED, BUILT 造 AND ITS ARCHITECTURAL STYLE 造.

RAD	STROKE	JME
162	10	662

造

N4701
tsao4
M6730
zào
create
make
build
prepare

辵
TO STOP & GO
R 162

⻌
TO STOP & GO
R 162 ABBRE.

造
STRUCTURE, PHYSIQUE, TO MAKE, CREATE, TO BUILD, MADE OF, WORK

告
TO TELL, INFORM
J 398

牛
BULL, OX, COW
J 62

口
MOUTH
J 27

JME 663 STROKE 12 RAD 152

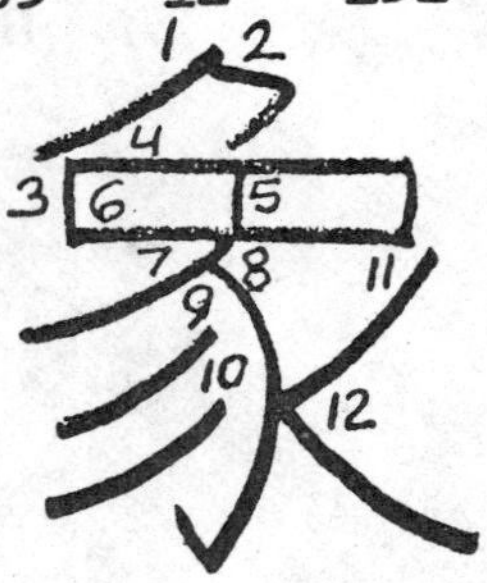

象

SHŌ, (IMAGE, SHAPE); ZŌ, ELEPHANT.

MAN BENDING OVER ク SUGGESTS MAHOUT. THE INDIAN ELEPHANT 象 CARRIES HEAD ⺈ HIGHER THAN SHOULDERS AND EATS 罒 TREMENDOUSLY (AS ZOO EVIDENCES). HE IS OF THE PIG 豕 FAMILY. AND HAS (UNUSUAL) IMAGE, SHAPE 象.

The Blind Men and the Elephant John Godfrey Saxe

N4472

hsiang4

M2568

xiàng

ivory

elephant

ク 象 罒 豕

MAHOUT BENDS | MAN BENDS R 20 | (IMAGE, SHAPE), ELEPHANT | MOUTHS J 27 | PIG R 152 | ARCHAIC KANJI PIG

Mandalay Rudyard Kipling

We useter watch the steamers
an' the hathis piling teak.
Elephints a-pilin' teak
In the sludgy pudgy creek,
Where the silence 'ung that 'eavy
you was 'arf afraid to speak!

JME 664 STROKE 14 RAD 9

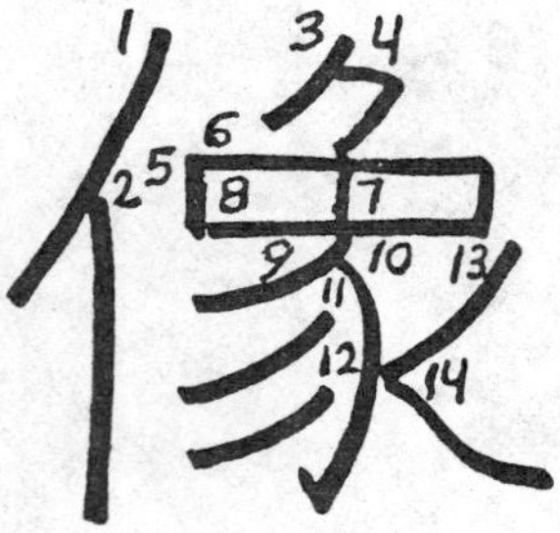

像

ZŌ, IMAGE, STATUE, FIGURE, PICTURE, PORTRAIT.

THE ELEPHANT 象 WITH HIS HAND-LIKE TRUNK, HIS INTELLIGENCE, HIS PERIODS OF LUST, HIS WRINKLED HIDE, AND PIG SHAPE IS OFTEN A PERSON'S 亻 IMAGE, STATUE, FIGURE, PICTURE 像.

The Romance of the Rose Jean de Meun
Pygmalion was a sculptor who wrought
In wax, wood, metal, stone, and ivory;
Wishing for his own pleasure to create,
He made an ivory image of a maid...

N540

hsiang4

M2569

xiàng

image

like

similar

appear-ance

resemblance

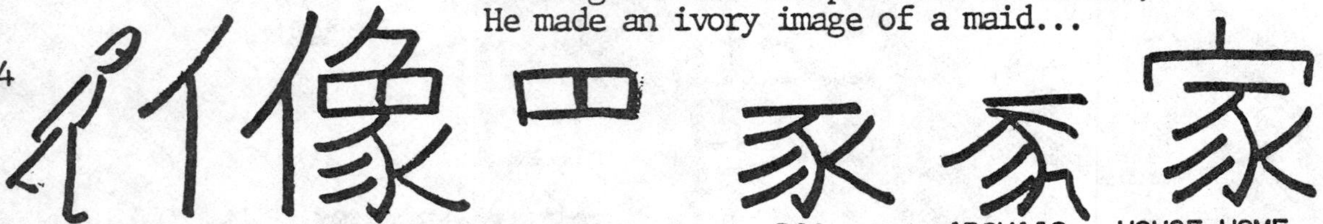

亻 像 罒 豕 家

PIC-TURE | PERSON, MAN R 9 | IMAGE, STATUE, FIGURE, PICTURE, PORTRAIT | MOUTHS J 27 | PIG R 152 | ARCHAIC KANJI PIG | HOUSE, HOME J 53

What is bigger than an elephant? But this is also become man's plaything, a spectacle at public solemnities; and it learns to skip, dance, & kneel.
Of Fortune Plutarch

The Mayan codices contain human figures with elephant heads..

ZŌ; MASU, TO INCREASE, TO ADD TO IV & TV.

RAD 32 STROKE 14 JME 665

PRIESTS 僧 ON EARTH 土 INCREASE, ARE ADDED TO 土曽. (IN CHINA AND JAPAN THEIR NUMBERS HAD TO BE REGULATED).

Masu, Masu, may his tribe increase
Increasingly, without surcease. A.D.

增

N1137
tseng 1
M6763
zēng
to add to increase

PICTURED EARTH AS ALTAR

土 EARTH, SOIL J 17

增 TO INCREASE, TO ADD TO

丷 HORNS (COIFFURE) J 12

曽 EYES TO SPEAK R 73

僧 BUDDHIST PRIEST

And God blessed Noah and his sons, and said unto them,
"Be fruitful and multiply and replenish the earth." Genesis

Farmers left their lands and became "privately ordained priests" to avoid excessive taxation. A Study of the ...Ryoiki Yoshiko K. Dykstra

SOKU, (LAW, RULE, BE BASED ON).

RAD 154 STROKE 9 JME 666

THE LAW, RULE 則 IS BASED ON 則 (OPENING THE BIVALVE) SEA SHELL 貝 WITH A KNIFE 刂.

The Merry Wives of Windsor Wm. Shakespear
Why, then the world's mine oyster,
Which I with sword will open.

則

N4487
tse2
M6746
zé
rule. law pattern standard list

目 EYE R 109

PICTURED SEA SHELL

貝 SEA SHELL J 169

則 LAW, RULE, BE BASED ON

刂 KNIFE R 18 ABBRE.

PICTURE

刀 KNIFE, SWORD R 18

667

JME 667 | STROKE 11 | RAD 9

SOKU; KAWA, (GAWA), SIDE.

PERSON 亻 WITH A KNIFE 刂 (OPENS) THE SIDE 側 OF THE (BIVALVE) SEA SHELL 貝.

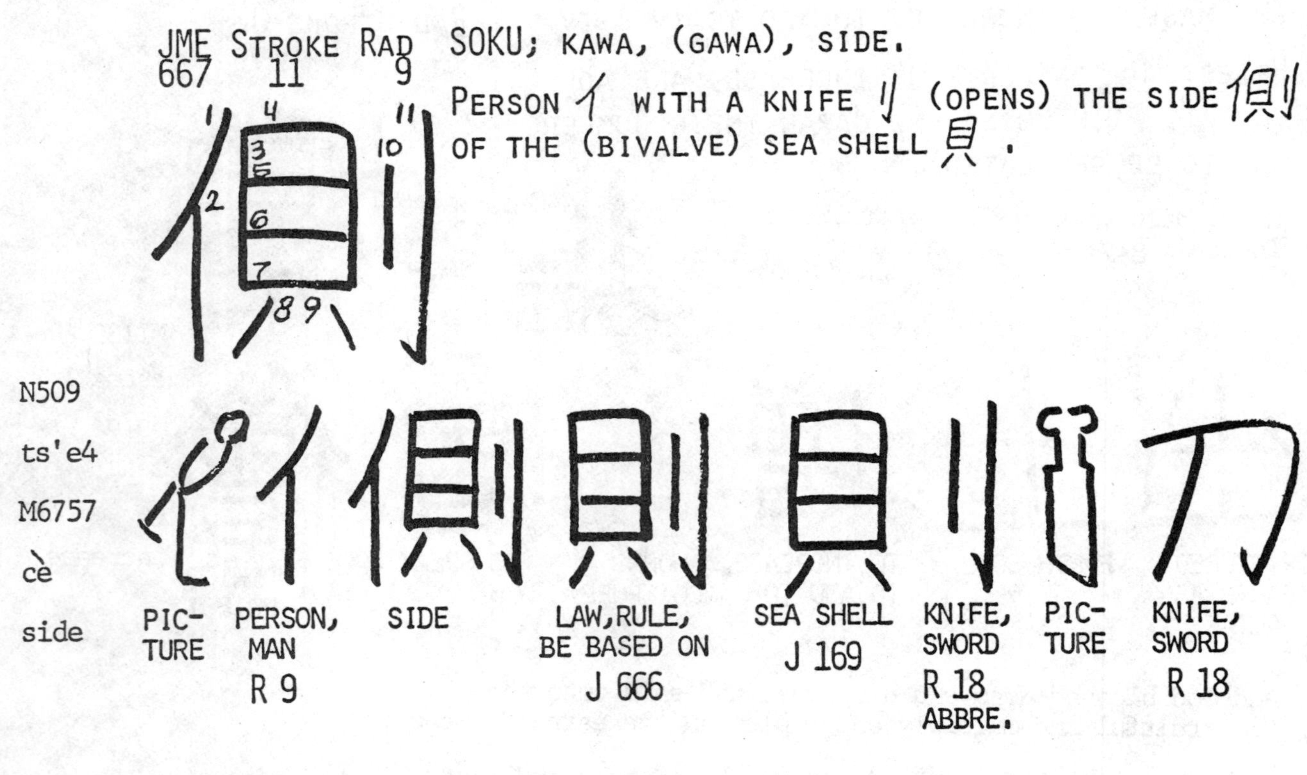

N509

ts'e4

M6757

cè

side

JME 668 | STROKE 12 | RAD 85

SOKU; HAKARU, TO MEASURE, TO FATHOM.

ON WATER 氵 THE LAW, RULE 則 BASED ON USING A SOUNDING LINE TO FIND THE DEPTH 測 FROM THE SIDE 側 (OF THE VESSEL) JUST AS ONE KNIFES 刂 THE SIDE 側 OF THE BIVALVE 貝.

The Tempest Wm. Shakespear
Full fathom five thy father lies;
Of his bones are coral made;
Those are pearls that were his eyes;

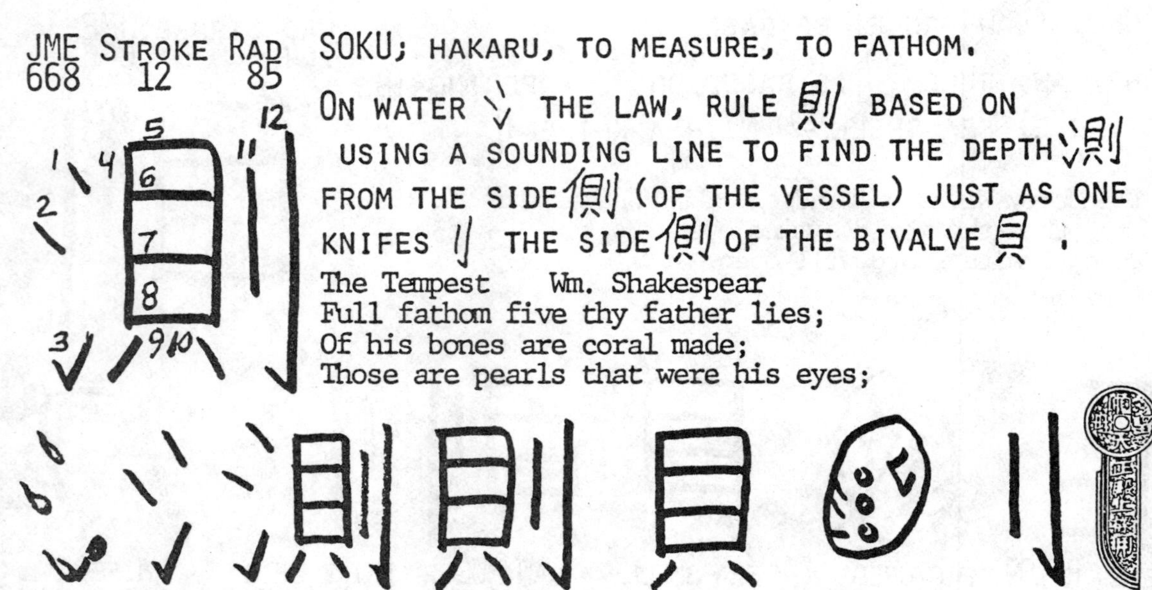

N2632

ts'e4

M6759

cè

to fathom

to measure

to estimate

Sir Patrick Spens
Half-owre, half-owre to Aberdour,
'Tis fifty fathoms deep;
And there lies gude Sir Patrick Spens,
Wi' the Scots lords at his feet!

TAI, BELT; OBI, OBI, BELT, GIRDLE; OBIRU, TAI SURU, TO WEAR AT THE BELT.

RAD 50 STROKE 10 JME 669

帯

A BELT, OBI 帯 IS LIKE A CROWN OF ANTLERS 卅 OR DOUBLE SKIRTS 巾 (ABOUT THE HEAD & BODY).

La Belle Dame Sans Merci John Keats
I made a garland for her head,
And bracelets too, and fragrant zone,
She look'd at me as she did love
And made sweet moan.

N1474 tai4 M6005 dài girdle sash belt

席 SEAT, PLACE J 444

卅 (CLOUD-GIRDED MOUNTAIN, WREATH, HORNS)

帯 OBI, BELT, GIRDLE

冖 CAP, CROWN R 14

巾 CLOTH R 50

(CLOTH IS DOUBLED FOR SKIRTS)

The Passionate Shepherd to His Love
A belt of straw and ivy buds
With coral clasps and amber studs:
Christopher Marlowe

On A Girdle
That which her tender waist confin'd
Shall now my joyful temples bind;
Edmund Waller

TAI, KASHI, BILL, DEBT, LOAN; KASU, TO LEND, TO LOAN, TO RENT.

RAD 154 STROKE 12 JME 670

貸

A BILL, DEBT, LOAN 貸 TO LEND, TO LOAN, TO RENT 貸 IS TO EXCHANGE, SUBSTITUTE, COMPENSATE 代 IN COWRIE 貝.

Wampum was made from white and purple quahog (Venus mercenaria) shells and could be exchanged for peag shell money on the American east coast. Western Indian trade routes can be discovered by remaining shells.

N4503 tai4 M6000 dài to lend borrow

PICTURE

亻 PERSON, MAN R 9

弋 ARCHAIC DART HAND

代 GENERATION, EXCHANGE, SUBSTITUTE J 463

貸 BILL, DEBT, LOAN, TO LEND, TO RENT

貝 SEA SHELL J 169

PICTURED SEA SHELL

Shells of various types were a worldwide basis of credit and debit. They were of course decorative and worn as ornaments.

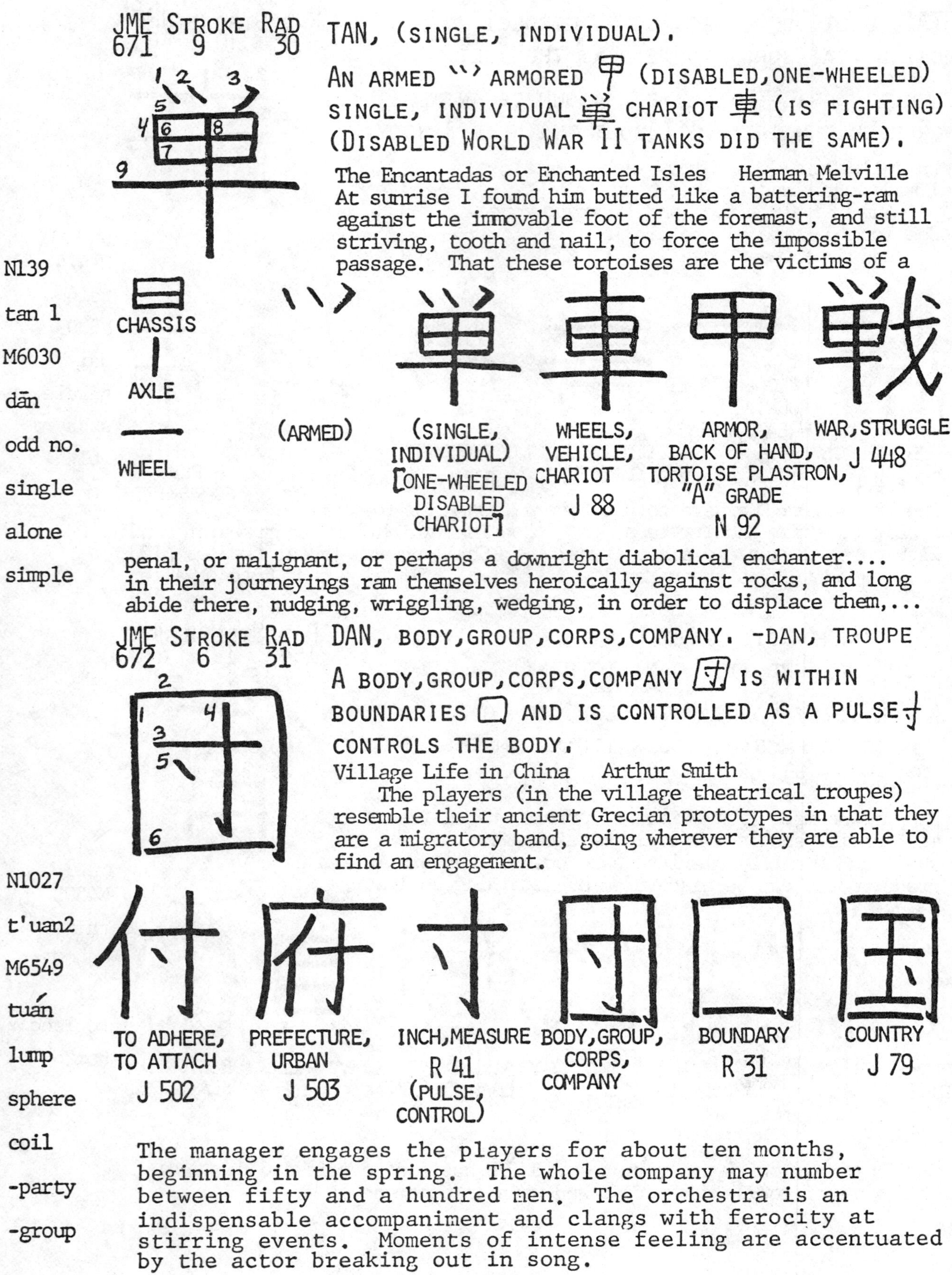

TAN, (SINGLE, INDIVIDUAL).

AN ARMED 丷 ARMORED 甲 (DISABLED, ONE-WHEELED) SINGLE, INDIVIDUAL 単 CHARIOT 車 (IS FIGHTING) (DISABLED WORLD WAR II TANKS DID THE SAME).

The Encantadas or Enchanted Isles Herman Melville
At sunrise I found him butted like a battering-ram against the immovable foot of the foremast, and still striving, tooth and nail, to force the impossible passage. That these tortoises are the victims of a penal, or malignant, or perhaps a downright diabolical enchanter.... in their journeyings ram themselves heroically against rocks, and long abide there, nudging, wriggling, wedging, in order to displace them,...

DAN, BODY, GROUP, CORPS, COMPANY. -DAN, TROUPE

A BODY, GROUP, CORPS, COMPANY 団 IS WITHIN BOUNDARIES 囗 AND IS CONTROLLED AS A PULSE 寸 CONTROLS THE BODY.

Village Life in China Arthur Smith
The players (in the village theatrical troupes) resemble their ancient Grecian prototypes in that they are a migratory band, going wherever they are able to find an engagement.

The manager engages the players for about ten months, beginning in the spring. The whole company may number between fifty and a hundred men. The orchestra is an indispensable accompaniment and clangs with ferocity at stirring events. Moments of intense feeling are accentuated by the actor breaking out in song.

CHIKU, KIZUKU, TO BUILD, TO CONSTRUCT.

RAD 118 STROKE 16 JME 673

TO BUILD, TO CONSTRUCT 築 IS GENERALLY 凡 THE WORKER 工 (PLUMBLINE) WITH BAMBOO ⺮ (SCAFFOLDING) OR WITH WOOD 木.

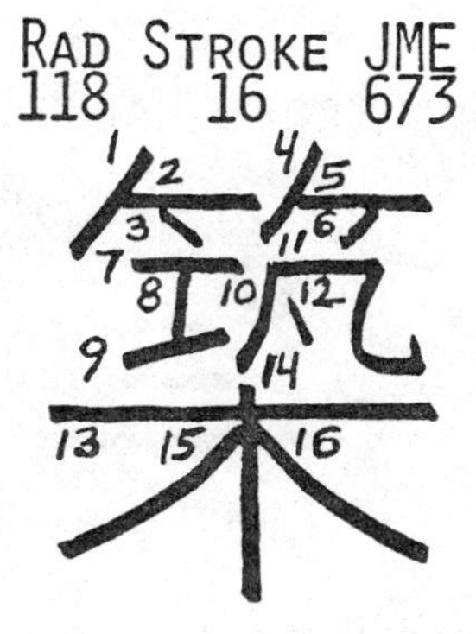

In Hongkong bamboo scaffolding is used instead of metal scaffolding, even in the construction of skyscrapers. Hollow dried lengths of bamboo have immense tensile strength and can be extended almost indefinitely.

木	竹	築	工	凡	几
TREE, WOOD J 15	BAMBOO J 113	TO BUILD, CONSTRUCT	WORKER, CONSTRUCTION J 71	GENERALLY, ALL, EVERY N 3098	TABLE R 16

N3435
chu4
M1376
zhù
build
ram earth

Ency. Brit. 11th ed. Bamboo is extensively used as a timber wood, and houses are frequently made entirely out of the products of the plant; complete sections of the stem form posts or columns; split up, it serves for floors or rafters; and, interwoven in lattice-work is used for the sides of rooms. The roof is sometimes only of bamboo, and split bamboo can become lathes and planks.

CHO, (TO STORE, TO SAVE).

RAD 154 STROKE 12 JME 674

COWRIES 貝 AND NAILS 丁 RUST-PROTECTED UNDER ROOFS 宀 WERE STORED, SAVED 貯

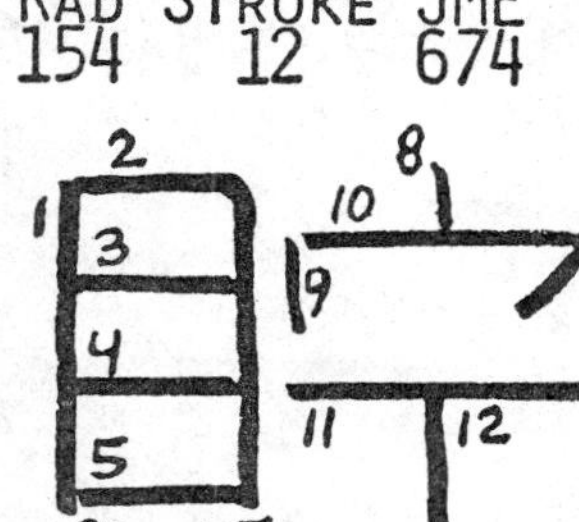

Concerning the Province of Karajang:

The Travels of Marco Polo

Their money is such as I will tell you. They use for the purpose white porcelain shells that are found in the sea...and eighty of these porcelain shells pass for a single weight of silver, equivalent to two Venice groats.

(shell)	貝	貯	丁	(nail)	宀
PICTURED SEA SHELL	SEA SHELL J 169	TO STORE, TO SAVE	(ARCHAIC NAIL KANJI)		ROOF R 40

N4502
chu3
M1368
zhù
to store
hoard

Old buildings in the American colonies were burnt down to recover the precious nails.

...we were agreeably surprised to find them of the same nation as the people of Otahiete...they exchanged a few fish they had in the Canoes for anything we offered them, but valued nails, or iron above every other thing.

Captain James Cook's Journal

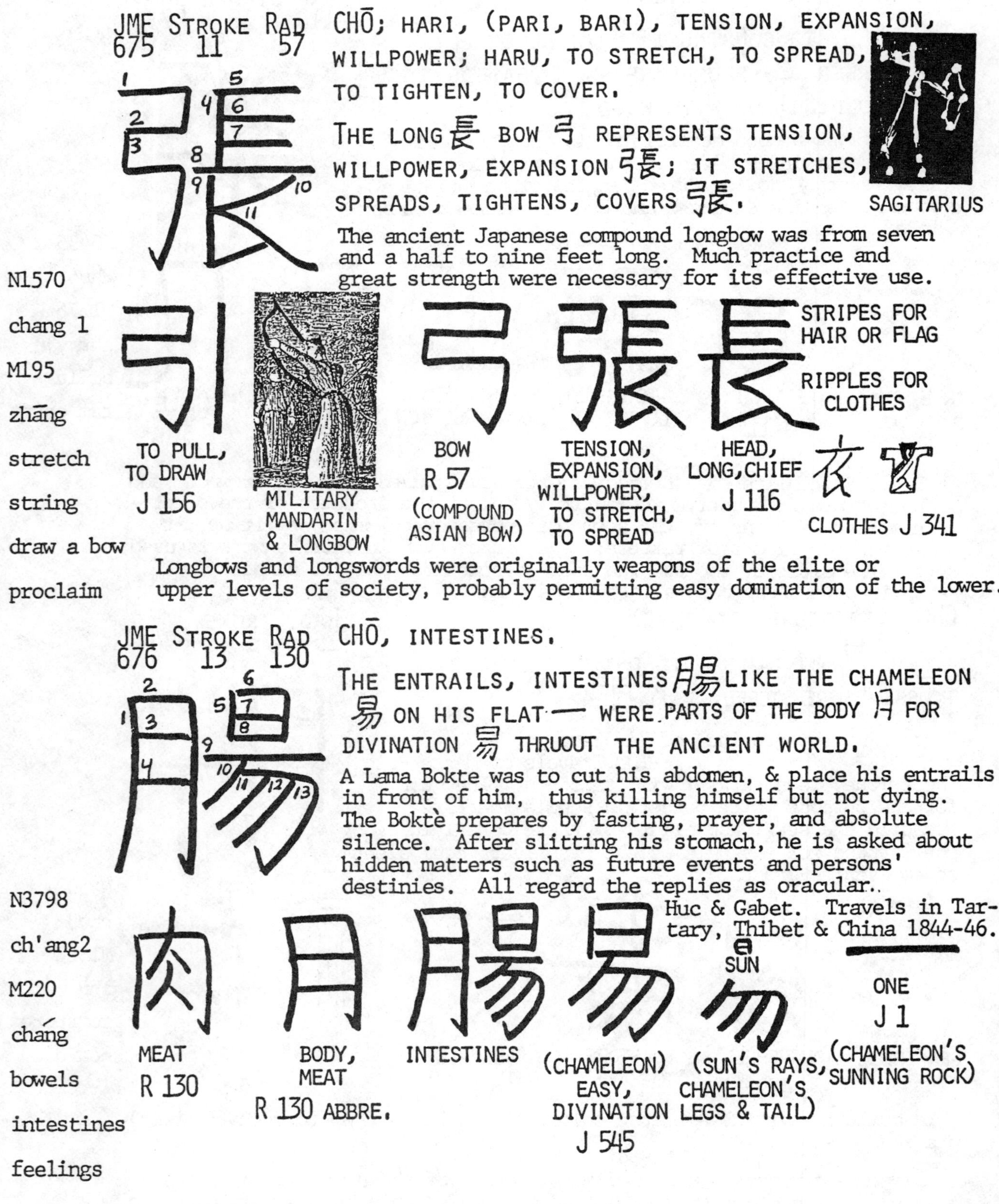

JME 675 STROKE 11 RAD 57

張

CHŌ; HARI, (PARI, BARI), TENSION, EXPANSION, WILLPOWER; HARU, TO STRETCH, TO SPREAD, TO TIGHTEN, TO COVER.

THE LONG 長 BOW 弓 REPRESENTS TENSION, WILLPOWER, EXPANSION 張; IT STRETCHES, SPREADS, TIGHTENS, COVERS 張.

SAGITARIUS

The ancient Japanese compound longbow was from seven and a half to nine feet long. Much practice and great strength were necessary for its effective use.

N1570

chang 1

M195

zhāng

stretch

string

draw a bow

proclaim

引 TO PULL, TO DRAW J 156

MILITARY MANDARIN & LONGBOW

弓 BOW R 57 (COMPOUND ASIAN BOW)

張 TENSION, EXPANSION, WILLPOWER, TO STRETCH, TO SPREAD

長 HEAD, LONG, CHIEF J 116

STRIPES FOR HAIR OR FLAG

RIPPLES FOR CLOTHES

衣 CLOTHES J 341

Longbows and longswords were originally weapons of the elite or upper levels of society, probably permitting easy domination of the lower.

JME 676 STROKE 13 RAD 130

腸

CHŌ, INTESTINES.

THE ENTRAILS, INTESTINES 腸 LIKE THE CHAMELEON 易 ON HIS FLAT 一 WERE PARTS OF THE BODY 月 FOR DIVINATION 易 THRUOUT THE ANCIENT WORLD.

A Lama Bokte was to cut his abdomen, & place his entrails in front of him, thus killing himself but not dying. The Boktè prepares by fasting, prayer, and absolute silence. After slitting his stomach, he is asked about hidden matters such as future events and persons' destinies. All regard the replies as oracular..

Huc & Gabet. Travels in Tartary, Thibet & China 1844-46.

N3798

ch'ang2

M220

cháng

bowels

intestines

feelings

肉 MEAT R 130

月 BODY, MEAT R 130 ABBRE.

腸 INTESTINES

易 (CHAMELEON) EASY, DIVINATION J 545

日 SUN

勿 (SUN'S RAYS, CHAMELEON'S LEGS & TAIL)

一 ONE J 1 (CHAMELEON'S SUNNING ROCK)

TEI; HIKUI, LOW, HUMBLE, SHORT.

THE PERSON 亻 AT THE BOTTOM, DEPTHS 底 OF THE CLAN, FAMILY 氏 IS LOW, HUMBLE, SHORT 低.

In contrast, recall that the kanji for long also means chief, leader. In Oriental societies as well as others, position and status are reflected by stance and posturing. The kowtow is not too different from the European feudal rite of kissing the lord's foot or even the current pope's ring.

RAD 9 STROKE 7 JME 677

低

N406
ti 1
M6188
dī
to bow
droop
lower
low
beneath

亻 低 底 氏 一 民

PICTURE

亻 PERSON, MAN R 9

低 LOW, HUMBLE, SHORT

底 BOTTOM, DEPTHS J 475 (SHED WATER-PLANT ATTACHES TO BOTTOM)

氏 MR., CLAN J 620 (FLOATING MULTI-BRANCHED WATER-PLANT)

一 ONE J 1 "BOTTOM LINE"

民 PEOPLE, SUBJECTS J 518 (MOUTH-HEAD IN CHARGE OF BRANCHED WATERPLANT PEOPLE)

TEKI, ENEMY, OPPONENT.

THE HARDENED 固 OLD 古 ENEMY, OPPONENT 敵 IS A PICTOGRAPH WITH A HEAD 立 AND FRAME 冂. HE HAS A STICK ノ IN HAND 攵.

Fuzzy-Wuzzy Rudyard Kipling
So, 'ere's to you, Fuzzy Wuzzy,
with your 'ayrick 'ead of hair---
You big black boundin' beggar---
for you broke a British square.

RAD 66 STROKE 15 JME 678

敵

N2060
ti2
M6221
dí
oppose
enemy
equal

十 TEN J 10

口 MOUTHS J 27

古 OLD, ANCIENT J 70

固 HARD J 393 (POTTED EARTH)

HEAD & FRAME

敵 ENEMY, OPPONENT (HARD HEAD & MOVING WITH STICK)

攵 STICK IN HAND R 66

Ein Feste Burg ist Unser Gott Martin Luther
For still our ancient foe
Doth seek to work us woe.

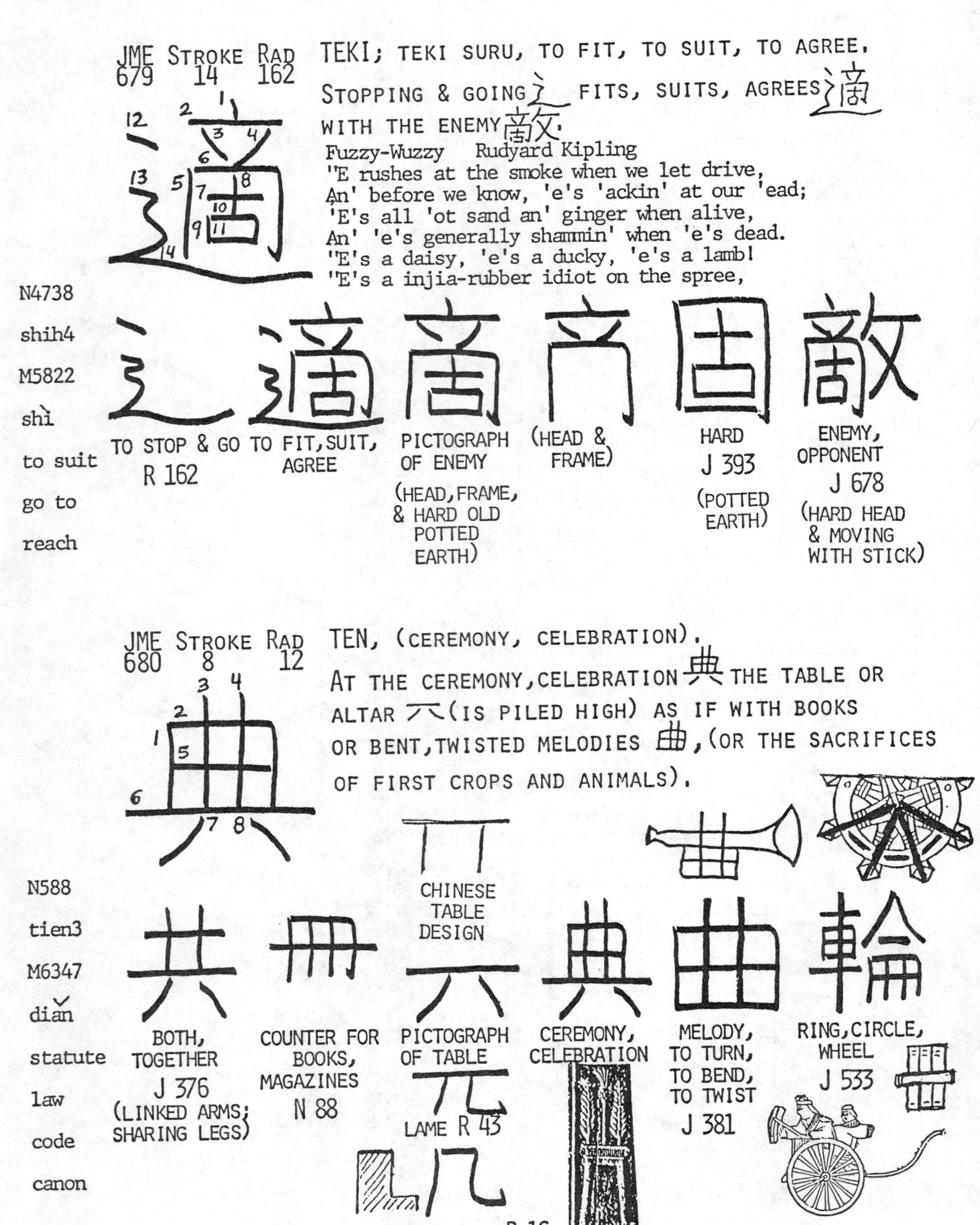

JME 679 Stroke 14 Rad 162

TEKI; TEKI SURU, TO FIT, TO SUIT, TO AGREE.

STOPPING & GOING ⻌ FITS, SUITS, AGREES 適 WITH THE ENEMY 敵.

Fuzzy-Wuzzy Rudyard Kipling
'E rushes at the smoke when we let drive,
An' before we know, 'e's 'ackin' at our 'ead;
'E's all 'ot sand an' ginger when alive,
An' 'e's generally shammin' when 'e's dead.
'E's a daisy, 'e's a ducky, 'e's a lamb!
'E's a injia-rubber idiot on the spree,

N4738
shih4
M5822
shì
to suit
go to
reach

⻌ TO STOP & GO R 162

適 TO FIT, SUIT, AGREE

啇 PICTOGRAPH OF ENEMY (HEAD, FRAME, & HARD OLD POTTED EARTH)

(HEAD & FRAME)

古 HARD J 393 (POTTED EARTH)

敵 ENEMY, OPPONENT J 678 (HARD HEAD & MOVING WITH STICK)

JME 680 Stroke 8 Rad 12

TEN, (CEREMONY, CELEBRATION).

AT THE CEREMONY, CELEBRATION 典 THE TABLE OR ALTAR 六 (IS PILED HIGH) AS IF WITH BOOKS OR BENT, TWISTED MELODIES 曲, (OR THE SACRIFICES OF FIRST CROPS AND ANIMALS).

N588
tien3
M6347
diǎn
statute
law
code
canon

CHINESE TABLE DESIGN

共 BOTH, TOGETHER J 376 (LINKED ARMS; SHARING LEGS)

冊 COUNTER FOR BOOKS, MAGAZINES N 88

六 PICTOGRAPH OF TABLE

尢 LAME R 43

几 SEAT, TABLE R 16

典 CEREMONY, CELEBRATION

曲 MELODY, TO TURN, TO BEND, TO TWIST J 381

輪 RING, CIRCLE, WHEEL J 533

DEN, LEGEND, TRADITION, LIFE, BIOGRAPHY; TSUTAERU, TO REPORT, TO TRANSMIT, TO TEACH; TSUTAWARU, TO BE REPORTED, TO BE TRANSMITTED.

RAD 9 STROKE 6 JME 681

伝

THE LEGEND, TRADITION, LIFE, BIOGRAPHY 伝 IS REPORTED, TRANSMITTED, TAUGHT 伝 BY PERSONS' SPEECH 云 AT A MEETING 会 WHERE THE FROSTY BREATH 二 FROM THE MOUTH 厶 IS LIKE CLOUDS 雲.

亻 伝 云 OR 言 雲 会

PICTURE	PERSON, MAN R 9	LEGEND, TRADITION, TRANSMIT	WORDS, SPEECH N 274	WORDS, SPEECH N 4309	CLOUD J 47	TO MEET, MEETING J 54

N379
ch'uan2
M1446
zhuàn
chuán
to preach
transmit
propagate

Buddha at Kamakura   Rudyard Kipling
And down the loaded air there comes
The thunder of Thibetan drums,
And droned-- "Om mane padme oms--"
A world's width from Kamakura.

Buddhist Mantra
Oh Thou Jewel of the Lotus
Om mani padme hum

TŌ; SUBERU, TO CONTROL, TO SUPERVISE, TO GOVERN.

RAD 120 STROKE 12 JME 682

統

AS THOUGH BY STRINGS 糸, THE CURRENT, FLOWING, WASHING AWAY 流 IS CONTROLLED, SUPERVISED, GOVERNED 統 AND BECOMES TWO MAIN STREAMS 儿.

Like the higher and then lower gait of a cripple 尢, the water level rises and falls according to the purpose of the one who controls, supervises, governs.

糸 統 充 流 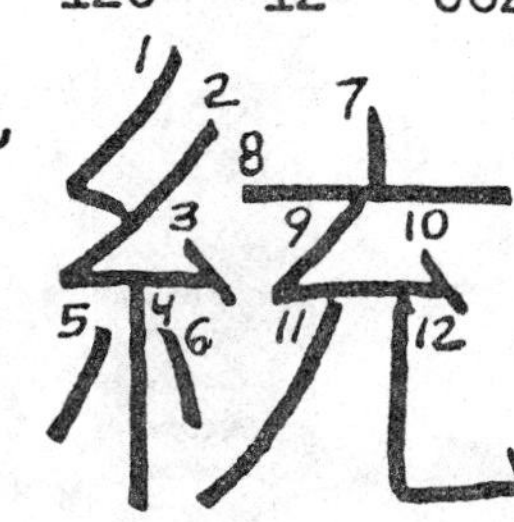

PICTURED COCOONS & THREADS	THREADS, SILK R 120	TO CONTROL, TO SUPERVISE, TO GOVERN	TO FILL N 289	CURRENT, TO FLOW J 334	PICTURED FLOWING STREAM

N3536
t'ung3
M6641
tǒng
govern
rule
control

When love with one another so
    Interinanimates two soules,
That abler soule, which thence doth flow,
    Defects of lonelinesse controules.   Donne   The Extasie

683

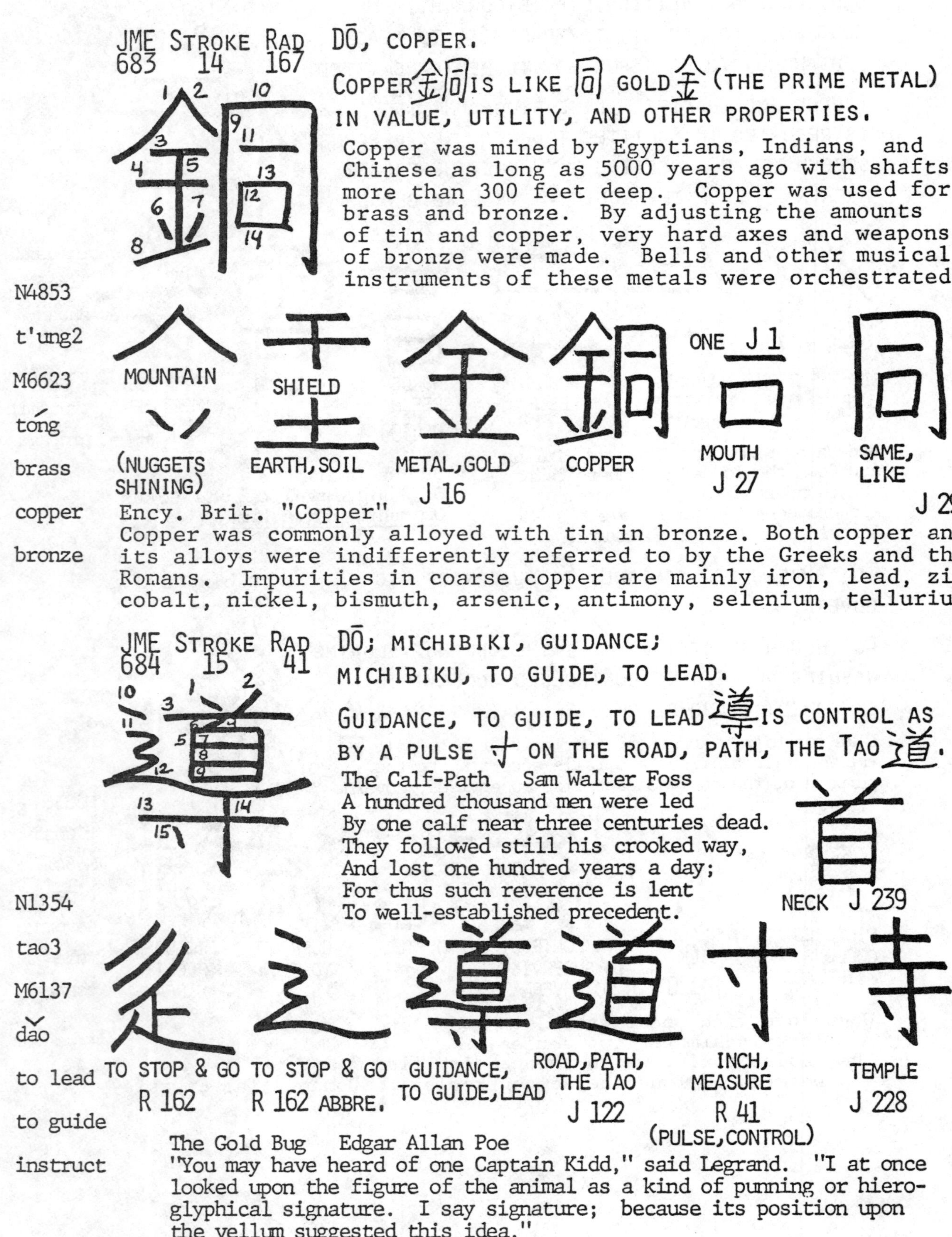

JME STROKE RAD
683 14 167

DŌ, COPPER.

COPPER 銅 IS LIKE 同 GOLD 金 (THE PRIME METAL) IN VALUE, UTILITY, AND OTHER PROPERTIES.

Copper was mined by Egyptians, Indians, and Chinese as long as 5000 years ago with shafts more than 300 feet deep. Copper was used for brass and bronze. By adjusting the amounts of tin and copper, very hard axes and weapons of bronze were made. Bells and other musical instruments of these metals were orchestrated.

N4853

t'ung2

M6623

tóng

brass

copper

bronze

Ency. Brit. "Copper"
Copper was commonly alloyed with tin in bronze. Both copper and its alloys were indifferently referred to by the Greeks and the Romans. Impurities in coarse copper are mainly iron, lead, zinc, cobalt, nickel, bismuth, arsenic, antimony, selenium, tellurium.

JME STROKE RAD
684 15 41

DŌ; MICHIBIKI, GUIDANCE; MICHIBIKU, TO GUIDE, TO LEAD.

GUIDANCE, TO GUIDE, TO LEAD 導 IS CONTROL AS BY A PULSE 寸 ON THE ROAD, PATH, THE TAO 道.

The Calf-Path Sam Walter Foss
A hundred thousand men were led
By one calf near three centuries dead.
They followed still his crooked way,
And lost one hundred years a day;
For thus such reverence is lent
To well-established precedent.

N1354

tao3

M6137

dǎo

to lead

to guide

instruct

The Gold Bug Edgar Allan Poe
"You may have heard of one Captain Kidd," said Legrand. "I at once looked upon the figure of the animal as a kind of punning or hieroglyphical signature. I say signature; because its position upon the vellum suggested this idea."

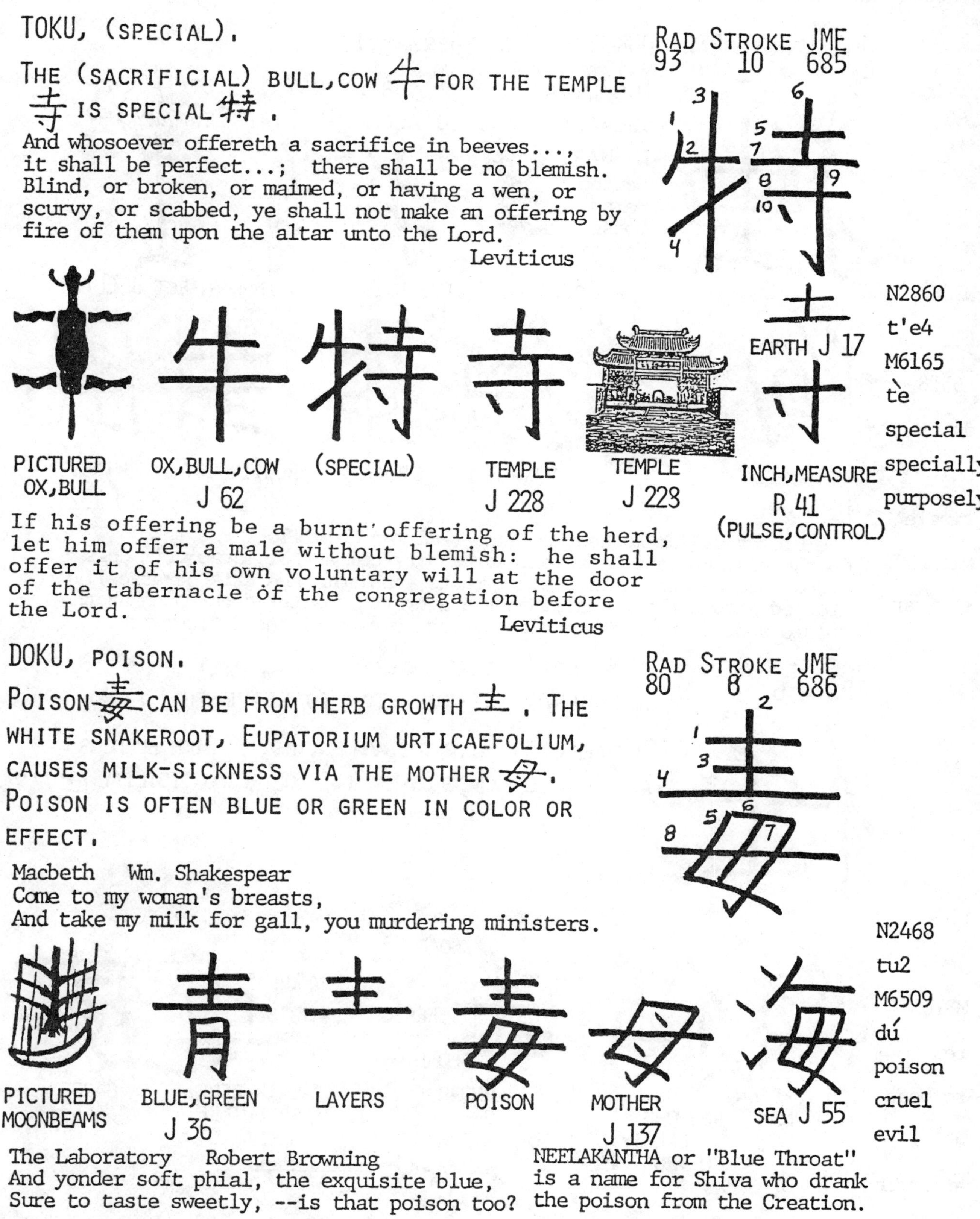

TOKU, (SPECIAL).

RAD 93 STROKE 10 JME 685

THE (SACRIFICIAL) BULL, COW 牛 FOR THE TEMPLE 寺 IS SPECIAL 特.

And whosoever offereth a sacrifice in beeves..., it shall be perfect...; there shall be no blemish. Blind, or broken, or maimed, or having a wen, or scurvy, or scabbed, ye shall not make an offering by fire of them upon the altar unto the Lord.

Leviticus

N2860
t'e4
M6165
tè
special
specially
purposely

PICTURED OX, BULL — 牛 OX, BULL, COW J 62 — 特 (SPECIAL) — 寺 TEMPLE J 228 — TEMPLE J 228 — 土 EARTH J 17 — 寸 INCH, MEASURE R 41 (PULSE, CONTROL)

If his offering be a burnt offering of the herd, let him offer a male without blemish: he shall offer it of his own voluntary will at the door of the tabernacle of the congregation before the Lord.

Leviticus

DOKU, POISON.

RAD 80 STROKE 8 JME 686

POISON 毒 CAN BE FROM HERB GROWTH 龶. THE WHITE SNAKEROOT, EUPATORIUM URTICAEFOLIUM, CAUSES MILK-SICKNESS VIA THE MOTHER 毋. POISON IS OFTEN BLUE OR GREEN IN COLOR OR EFFECT.

Macbeth Wm. Shakespear
Come to my woman's breasts,
And take my milk for gall, you murdering ministers.

N2468
tu2
M6509
dú
poison
cruel
evil

PICTURED MOONBEAMS — 青 BLUE, GREEN J 36 — 龶 LAYERS — 毒 POISON — 毋 MOTHER J 137 — 海 SEA J 55

The Laboratory Robert Browning
And yonder soft phial, the exquisite blue,
Sure to taste sweetly, --is that poison too?

NEELAKANTHA or "Blue Throat" is a name for Shiva who drank the poison from the Creation.

Verdigris is a green or bluish-green poison from copper treated with acetic acid.

687

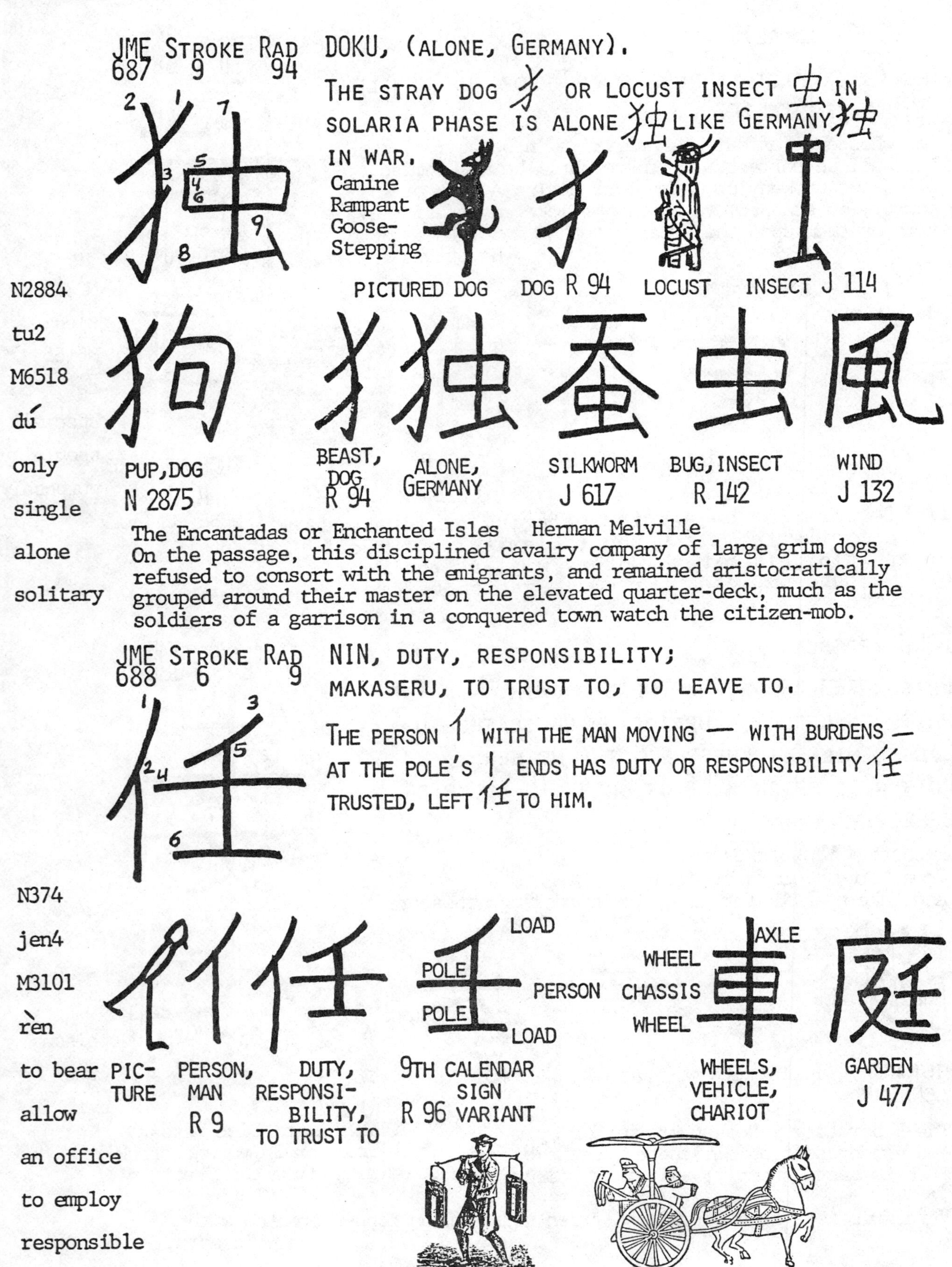

JME 687 Stroke 9 Rad 94

DOKU, (ALONE, GERMANY).

THE STRAY DOG 犭 OR LOCUST INSECT 虫 IN SOLARIA PHASE IS ALONE 独 LIKE GERMANY 独 IN WAR.

Canine Rampant Goose-Stepping

PICTURED DOG — DOG R 94 — LOCUST — INSECT J 114

N2884

tu2

M6518

dú

only

single

alone

solitary

狗 PUP, DOG N 2875 — 犭 BEAST, DOG R 94 — 独 ALONE, GERMANY — 蚕 SILKWORM J 617 — 虫 BUG, INSECT R 142 — 風 WIND J 132

The Encantadas or Enchanted Isles Herman Melville
On the passage, this disciplined cavalry company of large grim dogs refused to consort with the emigrants, and remained aristocratically grouped around their master on the elevated quarter-deck, much as the soldiers of a garrison in a conquered town watch the citizen-mob.

JME 688 Stroke 6 Rad 9

NIN, DUTY, RESPONSIBILITY;

MAKASERU, TO TRUST TO, TO LEAVE TO.

THE PERSON 亻 WITH THE MAN MOVING 一 WITH BURDENS 一 AT THE POLE'S 丨 ENDS HAS DUTY OR RESPONSIBILITY 任 TRUSTED, LEFT 任 TO HIM.

N374

jen4

M3101

rèn

to bear

allow

an office

to employ

responsible

PICTURE — 亻 PERSON, MAN R 9 — 任 DUTY, RESPONSIBILITY, TO TRUST TO — 壬 9TH CALENDAR SIGN R 96 VARIANT (LOAD, POLE, PERSON, POLE, LOAD) — 車 WHEELS, VEHICLE, CHARIOT (AXLE, WHEEL, CHASSIS, WHEEL) — 庭 GARDEN J 477

NEN, SENSE, THOUGHT, FEELING, DESIRE.

RAD 9/61 STROKE 8 JME 689

SENSE, THOUGHT, FEELING, DESIRE 念 ARE IN THE PERSON'S 人 HEART, MIND, SPIRIT 心 NOW, IN THE PRESENT 今.

The kanji for now, present 今 which shows the legs of the mother and the moving head of the neonate in childbirth (See J 81 in The Kanji ABC) has the kanji for heart, mind, spirit underneath to illustrate the sense, thought, feeling, desire which are related to childbirth.

N424
nien4
M4716
niàn
think of
recall
chant
repeat

PICTURED PERSON — PERSON, MAN R 9 — NOW, PRESENT J 81 (LEGS SPREAD; BIRTHING HEAD) — SENSE, THOUGHT, FEELING, DESIRE — MIND, HEART, SPIRIT J 95 — PICTURED ANATOMICAL HEART (R.A. R.V. L.A. L.V.)

The Aztec representation of Tlazolteotl as a mother in childbirth shows all the emotions of this kanji in her facial expressions perpetuated in nephrite.

NEN; MOERU, TO BURN, TO GLOW IV; MOYASU, TO BURN TV.

RAD 86 STROKE 16 JME 690

THE DOG'S 犬 BODY 月 OVER THE FIRE 灬 IS GLOWING, BURNING 燃 AS IT BAKES, GRILLS 焼.

Note the four legs of the fire like those of an animal.

The Egyptians believe that fire is a living animal which eats whatever it reaches, and dies after eating its food. (Therefore the quadruped legs). Herodotus

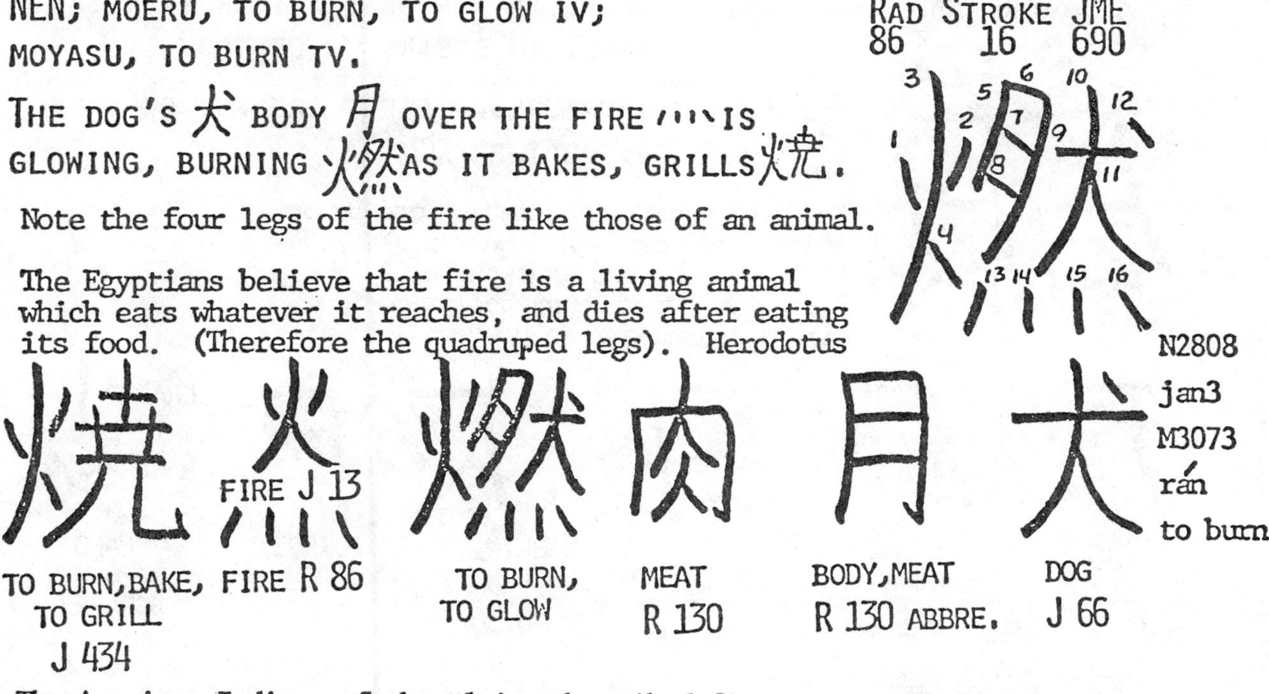

N2808
jan3
M3073
rán
to burn

The American Indians of the plains described fire as a red buffalo.

Faust Johann Wolfgang von Goethe

FAUST: And, if I err not, I see a trail of fire
Swirling in his wake.
WAGNER: I see nothing but a black poodle.

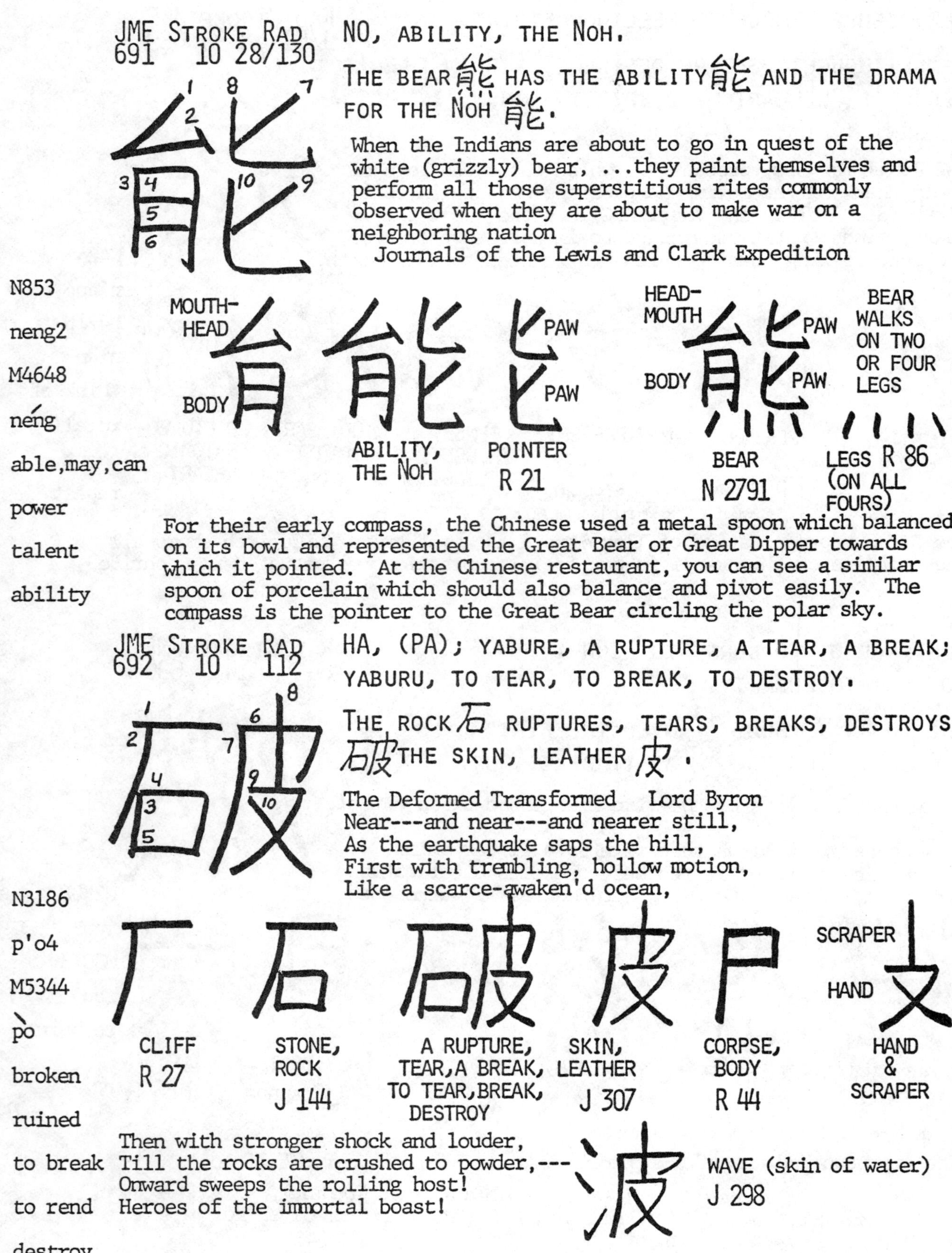

JME 691 STROKE 10 RAD 28/130

NO, ABILITY, THE NOH.

THE BEAR 熊 HAS THE ABILITY 能 AND THE DRAMA FOR THE NOH 能.

When the Indians are about to go in quest of the white (grizzly) bear, ...they paint themselves and perform all those superstitious rites commonly observed when they are about to make war on a neighboring nation

Journals of the Lewis and Clark Expedition

N853

neng2

M4648

néng

able, may, can

power

talent

ability

For their early compass, the Chinese used a metal spoon which balanced on its bowl and represented the Great Bear or Great Dipper towards which it pointed. At the Chinese restaurant, you can see a similar spoon of porcelain which should also balance and pivot easily. The compass is the pointer to the Great Bear circling the polar sky.

JME 692 STROKE 10 RAD 112

HA, (PA); YABURE, A RUPTURE, A TEAR, A BREAK; YABURU, TO TEAR, TO BREAK, TO DESTROY.

THE ROCK 石 RUPTURES, TEARS, BREAKS, DESTROYS 破 THE SKIN, LEATHER 皮.

The Deformed Transformed Lord Byron

Near---and near---and nearer still,
As the earthquake saps the hill,
First with trembling, hollow motion,
Like a scarce-awaken'd ocean,

N3186

p'o4

M5344

pò

broken

ruined

to break

to rend

destroy

Then with stronger shock and louder,
Till the rocks are crushed to powder,---
Onward sweeps the rolling host!
Heroes of the immortal boast!

HAI, (PAI); YABURU, TO DEFEAT;
YABURERU, TO BE DEFEATED.

THE COWRIES 貝 OF THE DEFEATED 敗 (GO TO)
THE HAND 攵 WITH THE STICK ノ OF THE ENEMY

What Dane-Geld Means Rudyard Kipling
If once you have paid him the Dane-geld,
You never get rid of the Dane.

RAD 154 STROKE 11 JME 693

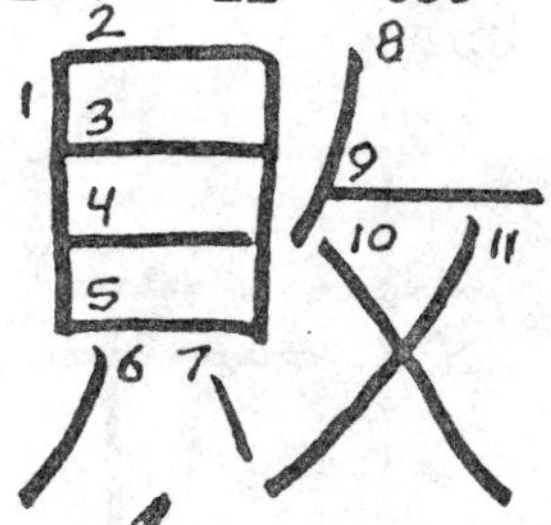

敗

N4494
pai4
M4866
bài
to ruin
destroy
spoil
defeat
carrion

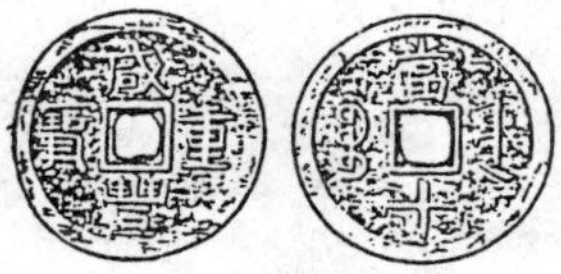

負 TO LOSE, BE DEFEATED J 312
貝 SEA SHELL, COWRIE J 169
敗 TO DEFEAT, BE DEFEATED
攵 HAND & STICK R 66
PICTURED HAND & STICK
敵 ENEMY J 678

CASH OF HIEN FUNG (R. 1851-61)

BAI, DOUBLE, TWICE, TIMES, -FOLD.

A PERSON 亻 TWICE, TIMES, MANYFOLD 倍
STANDS OVER 立 (INTERRUPTS THE SPEAKER'S
MOUTH 口.

RAD 9 STROKE 10 JME 694

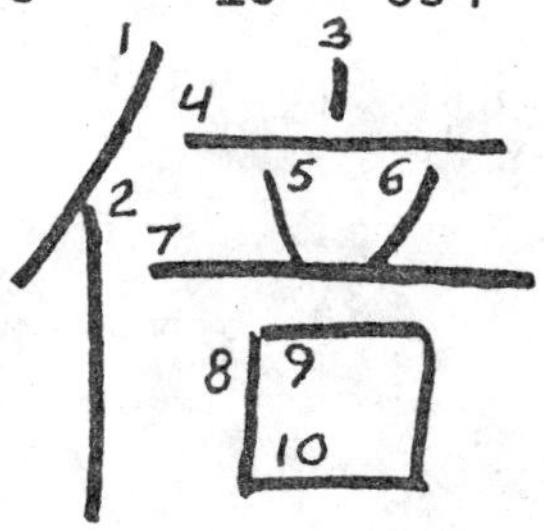

倍

N483
pei4
M5000
bèi
double
to double
-time
-fold

PICTURE
亻 PERSON, MAN R 9
倍 DOUBLE, TWICE, TIMES, -FOLD
立 TO STAND J 149
PICTURED STANDING
口 MOUTH J 27

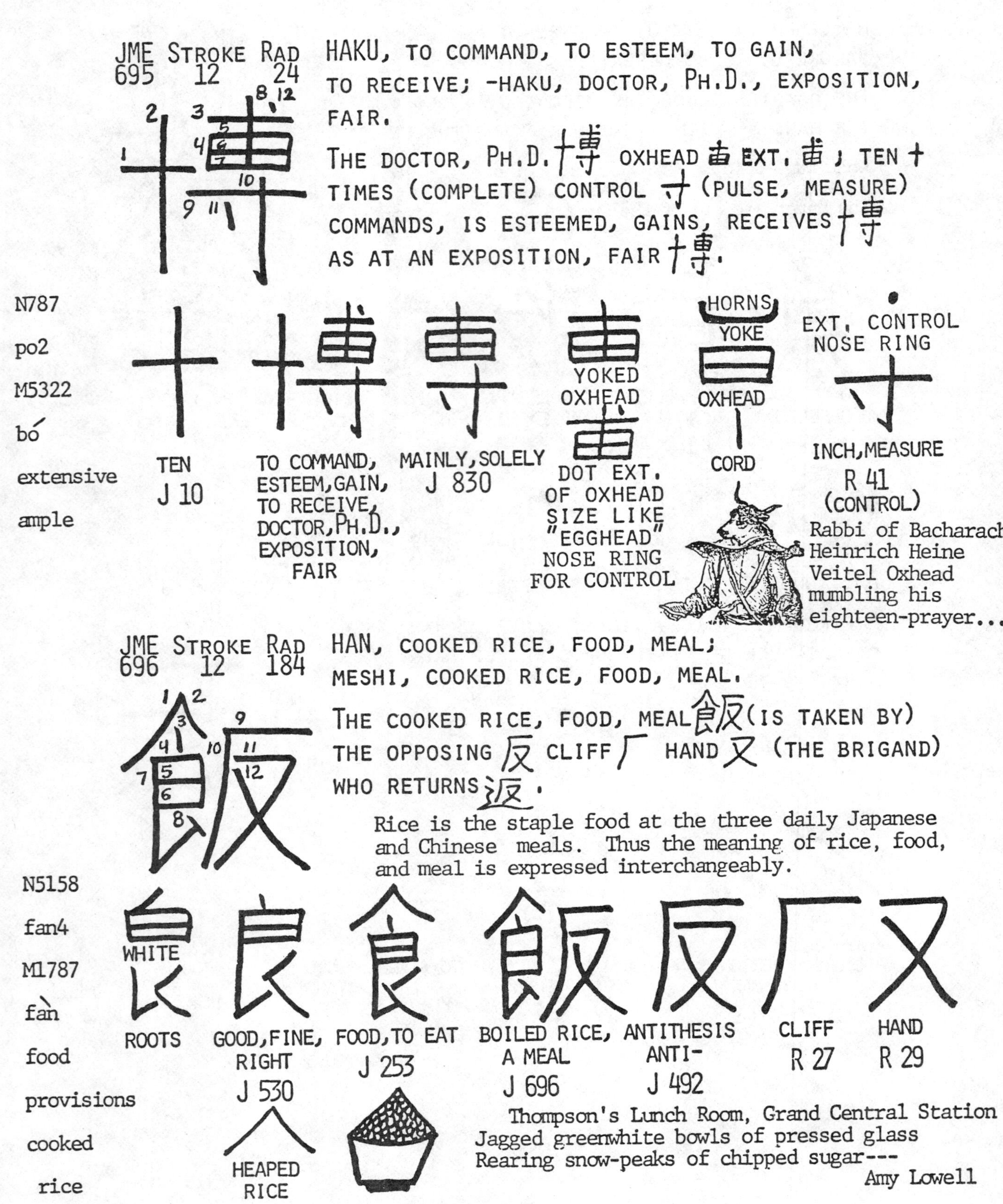

JME 695 STROKE 12 RAD 24

博

HAKU, TO COMMAND, TO ESTEEM, TO GAIN, TO RECEIVE; -HAKU, DOCTOR, PH.D., EXPOSITION, FAIR.

THE DOCTOR, PH.D. 博 OXHEAD 甫 EXT. 甫; TEN 十 TIMES (COMPLETE) CONTROL 寸 (PULSE, MEASURE) COMMANDS, IS ESTEEMED, GAINS, RECEIVES 博 AS AT AN EXPOSITION, FAIR 博.

N787
po2
M5322
bó
extensive
ample

十 TEN J 10

博 TO COMMAND, ESTEEM, GAIN, TO RECEIVE, DOCTOR, PH.D., EXPOSITION, FAIR

尃 MAINLY, SOLELY J 830

甫 YOKED OXHEAD — DOT EXT. OF OXHEAD SIZE LIKE "EGGHEAD" NOSE RING FOR CONTROL

HORNS, YOKE, OXHEAD, CORD

寸 EXT. CONTROL NOSE RING — INCH, MEASURE R 41 (CONTROL)

Rabbi of Bacharach
Heinrich Heine
Veitel Oxhead
mumbling his
eighteen-prayer...

JME 696 STROKE 12 RAD 184

飯

HAN, COOKED RICE, FOOD, MEAL; MESHI, COOKED RICE, FOOD, MEAL.

THE COOKED RICE, FOOD, MEAL 飯 (IS TAKEN BY) THE OPPOSING 反 CLIFF 厂 HAND 又 (THE BRIGAND) WHO RETURNS 返.

Rice is the staple food at the three daily Japanese and Chinese meals. Thus the meaning of rice, food, and meal is expressed interchangeably.

N5158
fan4
M1787
fàn
food
provisions
cooked
rice

皀 WHITE, ROOTS

良 GOOD, FINE, RIGHT J 530

食 FOOD, TO EAT J 253

飯 BOILED RICE, A MEAL J 696

反 ANTITHESIS ANTI- J 492

厂 CLIFF R 27

又 HAND R 29

HEAPED RICE

Thompson's Lunch Room, Grand Central Station
Jagged greenwhite bowls of pressed glass
Rearing snow-peaks of chipped sugar---
Amy Lowell

HI, RATIO, COMPARISON; KURABERU, TO COMPARE. RAD 81 STROKE 4 JME 697

TWO PERSONS IN PROFILE 比 (SPOON STYLE) FOR COMPARISON, TO COMPARE 比.

In form and feature, face and limb,
I grew so like my brother
That folks got taking me for him
And each for one another. Leigh

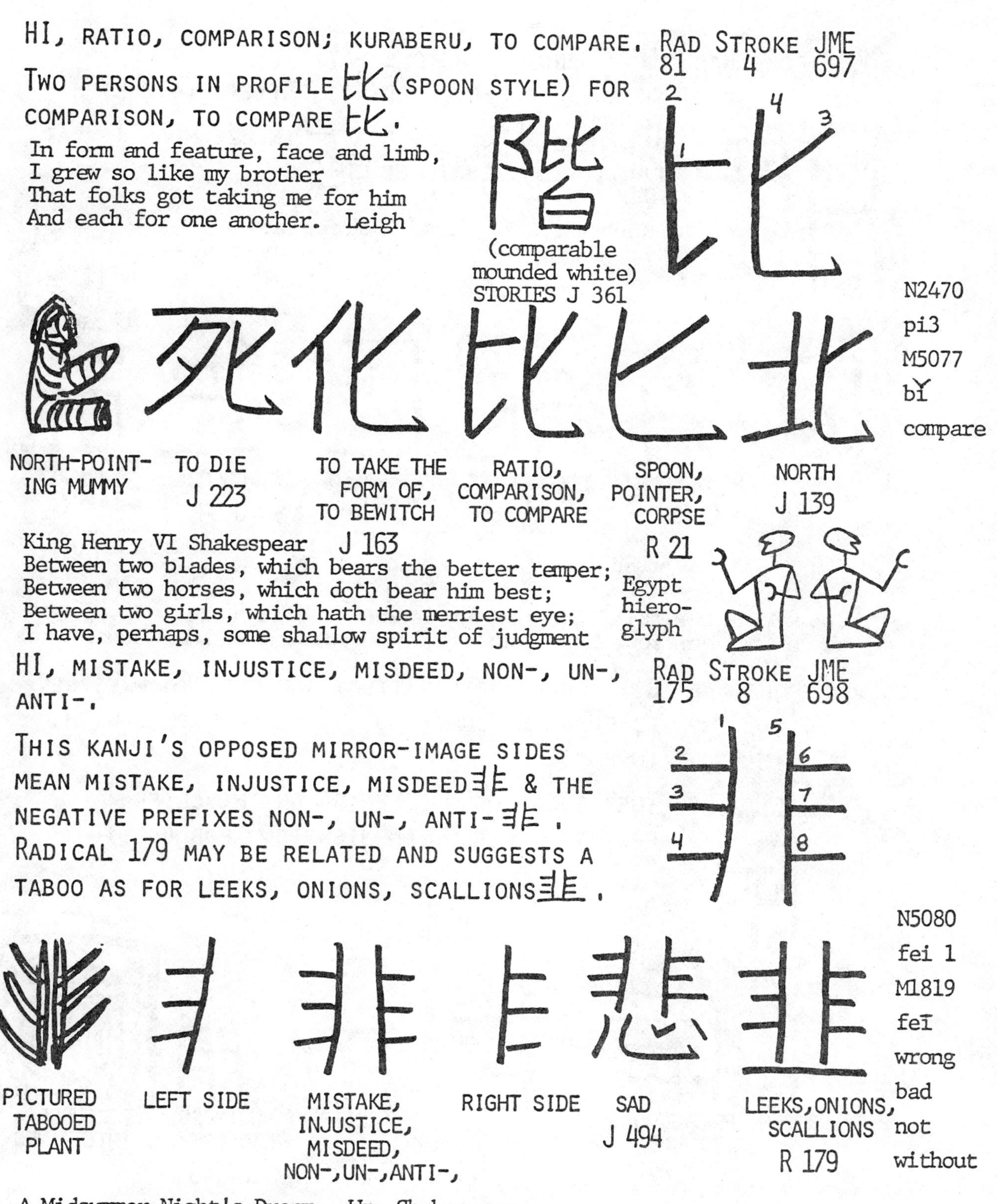

N2470
pi3
M5077
bǐ
compare

King Henry VI Shakespear
Between two blades, which bears the better temper;
Between two horses, which doth bear him best;
Between two girls, which hath the merriest eye;
I have, perhaps, some shallow spirit of judgment

HI, MISTAKE, INJUSTICE, MISDEED, NON-, UN-, ANTI-. RAD 175 STROKE 8 JME 698

THIS KANJI'S OPPOSED MIRROR-IMAGE SIDES MEAN MISTAKE, INJUSTICE, MISDEED 非 & THE NEGATIVE PREFIXES NON-, UN-, ANTI- 非. RADICAL 179 MAY BE RELATED AND SUGGESTS A TABOO AS FOR LEEKS, ONIONS, SCALLIONS 韭.

N5080
fei 1
M1819
fēi
wrong
bad
not
without

A Midsummer Night's Dream Wm. Shakespear
Eat no onions nor garlic, for we are to utter sweet breath.

Garlic makes a man stink. English Proverb

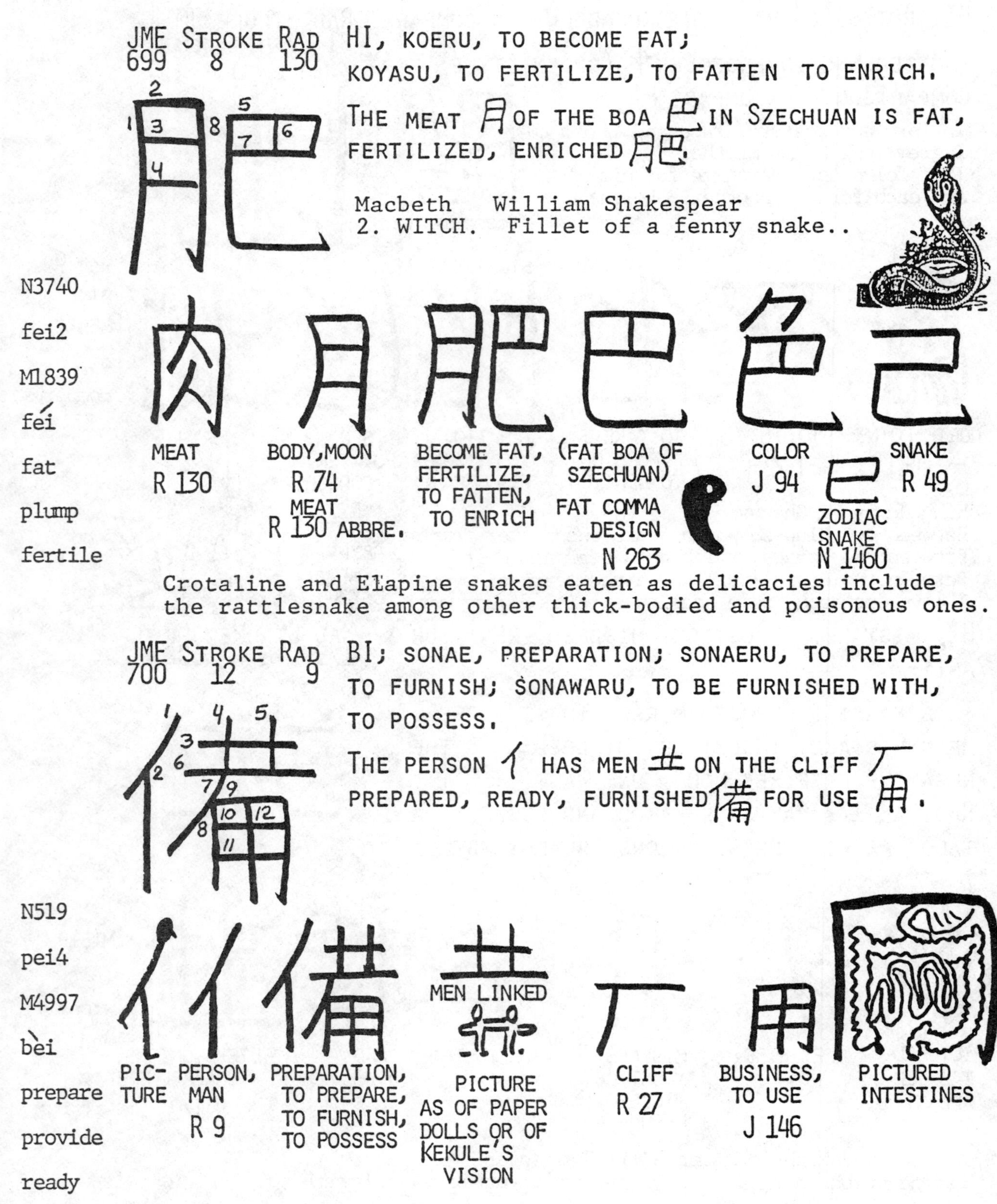

JME 699 STROKE 8 RAD 130

肥

HI, KOERU, TO BECOME FAT; KOYASU, TO FERTILIZE, TO FATTEN TO ENRICH.

THE MEAT 月 OF THE BOA 巴 IN SZECHUAN IS FAT, FERTILIZED, ENRICHED 肥.

Macbeth William Shakespear
2. WITCH. Fillet of a fenny snake..

N3740
fei2
M1839
féi
fat
plump
fertile

肉 MEAT R 130

月 BODY, MOON R 74 MEAT R 130 ABBRE.

肥 BECOME FAT, FERTILIZE, TO FATTEN, TO ENRICH

巴 (FAT BOA OF SZECHUAN) FAT COMMA DESIGN N 263

色 COLOR J 94

己 SNAKE R 49

巳 ZODIAC SNAKE N 1460

Crotaline and Elapine snakes eaten as delicacies include the rattlesnake among other thick-bodied and poisonous ones.

JME 700 STROKE 12 RAD 9

備

BI; SONAE, PREPARATION; SONAERU, TO PREPARE, TO FURNISH; SONAWARU, TO BE FURNISHED WITH, TO POSSESS.

THE PERSON 亻 HAS MEN 艹 ON THE CLIFF 厂 PREPARED, READY, FURNISHED 備 FOR USE 用.

N519
pei4
M4997
bèi
prepare
provide
ready

PICTURE

亻 PERSON, MAN R 9

備 PREPARATION, TO PREPARE, TO FURNISH, TO POSSESS

MEN LINKED — PICTURE AS OF PAPER DOLLS OR OF KEKULE'S VISION

厂 CLIFF R 27

用 BUSINESS, TO USE J 146

PICTURED INTESTINES

HITSU, (PITSU), FUDE, PEN, WRITING BRUSH.

RAD 118 STROKE 12 JME 701

THE PEN, WRITING BRUSH 筆 HAS A BAMBOO 竹 STOCK | WHICH MOVES 二 IN THE HAND ヨ.

Piping Down the Valleys Wild William Blake
Piper, sit thee down and write In a book that all may read. So he vanished from my sight; And I plucked a hollow reed, And I made a rural pen, And I stained the water clear, And I wrote my happy songs Every child may joy to hear.

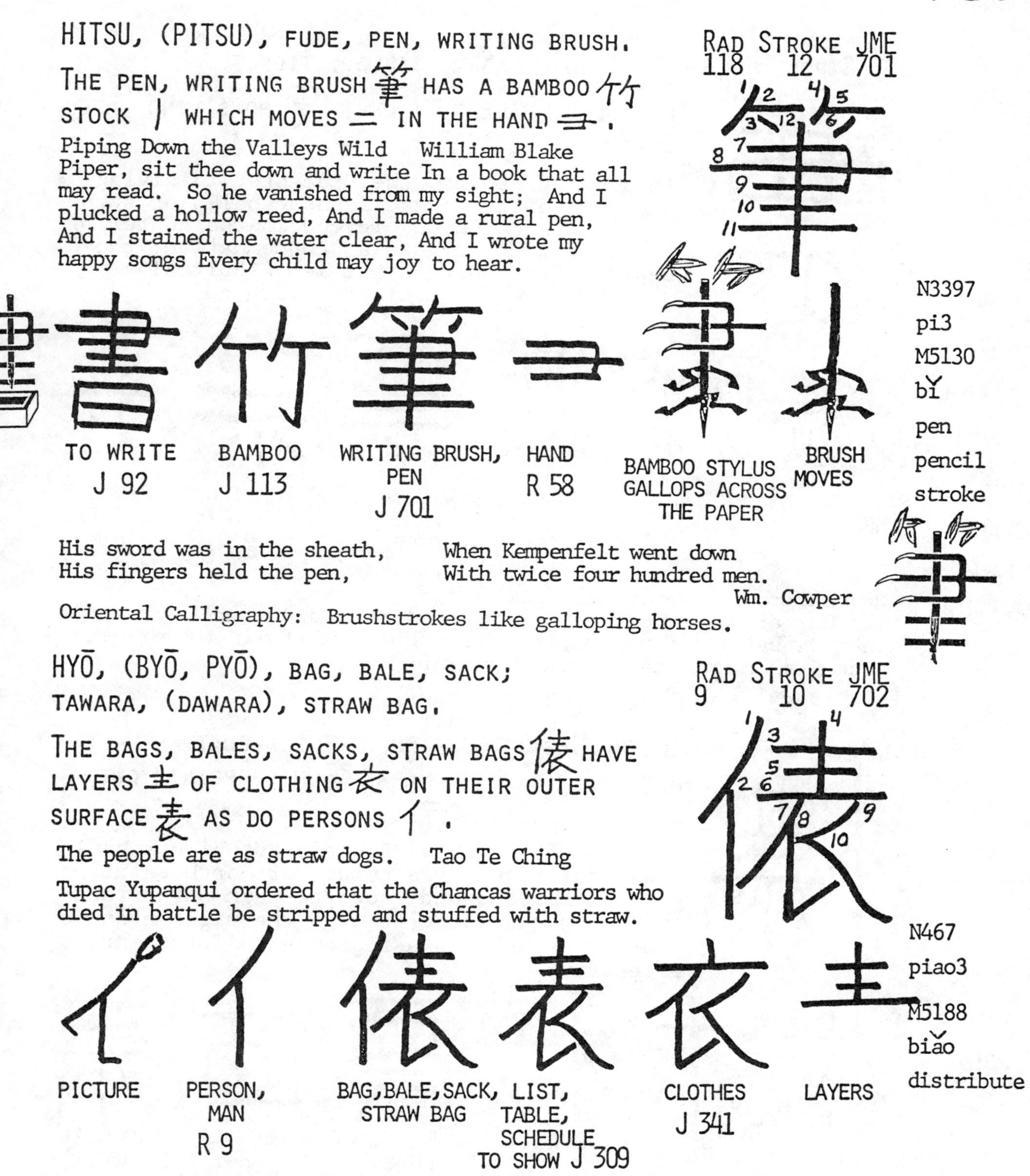

N3397
pi3
M5130
bǐ
pen
pencil
stroke

His sword was in the sheath,
His fingers held the pen,
When Kempenfelt went down
With twice four hundred men.
Wm. Cowper

Oriental Calligraphy: Brushstrokes like galloping horses.

HYŌ, (BYŌ, PYŌ), BAG, BALE, SACK;
TAWARA, (DAWARA), STRAW BAG.

RAD 9 STROKE 10 JME 702

THE BAGS, BALES, SACKS, STRAW BAGS 俵 HAVE LAYERS 丰 OF CLOTHING 衣 ON THEIR OUTER SURFACE 表 AS DO PERSONS 亻.

The people are as straw dogs. Tao Te Ching

Tupac Yupanqui ordered that the Chancas warriors who died in battle be stripped and stuffed with straw.

N467
piao3
M5188
biǎo
distribute

Fifty of the deceased Scythian king's best attendants and fifty of his most beautiful horses were strangled and their insides removed. The cavities were stuffed with chaff, and sewn up. Pairs of posts were driven into the ground. The corpses were mounted on the horses which were supported by the fellies of wheels attached to the posts. The mounted riders were placed in a circle about the tomb. Herodotus

JME 703 STROKE 11 RAD 146

HYŌ, (PYŌ), LABEL, BALLOT, TICKET.

THE LABEL, BALLOT, TICKET 票 SHOWS, INDICATES 示 IN THE WEST 西.

In ancient Athens, the diecasts, in giving their verdict, generally used balls of stone or of metal. Those pierced in the center or black in color signified condemnation; those unpierced or white signified acquittal.
Ency. Br. 11th ed.

N4276
p'iao4
M5192
piào
bill
banknote
ticket

PICTURED NEST — PICTURED BIRD — 西 WEST J 96 — 票 LABEL, BALLOT, TICKET — 示 TO SHOW, TO POINT OUT J 622 — 光 TO SHINE, LIGHT, RAY J 72

No tickee... no laundly!!

Henry Thoreau Slavery in Massachusetts
The fate of the country does not depend on what kind of paper you drop into the ballot box once a year, but on what kind of man you drop from your chamber into the street every morning.

JME 704 STROKE 15 RAD 75

HYŌ, (SIGNPOST, MARK).

IN THE WEST 西 THE WOOD 木 BLAZED TREE 木 HAS THE SIGNPOST, MARK 標 WHICH POINTS OUT, SHOWS, INDICATES 示.

Colonel Daniel Boone's Autobiography
I was solicited by a number of North Carolina gentlemen...and undertook to mark out a road in the best passage through the wilderness to Kentucky with such assistance as I thought necessary.

N2359
piao 1
M5180
biāo
mark
beacon
signal
flag
notice

PICTURED TREE — 木 TREE, WOOD J 15 — 標 SIGNPOST, MARK — 票 LABEL, BALLOT, TICKET J 703 — 西 WEST J 96 — 示 TO SHOW, POINT OUT J 622

HIN, BIN, POVERTY; MAZUSHII, POOR.

RAD 12 STROKE 11 JME 705

POVERTY, POOR, TO BE POOR 貧 IS FROM THE DIVIDING 分 OF THE COWRIES 貝 (INHERITANCE) AS BY KNIFING 刀 INTO PARTS, SHARES 分.

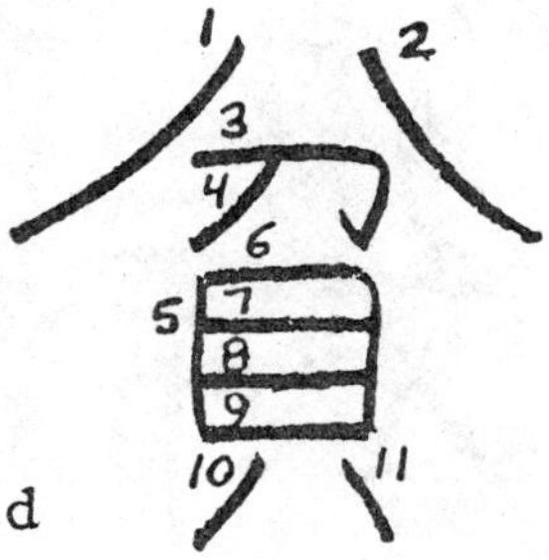

Village Life in China Arthur Smith

The Chinese ideal is to hold the family property in common indefinitely. But...the division of the land cannot always be postponed. ...one of the sons becomes discontented

貧

N600
p'in2
M5274
pín
poor

負 敗 八 貧 分 貝

TO BE INDEBTED TO, LOSE, BE DEFEATED J 312 | BE DEFEATED J 693 | EIGHT J 8 | POVERTY, POOR | TO DIVIDE, PARTS, SHARES J 133 | SEA SHELL, COWRIES J 169

and commissions a neighbor to tell the father that it is time to effect a division. It is often replied when we ask why a Chinese does not help his son or his brother who has a large family and nothing in the house to eat, "We have divided..."

FU, (PU), NUNO, CLOTH.

RAD 50 STROKE 5 JME 706

THE HAND 𠂇 IS ON CLOTH 巾 WHICH IS THE CLOTH 布

Except when required to be of the curtain shape, his undergarment was of silk cut narrow above and wide below. The Analects Confucius

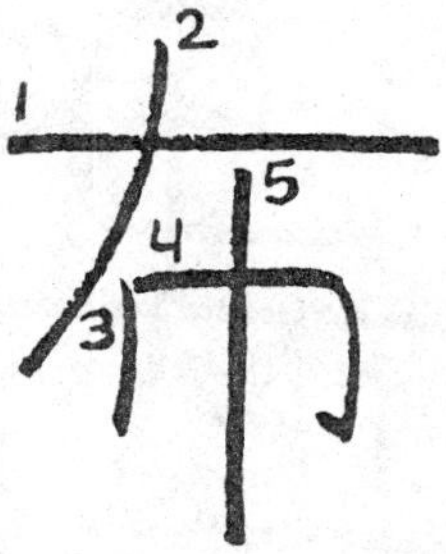

布

N1470
pu4
M5364
bù
cotton
cloth
calico
linen

𠂇 布 巾 帀 両

PICTURED HAND | HAND | CLOTH | CLOTH R 50 | BALANCE, SCALES (SILK WAS SOLD BY WEIGHT) | TWO, BOTH J 336

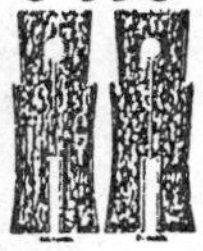

←LIBRA CONSTELLATION

希 市

RARE, DESIRE J 575 | MARKET J 222

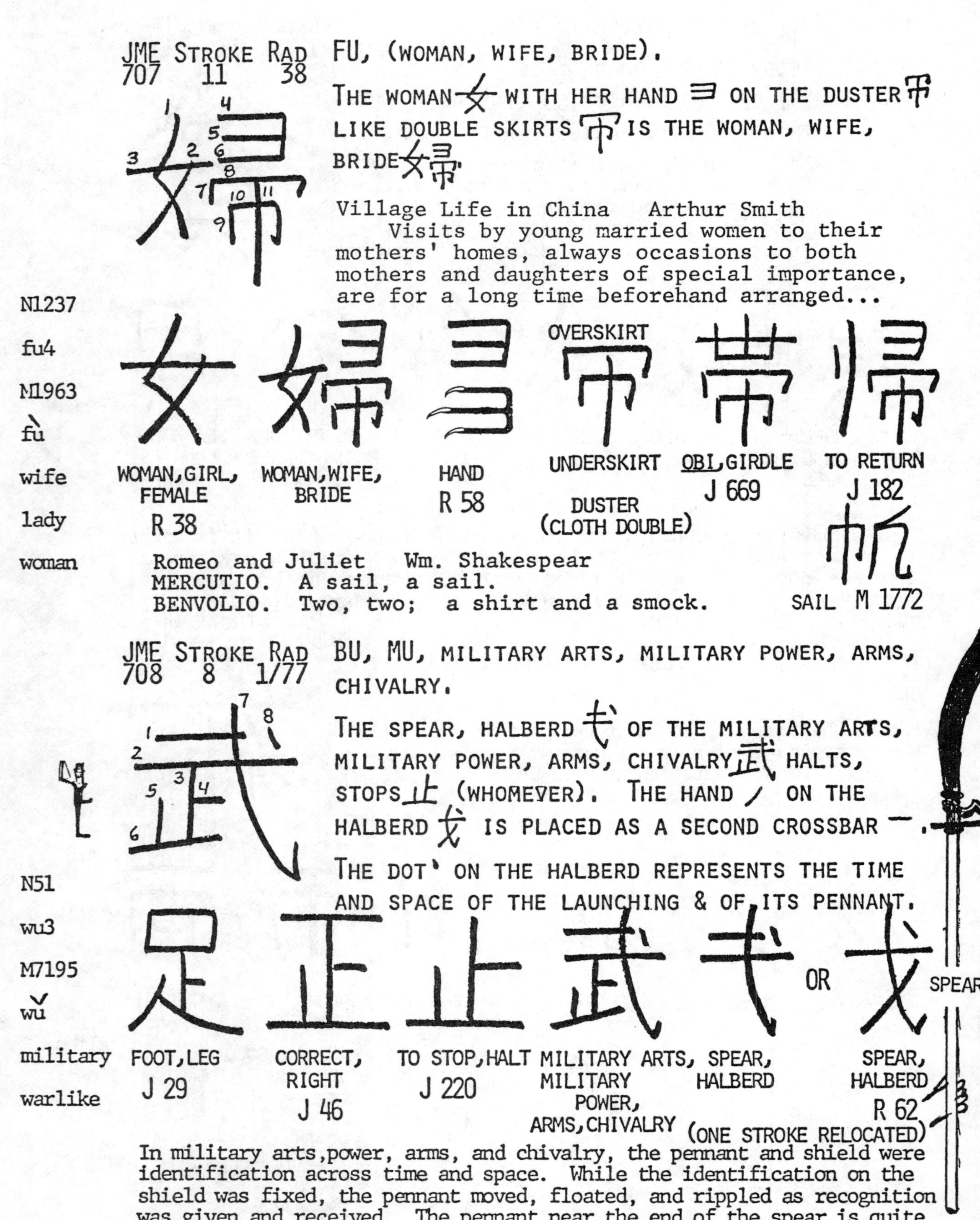

JME 707 Stroke 11 Rad 38

FU, (WOMAN, WIFE, BRIDE).

THE WOMAN 女 WITH HER HAND ⺕ ON THE DUSTER 帚 LIKE DOUBLE SKIRTS 巾 IS THE WOMAN, WIFE, BRIDE 婦.

婦

Village Life in China Arthur Smith
Visits by young married women to their mothers' homes, always occasions to both mothers and daughters of special importance, are for a long time beforehand arranged...

N1237
fu4
M1963
fù
wife
lady
woman

女 WOMAN, GIRL, FEMALE R 38

婦 WOMAN, WIFE, BRIDE

⺕ HAND R 58

巾 OVERSKIRT / UNDERSKIRT / DUSTER (CLOTH DOUBLE)

帯 OBI, GIRDLE J 669

帰 TO RETURN J 182

帆 SAIL M 1772

Romeo and Juliet Wm. Shakespear
MERCUTIO. A sail, a sail.
BENVOLIO. Two, two; a shirt and a smock.

JME 708 Stroke 8 Rad 1/77

BU, MU, MILITARY ARTS, MILITARY POWER, ARMS, CHIVALRY.

THE SPEAR, HALBERD 弋 OF THE MILITARY ARTS, MILITARY POWER, ARMS, CHIVALRY 武 HALTS, STOPS 止 (WHOMEVER). THE HAND ノ ON THE HALBERD 戈 IS PLACED AS A SECOND CROSSBAR 一. THE DOT ` ON THE HALBERD REPRESENTS THE TIME AND SPACE OF THE LAUNCHING & OF ITS PENNANT.

武

N51
wu3
M7195
wǔ
military
warlike

足 FOOT, LEG J 29

正 CORRECT, RIGHT J 46

止 TO STOP, HALT J 220

武 MILITARY ARTS, MILITARY POWER, ARMS, CHIVALRY

弋 SPEAR, HALBERD

OR

戈 SPEAR, HALBERD R 62 (ONE STROKE RELOCATED)

SPEAR

In military arts, power, arms, and chivalry, the pennant and shield were identification across time and space. While the identification on the shield was fixed, the pennant moved, floated, and rippled as recognition was given and received. The pennant near the end of the spear is quite universal.
A.D.

FUKU, (COPY, ASSISTANT, SECONDARY, ASSOCIATE, VICE-, SUB-).

RAD 18 STROKE 11 JME 709

THE GOOD FORTUNE, BLESSING, LUCK, WEALTH 福 HAS BEEN SLASHED 刂 (KNIFED TO THE STATUS) OF A COPY, ASSISTANT, SECONDARY, ASSOCIATE, VICE-, SUB- 副.

副

N699
fu4
M1951
fù
to aid
to second
ass't

福 FORTUNE, BLESSING, LUCK, WEALTH J 506 福

UNITED CONSUMPTION RICE FIELD 畐 TO FILL M 1975 畐

副 ASSISTANT, SECONDARY, ASSOCIATE, COPY, VICE-, SUB-

刂 KNIFE, SWORD R 18 ABBRE.

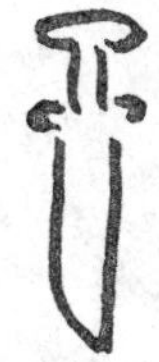

PICTURE

FUKU, (RE-, REPEAT); FUKU SURU, TO RETURN TO, TO BE RESTORED TO.

RAD 60 STROKE 12 JME 710

A PERSON 𠂉 WALKING 夂 WITH A FAN ′ UNDER THE SUN 日 WITH ATTENDANTS 彳 RETURNS, IS RESTORED 復

Some men a forward motion love,
But I by backward steps would move,
And when the dust falls in the urn,
In that state I came, return. The Retreat Vaughan

復

N1627
fu2
M1992
fù
return
repeat
reply
again

PICTURE

彳 TO STEP, WALK, TO FOLLOW R 60

復 (RE-, REPEAT) TO RETURN TO, BE RESTORED TO

𠂉 PERSON, MAN R 9

日 SUN R 72

夂 HAND OR WALKS WITH IMPLEMENT OR STICK

711

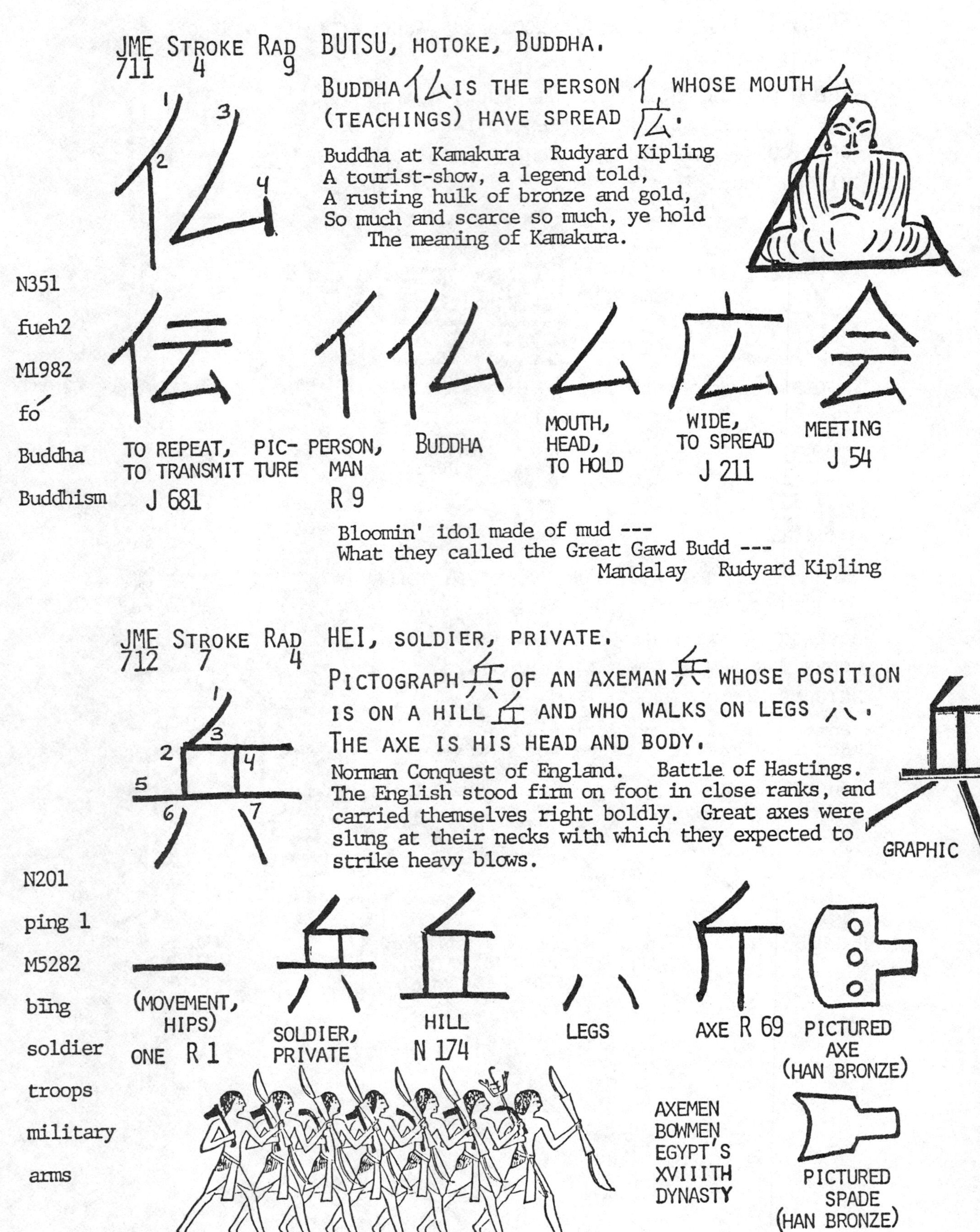
JME STROKE RAD
711 4 9
BUTSU, HOTOKE, BUDDHA.
BUDDHA 仏 IS THE PERSON 亻 WHOSE MOUTH ム (TEACHINGS) HAVE SPREAD 広.
Buddha at Kamakura Rudyard Kipling
A tourist-show, a legend told,
A rusting hulk of bronze and gold,
So much and scarce so much, ye hold
The meaning of Kamakura.
N351
fueh2
M1982
fó
Buddha
Buddhism
伝 亻 仏 ム 広 会
TO REPEAT, TO TRANSMIT J 681
PICTURE
PERSON, MAN R 9
BUDDHA
MOUTH, HEAD, TO HOLD
WIDE, TO SPREAD J 211
MEETING J 54
Bloomin' idol made of mud ---
What they called the Great Gawd Budd ---
Mandalay Rudyard Kipling
JME STROKE RAD
712 7 4
HEI, SOLDIER, PRIVATE.
PICTOGRAPH 兵 OF AN AXEMAN 兵 WHOSE POSITION IS ON A HILL 丘 AND WHO WALKS ON LEGS ハ.
THE AXE IS HIS HEAD AND BODY.
Norman Conquest of England. Battle of Hastings.
The English stood firm on foot in close ranks, and carried themselves right boldly. Great axes were slung at their necks with which they expected to strike heavy blows.
GRAPHIC
N201
ping 1
M5282
bīng
soldier
troops
military
arms
一 兵 丘 ハ 斤
(MOVEMENT, HIPS) ONE R 1
SOLDIER, PRIVATE
HILL N 174
LEGS
AXE R 69
PICTURED AXE (HAN BRONZE)
AXEMEN BOWMEN EGYPT'S XVIIITH DYNASTY
PICTURED SPADE (HAN BRONZE)

HEN, (PEN), SIDE, BOUNDARY, BORDER, DISTRICT, VICINITY.

RAD 162 STROKE 5 JME 713

ONE STOPS AND GOES 辶 WITH THE SWORD 刀 TO THE SIDE,BOUNDARY,BORDER,DISTRICT,VICINITY 辺.

辺

A border region or defense district called a march (as in marquis) and near the boundary, border, first established by Charlemagne on his frontiers and later by Germany. Both Prussia and Austria (Ostmark) had been such marches.

N4661 pian 1 M5243 biān side border edge margin frontier

足 FOOT,LEG J 29

辵 TO STOP & GO R 162

辶 TO STOP & GO R 162 ABBRE.

辺 SIDE,BORDER, BOUNDARY, DISTRICT, VICINITY

刀 KNIFE, SWORD R 18

EXECUTIONER'S CURVED SWORD

Basil Hall Chamberlain Things Japanese
The Japanese sword of medieval and modern times (the katana) is lighter, shorter, has an edge on one side, and is slightly curved towards the point.

側 SIDE J 667 (ALSO HAS A SWORD,KNIFE)

HEN, COMPILATION, EDITING;
AMU, TO KNIT, TO BRAID, TO CROCHET, TO TWIST.

RAD 120 STROKE 15 JME 714

THE BOOKS 冊 ARE BELOW A DOOR 戸 OF STRINGS 糸 (LIKE A BEADED CURTAIN) WHICH ARE COMPILED, EDITED, KNIT, BRAIDED, CROCHETED, TWISTED 編.

編

English Chant Fireside Encyclopedia
I knit this knot, this knot I knit
To know the thing I know not yet,
That I may see

N3583 pien 1 M5231 biān plait weave arrange enroll edit

結 KNOT,TO TIE. J 390

糸 THREADS, SILK R 120

編 COMPILATION, EDITING, TO KNIT,BRAID,

戸 DOOR R 63

冊 BOOKS N 88

曲 MELODY, TO BEND J 381

The man that shall my husband be,
Not in his best or worst array,
But what he weareth every day;
That I tomorrow may him ken
From among all other men.

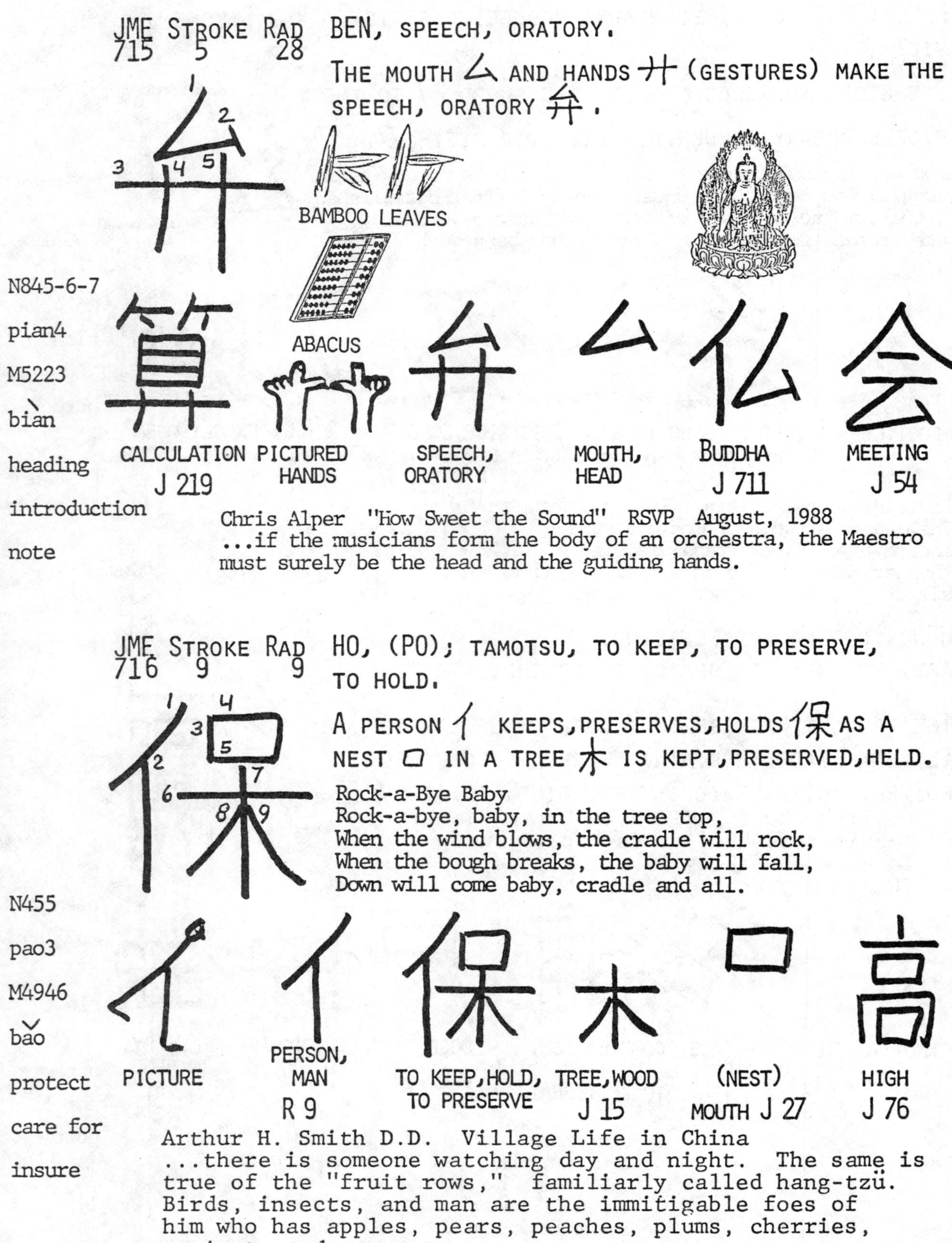

JME 715 STROKE 5 RAD 28

BEN, SPEECH, ORATORY.

THE MOUTH 厶 AND HANDS 廾 (GESTURES) MAKE THE SPEECH, ORATORY 弁.

N845-6-7

pian4

M5223

bìan

heading

introduction

note

算 CALCULATION J 219

PICTURED HANDS

弁 SPEECH, ORATORY

厶 MOUTH, HEAD

仏 BUDDHA J 711

会 MEETING J 54

Chris Alper "How Sweet the Sound" RSVP August, 1988
...if the musicians form the body of an orchestra, the Maestro must surely be the head and the guiding hands.

JME 716 STROKE 9 RAD 9

HO, (PO); TAMOTSU, TO KEEP, TO PRESERVE, TO HOLD.

A PERSON 亻 KEEPS, PRESERVES, HOLDS 保 AS A NEST 口 IN A TREE 木 IS KEPT, PRESERVED, HELD.

Rock-a-Bye Baby
Rock-a-bye, baby, in the tree top,
When the wind blows, the cradle will rock,
When the bough breaks, the baby will fall,
Down will come baby, cradle and all.

N455

pao3

M4946

bǎo

protect

care for

insure

PICTURE

亻 PERSON, MAN R 9

保 TO KEEP, HOLD, TO PRESERVE

木 TREE, WOOD J 15

口 (NEST) MOUTH J 27

高 HIGH J 76

Arthur H. Smith D.D. Village Life in China
...there is someone watching day and night. The same is true of the "fruit rows," familiarly called hang-tzü. Birds, insects, and man are the immitigable foes of him who has apples, pears, peaches, plums, cherries, apricots and grapes.

HŌ, (PŌ), NEWS, REPORT, REWARD; MUKUI, REWARD, RETRIBUTION; MUKUIRU, TO REWARD, TO REVENGE.

RAD	STROKE	JME
32	12	717

THE HAND 又 WITH THE SEAL 卩 GIVES THE EARTH 土 (HOLDER) WITH THE SHINING ソ SHIELD 干 THE BLESSINGS, GOOD LUCK, FORTUNE, HAPPINESS 幸 FOR HIS NEWS REPORT, REWARD, RETRIBUTION, REVENGE 報.

報

土 EARTH, SOIL R 32

ソ (SHINING) EIGHT J 12

干 SHIELD R 51

報 NEWS, REPORT, REWARD, RETRIBUTION, TO REVENGE

卩 SEAL R 26

又 HAND R 29

N1114
pao4
M4955
bào
announce
report
inform
declare

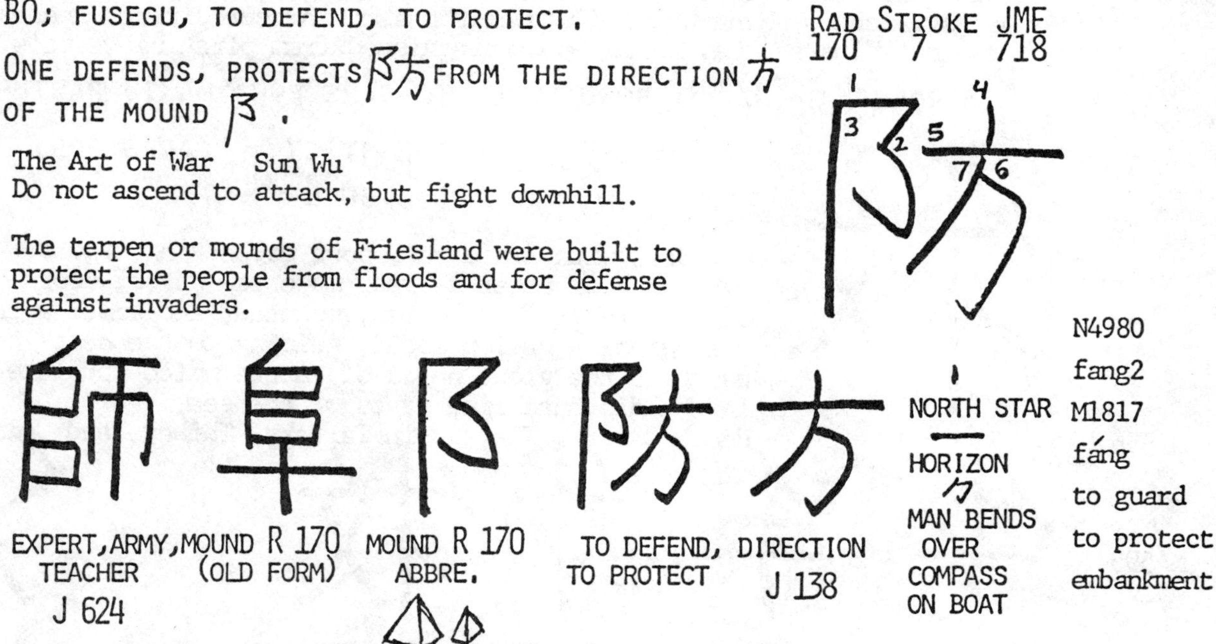

BŌ; FUSEGU, TO DEFEND, TO PROTECT.

RAD	STROKE	JME
170	7	718

ONE DEFENDS, PROTECTS 防 FROM THE DIRECTION 方 OF THE MOUND 阝.

The Art of War   Sun Wu
Do not ascend to attack, but fight downhill.

The terpen or mounds of Friesland were built to protect the people from floods and for defense against invaders.

防

師 EXPERT, ARMY, TEACHER J 624

阜 MOUND R 170 (OLD FORM)

阝 MOUND R 170 ABBRE.

防 TO DEFEND, TO PROTECT

方 DIRECTION J 138

丶 NORTH STAR
一 HORIZON
勹 MAN BENDS OVER COMPASS ON BOAT

N4980
fang2
M1817
fáng
to guard
to protect
embankment

A city wall is an inner circular mound made from the earth dug out of the outer circular moat.   A.D.

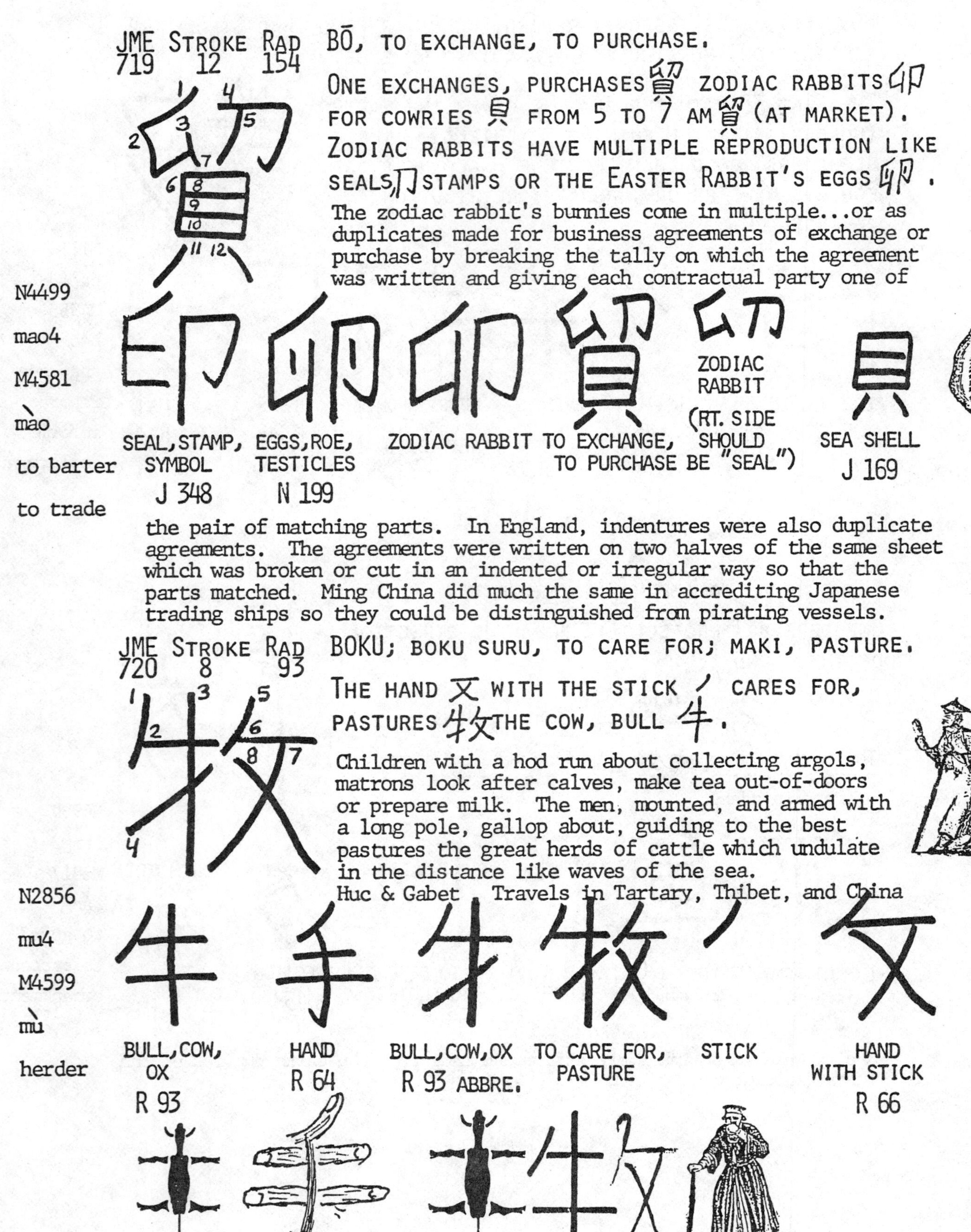

JME 719 Stroke 12 Rad 154

BŌ, TO EXCHANGE, TO PURCHASE.

ONE EXCHANGES, PURCHASES 貿 ZODIAC RABBITS 卯 FOR COWRIES 貝 FROM 5 TO 7 AM 貿 (AT MARKET). ZODIAC RABBITS HAVE MULTIPLE REPRODUCTION LIKE SEALS 卩 STAMPS OR THE EASTER RABBIT'S EGGS 卵.

The zodiac rabbit's bunnies come in multiple...or as duplicates made for business agreements of exchange or purchase by breaking the tally on which the agreement was written and giving each contractual party one of the pair of matching parts. In England, indentures were also duplicate agreements. The agreements were written on two halves of the same sheet which was broken or cut in an indented or irregular way so that the parts matched. Ming China did much the same in accrediting Japanese trading ships so they could be distinguished from pirating vessels.

N4499
mao4
M4581
mào
to barter
to trade

印 SEAL, STAMP, SYMBOL J 348

卵 EGGS, ROE, TESTICLES N 199

卯 ZODIAC RABBIT

貿 TO EXCHANGE, TO PURCHASE

ZODIAC RABBIT (RT. SIDE SHOULD BE "SEAL")

貝 SEA SHELL J 169

JME 720 Stroke 8 Rad 93

BOKU; BOKU SURU, TO CARE FOR; MAKI, PASTURE.

THE HAND 又 WITH THE STICK ノ CARES FOR, PASTURES 牧 THE COW, BULL 牛.

Children with a hod run about collecting argols, matrons look after calves, make tea out-of-doors or prepare milk. The men, mounted, and armed with a long pole, gallop about, guiding to the best pastures the great herds of cattle which undulate in the distance like waves of the sea.
Huc & Gabet, Travels in Tartary, Thibet, and China

N2856
mu4
M4599
mù
herder

牛 BULL, COW, OX R 93

手 HAND R 64

牜 BULL, COW, OX R 93 ABBRE.

牧 TO CARE FOR, PASTURE

ノ STICK

攵 HAND WITH STICK R 66

MAN, FULLNESS; MICHIRU, TO BE FULL, TO RISE (TIDE), TO WAX (MOON).

RAD 85 STROKE 12 JME 721

PERSONS 廿 (VIEWING) THE WAXING 満 BOTH SIDES 両 OF THE FULL 満 (MOON) WHICH CAUSES WATER 氵 (TIDES) TO RISE 満.

The sea is calm tonight,
The tide is full, the moon lies fair
Upon the Straits. Dover Beach Matthew Arnold

満

N2636
man3
M4326
mǎn
full
satisfied
complete

DROPS

氵 WATER R 85

満 FULLNESS, TO BE FULL, TO RISE, WAX

廿 (LINKED PERSONS)

両 TWO, BOTH, GOLD COIN J 336

円 CIRCLE, YEN J 48

FIVE YEN

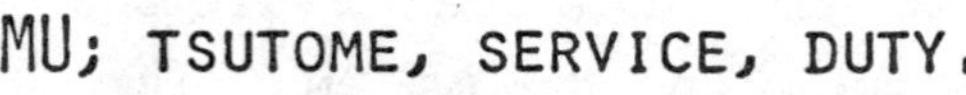

MU; TSUTOME, SERVICE, DUTY.

RAD 110 STROKE 11 JME 722

THE STRENGTH 力 OF THE HAND WITH THE STICK 攵 AND THE 3-PRONGED HALBERD 矛 (PERFORM) DUTY, SERVICE 務

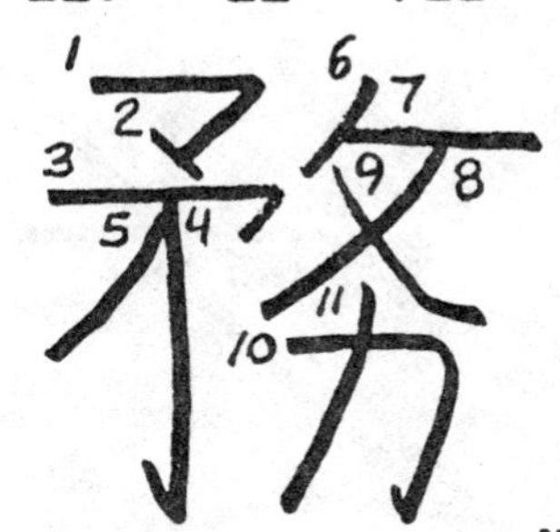

N3167
wu4
M7198
wù
must
-business
-duties
-affairs

予 PREVIOUS J 525 (HALBERD STOCK OR SHAFT BEFORE FINISHED)

矛 HALBERD R 110

務 SERVICE, DUTY

力 STRENGTH, POWER R 19

丿 STICK

攵 STICK IN HAND J 66

723

JME 723 STROKE 12 RAD 86

MU, BU; NAI, NASHI, NOTHING, NIL, NEGATIVE, NON-EXISTENT.

PICTOGRAPH OF A HORNED PLATED QUADRUPED (EXTINCT AND THEREFORE) NON-EXISTENT, NOTHING, NIL, NEGATIVE 無. (PERHAPS THE SQUARE-HEADED RECTANGULAR-BODIED MONSTER IN THE LASCAUX CAVERN PAINTING). THE SUN AT MIDNIGHT. NIRVANA IS THE NOTHINGNESS IN THE WHEEL'S HUB.

N2773
wu2
M7180
wu
without
none
negative

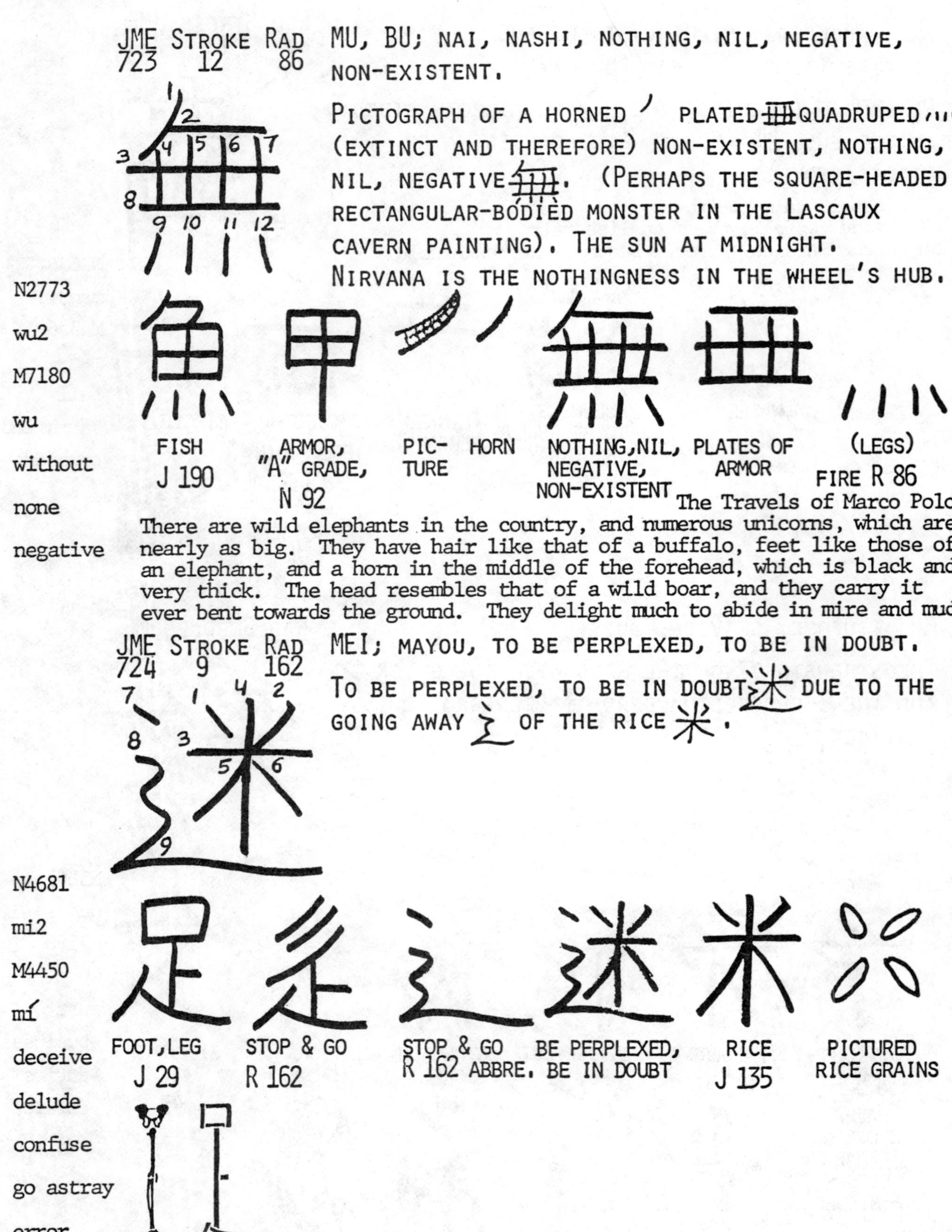

The Travels of Marco Polo

There are wild elephants in the country, and numerous unicorns, which are nearly as big. They have hair like that of a buffalo, feet like those of an elephant, and a horn in the middle of the forehead, which is black and very thick. The head resembles that of a wild boar, and they carry it ever bent towards the ground. They delight much to abide in mire and mud.

JME 724 STROKE 9 RAD 162

MEI; MAYOU, TO BE PERPLEXED, TO BE IN DOUBT.

TO BE PERPLEXED, TO BE IN DOUBT 迷 DUE TO THE GOING AWAY 辶 OF THE RICE 米.

N4681
mi2
M4450
mí
deceive
delude
confuse
go astray
error

MEN; WATA, COTTON, COTTON THREADS, COTTON CLOTH.

RAD STROKE JME
120 14 725

THREADS 糸 AND CLOTH 巾 OF COTTON 綿, OFTEN WHITE 白 CLOTH 巾.

線 LINE, TRACT, WIRE, STRING J 447

綿

糸 THREADS, SILK R 120

綿 COTTON, COTTON THREADS, COTTON CLOTH

帛 CLOTH N 3096

白 WHITE R 106 COTTON POD OR BOLL

巾 CLOTH R 50

吊 TO HANG, TO SUSPEND, TO WEAR (AS A SWORD) N 884

N3566
mien2
M4506
mián
soft
downy
silk floss

William Butler Yeats Byzantium
For Hades bobbin bound in mummy-cloth
May unwind the winding path;

YAKU, PROMISE, APPROXIMATELY;
YAKUSURU, TO PROMISE.

RAD STROKE JME
120 9 726

A PROMISE, APPROXIMATELY 約 IS A STRUNG- 糸 OUT (CONTINUOUS AFFAIR) RELATED TO CAPACITY, AREA 勹.

約

糸 THREADS, SILK R 120

約 PROMISE, APPROXIMATELY, TO PROMISE

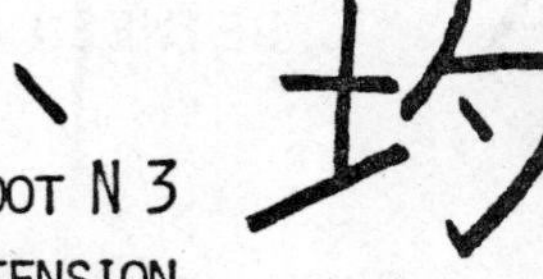

勹 UNIT OF AREA & CAPACITY N 740

、 DOT N 3 (EXTENSION IN SPACE, TIME, ETC.)

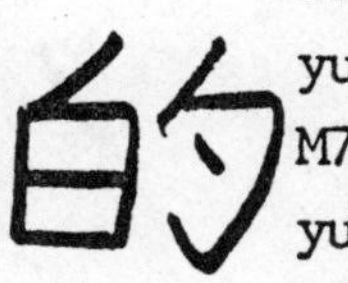

均 LEVEL, EQUALITY J 590

的 TARGET, LIKE, SIMILAR J 478

N3499
yueh 1
M7493
yuē
treaty
agreement
to agree
to bind

The Near Eastern shadoof with a container at the end of a rope attached to a counter-balanced pole promises capacity for area.

JME STROKE RAD
727 16 159

YU, (TO SEND, TO TRANSPORT).

A CHARIOT, CARRIAGE, CART 車 OR (WATER-) TIGHT 亼 BOAT 俞 CURVED LIKE A SICKLE MOON 月 OR A SCIMITAR SWORD 刀 SENDS, TRANSPORTS 輸.

輸

Peter Bell: A Tale Wm. Wordsworth
There's something in a flying horse,
There's something in a huge balloon;
But through the clouds I'll never float
Until I have a little Boat
Shaped like the crescent moon.

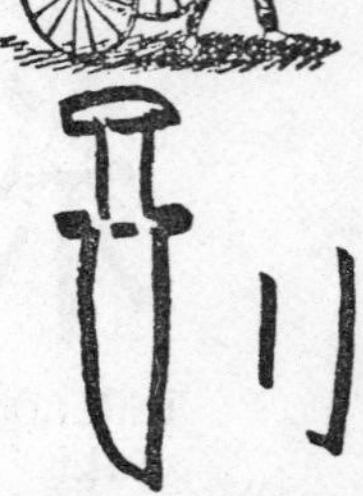

N4634
shu 1
M5864
shū
transport
lose

車 WHEELS, VEHICLE, CHARIOT J 88

輸 TO SEND, TO TRANSPORT

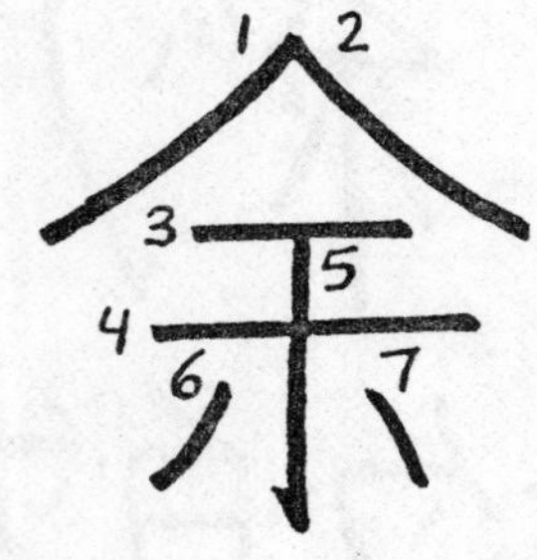

俞 (BOAT) ANSWER AFFIRMATIVELY M 7628

亼 (TIGHT RIGID TRIANGLES OF THE WHEEL'S RIM & SPOKES OR SHIP'S BOW & STERN)

月 MOON, BODY J 12

刂 PICTURE KNIFE, SWORD R 18

Paul Revere's Ride Henry Wadsworth Longfellow
One if by land, and two if by sea;
And I on the opposite shore will be,
Ready to ride and spread the alarm
Through every Middlesex village & far

JME STROKE RAD
728 7 9

YO, I, MYSELF, SURPLUS; AMARI, REMAINDER, EXCESS; -AMARI, MORE THAN; AMARU, TO REMAIN, TO EXAMINE; AMASU, TO LEAVE, TO SPARE.

余

I, MYSELF, SURPLUS, REMAINDER, EXCESS, MORE, THAN, TO REMAIN, TO EXAMINE, TO SPARE 余 IS THE DIVIDED 八 NAIL BODY 亅 FROM TIGHTLY 亼 BETWEEN THE LEGS 人 (RELEASED AS WASTE).

N408
yu2
M7605
yú
I
me
excess
surplus

亅 NAIL BODY R 6

八 EIGHT J 8 (TO DIVIDE)

于 GOING, FROM N 5

余 I, MYSELF, SURPLUS, REMAINDER, EXCESS, MORE THAN, TO REMAIN, TO LEAVE, SPARE TO EXAMINE

亼 TIGHTLY, JOINED (RIGID TRIANGLES OF WHEEL RIM AND SPOKES OR THE SHIP'S BOW & STERN)

人 PERSON, MAN R 9 (LEGS)

YŌ, THE MAIN POINT, NECESSITY, NEED;
YŌ SURU, TO NEED, TO REQUIRE.

RAD 146 STROKE 9 JME 729

要

THE MAIN POINT, NECESSITY, NEED, REQUIREMENT 要 OF A WESTERN 西 WOMAN 女 IS A HEADDRESS 覀

There is not so variable a thing in nature as a lady's head-dress.
The Spectator Addison

N4274
yao4
M7300
yào
impor-tant
necessary
must
want

価	西	要	女	妻	腰
PRICE,VALUE J 563	WEST J 95	THE MAIN POINT, NECESSITY, NEED, TO REQUIRE	WOMAN, GIRL,FEMALE	WIFE, MY WIFE, J 790	WAIST,LOINS N 3799

Western Wind Anony.
Western wind, when wilt thou blow?
The small rain down can rain, ...
Christ, if my love were in my arms
And I in my bed again.

YŌ, (FORM, LOOKS).

RAD 40 STROKE 10 JME 730

容

FORM, LOOKS 容 LIKE A (LUSCIOUS) VALLEY 谷 UNDER THE ROOF 宀.

Chin P'ing Mei (Plum Blossoms in a Golden Vase)
His hand wandered lightly over the secret valleys and mounds of her body, caressing her abdomen and separating her thighs.

In Open-Roofed Seraglios A.D.
The Irish colleens' mossy mounds,
The Quartier Francais' golden rounds---

N1309
jung 1
M7560
rōng
appearance
manner
allow
permit

口	八	谷	容	宀	
MOUTH R 30	MT.RANGES	VALLEY J 78	FORM,LOOKS	ROOF R 40	PICTURED ROOF

In open-roofed seraglios
The harem mouths make pulsing sounds.

Song of Solomon
I am the rose of Sharon, and the lily of the valley

731

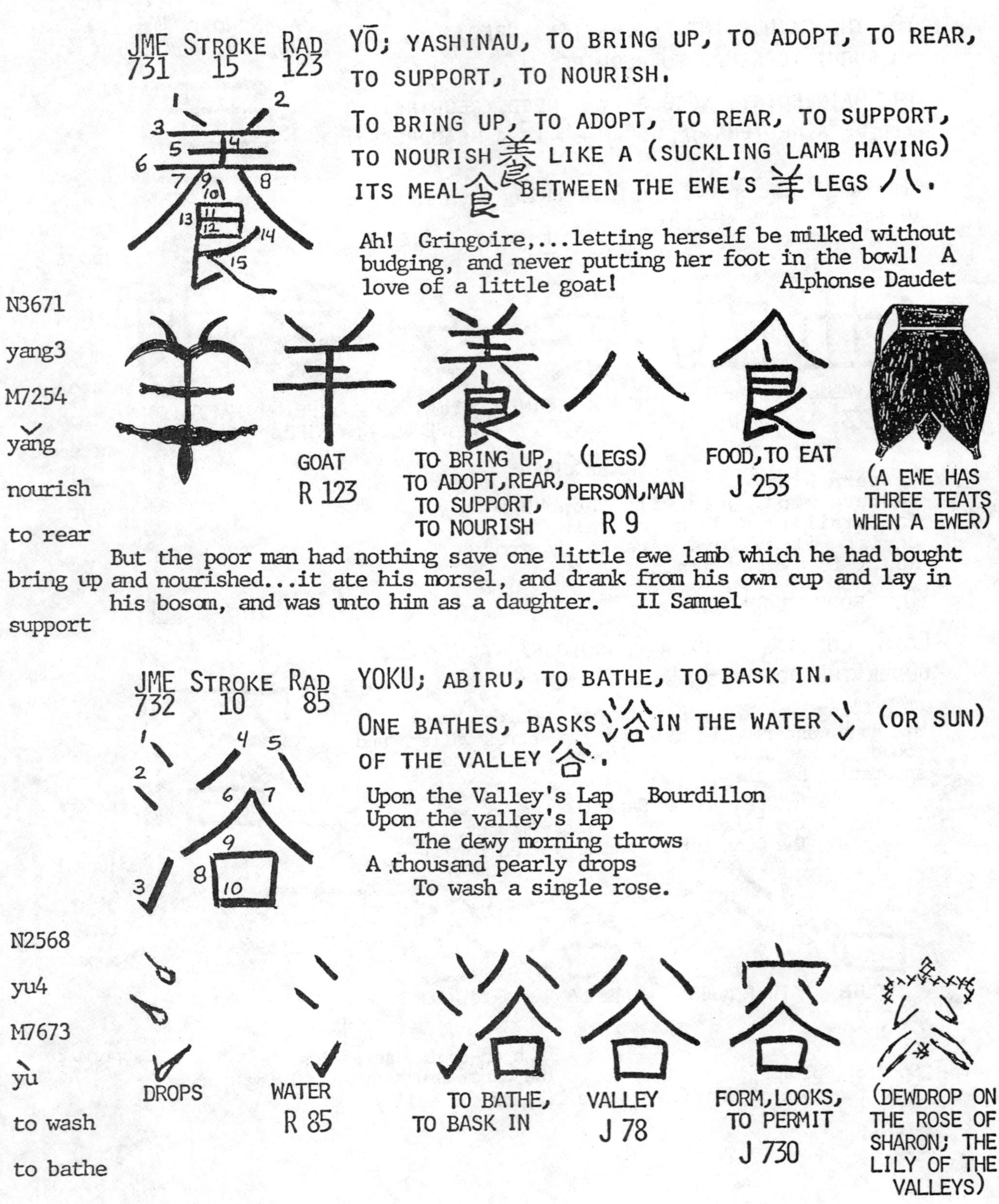

JME 731 STROKE 15 RAD 123

YŌ; YASHINAU, TO BRING UP, TO ADOPT, TO REAR, TO SUPPORT, TO NOURISH.

TO BRING UP, TO ADOPT, TO REAR, TO SUPPORT, TO NOURISH 養 LIKE A (SUCKLING LAMB HAVING) ITS MEAL 食 BETWEEN THE EWE'S 羊 LEGS 八.

Ah! Gringoire,...letting herself be milked without budging, and never putting her foot in the bowl! A love of a little goat! Alphonse Daudet

N3671

yang3

M7254

yǎng

nourish

to rear

bring up

support

But the poor man had nothing save one little ewe lamb which he had bought and nourished...it ate his morsel, and drank from his own cup and lay in his bosom, and was unto him as a daughter. II Samuel

JME 732 STROKE 10 RAD 85

YOKU; ABIRU, TO BATHE, TO BASK IN.

ONE BATHES, BASKS 浴 IN THE WATER 氵 (OR SUN) OF THE VALLEY 谷.

Upon the Valley's Lap Bourdillon

Upon the valley's lap
The dewy morning throws
A thousand pearly drops
To wash a single rose.

N2568

yu4

M7673

yù

to wash

to bathe

RYŪ, RU; TOMARU, TO STOP, TO HALT, TO CEASE; TOMERU, TO STOP, TO FASTEN, TO DETAIN.

RAD 102 STROKE 10 JME 733

THE ZODIAC RABBIT 卯 STOPS, HALTS, CEASES 留 STOPS, FASTENS, DETAINS 留 IN THE RICE FIELD 田

The Tale of Peter Rabbit Beatrix Potter
Peter, who was very naughty, ran straight away to Mr. McGregor's garden... First he ate some lettuces and some French beans, and then he ate some radishes... Around the end of a cucumber frame, whom should he

印 貿 卯 卯 留 田

SEAL, STAMP, SYMBOL J 348

TO EXCHANGE, TO PURCHASE J 719

ZODIAC RABBIT N 806 (MULTIPLIES LIKE A SEAL)

(BY ERROR SEAL ON RT. HAS BECOME SWORD, KNIFE IN THE KANJI TO THE RT.)

TO STOP, HALT, CEASE, TO FASTEN, TO DETAIN

PADDY, RICE FIELD J 102

N3003
liu2
M4083
liú
detain
keep

meet but Mr. McGregor! Mr. McGregor was on his hands and knees planting out young cabbages, but he jumped up and ran after Peter, waving a rake and calling out, "Stop, thief!"

RYŌ, QUANTITY, MEASURE; HAKARU, TO MEASURE, TO WEIGH.

RAD 72 STROKE 12 JME 734

THE QUANTITY, MEASURE 量 IS MEASURED, WEIGHED 量 (WHEN WELL-VIEWED) IN THE DAYTIME 昼.

里 量 旦 昼 尺

JPN. LEAGUE = 2.44 MI. (DISTANCE OF PADDY ACROSS EARTH)

QUANTITY, MEASURE, TO MEASURE, TO WEIGH

DAWN, MORNING N 2098 (SUN OVER HORIZON)

NOON, DAYTIME J 279 (SUN IS OVERHEAD LIKE A STRIDING BODY)

LINEAR MEASURE, = 0.995 FT. (LENGTH OF THE BODY'S FOOT)

N2141
liang4
M3943
liàng
to measure
to buy

735

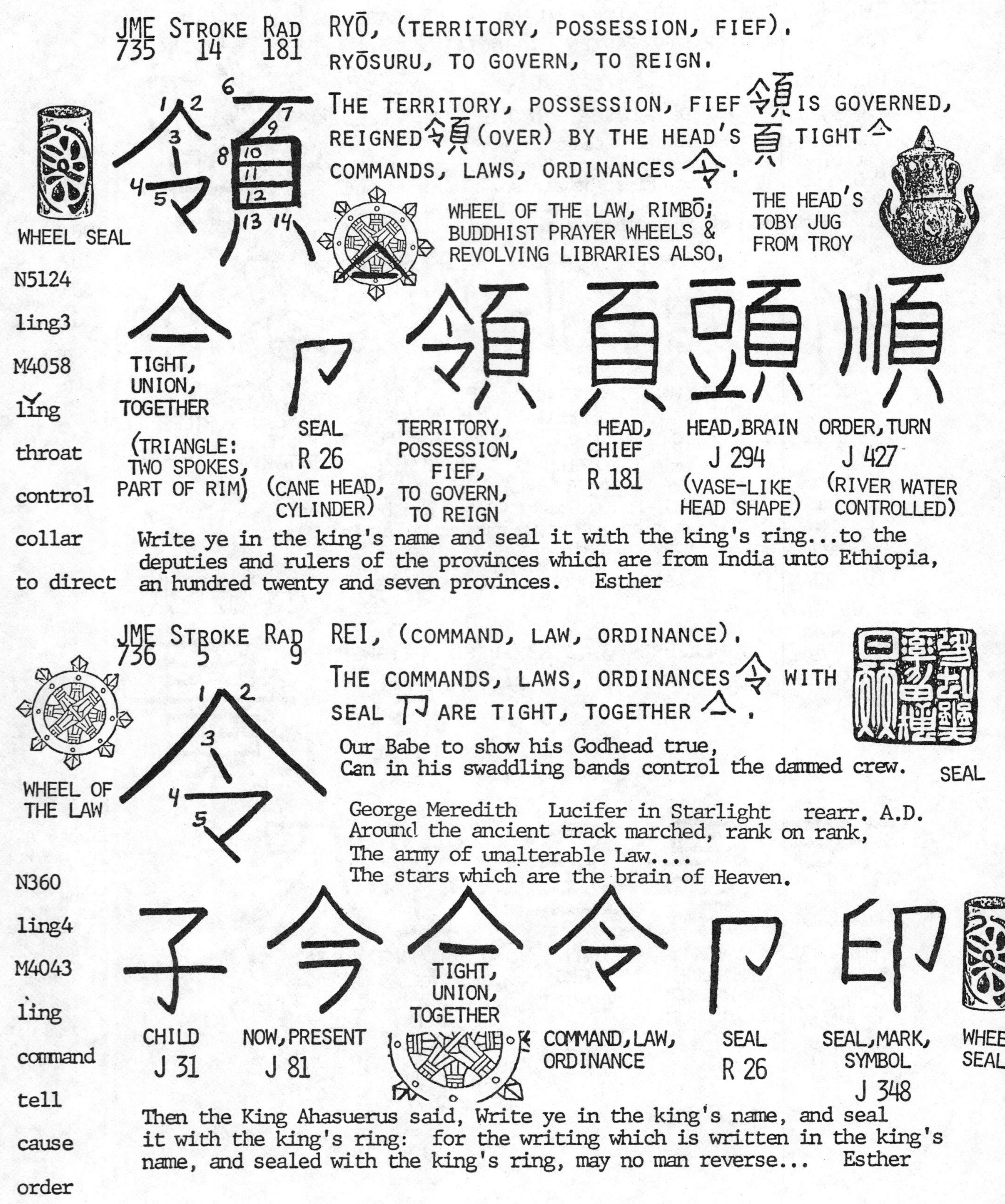

JME 735 Stroke 14 Rad 181

RYŌ, (TERRITORY, POSSESSION, FIEF).
RYŌSURU, TO GOVERN, TO REIGN.

THE TERRITORY, POSSESSION, FIEF 領 IS GOVERNED, REIGNED 領 (OVER) BY THE HEAD'S 頁 TIGHT 亼 COMMANDS, LAWS, ORDINANCES 令.

WHEEL SEAL

WHEEL OF THE LAW, RIMBŌ; BUDDHIST PRAYER WHEELS & REVOLVING LIBRARIES ALSO.

THE HEAD'S TOBY JUG FROM TROY

N5124
ling3
M4058
lǐng
throat
control
collar
to direct

亼 TIGHT, UNION, TOGETHER (TRIANGLE: TWO SPOKES, PART OF RIM)

卩 SEAL R 26 (CANE HEAD, CYLINDER)

領 TERRITORY, POSSESSION, FIEF, TO GOVERN, TO REIGN

頁 HEAD, CHIEF R 181

頭 HEAD, BRAIN J 294 (VASE-LIKE HEAD SHAPE)

順 ORDER, TURN J 427 (RIVER WATER CONTROLLED)

Write ye in the king's name and seal it with the king's ring...to the deputies and rulers of the provinces which are from India unto Ethiopia, an hundred twenty and seven provinces. Esther

JME 736 Stroke 5 Rad 9

REI, (COMMAND, LAW, ORDINANCE).

THE COMMANDS, LAWS, ORDINANCES 令 WITH SEAL 卩 ARE TIGHT, TOGETHER 亼.

WHEEL OF THE LAW

SEAL

Our Babe to show his Godhead true,
Can in his swaddling bands control the damned crew.

George Meredith Lucifer in Starlight rearr. A.D.
Around the ancient track marched, rank on rank,
The army of unalterable Law....
The stars which are the brain of Heaven.

N360
ling4
M4043
lìng
command
tell
cause
order

子 CHILD J 31

今 NOW, PRESENT J 81

亼 TIGHT, UNION, TOGETHER

令 COMMAND, LAW, ORDINANCE

卩 SEAL R 26

印 SEAL, MARK, SYMBOL J 348

WHEEL SEAL

Then the King Ahasuerus said, Write ye in the king's name, and seal it with the king's ring: for the writing which is written in the king's name, and sealed with the king's ring, may no man reverse... Esther

REI, CUSTOM, USAGE, EXAMPLE.

RAD 9 STROKE 8 JME 737

THE CORPSE, BONES 歹 (OF A CRIMINAL) PERSON 亻 SLICED 刂 (WITH A SWORD) HANG ACCORDING TO CUSTOM, USAGE 例 AS AN EXAMPLE 例. THE "DEATH OF A THOUSAND CUTS" IN CHINA WAS A PUNISHMENT IN WHICH AS MUCH FLESH AS POSSIBLE WOULD BE SLICED OFF BEFORE DEATH AFTER WHICH THE CORPSE COULD BE EXPOSED.

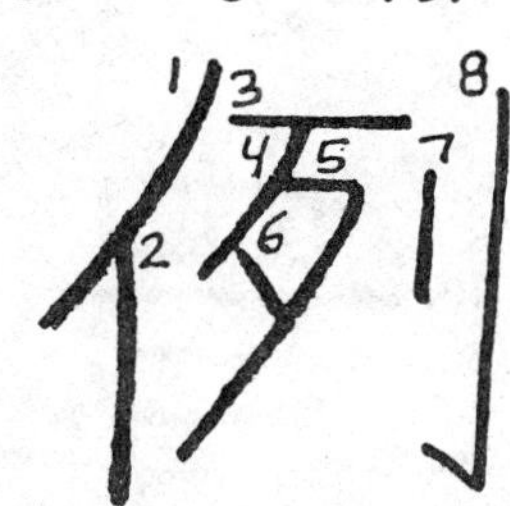

N428
lieh4
M3890
lì
law
custom
usage

亻	亻	例	列	歹	刂	残
PICTURE	PERSON, MAN R 9	CUSTOM, USAGE, EXAMPLE	ROW, RANK, FILE, COLUMN, LINE J 537	CORPSE, BONES R 78	SWORD, KNIFE R 18	REMAINDER, LEAVE BEHIND J 409

I; KOTONARU, TO DIFFER, TO VARY, TO BE UNUSUAL

RAD 102 STROKE 11 JME 738

PICTOGRAPH OF A PERSON WHO DIFFERS, VARIES, IS UNUSUAL 異 (IN HAVING OR BEING AS LARGE AS) BOTH 共 (BODIES) TOGETHER 共 BUT ONE HEAD 田 AND TWO FEET ノ丶.

N3008
i4
M3009
yì
strange
other
different
foreign

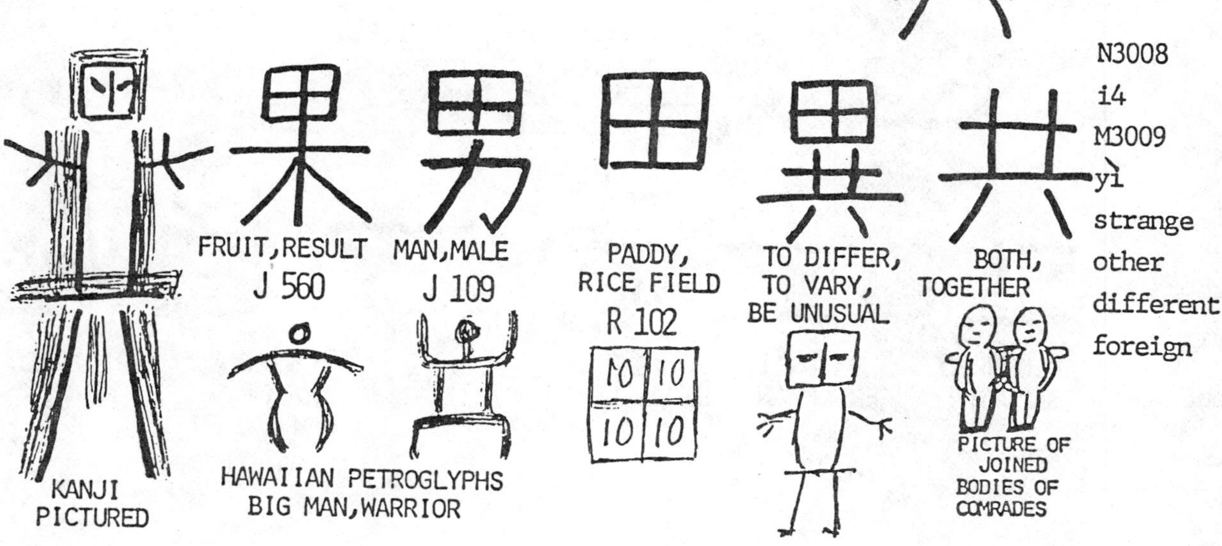

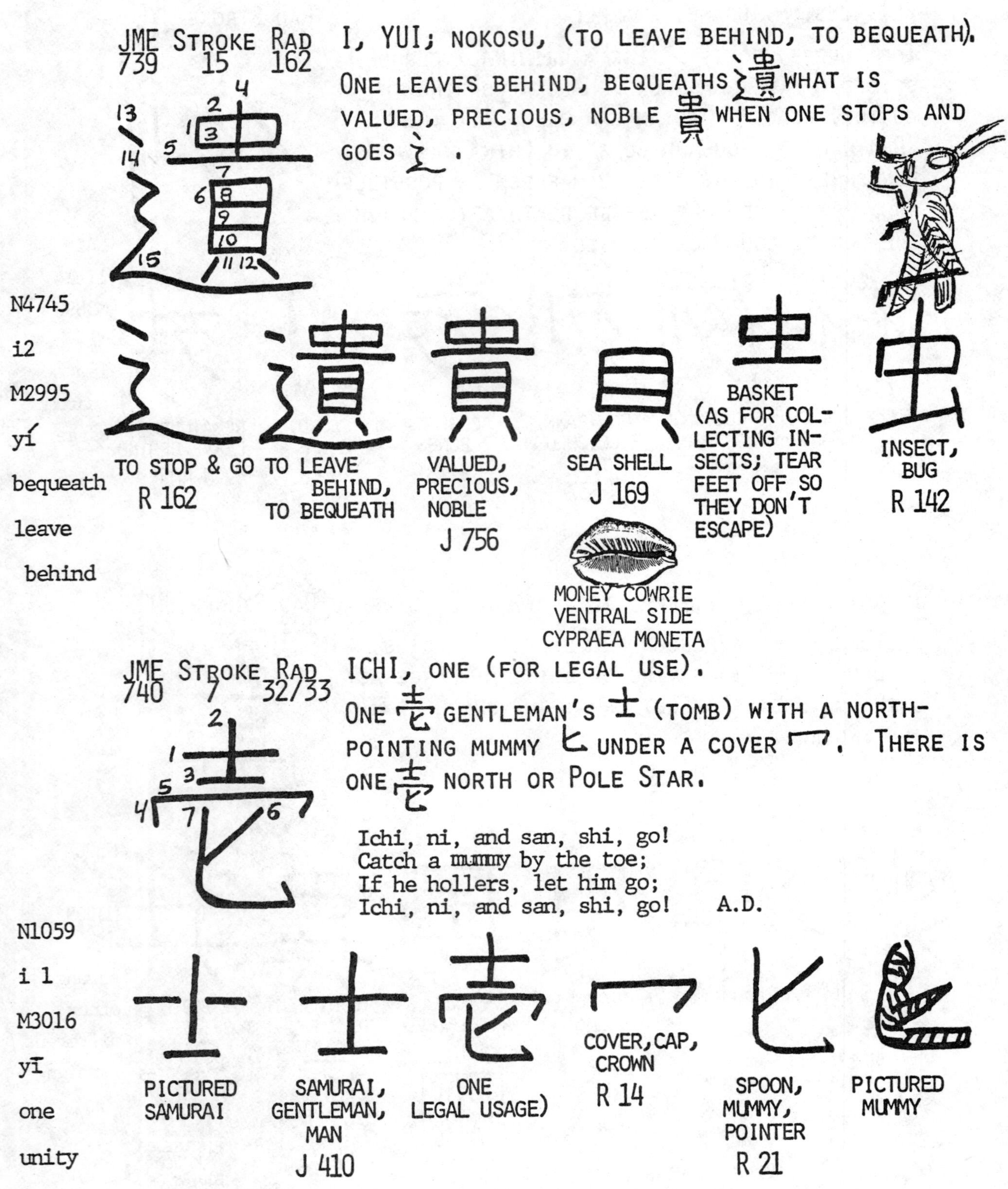

JME 739 | STROKE 15 | RAD 162

I, YUI; NOKOSU, (TO LEAVE BEHIND, TO BEQUEATH).

ONE LEAVES BEHIND, BEQUEATHS 遺 WHAT IS VALUED, PRECIOUS, NOBLE 貴 WHEN ONE STOPS AND GOES 辶.

遺

N4745
i2
M2995
yí
bequeath
leave behind

辶 TO STOP & GO R 162

遺 TO LEAVE BEHIND, TO BEQUEATH

貴 VALUED, PRECIOUS, NOBLE J 756

貝 SEA SHELL J 169

BASKET (AS FOR COLLECTING INSECTS; TEAR FEET OFF SO THEY DON'T ESCAPE)

虫 INSECT, BUG R 142

MONEY COWRIE
VENTRAL SIDE
CYPRAEA MONETA

JME 740 | STROKE 7 | RAD 32/33

ICHI, ONE (FOR LEGAL USE).

ONE 壱 GENTLEMAN'S 士 (TOMB) WITH A NORTH-POINTING MUMMY 匕 UNDER A COVER 冖. THERE IS ONE 壱 NORTH OR POLE STAR.

Ichi, ni, and san, shi, go!
Catch a mummy by the toe;
If he hollers, let him go;
Ichi, ni, and san, shi, go! A.D.

壱

N1059
i 1
M3016
yī
one
unity

PICTURED SAMURAI

士 SAMURAI, GENTLEMAN, MAN J 410

壱 ONE LEGAL USAGE)

冖 COVER, CAP, CROWN R 14

匕 SPOON, MUMMY, POINTER R 21

PICTURED MUMMY

EI; ITONAMI, BUSINESS, OCCUPATION; ITONAMU, PERFORM (CEREMONIES), CONDUCT (A BUSINESS).

ONE PERFORMS (CEREMONIES), CONDUCTS BUSINESS, OCCUPATION 営 IN A PALACE 宮 WITH LAURELS, RECEIPTS ⺍.

RAD	STROKE	JME
30	12	741

学 ⺍ 営 呂 高 宮

LEARNING, SCIENCE J 57 — (LAURELS, RECEIPTS) — BUSINESS, OCCUPATION, PERFORM, CONDUCT — DISC, SPINE, DISC, BACKBONE — HIGH J 76 — PALACE, PRINCE OF THE BLOOD J 374

N963
ying2
M7467
yíng
manage
camp
barracks

EKI, GAIN, BENEFIT, PROFIT;
EKI SURU, TO BENEFIT.

THE GAIN, BENEFIT, PROFIT 益 MAKES THE DISH OVERFLOW 䒑. (WATER 水 KANJI TURNED 90°).

My cup runneth over. Psalms

RAD	STROKE	JME
12	10	742

N597
yi4
M3052
yì
advantage
profit
benefit

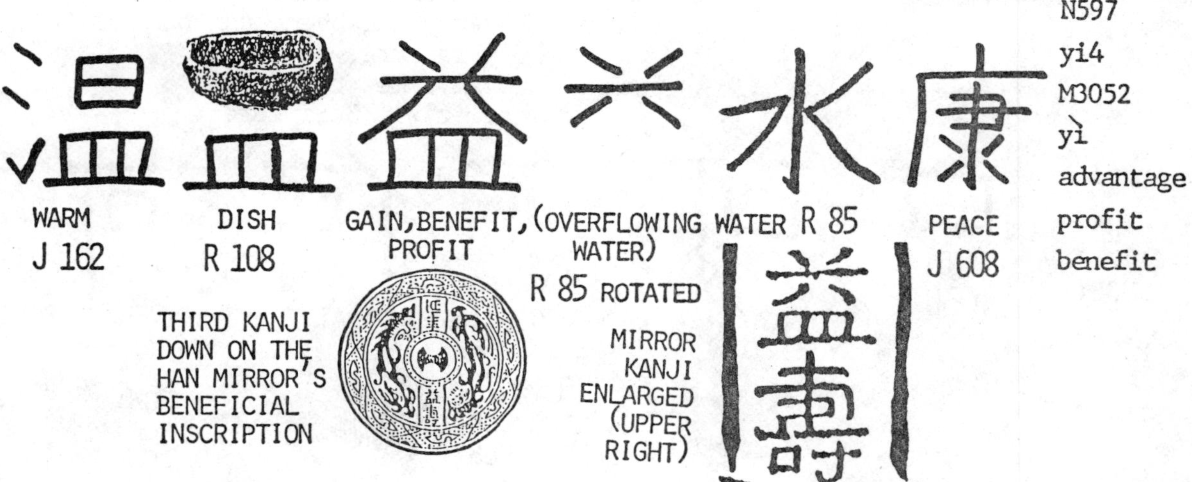

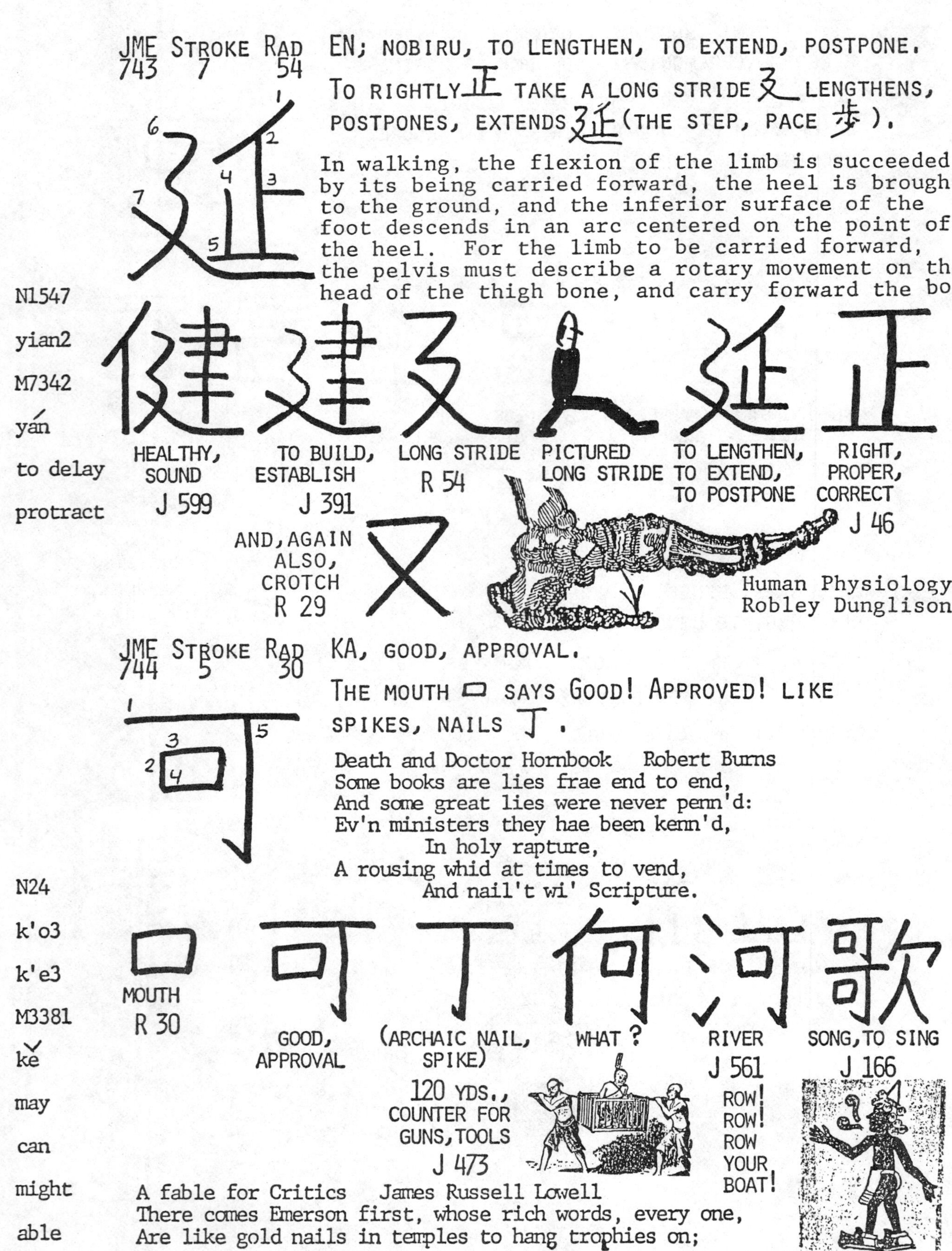

JME 743 STROKE 7 RAD 54

EN; NOBIRU, TO LENGTHEN, TO EXTEND, POSTPONE.

TO RIGHTLY 正 TAKE A LONG STRIDE 廴 LENGTHENS, POSTPONES, EXTENDS 延 (THE STEP, PACE 歩).

延

In walking, the flexion of the limb is succeeded by its being carried forward, the heel is brought to the ground, and the inferior surface of the foot descends in an arc centered on the point of the heel. For the limb to be carried forward, the pelvis must describe a rotary movement on the head of the thigh bone, and carry forward the body.

N1547

yian2

M7342

yán

to delay

protract

健	建	廴		延	正
HEALTHY, SOUND	TO BUILD, ESTABLISH	LONG STRIDE	PICTURED LONG STRIDE	TO LENGTHEN, TO EXTEND, TO POSTPONE	RIGHT, PROPER, CORRECT
J 599	J 391	R 54			J 46

AND, AGAIN ALSO, CROTCH R 29 又

Human Physiology
Robley Dunglison

JME 744 STROKE 5 RAD 30

KA, GOOD, APPROVAL.

THE MOUTH 口 SAYS GOOD! APPROVED! LIKE SPIKES, NAILS 丁.

可

Death and Doctor Hornbook Robert Burns
Some books are lies frae end to end,
And some great lies were never penn'd:
Ev'n ministers they hae been kenn'd,
In holy rapture,
A rousing whid at times to vend,
And nail't wi' Scripture.

N24

k'o3

k'e3

M3381

kě

may

can

might

able

口	可	丁	何	河	歌
MOUTH R 30	GOOD, APPROVAL	(ARCHAIC NAIL, SPIKE) 120 YDS., COUNTER FOR GUNS, TOOLS J 473	WHAT?	RIVER J 561	SONG, TO SING J 166

ROW! ROW! ROW YOUR BOAT!

A fable for Critics James Russell Lowell
There comes Emerson first, whose rich words, every one,
Are like gold nails in temples to hang trophies on;

GA; WARE, I, SELF, ONESELF.

RAD 4 STROKE 7 JME 745

I, SELF, ONESELF 我 AM A SPEAR 戈 AND (THROWING) HAND 扌. I AM A WEAPONED SUPPLIED WARRIOR. NOTE RELATION OF GUARD AND GARDEN.

A Tour on the Prairies Washington Irving
Thus equipped and provided, an Indian hunter on a prairie is like a cruiser on the ocean, perfectly independent of the world, and competent to self-protection and self-maintenance.

我

N200
wo3
M4778
wǒ
I
my
me
we
our

牛 : 牜 :: 手 : 扌 我 戈

BULL,OX,COW J 62 | BULL,OX,COW R 93 ABBRE. | HAND J 28 | HAND (LEFT SIDE) R 64 | I,SELF, ONESELF | SPEAR R 62

...in government employ, being engaged by the commissioner, he had drawn rations of flour and bacon, and put them up so as to be weather-proof. He came prepared at all points for war or hunting: his rifle on his shoulder, his powder-horn and bullet-pouch at his side, his hunting-knife stuck in his belt...A Tour on the Prairies Washington Irving

KAKU, TANNED LEATHER.

RAD 177 STROKE 9 JME 746

TANNED LEATHER 革 IS A PICTOGRAPH OF A HORNED AND TANNED ANIMAL HIDE.

Old Hec's Idolatry James Whitcomb Riley
"Old Hec," said we
Who knew him, hide-and-tallow, hoof-and-horn!

Let the horns gang wi' the hide. Scottish Proverb

革

N5088
ke2
M3314
gé
hide
skin
to reform

午 牛 帯 革 席

ZODIAC HORSE J 207 | BULL,COW,OX J 62 | OBI, TO WEAR J 669 | PICTURED HORNS & HIDE | TANNED LEATHER | SEAT,PLACE J 444

As You Like It William Shakespear
SONG: What shall he have that killed the deer?
His leather skin and horns to wear.
Then sing him home.

747

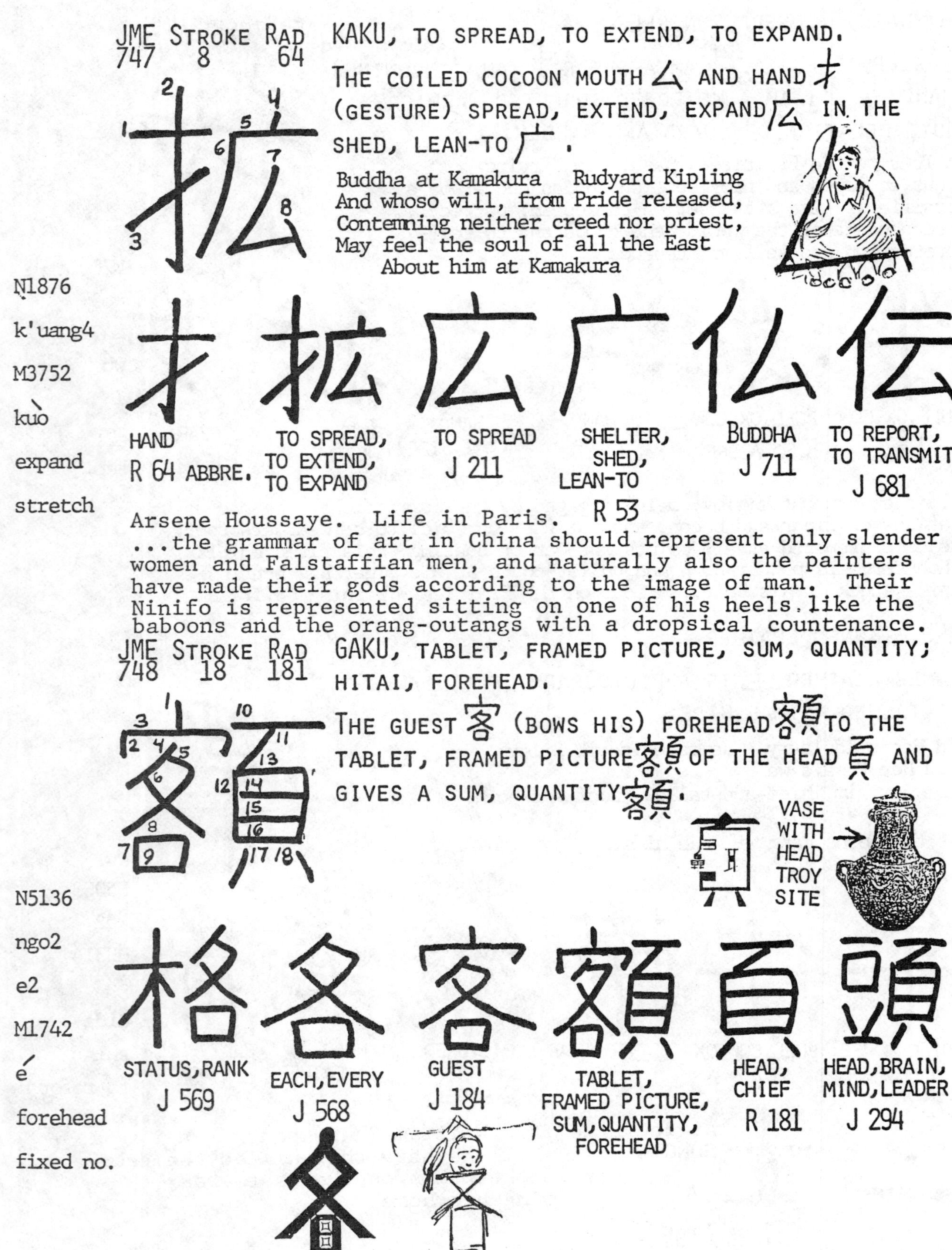

JME 747 | STROKE 8 | RAD 64

拡

KAKU, TO SPREAD, TO EXTEND, TO EXPAND.

THE COILED COCOON MOUTH 厶 AND HAND 扌 (GESTURE) SPREAD, EXTEND, EXPAND 広 IN THE SHED, LEAN-TO 广.

Buddha at Kamakura   Rudyard Kipling
And whoso will, from Pride released,
Contemning neither creed nor priest,
May feel the soul of all the East
About him at Kamakura

N1876
k'uang4
M3752
kuò
expand
stretch

扌 HAND R 64 ABBRE.
拡 TO SPREAD, TO EXTEND, TO EXPAND
広 TO SPREAD J 211
广 SHELTER, SHED, LEAN-TO R 53
仏 BUDDHA J 711
伝 TO REPORT, TO TRANSMIT J 681

Arsene Houssaye. Life in Paris.
...the grammar of art in China should represent only slender women and Falstaffian men, and naturally also the painters have made their gods according to the image of man. Their Ninifo is represented sitting on one of his heels like the baboons and the orang-outangs with a dropsical countenance.

JME 748 | STROKE 18 | RAD 181

額

GAKU, TABLET, FRAMED PICTURE, SUM, QUANTITY; HITAI, FOREHEAD.

THE GUEST 客 (BOWS HIS) FOREHEAD 額 TO THE TABLET, FRAMED PICTURE 額 OF THE HEAD 頁 AND GIVES A SUM, QUANTITY 額.

VASE WITH HEAD TROY SITE

N5136
ngo2
e2
M1742
é
forehead
fixed no.

格 STATUS, RANK J 569
各 EACH, EVERY J 568
客 GUEST J 184
額 TABLET, FRAMED PICTURE, SUM, QUANTITY, FOREHEAD
頁 HEAD, CHIEF R 181
頭 HEAD, BRAIN, MIND, LEADER J 294

KABU, SHARES, STOCKS.

RAD 75 STROKE 10 JME 749

SHARES, STOCKS 株 ARE LIKE THE SAP OF THE GASHED ノ NOT YET 未 TAPPED TREE 木 OR THE ZODIAC SHEEP 未. (TREES AND SHEEP GIVE DIVIDENDS LIKE SHARES, STOCK).

株

N2257
chu 1
M1348
zhū
tree
trunk
NA trees

木 TREE, WOOD J 15

株 SHARES, STOCKS

朱 CINNABAR, VERMILION N 184

ノ KNIFE, HORN

未 NOT YET, ZODIAC SHEEP J 872

味 TASTE, RELISH, EXPERIENCE J 516

EWER

(EWE'S MILK FOR TASTE AND RELISH)

KAN, (PUBLISHING, TO CARVE, TO ENGRAVE).

RAD 51 STROKE 5 JME 750

THE SHIELD 干 IS THE FLAT WOODEN PRINTING BLOCK WHICH THE KNIFE 刂 CARVES, ENGRAVES TO PUBLISH 刊 WHAT IS LEFT IN RELIEF.

Justus Doolittle. Social Life of the Chinese. An exact facsimile of the page desired is made on very thin bamboo paper by a hair pencil and black ink. This is pasted with the written side down on a smooth block of hard wood. The moistened

刊

N1493
k'an 1
M3242
kān
cut
carve
engrave

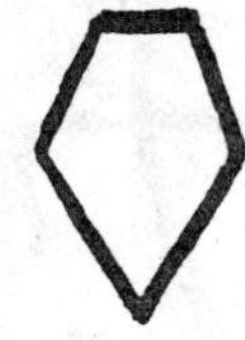

PICTURED SHIELD OUTLINES

干 SHIELD N 1492

刊 PUBLISHING, TO CARVE, TO ENGRAVE

刂 KNIFE, SWORD R 18 ABBRE.

PICTURED KNIFE

paper is rubbed off, leaving the characters and punctuation traced on the block in black ink. The space taken up by the white portion of the block is cut out, an eighth of an inch deep, by small sharp knives, leaving the parts of the block occupied by black lines or dots. The characters are wetted with printing ink and a sheet pressed on them.

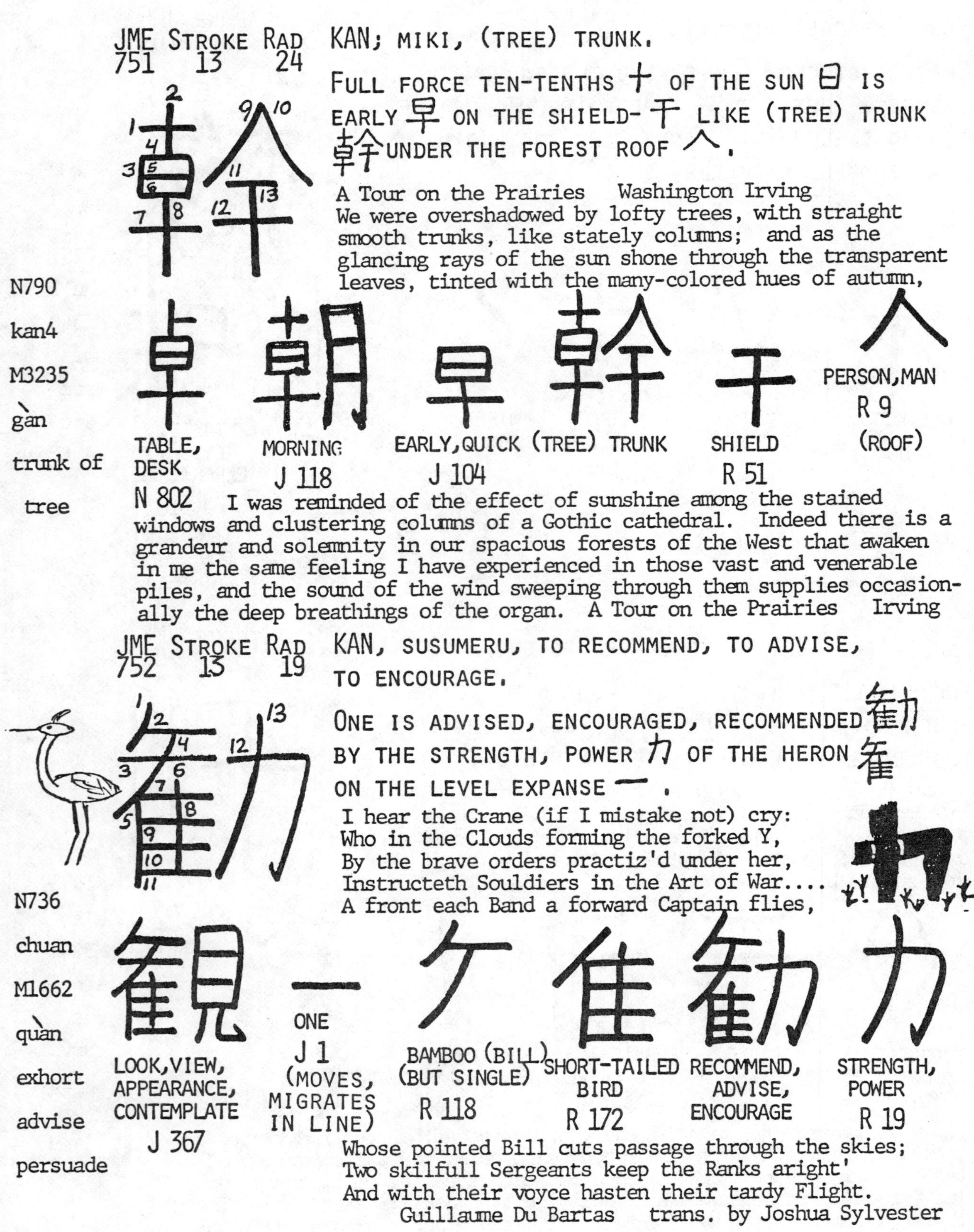

JME STROKE RAD 751 13 24

KAN; MIKI, (TREE) TRUNK.

FULL FORCE TEN-TENTHS 十 OF THE SUN 日 IS EARLY 早 ON THE SHIELD- 干 LIKE (TREE) TRUNK 幹 UNDER THE FOREST ROOF 人.

A Tour on the Prairies Washington Irving
We were overshadowed by lofty trees, with straight smooth trunks, like stately columns; and as the glancing rays of the sun shone through the transparent leaves, tinted with the many-colored hues of autumn,

N790
kan4
M3235
gàn
trunk of tree

卓 TABLE, DESK N 802
朝 MORNING J 118
早 EARLY, QUICK J 104
幹 (TREE) TRUNK
干 SHIELD R 51
人 PERSON, MAN R 9 (ROOF)

I was reminded of the effect of sunshine among the stained windows and clustering columns of a Gothic cathedral. Indeed there is a grandeur and solemnity in our spacious forests of the West that awaken in me the same feeling I have experienced in those vast and venerable piles, and the sound of the wind sweeping through them supplies occasionally the deep breathings of the organ. A Tour on the Prairies Irving

JME STROKE RAD 752 13 19

KAN, SUSUMERU, TO RECOMMEND, TO ADVISE, TO ENCOURAGE.

ONE IS ADVISED, ENCOURAGED, RECOMMENDED 勧 BY THE STRENGTH, POWER 力 OF THE HERON 雈 ON THE LEVEL EXPANSE 一.

I hear the Crane (if I mistake not) cry:
Who in the Clouds forming the forked Y,
By the brave orders practiz'd under her,
Instructeth Souldiers in the Art of War....
A front each Band a forward Captain flies,

N736
chuan
M1662
quàn
exhort
advise
persuade

観 LOOK, VIEW, APPEARANCE, CONTEMPLATE J 367
一 ONE J 1 (MOVES, MIGRATES IN LINE)
ケ BAMBOO (BILL) (BUT SINGLE) R 118
隹 SHORT-TAILED BIRD R 172
勧 RECOMMEND, ADVISE, ENCOURAGE
力 STRENGTH, POWER R 19

Whose pointed Bill cuts passage through the skies;
Two skilfull Sergeants keep the Ranks aright'
And with their voyce hasten their tardy Flight.
Guillaume Du Bartas trans. by Joshua Sylvester

KAN, JOY, PLEASURE.

RAD STROKE JME
76 15 753

AFTER CATCHING A FISH, THE HERON雚 DRAWS A BREATH 欠 AND EXCLAIMS IN JOY, PLEASURE歓.

The Book of Songs James Legge
All true words spread, as from the marsh's eye
The crane's sonorous note ascends the sky.
Goodness throughout the widest sphere abides,
As fish round isle and through the ocean glides.

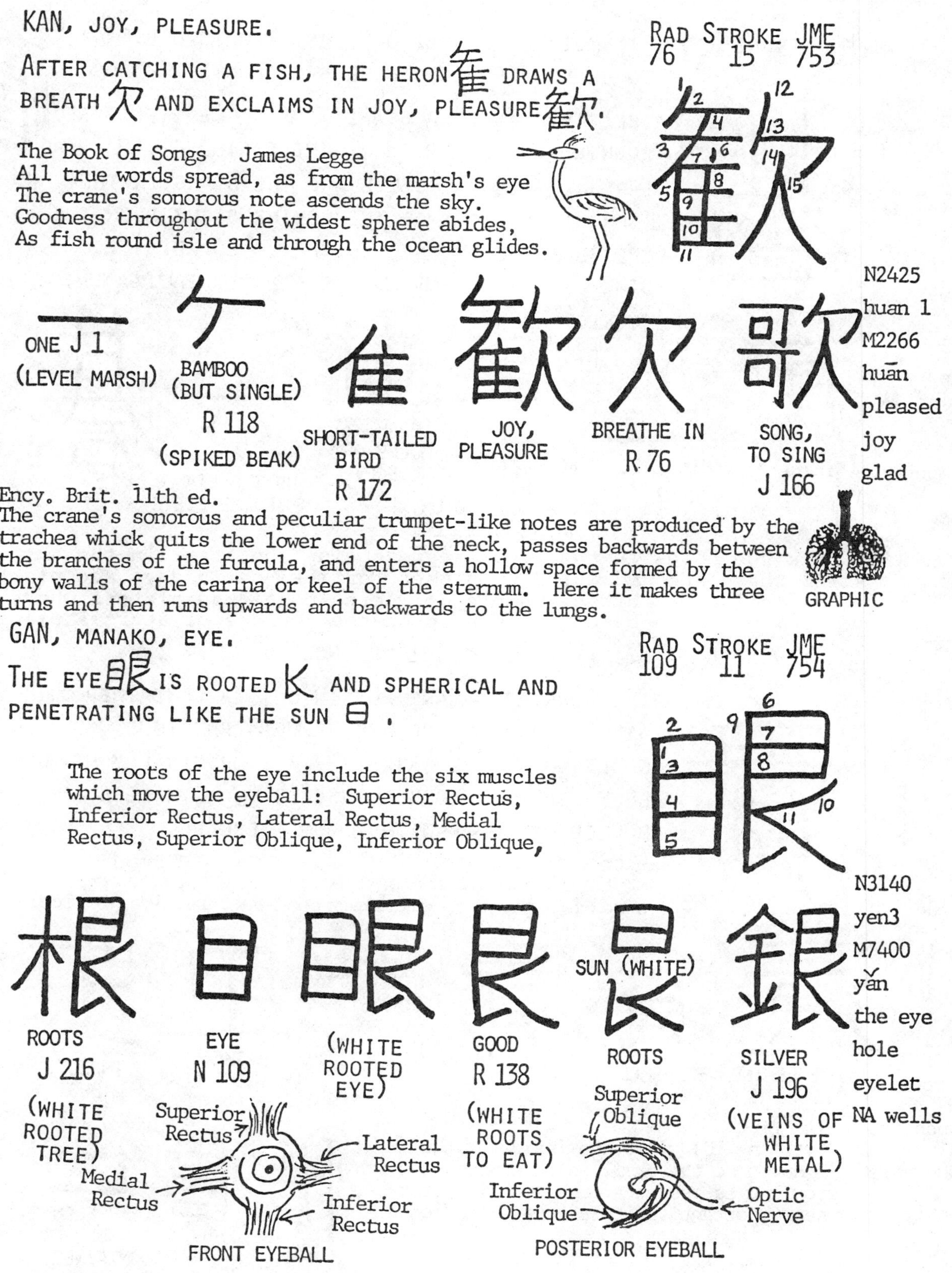

N2425
huan 1
M2266
huān
pleased
joy
glad

Ency. Brit. 11th ed.
The crane's sonorous and peculiar trumpet-like notes are produced by the trachea whick quits the lower end of the neck, passes backwards between the branches of the furcula, and enters a hollow space formed by the bony walls of the carina or keel of the sternum. Here it makes three turns and then runs upwards and backwards to the lungs.

GAN, MANAKO, EYE.

RAD STROKE JME
109 11 754

THE EYE眼 IS ROOTED 艮 AND SPHERICAL AND PENETRATING LIKE THE SUN 日.

The roots of the eye include the six muscles which move the eyeball: Superior Rectus, Inferior Rectus, Lateral Rectus, Medial Rectus, Superior Oblique, Inferior Oblique,

N3140
yen3
M7400
yǎn
the eye
hole
eyelet
NA wells

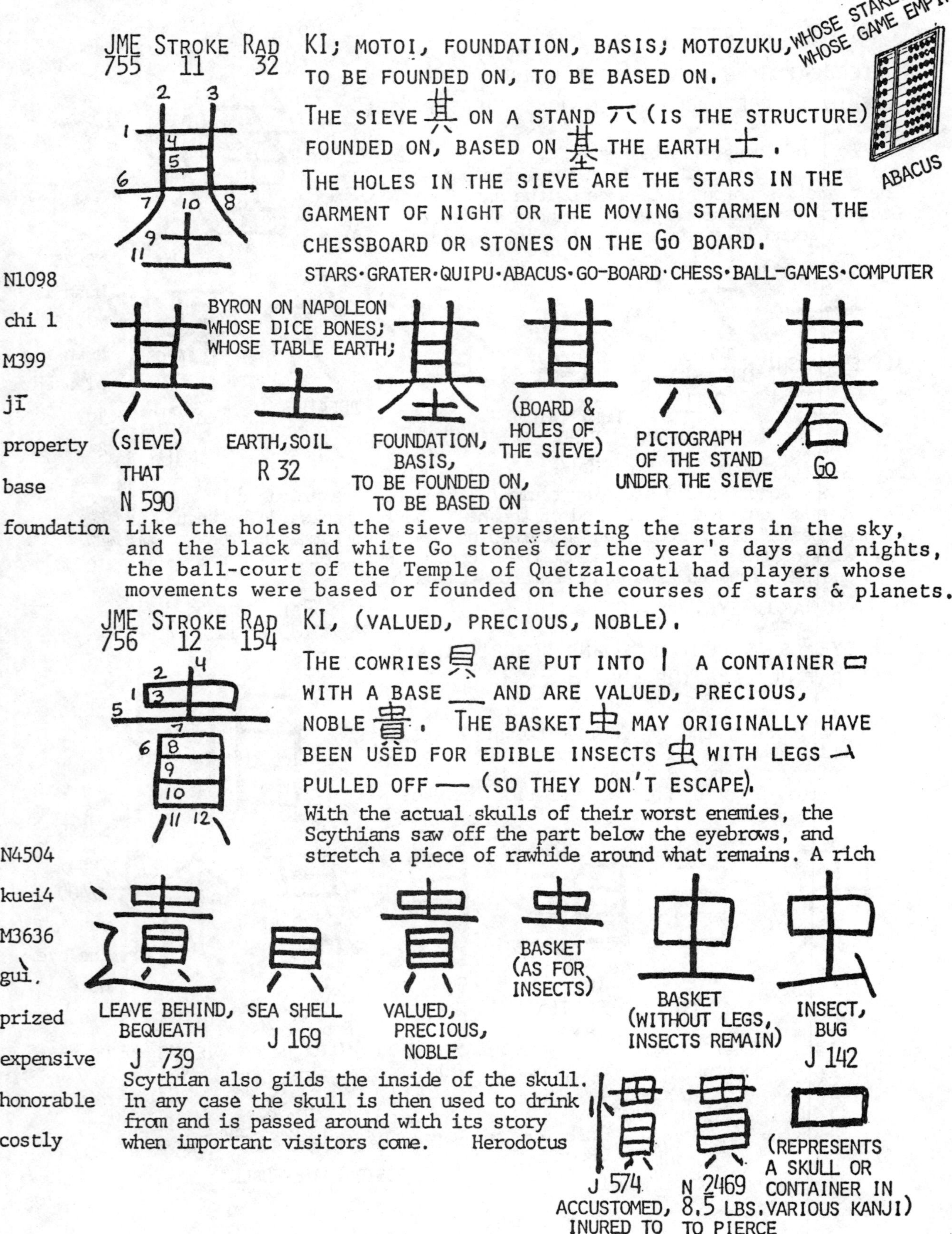

755

JME 755 STROKE 11 RAD 32

KI; MOTOI, FOUNDATION, BASIS; MOTOZUKU, TO BE FOUNDED ON, TO BE BASED ON.

THE SIEVE 其 ON A STAND 六 (IS THE STRUCTURE) FOUNDED ON, BASED ON 基 THE EARTH 土.

THE HOLES IN THE SIEVE ARE THE STARS IN THE GARMENT OF NIGHT OR THE MOVING STARMEN ON THE CHESSBOARD OR STONES ON THE GO BOARD.

STARS·GRATER·QUIPU·ABACUS·GO-BOARD·CHESS·BALL-GAMES·COMPUTER

N1098

chi 1

M399

jī

property

base

foundation

BYRON ON NAPOLEON
WHOSE DICE BONES;
WHOSE TABLE EARTH;

其 (SIEVE) THAT N 590

土 EARTH, SOIL R 32

基 FOUNDATION, BASIS, TO BE FOUNDED ON, TO BE BASED ON

甘 (BOARD & HOLES OF THE SIEVE)

六 PICTOGRAPH OF THE STAND UNDER THE SIEVE

碁 Go

Like the holes in the sieve representing the stars in the sky, and the black and white Go stones for the year's days and nights, the ball-court of the Temple of Quetzalcoatl had players whose movements were based or founded on the courses of stars & planets.

JME 756 STROKE 12 RAD 154

KI, (VALUED, PRECIOUS, NOBLE).

THE COWRIES 貝 ARE PUT INTO | A CONTAINER 口 WITH A BASE — AND ARE VALUED, PRECIOUS, NOBLE 貴. THE BASKET 虫 MAY ORIGINALLY HAVE BEEN USED FOR EDIBLE INSECTS 虫 WITH LEGS 一 PULLED OFF — (SO THEY DON'T ESCAPE).

With the actual skulls of their worst enemies, the Scythians saw off the part below the eyebrows, and stretch a piece of rawhide around what remains. A rich Scythian also gilds the inside of the skull. In any case the skull is then used to drink from and is passed around with its story when important visitors come. Herodotus

N4504

kuei4

M3636

guì

prized

expensive

honorable

costly

遺 LEAVE BEHIND, BEQUEATH J 739

貝 SEA SHELL J 169

貴 VALUED, PRECIOUS, NOBLE

中 BASKET (AS FOR INSECTS)

中 BASKET (WITHOUT LEGS, INSECTS REMAIN)

虫 INSECT, BUG J 142

慣 J 574 ACCUSTOMED, INURED TO

貫 N 2469 8.5 LBS. TO PIERCE

口 (REPRESENTS A SKULL OR CONTAINER IN VARIOUS KANJI)

GI; UTAGAI, DOUBT, SUSPICION, UNCERTAINTY; UTAGAU, TO DOUBT, TO DISTRUST.

RAD STROKE JME
21/103 14 757

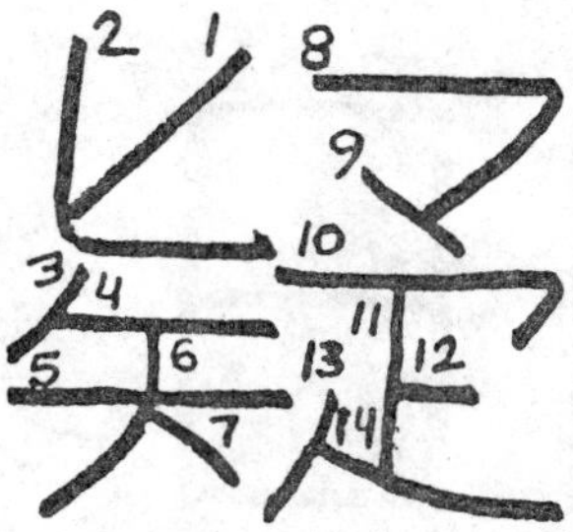

ONE IS RUNNING 走 DIRECTLY 疋 WITH ALL EFFORT マ TO POINTED OUT 匕 ARROW 矢 BUT THERE IS DOUBT, SUSPICION, UNCERTAINITY 疑 (AS TO LOCATION). There is suspicion and distrust with stiffness of pointer, arrow, & leg. Dog's hackles are erect like pointer, arrow, or man poised to leap with effort when dog is doubtful, suspicious.

疑

矢 ARROW R 111

匕 POINTER, SPOON, MUMMY

疑 DOUBT, SUSPICION, UNCERTAINTY

疋 RUN DIRECTLY R 103

マ DO WITH ALL ENERGY, GO ALL OUT

勇 BRAVE J 524

N755
i2
M2940
yí
distrust
doubt
suspect

Jonathan Distrusts Saul

And Jonathan said unto his lad, Run, find out now the arrows which I shot. And as the lad ran, he shot an arrow beyond him. And when the lad was come to the place of the arrow which Jonathan had shot, Jonathan cried after the lad, and said, Is not the arrow beyond thee? And Jonathan cried after the lad, Make speed, haste, and stay not. And Jonathan's lad gathered up the arrows and came to his master. I Samuel (refer for context)

GYAKU, GEKI, REVERSE, INVERSE; GYAKU NI, CONVERSELY, INVERSELY; SAKARAU, TO OPPOSE, TO ACT CONTRARY TO, TO OFFEND.

RAD STROKE JME
162 9 758

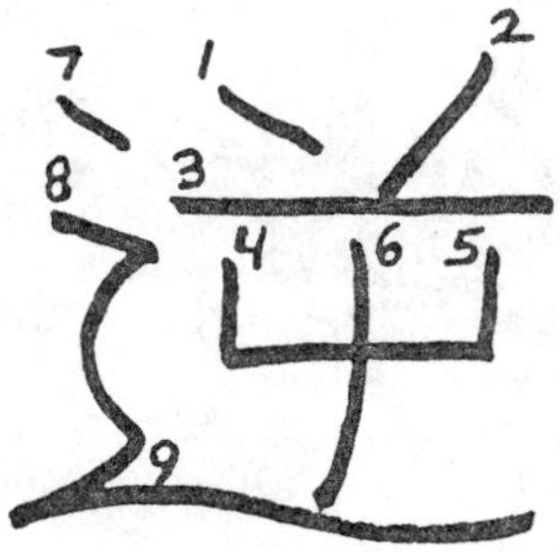

THE GRASS, PLANT 屮 WITH HORNS 丷 WHICH GOES QUICKLY AND STOPS SUDDENLY 辶 OPPOSES, ACTS CONTRARY TO, OFFENDS 逆 AND IS THE REVERSE, INVERSE, 逆 (ACTS) CONVERSELY, INVERSELY 逆 TO THE TENDER SHORT-LIVED GRASS 屮

逆

辵 STOP & GO R 162

辶 STOP & GO R 162 ABBRE.

逆 REVERSE, INVERSE, TO OPPOSE, TO OFFEND

屰 BATTERING RAM (DOUBLED)

屮 GRASS (SINGLE FORM) R 140

丷 HORNS AS IN GOAT R 123

N4685
ni4
M4677
nì
destroy
rebel
oppose
contrary

Horace Epistles
You may drive out Nature with a pitchfork, still she will return.

Tendrils and horned tentacles.

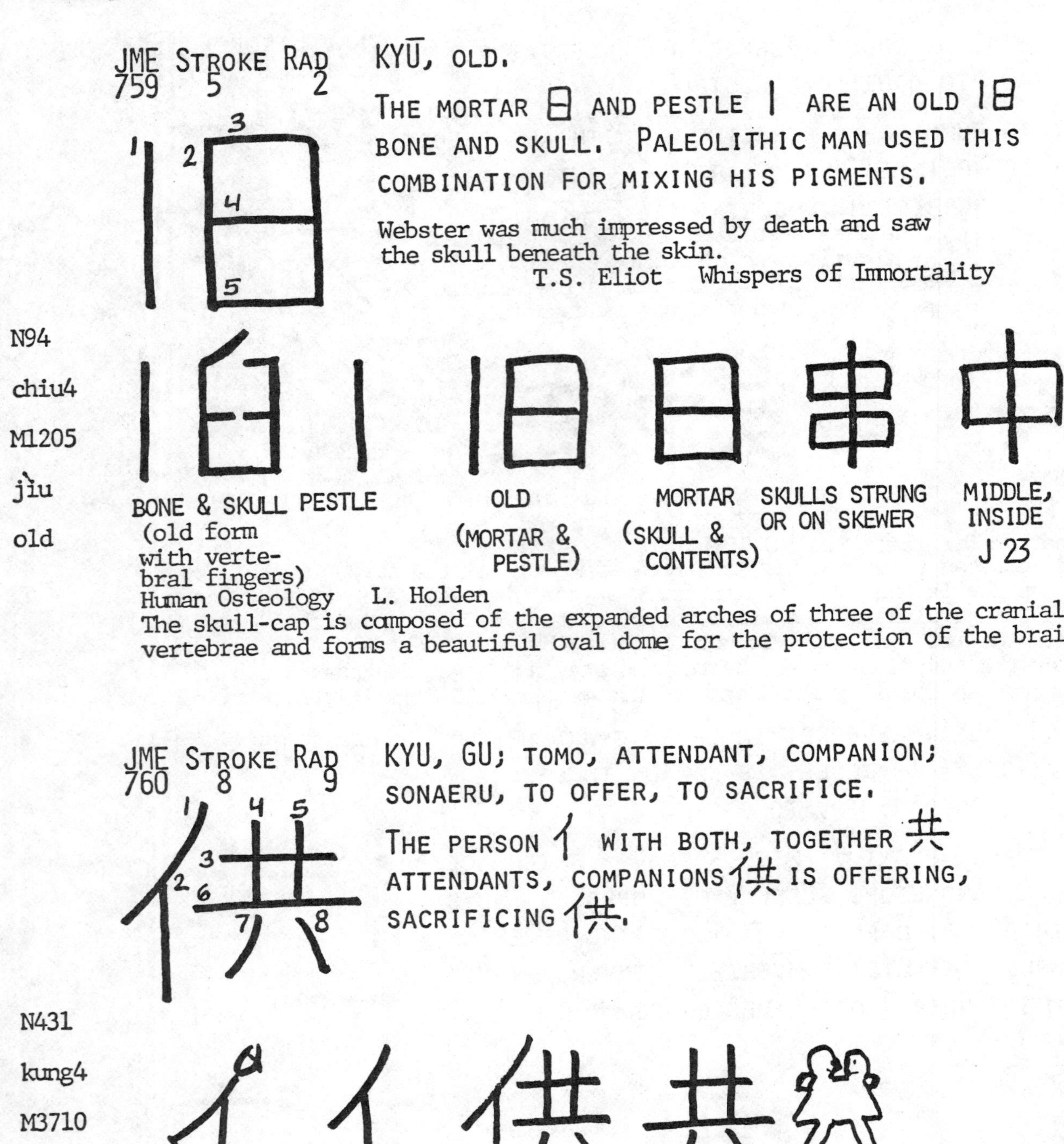

JME Stroke Rad
759 5 2

KYŪ, OLD.

THE MORTAR 日 AND PESTLE | ARE AN OLD 旧 BONE AND SKULL. PALEOLITHIC MAN USED THIS COMBINATION FOR MIXING HIS PIGMENTS.

Webster was much impressed by death and saw
the skull beneath the skin.
T.S. Eliot Whispers of Immortality

N94
chiu4
M1205
jìu
old

BONE & SKULL (old form with verte-bral fingers) — PESTLE — OLD (MORTAR & PESTLE) — MORTAR (SKULL & CONTENTS) — SKULLS STRUNG OR ON SKEWER — MIDDLE, INSIDE J 23

Human Osteology L. Holden
The skull-cap is composed of the expanded arches of three of the cranial vertebrae and forms a beautiful oval dome for the protection of the brain.

JME Stroke Rad
760 8 9

KYU, GU; TOMO, ATTENDANT, COMPANION; SONAERU, TO OFFER, TO SACRIFICE.

THE PERSON 亻 WITH BOTH, TOGETHER 共 ATTENDANTS, COMPANIONS 供 IS OFFERING, SACRIFICING 供.

N431
kung4
M3710
gòng
supply
offer

PICTURED PERSON, MAN — PERSON, MAN R 9 — ATTENDANT, COMPANION, TO OFFER, TO SACRIFICE — BOTH, TOGETHER J 376 — PICTURED BOTH, TOGETHER

KYŌ, KEI; SAKAI, BOUNDARY, BORDER, FRONTIER.

RAD 32 STROKE 14 JME 761

LAND'S 土 END 竟 IS THE SOUTHWESTERN BORDER, BOUNDARY, FRONTIER 境 OF ENGLAND

境

Land's End, England
Lands End, Canada
Finisterre, Spain
Finisterra, Mexico
Finistère, France

Beyond the frontier of our living world through the mirrors of the shaman, of the Shinto shrine, of the Jewish shivah, of the schizophrenic and Alice into the reversed realms of anti-matter, antipodes & Spiegelschrift

鏡	土	境	竟	音
MIRROR	EARTH, SOIL	BOUNDARY, BORDER, FRONTIER	TO END, TERMINATE	SOUND, NOISE
J 378	R 32		N 5111	J 50

N1135
ching4
M1136
jìng
boundary
frontier
region

Tom o'Bedlam
With a host of furious fancies Whereof I am commander,
With a burning spear, and a horse of air, To the wilderness I wander;
By a knight of ghosts and shadows I summoned am to tourney
Ten leagues beyond the wide world's end. Methinks it is no journey.

KIN; TSUTOME, SERVICE, DUTY;
TSUTOMERU, TO SERVE, TO FILL A POST.

RAD 19 STROKE 12 JME 762

ONE SERVES, FILLS A POST 勤 HAS SERVICE, DUTY 勤 WHEN HIS STRENGTH, POWER 力 (IS EXERTED) ON YELLOW 黄 LOAM 堇 (LOESS), POTTERS' CLAY.

勤

Hamlet Wm. Shakespear
Imperial Caesar, dead and turned to clay,
might stop a hole to keep the wind away.

菫
VIOLET
N3972

黄	+ PLUS	土	= EQUALS	堇	勤	力	漢
YELLOW		EARTH, SOIL		YELLOW EARTH	SERVICE, DUTY TO SERVE, FILL A POST	STRENGTH, POWER	CHINA, HAN ERA, MASCULINE SUFFIX
R 201		R 32		M 1065			J 572 N 2662

N732
ch'in2
M1097
qín
diligent
industrious

The Book of Poetry James Legge
The plain of Chou, with violets o'erspread lay wide and rich;
Ancient Duke T'an-fu asked his men their mind: "Now is the time and here!"
He named two officers who should preside over labor and the people guide.

JME 763 STROKE 13 RAD 113

KIN, PROHIBITION, BAN.
KINJIRU, KINZURU, TO PROHIBIT, TO FORBID.

THE WOODS 林 WHERE THE GODS 神 SHOW, POINT OUT, INDICATE 示 ARE PROHIBITED, BANNED, FORBIDDEN 禁.

禁

Lays of Ancient Rome Macaulay
The trees in whose dim shadow
The ghastly priest doth reign,
The priest who slew the slayer
And shall himself be slain.

N3251
chin4
M1077
jìn
prohibit
forbid
warn

林	禁	示	礻	神
WOODS J 150	PROHIBITION, BAN, TO PROHIBIT, TO FORBID	TO SHOW, POINT OUT J 622	TO SHOW, TO INFORM R 113 ABBRE.	GOD, DEITY, SPIRIT J 257

In Hawaii, a taboo or kapu camp or enclosure had kapu sticks placed to indicate that it was off limits. A chief of very high status would have runners brandishing ti branches precede him to show he had the kapu moe.

JME 764 STROKE 10 RAD 149

KIN, KUN, (RULE); THE "KUN" READING, JAPANESE READING OF A KANJI AS DISTINCT FROM THE "ON" OR ORIGINALLY DERIVED CHINESE READING.

THE RIVER 川 OF WORDS 言 IS THE JAPANESE KUN 訓 READING OR RULE 訓.

RULE 訓 IS BY WORDS 言 ABOUT THE RIVER 川 (IRRIGATION) WHICH IS BY ORDER, TURN 順.

訓

N4317
hsun4
M2914
xùn
instruct
advise
adminish
counsel

言 (sound)	言	訓	川	順	
SOUND VIBRATIONS	WORDS J 392	(RULE), KUN READING	RIVER J 39	ORDER, TURN J 427	TERRACOTTA CONTAINER TROY SITE

KEI, (SYSTEM, LINEAGE, FAMILY LINE).

RAD 4 STROKE 7 JME 765

THE SYSTEM, LINEAGE, FAMILY LINE 系 IS ANALOGOUS TO THE KNOTTED STRING 糸 RECORDS OF THE HORNED ノ DOMESTIC ANIMALS' BLOODLINES, SYSTEM, LINEAGE, FAMILY LINES 系.

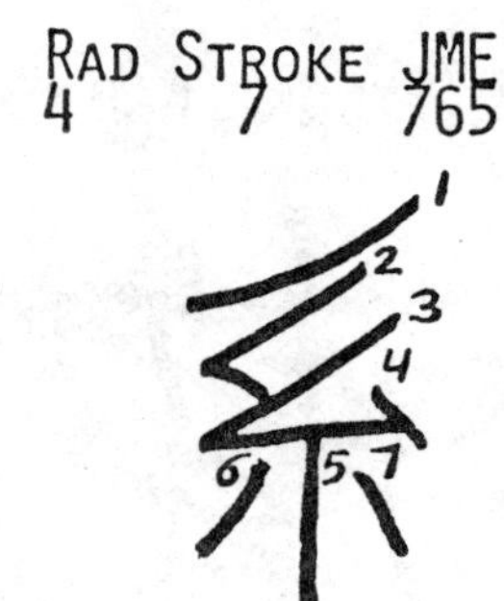

牛 BULL, COW, OX R 93

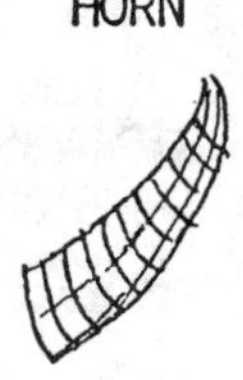

ノ HORN

系 SYSTEM, LINEAGE, FAMILY LINE (HORN & THREADS, STRINGS OF RELATIONSHIP)

糸 STRINGS, THREADS, SILK J 83

PICTURED COCOONS & THREADS

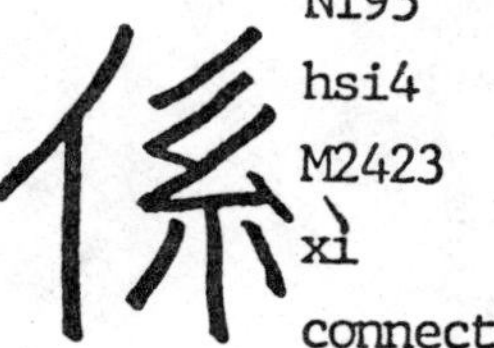

係 DUTY, IN CHARGE OF J 385 (DUTY, IN CHARGE OF BREEDING, BLOODLINES)

N195 hsi4 M2423 xì connection succession family line

KEI, UYAMAU, TO RESPECT.

RAD 140 STROKE 12 JME 766

RESPECTING 敬 ANY, AT ALL, IN THE SLIGHTEST DEGREE 苟 THE STICK ノ IN HAND 又 OR THE CLAUSE, PHRASE, LINE 句 (WHEN CARRYING) A LOAD, BURDEN 荷.

Cadence and song are closely related to work, whether carrying burdens or towing boats from bank or cliffside. Respect is given to those working and those directing.

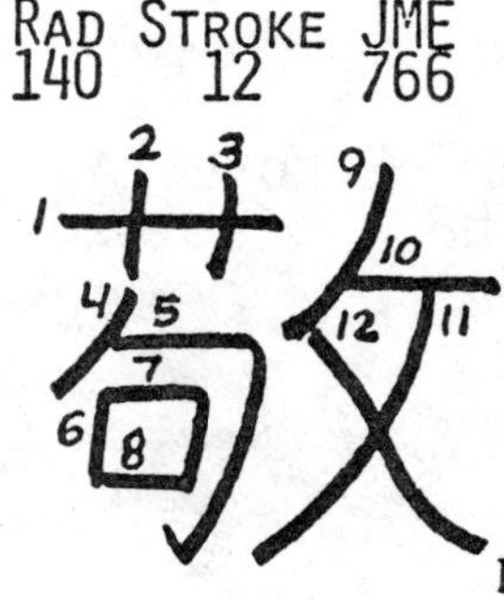

N2055 ching4 M1138 jìng to respect to honor

歌 SONG, TO SING J 166

荷 A LOAD, A BURDEN J 165

句 CLAUSE, PHRASE, VERSE, LINE J 592 (WRAPPED AROUND THE MOUTH)

苟 ANY, AT ALL, IN THE SLIGHTEST DEGREE N 3918

敬 TO RESPECT

攵 STICK IN HAND R 66

767

JME 767 Stroke 15 Rad 85

KETSU; ISAGIYOI, PURE, CLEAN, RIGHTEOUS, MANLY.

THE LONG THREADS 糸 WERE CUT 刀 ROLLED ON A MANLY 絜 SPINDLE 主 WITH PROJECTIONS 三 AND WASHED 氵 TO BE PURE, CLEAN, RIGHTEOUS AND MANLY 潔 THEREFORE.

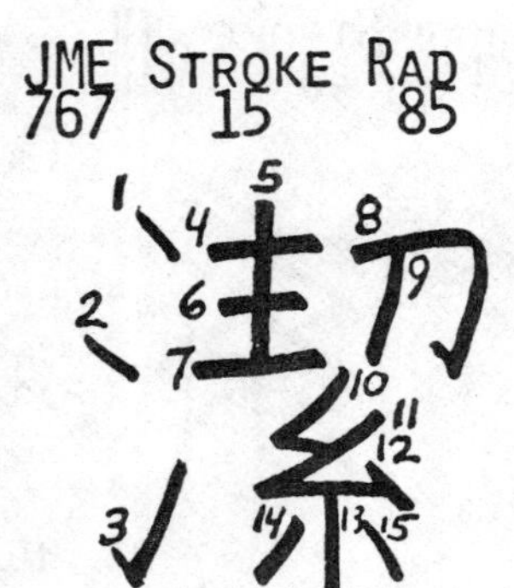

N2698
chieh2
M772
jié
clean
pure
clear

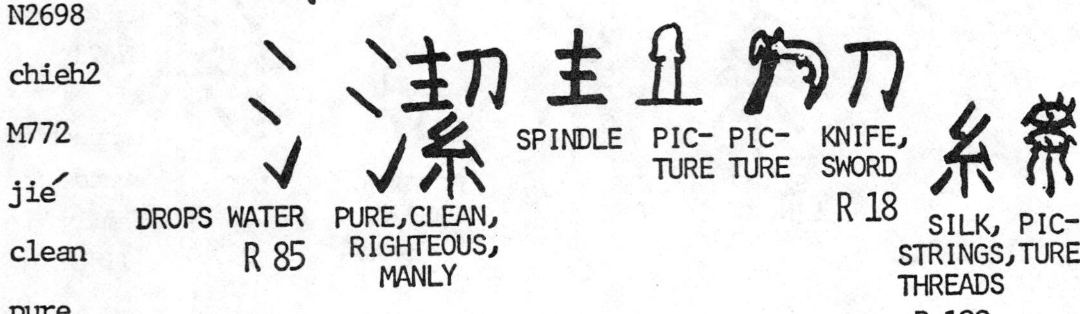

JME 768 Stroke 8 Rad 18

KEN, TICKET, COUPON, BOND.

THE FOUR-LEGGED 二 HIDE OF THE HALVED 半 ANIMAL DIVIDED 丷 AND CUT 刀 (AS BY A KNIFE IN GELDING) INTO TICKETS, COUPONS, BONDS 券.

Coupons are clipped. Cut leather was early used for tickets, coupons, etc. of value.

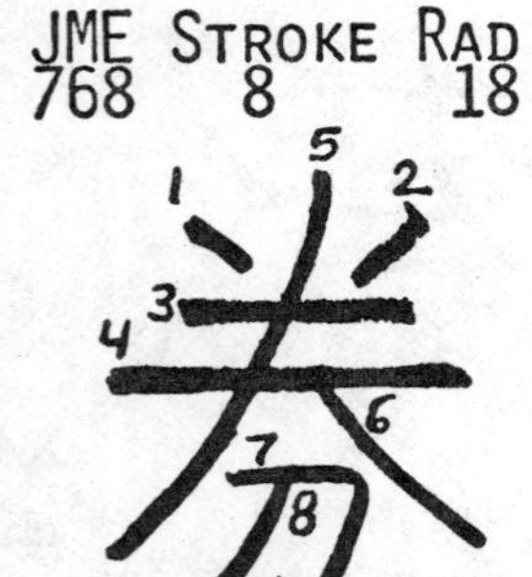

N678
chuan4
M1652
juàn
deed
contract
bond

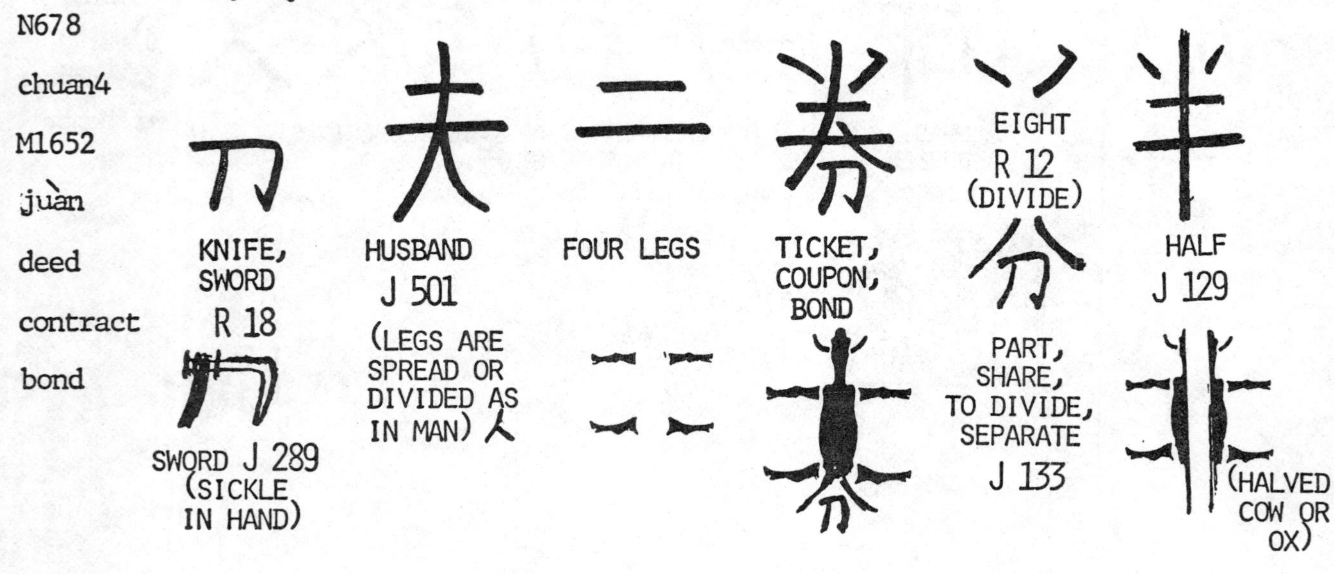

KEN, AND, IN ADDITION, CONCURRENTLY; KANERU, COMBINE WITH, SERVE AS BOTH; -KANERU, CANNOT.

RAD 12 STROKE 10 JME 769

兼

A HAND ⺕ HOLDING TWO TREES 仆 PAIRED LIKE GOAT HORNS 丷 MEANS AND, IN ADDITION, CONCURRENTLY, TO COMBINE WITH, SERVE AS BOTH 兼. IF A CONFLICT OF INTERESTS OR IF PROHIBITED, THIS CANNOT 兼 BE DONE.

林 WOODS J 150

仆 (TWO TREES)

兼 IN ADDITION, CONCURRENTLY, AND, CANNOT, COMBINE WITH

⺕ HAND R 58

丷 HORNS (AS IN GOAT, R 123)

羊 GOAT R 123

N598
chien 1
M830
jiān
to combine
connect
and
also
together
with
both
equally

Baucis and Philemon Jonathan Swift

When Baucis hastily cried out,
'My dear, I see your forehead sprout";
    Description would but tire my Muse;
In short, they both were turned to yews.

KEN, STRATEGIC POSITION AS INACCESSIBLE, IMPREGNABLE; KEWASHII, STEEP.

RAD 170 STROKE 11 JME 770

険

ALL, THE WHOLE 㑒 OF THE MOUND 阝 IS TIGHT 亼, STRATEGICALLY INACCESSIBLE, IMPREGNABLE, STEEP 険. LIKE A FACE 僉 FROM A PEAK 人.

The Book of Songs James Legge
How high those frowning rocks arise!
With awe they fill the mind.

(ROTATED 90 DEGREES LEFT)

阝 MOUND R 170

険 INACCESSIBLE, IMPREGNABLE, STEEP

㑒 ALL, THE WHOLE M 914

亼 JOINED, TOGETHER

人 PERSON, MAN

口 NOISE

臉 FACE

人 PEAK

N5000
hsien3
M2689
xiǎn
dangerous
danger
risk
mt. pass

Those frowning rocks the heights surmount,
And fill the mind with dread.
Our warrior hastens on the track,
Nor thinks he of our turning back.

The Book of Songs
James Legge

JME 771 STROKE 12 RAD 75

KEN, (TO INVESTIGATE).

TO INVESTIGATE 検 ALL, THE WHOLE 㑒 TREE 木.

The Republic   Plato
...your dog is a true philosopher.
Why?
Because he distinguishes the face of a friend from that of an enemy only by the criterion of knowing and not knowing. And must not an animal love learning if he decides what he likes and dislikes by the test of knowledge and of ignorance?
Most certainly.
And is not love of learning the love of wisdom which is philosophy?
They are the same, he answered.

N2304
chien3
M851
jiǎn
examine
search

険	木	検	㑒	臉	
INACCESSIBLE, IMPREGNABLE, STEEP J 770	TREE, WOOD J 15	TO INVESTIGATE	ALL, THE WHOLE M 914	"FACE", HONOR, FACE	JOINED, TIGHT

JME 772 STROKE 13 RAD 120

KEN; KINU, SILK.

THE WORM'S BODY 月 WITH ITS MOUTH 口 EJECTS THE THREAD 糸 OF SILK 絹.

The Bait   John Donne
Come live with me, and be my love,
And we will some new pleasures prove
of golden sands, and crystal brooks,
With silken lines and silver hooks.

N3543
chuan4
M1635
juàn
silk
pongee

	糸	絹	口	肙	月	育
PICTURED COCOONS & THREADS	SILK, STRINGS, THREADS R 120	SILK	MOUTH R 30	WORM, EMPTY G 13731	BODY R 74	TO BRING UP, TO EDUCATE, TO RAISE J 347

Where Wormes and Food doe naturally abound
A gallant Silken Trade must there be found.   Anony.

KEN, LAW.

RAD STROKE JME
40/61 16 773

THE NET 罒 WHICH PENETRATES 丨 THE LAYERS 主 UNDER THE ROOF 宀 TO CATCH THE MINDS, HEARTS, SPIRITS 心 BREAKING LAWS 憲.

In China, on occasion, a net was thrown over the head of the condemmed violator of laws.

心	罒 OR 网	主	憲	宀	害
MIND, HEART, SPIRIT J 95	NET R 122	LAYERS	LAW	ROOF R 40	HARM, CALAMITY J 362

N1342
hsien4
M2697
xiàn
law
regulation
constitution
problem

Essays on Men and Manners: On Politics. Wm. Shenstone
Laws are generally found to be nets of such a texture, as the little creep through, the great ones break through, and the middle-sized alone become entangled.

GON, KEN, AUTHORITY, POWER.

RAD STROKE JME
75 15 774

THE HERON 雚 HAS THE AUTHORITY, POWER 權 LIKE A TREE 木 AS THIS SHORT-TAILED BIRD 隹 POISES HIS BAMBOO ⺮ BILL ON THE FLATS 一.

The steelyard is the balance of a beam of unequal arms (the heron's legs) used in weighing and has the power, authority of measurement. One of China's six measures.

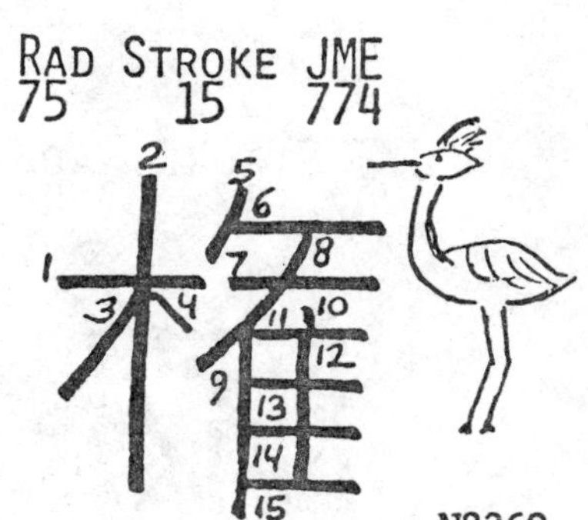

木	權	雚	歡	勸	觀
TREE, WOOD J 15	AUTHORITY, POWER	HERON	JOY, PLEASURE J 753	RECOMMEND, ADVISE, ENCOURAGE J 752	TO SHOW, TO LOOK AT CAREFULLY J 367

N2360
ch'uan2
M1663
quán
authority
power
influence
to weigh
weight

Shuo Wen is of the opinion that the heron is very intelligent and knows when it will rain. His balanced and poised position as he waits for fish has gotten him the Chinese name of Old Waiter. The crested crane is the totem of the Watusi rulers in Africa. Both birds share anthropomorphic characteristics.

775

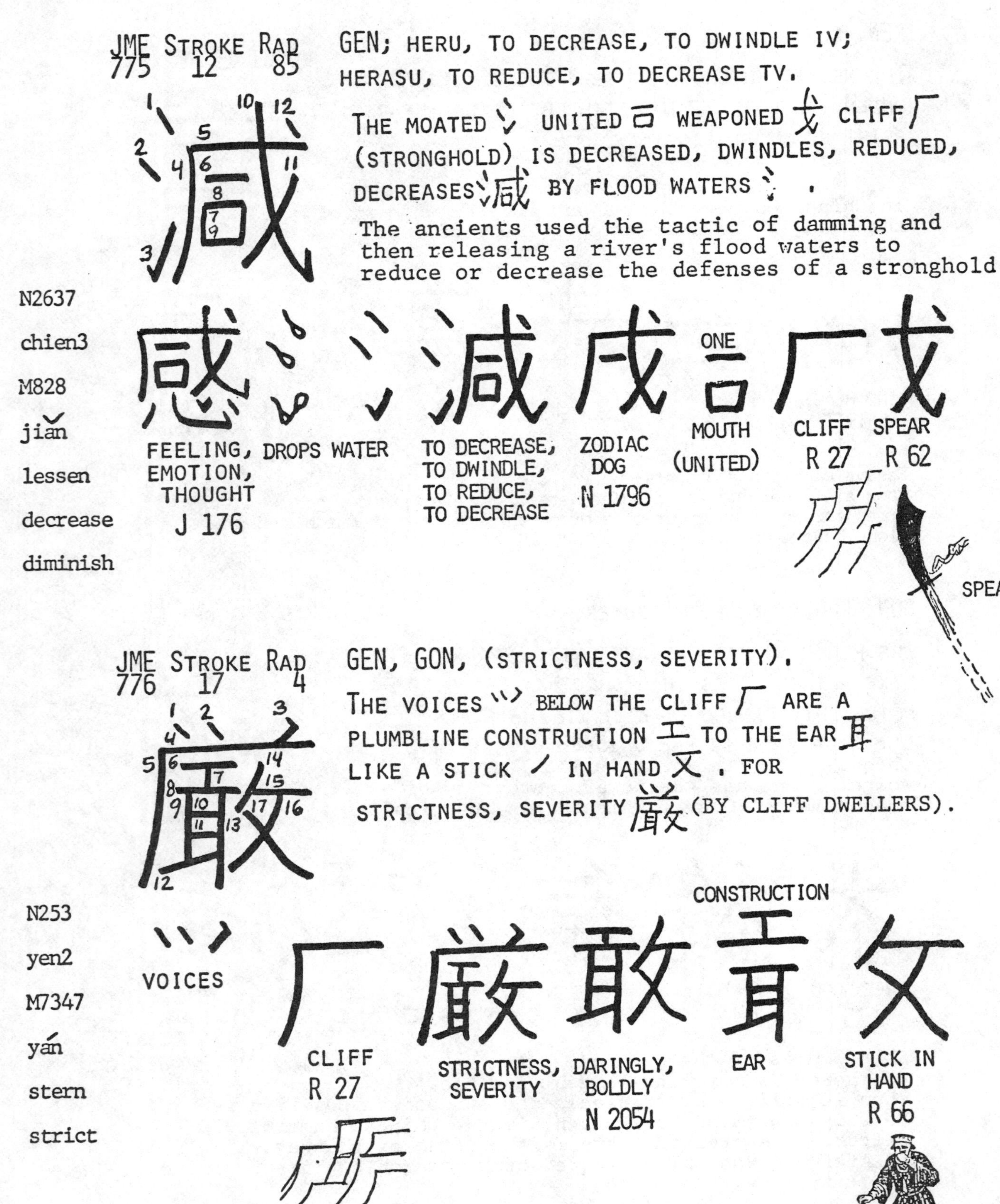

JME 775 | Stroke 12 | Rad 85

減

GEN; HERU, TO DECREASE, TO DWINDLE IV; HERASU, TO REDUCE, TO DECREASE TV.

THE MOATED 氵 UNITED 口 WEAPONED 戈 CLIFF 厂 (STRONGHOLD) IS DECREASED, DWINDLES, REDUCED, DECREASES 減 BY FLOOD WATERS 氵.

The ancients used the tactic of damming and then releasing a river's flood waters to reduce or decrease the defenses of a stronghold.

N2637
chien3
M828
jiǎn
lessen
decrease
diminish

感 FEELING, EMOTION, THOUGHT J 176
氵 DROPS WATER
減 TO DECREASE, TO DWINDLE, TO REDUCE, TO DECREASE
戌 ZODIAC DOG N 1796
一 ONE
口 MOUTH (UNITED)
厂 CLIFF R 27
戈 SPEAR R 62

SPEAR

JME 776 | Stroke 17 | Rad 4

嚴

GEN, GON, (STRICTNESS, SEVERITY).

THE VOICES ⺍ BELOW THE CLIFF 厂 ARE A PLUMBLINE CONSTRUCTION 工 TO THE EAR 耳 LIKE A STICK ノ IN HAND 又. FOR STRICTNESS, SEVERITY 厳 (BY CLIFF DWELLERS).

N253
yen2
M7347
yán
stern
strict

⺍ VOICES
厂 CLIFF R 27
厳 STRICTNESS, SEVERITY
敢 DARINGLY, BOLDLY N 2054
工 CONSTRUCTION
耳 EAR
夂 STICK IN HAND R 66

KO, KI, ONESELF, MYSELF, YOURSELF.

RAD 49 STROKE 3 JME 777

THE REFLEXIVE PRONOUNS ONESELF, MYSELF, YOURSELF 己 TURN ON THEMSELVES LIKE A SNAKE 己.

The evil streak came through the grass and flowers,
now and then turning its head to its back,
licking like an animal to sleek itself.
Purgatory Dante

己

N1462
chi3
M429
jǐ
self
personal
private

EGYPTIAN SNAKE HIEROGLYPH

己 ZODIAC SNAKE R 49 ONESELF, MYSELF, YOURSELF

巴 (FAT BOA OF SZECHUAN) HUGE COMMA DESIGN N 263

色 COLOR J 94

池 POND, LAKE J 110

PICTURED SNAKE

The Snake is the sixth of the Twelve Oriental Zodiac Creatures which are Rat, Ox, Tiger, Hare, Dragon, Snake, Horse, Sheep, Monkey, Cock, Dog, Boar.

KO, (OLD, FORMER TIMES; REASON).

RAD 66 STROKE 9 JME 778

AS IN OLD, FORMER TIMES 故 IS THE OLD 古 REASON 古攵 LIKE A STICK ノ IN HAND 攵.

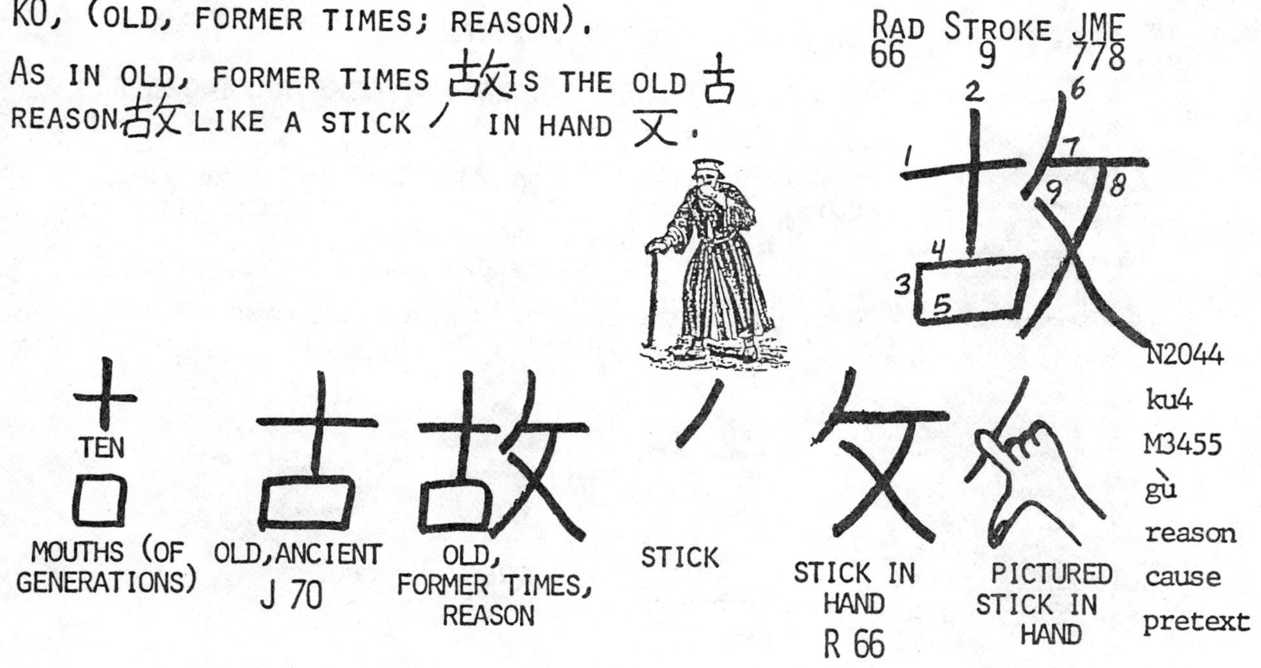

故

N2044
ku4
M3455
gù
reason
cause
pretext

十 TEN 口 MOUTHS (OF GENERATIONS)

古 OLD, ANCIENT J 70

故 OLD, FORMER TIMES, REASON

ノ STICK

攵 STICK IN HAND R 66

PICTURED STICK IN HAND

JME 779 STROKE 14 RAD 149

GO; AYAMARI, MISTAKE, ERROR;
AYAMARU, TO MISTAKE, TO BE MISTAKEN IV & TV.

DIFFERENT CHINESE DIALECTS AND PRONUNCIATIONS REACHED JAPAN AT DIFFERENT TIMES FROM VARIOUS PARTS OF CHINA. THE SPEECH 言 OF GO 呉 (WU) ARRIVED LATER AND WAS MISTAKEN, IN ERROR 誤 TO THE JAPANESE.

N4372
wu4
M7204
wù
impede
interfere w/
be mistaken

SOUND VIBRATIONS | SPEECH, WORDS J 392 | MISTAKE, ERROR | GO CHINESE STATE OF WU | (CITIZEN OF WU PICTURED)

Give Me a Ukelele Lew Brown & Gene Williams
Don't know how to act with girls who talk Chinese
Don't know how to ask 'em for a hug and squeeze
I'll admit I'm kind of slow But oh! OH!
Give me a Ukelele, And a Ukelele baby, You can leave the rest to me.

JME 780 STROKE 6 RAD 4

KŌ, (GŌ), EMPRESS, QUEEN.

AN AXE WITH THE LAST STROKE REPLACED BY MOUTH 口 IS EMPRESS, QUEEN 后.

The Queen turned crimson with fury, and after glaring at her for a moment like a wild beast, began screaming
"Off with her head! Off with---"
Alice in Wonderland Lewis Carroll

"Was, du redest von Axt?" sagte die Herzogin.
"Hau' ihr den Kopf ab!"

N181
hou4
M2144
hòu
empress
king
ruler

PICTURED AXE | AXE R 69 | AXE WITH STROKE DELETED | EMPRESS, QUEEN | MOUTH R 30

Old Hatchetface and Old Battleaxe.

Ovid: The battleaxe was the favorite weapon of the Amazons.

KŌ, FILIAL PIETY.

RAD 24 STROKE 7 JME 781

THE CHILD 子 WITH FILIAL PIETY 孝 CARRIES THE EARTH 土 (-LY BURDEN).

The traditional Chinese period of mourning for a parent was three years, shortened to thirty months, because that was the period during which the mourner had been carried as an infant and child. The mourner should thus reciprocate.

孝

老 土 ノ 孝 子 教

OLD MAN J 541 — EARTH, SOIL R 32 — (BEARING, SUPPORTING) — FILIAL PIETY — CHILD R 39 — TO TEACH J 191

N773
hsiao4
M2601
xiào
filial
to honor parents

Korean Proverb: Now one is taught by a child whom one formerly carried on one's back.

KŌ, EFFICACY, EFFECT.

RAD 19 STROKE 8 JME 782

THE STRENGTH, POWER 力 OF MIXING, OF ASSOCIATION 交 HAS EFFICACY, EFFECT 効.

効

文 交 効 力

WRITINGS, SENTENCE J 134 — TO MIX, TO ASSOCIATE J 212 — EFFICACY, EFFECT — STRENGTH, POWER — PICTURED STRENGTH, POWER

N722
hsiao4
M2597
xiào
to toil
imitate
similar
like

JME 783 STROKE 9 RAD 106

KŌ, Ō, (EMPEROR).

THE WHITE 白 KING 王 IS EMPEROR 皇.

White as with the Imperial Japanese stallions, Alexander's Bucephalus, the Ferghana trans-Oxianic studs imported to Han China, the rajah's albino elephants, and the giant white stars. A.D.

Hellas Percy Bysshe Shelley
Kings are like stars-- they rise and set,
they have the worship of the world but no repose.

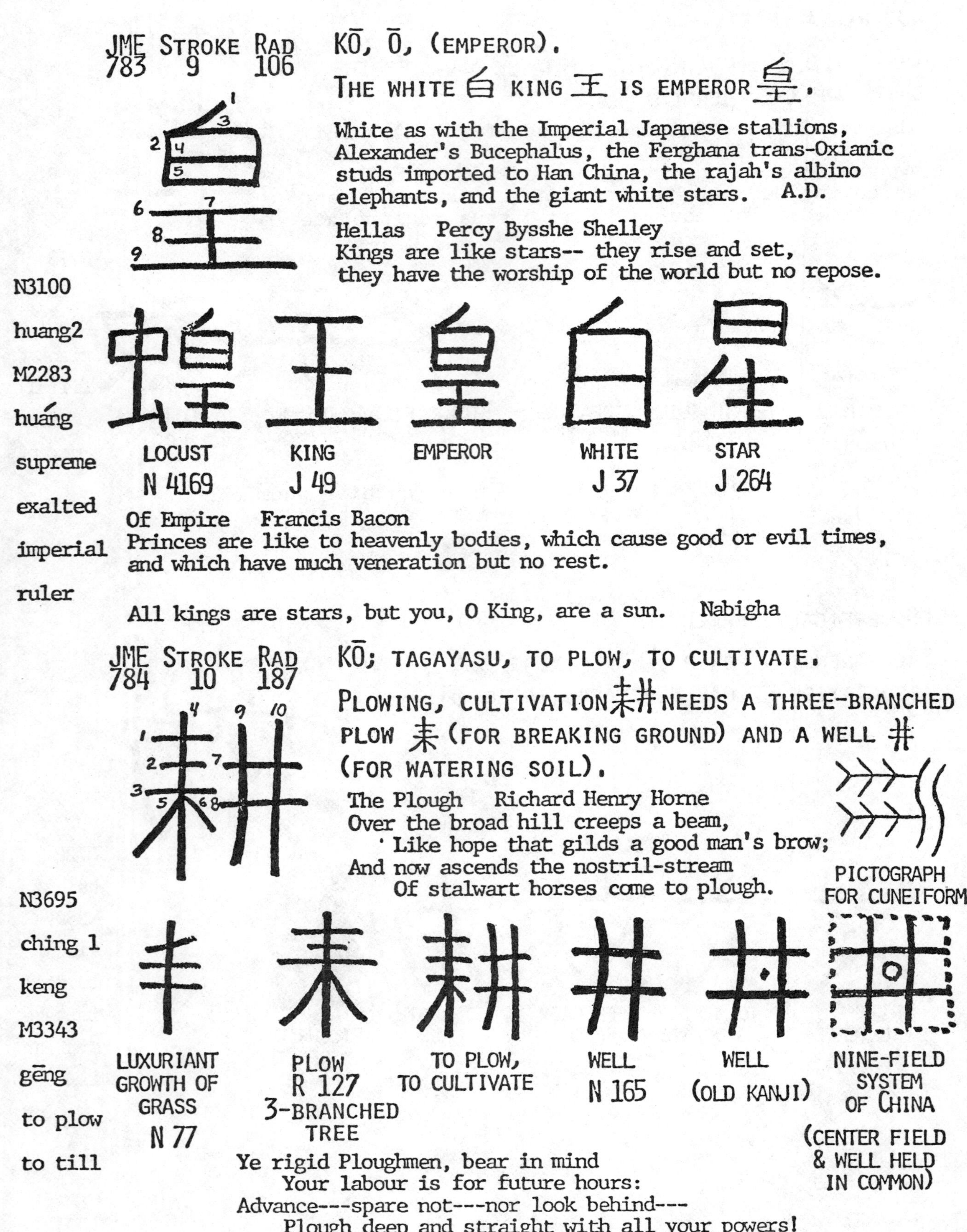

N3100
huang2
M2283
huáng
supreme
exalted
imperial
ruler

Of Empire Francis Bacon
Princes are like to heavenly bodies, which cause good or evil times, and which have much veneration but no rest.

All kings are stars, but you, O King, are a sun. Nabigha

JME 784 STROKE 10 RAD 187

KŌ; TAGAYASU, TO PLOW, TO CULTIVATE.

PLOWING, CULTIVATION 耕 NEEDS A THREE-BRANCHED PLOW 耒 (FOR BREAKING GROUND) AND A WELL 井 (FOR WATERING SOIL).

The Plough Richard Henry Horne
Over the broad hill creeps a beam,
Like hope that gilds a good man's brow;
And now ascends the nostril-stream
Of stalwart horses come to plough.

N3695
ching 1
keng
M3343
gēng
to plow
to till

Ye rigid Ploughmen, bear in mind
Your labour is for future hours:
Advance---spare not---nor look behind---
Plough deep and straight with all your powers!
The Plough Richard Henry Horne

KŌ; KAMAE, (GAMAE), CONSTRUCTION, ARCHITECTURE, POSTURE; KAMAERU, (GAMAERU), TO BUILD, TO KEEP HOUSE, TO TAKE A POSTURE.

RAD 75 STROKE 14 JME 785

CONSTRUCTION, ARCHITECTURE, TO BUILD IS THE REPEATED 再 PILING UP OF LOGS 井 LIKE TREES, WOOD 木 THAT TAKES A POSTURE 構 SO ONE CAN KEEP HOUSE 構.

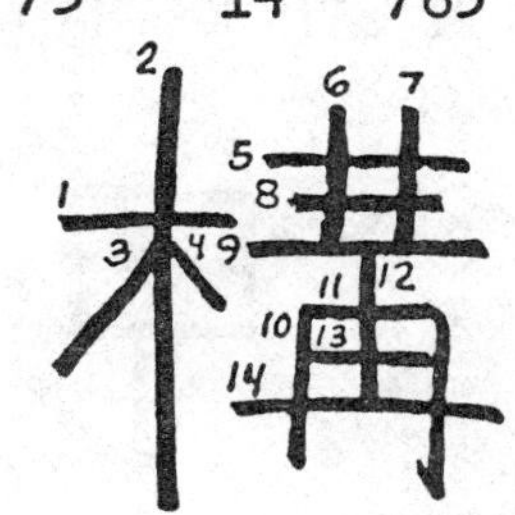

N2343
kou4
M3428
gòu
to roof w/ beams
to unite

講	木	構	再	井	寒
LECTURE, INVESTIGATION J 609	TREE, WOOD R 75	CONSTRUCTION, ARCHITECTURE, POSTURE, TO BUILD, KEEP HOUSE	REPEATED J 788	LOGS OF BLDG. STRUCTURE (LAYERS DOUBLED)	COLD J 175

The Book of Songs
James Legge

To mold the walls, the frames they firmly tie;
The walls shall vermin, storm, and bird defy;
In height, like human form most reverent, grand;
And straight, as flies the shaft when bow unbends;

KOKU, (CEREALS, GRAIN).

RAD 79/115 STROKE 14 JME 786

THE MAN, FIGURE 士 STRIKES 殳 THE COVER 冖 (HUSK) FROM THE GRAIN 禾.

John Barleycorn: A Ballad Robert Burns
They laid him down upon his back,
And cudgelled him full sore;
They hung him up before the storm,
And turned him o'er and o'er.

N2461
ku3
M3490
gǔ
grain
corn

士	冖	禾	穀	殳	殺
MAN, FIGURE, SAMURAI J 410	CROWN COVER R 14	GRAIN, RICE R 115	CEREALS, GRAIN	TO STRIKE R 79 (WING & HAND)	TO KILL J 614

Kubla Khan Samuel Taylor Coleridge
Huge fragments vaulted like rebounding hail,
Or chaffy grain beneath the thresher's flail.

EMPEROR KUANG WU CROWNED COVERED

JME 787 STROKE 11 RAD 85

KON: KONZURU, TO MIX, TO ADULTERATE, TO CONFUSE IV & TV; MAJIRU, TO BE MINGLED, TO BE MIXED IV; MAZERU, TO MINGLE, TO MIX.

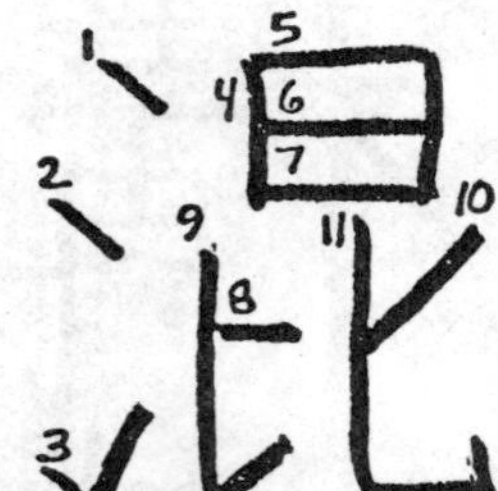

TO MIX, TO MINGLE, TO ADULTERATE, TO CONFUSE 混 THE FOETAL SPOON-STYLE MUMMIES 比 WITH THE SUNSHINE 日 AND WATER 氵 (OF LIFE).

N2604
hun3
M2371
hùn
muddy
disorderly
mixed
confused

氵 WATER R 85

混 TO ADULTERATE, TO MIX, CONFUSE, BE MINGLED, BE MIXED

比 TO COMPARE J 697

日 SUN J 11

Antigone Sophocles
ANTIGONE:
But for the corpse
of Polynices, slain
So piteously, they say,
he has proclaimed
To all the citizens,
that none should give
His body burial,
or bewail his fate,
But leave it still
unsepulchred, unwept..
So Creon bids, they say...

JME 788 STROKE 6 RAD 13

SAI, FUTATABI, AGAIN, TWICE.

AGAIN, TWICE 再 ON THE BALANCE, SCALES 冂. (CHECK AND DOUBLE CHECK).

再

Village Life in China Arthur H. Smith
The architecture of the Chinese has been described as consisting essentially of two sticks placed upright, with a third laid across them at the top.

N35
tsai4
M6658
zài
again
2nd time
repeated

構 CONSTRUCTION, ARCHITECTURE, TO BUILD J 785

二 TWO, TWICE, TWO TIMES J 2

再 AGAIN, TWICE

冂 BALANCE, SCALE

両 BOTH, TWO, J 336 N 34

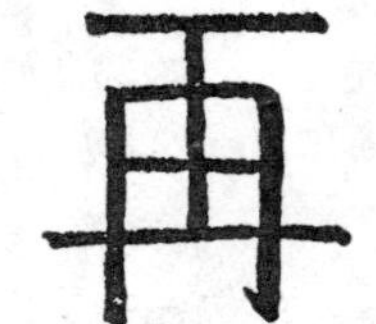

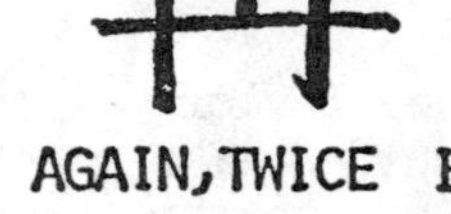

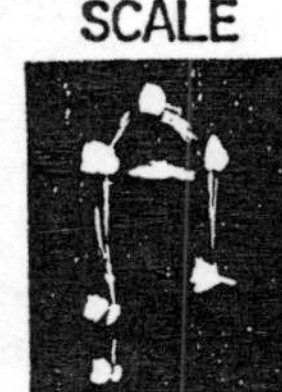

LIBRA
THE SCALES

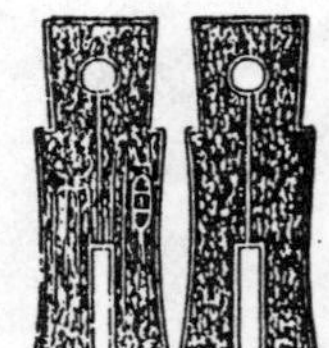

HAN DY. CASH

SAI; WAZAWAI, CALAMITY, MISFORTUNE.

CALAMITIES, MISFORTUNES 災 ARE FROM STREAMS 巛 AND FIRES 火.

RAD 86 STROKE 7 JME 789

災

水 川 巛 災 火

WATER R 85 | RIVER J 39 | STREAMS (MOVEMENT) | CALAMITY, MISFORTUNE | FIRE R 86 | PICTURED FIRE

N448
tsai 1
M6652
zāi
flood
famine
pestilence
misery
suffering
evil

Ladybird, ladybird,
Fly away home,
Your house is on fire
And your children are gone;
All except one
And that's little Anne
And she has crept under
The warming pan.

SAI, (MY) WIFE; TSUMA, WIFE.

THE WIFE 妻 IS THE WOMAN 女 WITH DUSTER 十 IN HAND ヨ.

RAD 38 STROKE 8 JME 790

妻

帰 十 ヨ 妻 女

TO RETURN J 182 | DUSTER | HAND R 58 | DUSTER IN HAND | (MY) WIFE (HUMBLE FORM) | WOMAN, GIRL, FEMALE R 38

N1206
ch'i 1
M555
qī
legal wife

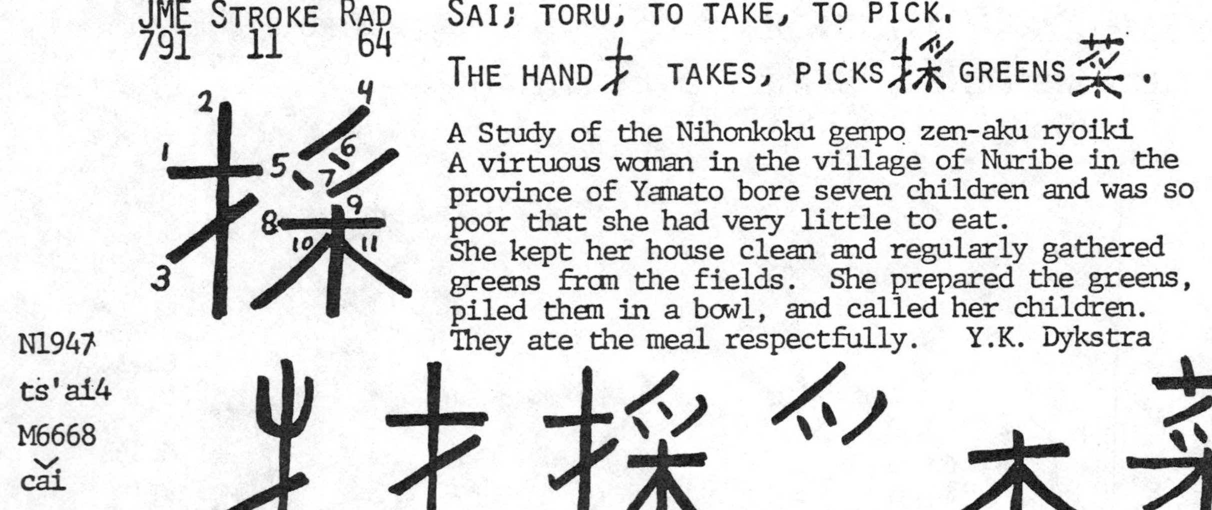

JME 791 STROKE 11 RAD 64

採

SAI; TORU, TO TAKE, TO PICK.

THE HAND 扌 TAKES, PICKS 採 GREENS 菜.

A Study of the Nihonkoku genpo zen-aku ryoiki
A virtuous woman in the village of Nuribe in the province of Yamato bore seven children and was so poor that she had very little to eat.
She kept her house clean and regularly gathered greens from the fields. She prepared the greens, piled them in a bowl, and called her children.
They ate the meal respectfully. Y.K. Dykstra

N1947
ts'ai4
M6668
cǎi
pick
gather
choose
collect

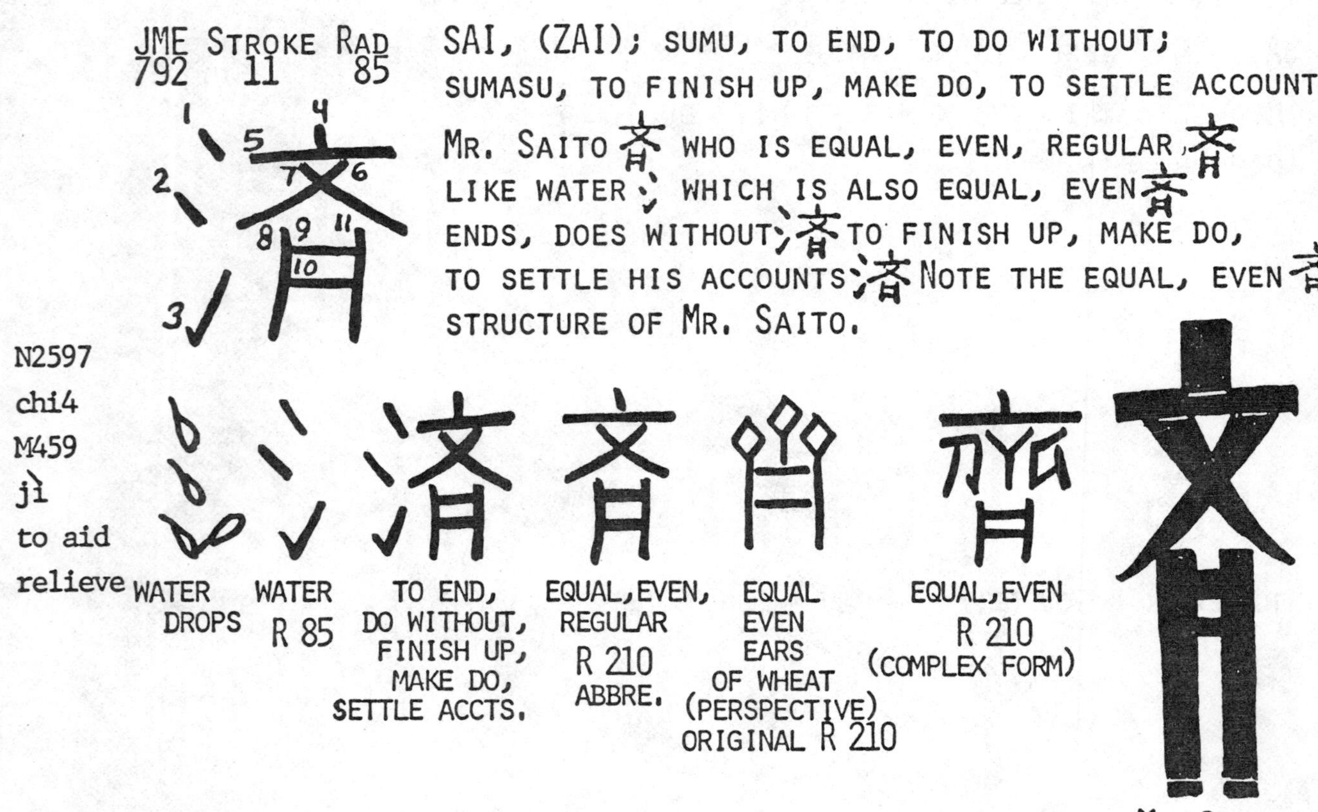

JME 792 STROKE 11 RAD 85

済

SAI, (ZAI); SUMU, TO END, TO DO WITHOUT;
SUMASU, TO FINISH UP, MAKE DO, TO SETTLE ACCOUNTS

MR. SAITO 斉 WHO IS EQUAL, EVEN, REGULAR 斉 LIKE WATER 氵 WHICH IS ALSO EQUAL, EVEN 斉 ENDS, DOES WITHOUT 済 TO FINISH UP, MAKE DO, TO SETTLE HIS ACCOUNTS 済 NOTE THE EQUAL, EVEN 斉 STRUCTURE OF MR. SAITO.

N2597
chi4
M459
jì
to aid
relieve

ZAI, (WEALTH, MONEY, ASSETS).

WEALTH, MONEY, ASSETS 財 ARE IN COWRIES 貝 AND IN TALENT 才.

Ability or talent is like the tree that has been pruned or trimmed for effective growth. Dead wood is removed and the good timber remains. The same is true of a person whose abilities have been well developed like a tree whose fruit or timber capacities are improved by analogous methods.

RAD 154 STROKE 10 JME 793

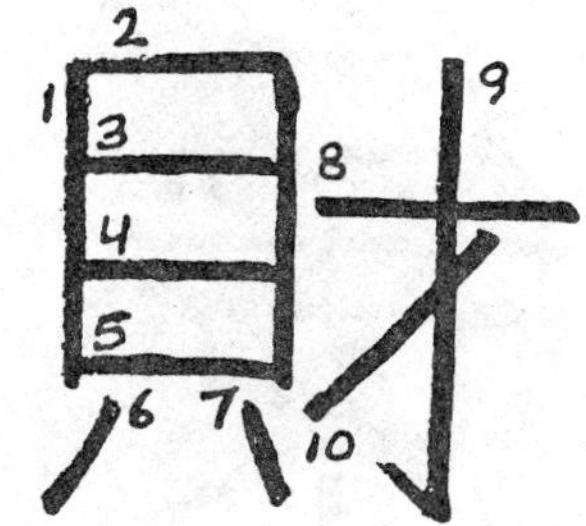

N4490
ts'ai2
M6662
cái
wealth
property
valuables
bribes

PICTURED SEA SHELL

貝 SEA SHELL R 154

財 WEALTH, MONEY, ASSETS

才 TALENT J 217

木 TREE, WOOD R 75

材 LUMBER, LOG, MATERIAL, ABILITY J 403

CHINESE COIN

MAYAN ZERO

The cowrie (Cypraea moneta) was used for exchange throughout Asia. Indian trade routes in the American West are marked by sea shells shared by Hopi, Zuni, Papago, and Pima tribes. Peag and wampum shells were used in the East. The shell shape suggested a woman and the eye. A dotted shell was the Mayan symbol for zero.

ZAI; TSUMI, CRIME, SIN, GUILT.

CRIMES, SINS, GUILT 罪 ARE THE FAULTS, WRONGS, "NO-NO'S" 非 FOR WHICH ONE IS NETTED 罒.

In ancient times, a net was thrown over the head of the criminal taken by law enforcers.

RAD 122 STROKE 13 JME 794

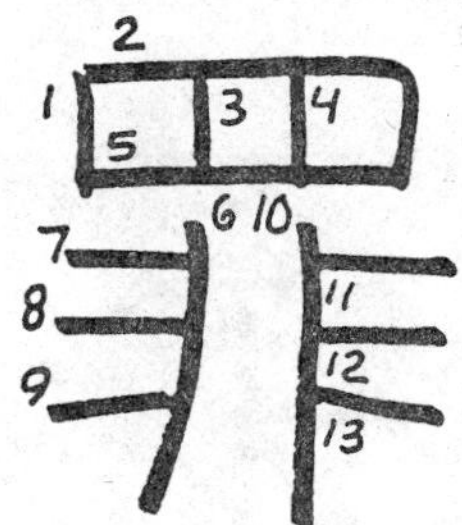

N3643
tsui4
M6860
zuì
sin
crime
wrong
to blame

憲 LAW J 773

罒 OR 网 NET R 122

罪 CRIME, SIN, GUILT

非 FAULT, WRONG, NON-, UN- J 698

韭 GARLIC, ONIONS, SCALLIONS R 179

Laws are like cobwebs, which may catch small flies, but let wasps and hornets break through.

A Critical Essay Upon the Faculties of the Mind — Swift

795

JME 795 | Stroke 12 | Rad 118

策

SAKU, SCHEME, POLICY, PLAN.

THE SCHEME, POLICY, PLAN 策 IS TO COVER 冂 THE THORNY 朿 STICKS 木 WITH ONE 一 WITHE 冂 OR BAND OF BAMBOO ⺮ (FOR EASY HANDLING).

Scilurus, on his death-bed, being about to leave four-score sons surviving, offered a bundle of darts to each of them, and bade them break them. When all refused, drawing out one by one, he easily broke them,

N3393
t'se4
M6760
cè
plan
scheme
bundle of bamboo slips

速 SPEEDY, QUICK J 453
朿 BUNDLE, SHEAF N 196
竹 BAMBOO R 118
策 SCHEME, POLICY, PLAN
木 TREE, WOOD R 75
一 ONE J 1
冂 COVER R 14

---thus teaching them that if they held together, they would continue strong; but if they fell out and were divided, they would become weak.

Plutarch's Lives

BAMBOO BUNDLE

"IN UNION IS STRENGTH"

GRAPHIC

JME 796 | Stroke 6 | Rad 133

至

SHI, (JI), ITARU, TO GO, TO REACH, TO COME. TO ARRIVE.

A BODY COILED 厶 FLAT 一 ON THE EARTH 土 HAS GONE, REACHED, COME, ARRIVED 至.

Go play with the towns you have built of blocks
The towns where you would have bound me!
I sleep in my earth like a tired fox,
And my buffalo have found me.

The Ballad of Wm. Sycamore Stephen Vincent Binet

N3845
chih4
M982
zhì
to reach
arrive
very
extreme
best

去 PAST, TO LEAVE, TO DEPART J 189

PICTURED ALTAR OR GRAVE-MOUND

土 EARTH, SOIL R 32

至 TO GO, REACH, TO COME, TO ARRIVE

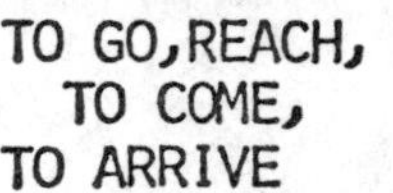

厶 (COILED, PRIVATE, COCOON)

一 ONE J 1 (FLAT)

ṢHI, I, PRIVATE;
WATASHI, WATAKUSHI, I, MYSELF, PRIVATE.
I, MYSELF, PRIVATE 私 IS MY BAG 厶 OF GRAIN 禾

RAD 115 STROKE 7 JME 797

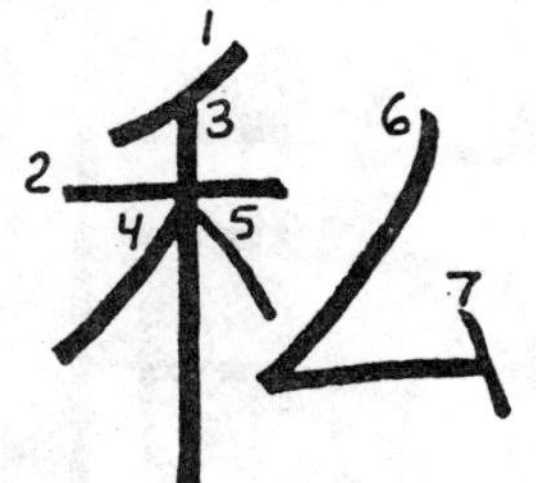

I, SELF J 745 — SPEAR — GRAIN, RICE R 115 — I, PRIVATE — (COILED, COCOON, PRIVATE, MOUTH)

N3265
szu 1
M5569
sī
private
personal
selfish
secret

SHI, MIRU, TO SEE, TO LOOK AT.
TO SEE, TO LOOK AT 視 IS TO SEE, TO LOOK 見 AND TO SHOW, INDICATE, POINT OUT 礻.

RAD 115 STROKE 11 JME 798

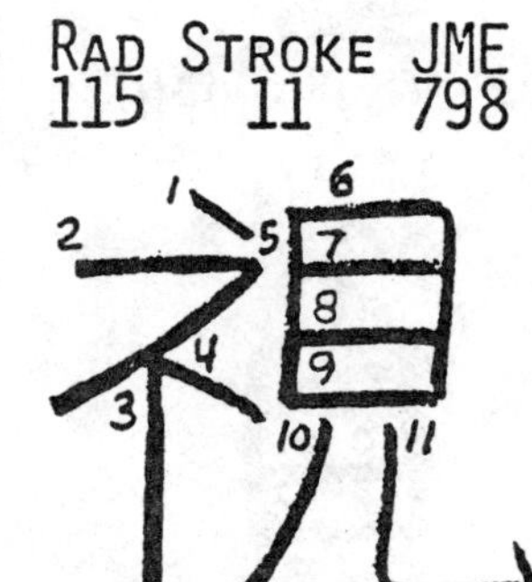

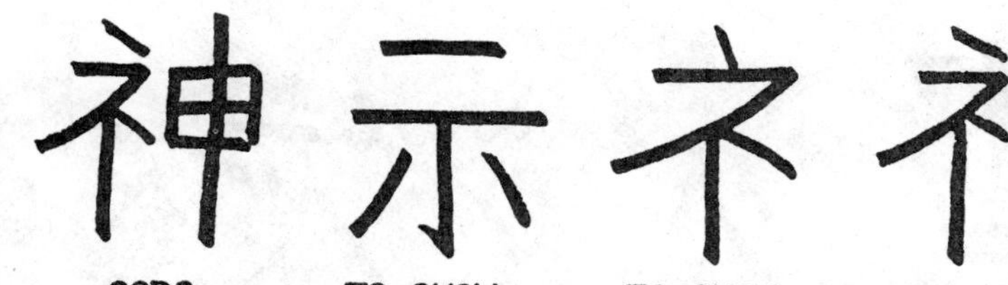

GODS J 257 — TO SHOW, POINT OUT J 622 R 113 — TO SHOW, TO POINT OUT R 113 ABBRE. — TO SEE, TO LOOK AT — TO SEE, LOOK J 67 — PICTURED EYE ON LEGS

N3248
shih4
M5789
shì
look at
regard
inspect

799

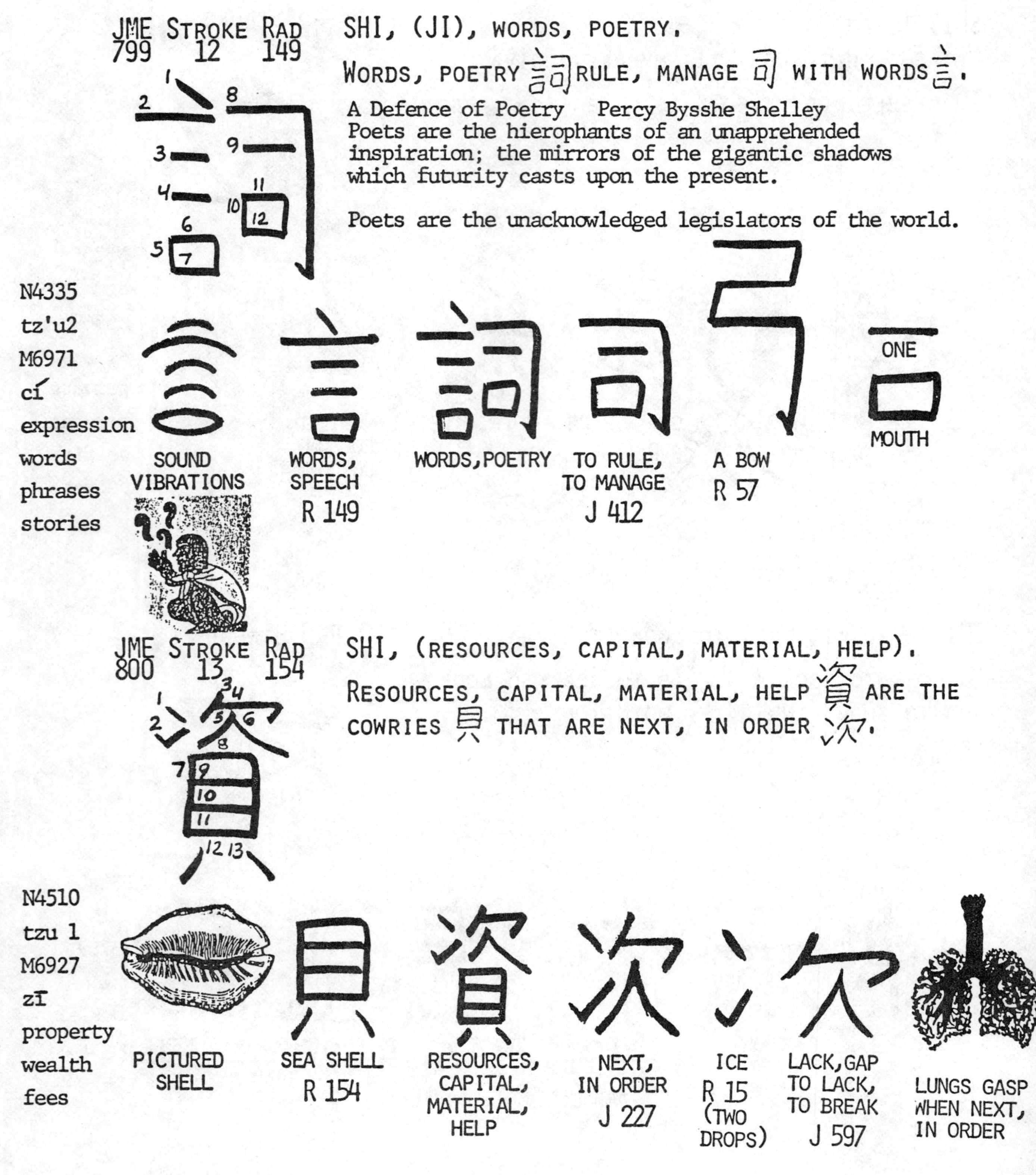

JME 799 STROKE 12 RAD 149

SHI, (JI), WORDS, POETRY.

WORDS, POETRY 詞 RULE, MANAGE 司 WITH WORDS 言.

A Defence of Poetry Percy Bysshe Shelley
Poets are the hierophants of an unapprehended inspiration; the mirrors of the gigantic shadows which futurity casts upon the present.

Poets are the unacknowledged legislators of the world.

N4335
tz'u2
M6971
cí
expression
words
phrases
stories

SOUND VIBRATIONS — 言 WORDS, SPEECH R 149 — 詞 WORDS, POETRY — 司 TO RULE, TO MANAGE J 412 — A BOW R 57 — ONE, MOUTH

JME 800 STROKE 13 RAD 154

SHI, (RESOURCES, CAPITAL, MATERIAL, HELP).

RESOURCES, CAPITAL, MATERIAL, HELP 資 ARE THE COWRIES 貝 THAT ARE NEXT, IN ORDER 次.

N4510
tzu 1
M6927
zī
property
wealth
fees

PICTURED SHELL — 貝 SEA SHELL R 154 — 資 RESOURCES, CAPITAL, MATERIAL, HELP — 次 NEXT, IN ORDER J 227 — 冫 ICE R 15 (TWO DROPS) — 欠 LACK, GAP TO LACK, TO BREAK J 597 — LUNGS GASP WHEN NEXT, IN ORDER

JI, NI, CHILD.

RAD 10 STROKE 7 JME 801

THE CHILD 児 IS A PESTLE | AND MORTAR 日 ON LEGS 儿. ITS SKULL STILL HAS THE OPENING FOR THE PESTLE AT THE MEMBRANE-COVERED FONTANEL BETWEEN THE ANGLES OF THE PARIETAL AND NEIGHBORING BONES.

児

Old age is just a second childhood. — Clouds, Aristophanes

兄 OLDER BROTHER J 199

儿 LEGS R 10

児 CHILD (SONNY)

| PESTLE

臼 CRANIAL LOBAL FINGERS HOLD THE BRAIN & LATER FUSE

旧 J 759 OLD

N572
er 1
M1759
ér
son
child
noun suffix

Both young and old skulls are fragile.

In Japanese art, faces are often simplified: A line for the eye (hikime), and a hook for the nose (kagibana). (if you prefer the skull covered)

Little Ah Sid was a Chinese kid,
A neat little cuss, I declare,
With eyes full of fun,
And a nose that begun
Way up in the roots of his hair.

Little Ah Sid

SHAKU, (TO INTERPRET, TO EXPLAIN).

RAD 165 STROKE 11 JME 802

ANIMAL TRACKS 釆 AND FOOT, MEASURE 尺 ARE INTERPRETED, EXPLAINED 釈.

釈

James Fenimore Cooper — Last of the Mohicans

One moccasin like another! You may as well say that one foot is like another; though we all know that some are long, and others short; some broad and others narrow; some with high and some with low insteps; some in-toed, and some out. Sagamore: you measured the prints more than once, when we hunted the varmints....

番 WATCH, GUARD J 306

釆 (TRACK IN RICE, GRAIN) TO DISTINGUISH, TO DIVIDE R 165

釈 TO INTERPRET, TO EXPLAIN

尺 MEASURE, JPN. FOOT, N 1377

尸 BODY R 44

駅 STATION J 158

N4809
shih3
M5824
shì
to release
unloose
explain

DEER TRACKS IN THE RICE FIELD

JME 803 STROKE 11 RAD 64

JU; SAZUKERU, TO GIVE, TO GRANT, TO TEACH; SAZUKARU, TO BE GRANTED, TO BE AWARDED, TO BE TAUGHT.

授

THE HAND 爫 (ABOVE) RECEIVES 受 THE CROWN 冖 FROM THE HAND 又 (BELOW) AS GIVEN, GRANTED, TAUGHT, AWARDED 授 BY THE (SUPERVISING) HAND 扌

N1946
shou4
M5841
shòu
give
confer
transmit

扌	授	受	爫	冖	又
HAND	TO GIVE, GRANT, TO TEACH, TO BE GRANTED, TO BE AWARDED, TO BE TAUGHT	TO RECEIVE	HAND, CLAW	CROWN	HAND
R 64		J 240	R 87	R 14	R 29

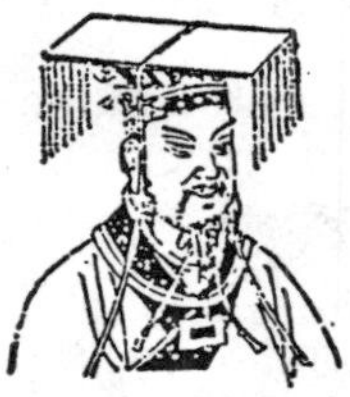

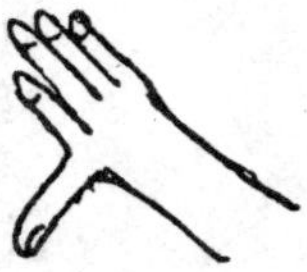

JME 804 STROKE 14 RAD 173

JU, (REQUEST, NEED).

需

THE REQUEST, NEED 需 OF THE BEARDED 而 ONE IS FOR RAIN 雨. The urgency of the request and need causes saliva to rain upon the beard.

The Canterbury Tales   Geoffrey Chaucer
His beard, like any sow or fox, was red
And broadly built, as though it were a spade.

雨 MYCENAE LIQUID MEASURE

Note the Chinese-Mycenae connection:

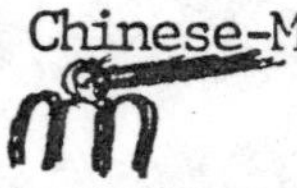

N5052
hsu 1
M2844
xū
require
need
essen-tial

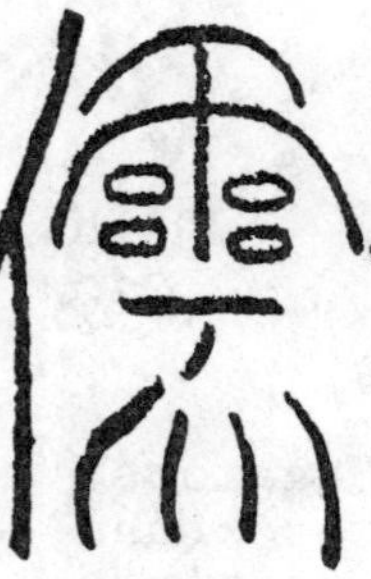

	儒	而	雲	電	雨
PICTURED CONFUCIANIST	CONFUCIANIST, CHINESE SCHOLAR	HARROW / BEARD	CLOUD	ELECTRICITY, LIGHTNING	RAIN
	N 561	R 126	J 47	J 286	J 42 R 173 (SALIVA DROPS)

Reisebilder   Heinrich Heine
...a day will arrive when the fire in my veins will be put out, when winter will live in my heart, when his snowflakes will whiten my tresses of hair, and his mists will dim my eyes.

SŌ, SHŪ, RELIGION, SECT.

THE RELIGION, SECT 宗 POINTS OUT, SHOWS 示 UNDER THE ROOF 宀.

RAD 40 STROKE 8 JME 805

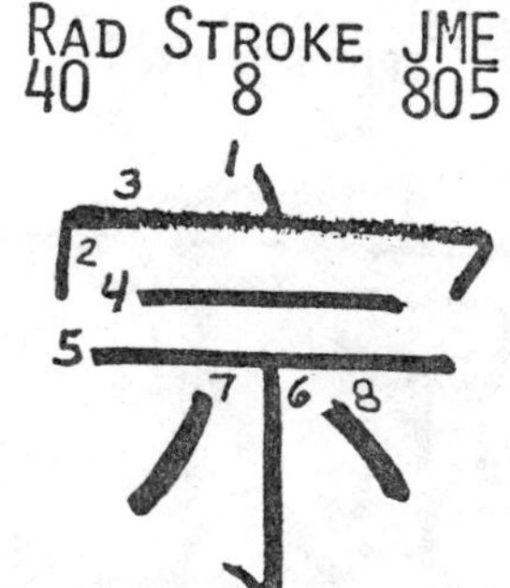

禁 示 宗 宀

FORBIDDEN J 763 | TO SHOW, TO POINT OUT J 622 | RELIGION, SECT | ROOF R 40 | PICTURED ROOF

N1294 tsung 1 M6896 zōng ancestral kindred class kind sect

SHŪ, (MANY, POPULACE, COMPANIONS).

THE MANY, THE POPULACE, THE COMPANIONS 衆 ARE LIKE PIGS 豕 OF A BLOOD 血.

Reflections on the Revolution in France Edmund Burke
Learning will be cast into the mire and trodden under the hoofs of a swinish multitude.

"Your people, sir, is nothing but a great beast."
Alexander Hamilton

RAD 143 STROKE 12 JME 806

衆

家 豕 豕 衆 血 皿

HOME J 53 | PIG R 152 | PIG R 152 VARIANT | MANY, POPULACE, COMPANIONS | BLOOD R 143 | BOWL R 108

N4210 tsung4 M1517 zhòng all the whole crowd

...it is that great enemy of reason, virtue, and religion, the multitude ...one great beast and a monstrosity...
Religio Medici Sir Thomas Browne

And he took the cup and gave thanks, and gave it to them, saying, "Drink ye all of it. This is my blood shed for many...
St. Matthew

JME	Stroke	Rad
807	12	8

就

SHŪ, JU, TSUKU, SETTLE (IN PLACE), TAKE (A SEAT), STUDY (WITH A TEACHER), TAKE (A POSITION); NI TSUITE, CONCERNING.

THE SUPERB, OUTSTANDING 尤 (ONES) IN THE CAPITAL 京 SETTLE (IN PLACE), TAKE (A SEAT), STUDY (WITH A TEACHER), TAKE (A POSITION), CONCERNING 就 (THEM).

N323
chiu4
M1210
jiù
then
acc. to
at once
in consequence

亠口	京	就	尤	丶	尢
PICTURED STONE LANTERN	CAPITAL J 63 (head-city; caput)	TO SETTLE, TAKE (A SEAT), STUDY W/ TCHR, CONCERNING	SUPERB, OUTSTANDING, RIGHT, NATURAL N 128 (DOTTED EXT. OF LAMENESS)	DOT R 4	LAME, CROOKED LEG R 43

He had a head which statuaries loved to copy, and a foot the deformity of which the beggars in the street mimicked. Macaulay on Byron

THE COMPENSATED CRIPPLE IS THE SUPERB HORSEMAN AND PLANNER, WHETHER TIMUR THE LAME OR CRIPPLED PHILIP OF MACEDON OR FDR

JME	Stroke	Rad
808	10	60

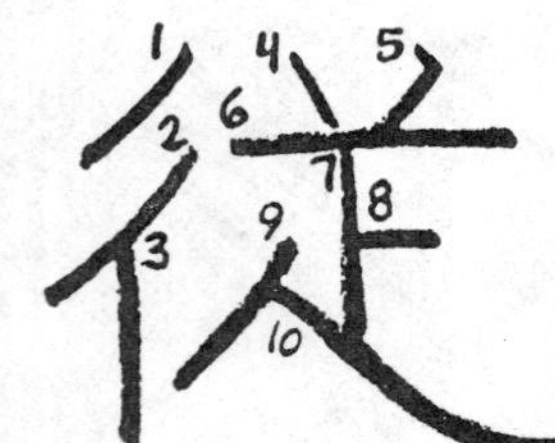

JŪ, SHITAGAU, TO OBEY, TO COMPLY WITH, TO SUBMIT TO, TO FOLLOW.

PERSONS 彳 OBEY, COMPLY WITH, SUBMIT TO, FOLLOW 従 LIKE GOATS, SHEEP 羊 RUNNING 走.

A Nation of Sheep: (book title).

Ein Schaf geht voraus und Alle folgen ihm.
One sheep goes ahead and all follow him.
German Proverb

N1613
ts'ung2
M6919
cóng
follow
comply
obey

	彳	従	走		羊	徒
PICTURE	STEP, WALK, FOLLOW R 60	TO OBEY, COMPLY WITH, SUBMIT TO, FOLLOW	TO RUN J 105	GOAT HORNS	SHEEP, GOAT R 123	COMPANION J 480

The Mysterious Stranger Mark Twain

Satan speaks: "Oh, it's true. I know your race. It is made up of sheep. It is governed by minorities, seldom or never by majorities. It suppresses its feelings and its beliefs and follows the handful that makes the most noise.

JUTSU, NOBERU, TO EXPRESS, TO SPEAK, TO RELATE.

RAD 162 STROKE 8 JME 809

述

THE USERS OF THE HEMP, SOMA 朮 (ETC.) WILL GO AND STOP ⻌ EXPRESSING, SPEAKING, RELATING 述.

La Belle Dame Sans Merci John Keats
She found me roots of relish sweet
And honey wild and manna dew,
And sure in language strange she said--
"I love thee true."

⻌	述	朮	丶	木	術
TO STOP & GO R 162	TO EXPRESS, TO SPEAK, TO RELATE	HEMP, HASHISH M 5886 (DOTTED EXT. OF TREE)	DOT R 4 ADDED DOT CREATES PODOPHYLLUM VERSIPELLE	TREE, WOOD R 75	ART, MAGIC, ARTIFICE J 636

N4675
shu4
M5890
shù
narrate
state
tell detail
transmit

Romeo and Juliet
And shrieks like mandrakes' torn out of the earth...

The hemp of the Scythians, the cannabis sativa of ancient China, and the mandrake of Pliny, Isodorus, and Rachel produced babblings, prophesies, and sexual encounters credited to the mannikin's rootlike powers.

JUN, INNOCENCE, PURITY.

RAD 120 STROKE 10 JME 810

純

INNOCENT, PURE 純 LIKE A SPROUT, A SPROUTING PLANT 屯 OR LIKE STRANDS 糸 OF SILK.

Patience Wm. Schwenck Gilbert
If you walk down Piccadilly with a poppy or a lily in your medieval hand, And everyone will say, As you walk your flowery way, "If he's content with a vegetable love which would certainly not suite ME, Why what a most particularly pure young man this pure young man must be!" ...a sentimental passion of a vegetable fashion...

	糸	純	屯	艸	艹
PICTURED COCOONS & THREADS	THREADS, STRINGS, SILK R 120	INNOCENCE, PURITY	SPROUT, SPROUTING PLANT R 45	GRASS R 140	GRASS R 140 ABBR.

N3509
shun2
M5930
chún
pure
simple
sincere
monochrome
unmixed

The simple test of pure silk is that when burned it leaves no ash.

Marvell To His Coy Mistress I would Love you ten years before the Flood, And you should, if you please, refuse Till the conversion of the Jews. My vegetable love should grow Vaster than empires, and more slow.

JME 811 · Stroke 5 · Rad 34

KING GYDES OF LYDIA

処

SHO, SHOSURU, TO MANAGE, TO DEAL WITH, TO SENTENCE, TO BEHAVE, TO CONDUCT ONESELF (WELL); TOKORO, PLACE.

PERSON 夂 WALKING 又 WITH A STICK ㇒ TAKES A SEAT 几 IN THE PLACE 処 WHERE HE MANAGES, DEALS WITH, SENTENCES, BEHAVES, CONDUCTS HIMSELF (WELL) 処.

N1162
ch'u4
M1407
chù
manage
decide
settle
dwell

冬 夂 処 几 机 売

冬	夂	処	几	机	売
WINTER J 120	STICK IN HAND WALK W/ STICK R 34	PLACE, TO MANAGE, TO DEAL WITH, TO SENTENCE, TO BEHAVE	SEAT, TABLE R 16 (BENT LEG IS PEG LEG, WOODEN OR CRIPPLE)	DESK N 2174 (WOODEN & PEG LEG)	TO SELL, SALE J 301 (SITTING SELLER = CRIPPLE AT PEG LEG DESK/TABLE)

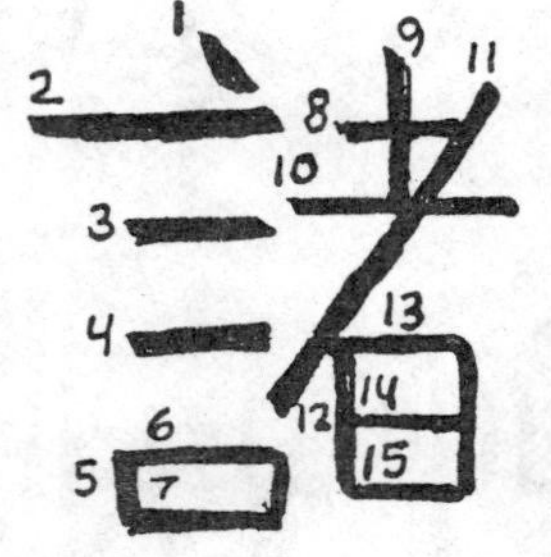

JME 812 · Stroke 15 · Rad 149

諸

SHO, (SEVERAL, MANY, VARIOUS).

THE WORDS 言 OF PERSONS 者 (INDICATE THAT THEY ARE) SEVERAL, MANY, VARIOUS 諸.

SOUND VIBES MAYAN CODEX

N4393
chu 1
M1362
zhū
all
every

言 諸 者 老 日 暑

言	諸	者	老	日	暑
SPEECH, WORDS J 392	SEVERAL, MANY, VARIOUS	PERSON J 235 (TUMPLINE BURDENED PERSON CHANTS)	OLD AGE, OLD J 541 (TUMPLINE BURDENED NEAR DEATH)	SUN J 11 (SUN OR PERSON SPEAKS CHANTS)	HOT J 247 (HOT SUN: TUMPLINE BURDENED PERSON IS CHANTING: AS THO SUN) ABOVE & BELOW

JO, DIVISION (IN MATH);
NOZOKU, TO REMOVE, TO ABOLISH, TO EXCLUDE.

RAD 170 STROKE 10 JME 813

THE MOUND 阝 OF THE NAIL BODIES 亅 DIVIDED 八 FROM 于 TIGHTLY 亼 BETWEEN THE LEGS 人 IS REMOVED, ABOLISHED, EXCLUDED 除, OR DIVIDED 除 (AS A REMAINDER).

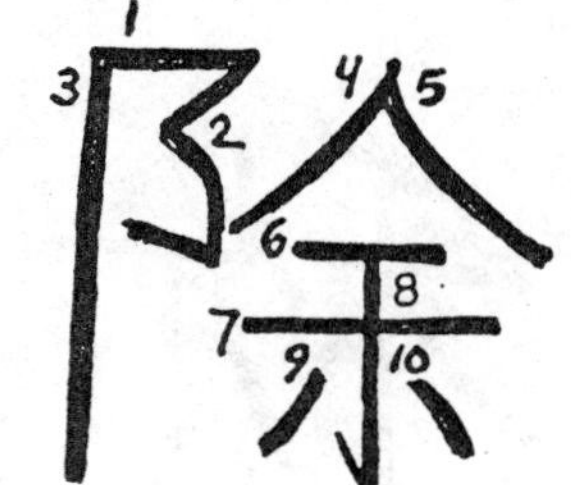

N4993
ch'u2
M1391
chú
to remove
do away w/

阝 MOUND R 170

除 DIVISION (MATH), TO REMOVE, TO ABOLISH, TO EXCLUDE

亼 TIGHTLY, JOINED

于 GOING, FROM N 5

八 EIGHT J 8 TO DIVIDE

亅 NAIL BODY N 5

SHŌ, MANEKU, TO BECKON TO, TO SUMMON, INVITE.

RAD 64 STROKE 8 JME 814

TO BECKON, TO SUMMON, TO INVITE 招 IS THE HAND 扌 CALLING, SENDING FOR, TO WEAR 召.

The Maneki-Neko, "Beckoning Cat," invites or beckons customers into a Japanese shop. The beckoning paw is raised with the palm and digits down in typical Japanese fashion. These cat figurines are amulets or good luck charms. They may be used as "kitty banks" and often have the kanji "Hundred Ten-Thousand Ryō on their front for profit and good fortune.

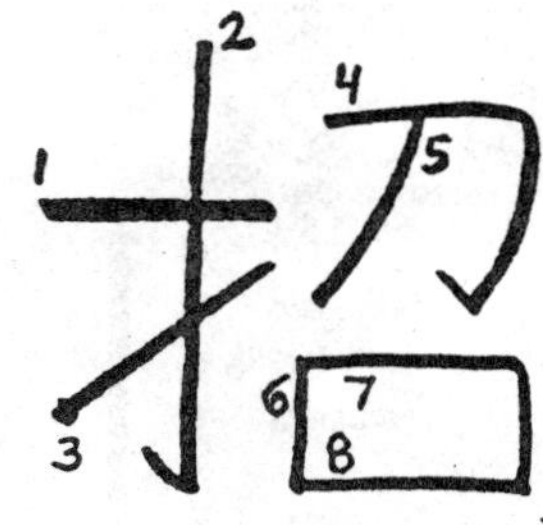

N1882
chao 1
M235
zhāo
beckon
call
proclaim

MANEKI-NEKO

扌 HAND R 64 ABBRE.

招 TO BECKON TO, TO SUMMON, TO INVITE

召 TO CALL, TO SEND FOR, TO WEAR N 668

刀 KNIFE, SWORD R 18

口 MOUTH J 30

百 J 130 HYAKU hundred

万 J 320 MAN 10,000

両 J 336 RYO gold coin

JME 815 STROKE 10 RAD 115

SHŌ, (TO PRAISE); SHŌ SURU, TO NAME, TO ENTITLE, TO PRETEND TO BE, TO PRAISE.

YOU 尓 ARE NAMED, ENTITLED, PRETEND TO BE, PRAISED 称 WITH GRAIN 禾 (ALLOTMENT).

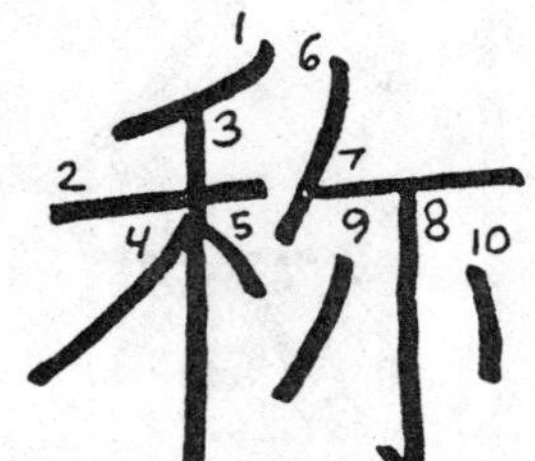

N3280
ch'eng 1
M383
chēng
praise

HORN (HEAD OF GRAIN, CORNUCOPIA)

木 TREE, WOOD R 75

禾 GRAIN, RICE R 115

称 TO PRAISE, TO NAME, TO ENTITLE, PRETEND TO BE

尓 THOU, YOU, SO, IN THAT WAY N 69

MAN R 9

SMALL R 42

JME 816 STROKE 12 RAD 149

SHŌ, (PROOF, EVIDENCE, TESTIMONY).

CORRECT, RIGHT 正 WORDS 言 ARE PROOF, EVIDENCE, TESTIMONY 証.

FERTILITY GOD MIN OF EGYPT

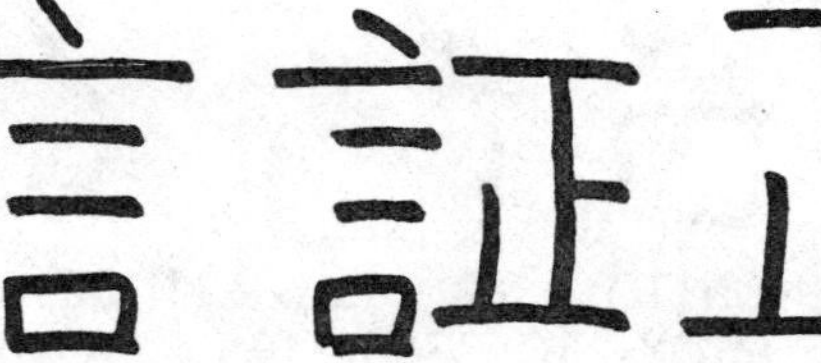

N4341
cheng4
M357
zhèng
evidence
proof
testify

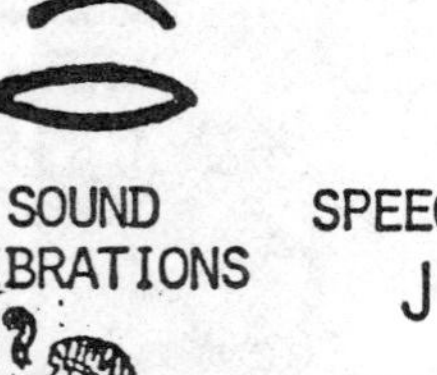

SOUND VIBRATIONS

言 SPEECH, WORDS J 149

証 PROOF, EVIDENCE, TESTIMONY

正 CORRECT, RIGHT

止 TO STOP J 220

上 ABOVE, TOP, UP J 20

SOUND VIBES MAYAN CODEX

JŌ, (ARTICLE, CLAUSE OF THE TREATY, LAW).

PERSON 夂 WITH A STICK ノ IN HAND 又 AND A POLE 木 (FEELING OUT AS IN A FORD THE NEGOTIATED) ARTICLES, CLAUSES OF THE TREATY, LAW 条.

RAD 34 STROKE 7 JME 817

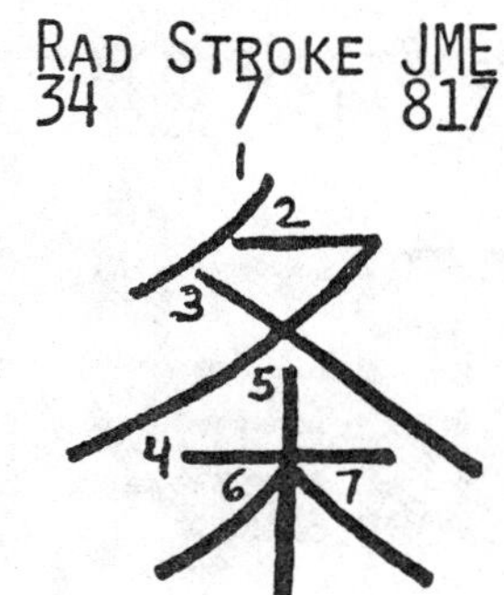

木	条	夂	冬	深
PICTURED TREE				
TREE, WOOD J 15	ARTICLE, TREATY CLAUSE, LAW	STICK IN HAND J 34	WINTER J 120	DEEP J 258

N1164
t'iao3
M6300
tiáo
length
section
clause
branch

ICE (TWO DOTS)

JŌ, CONDITION, CIRCUMSTANCES, LETTER.

THE DOG 犬 UNDER CONDITIONS, CIRCUMSTANCES 状 LEAVES A BILLET-DOUX OR FRENCH LETTER 状 ON THE LEFT-SIDED 丬 (TREE). HE IS A RIGHT-REAR-LEGGED DOG, NATURELLEMENT.

The dog's act is analogous to that of the person who leaves a scented or perfumed letter: simply another way of cocking a leg and leaving a personalized mark.

RAD 90 STROKE 7 JME 818

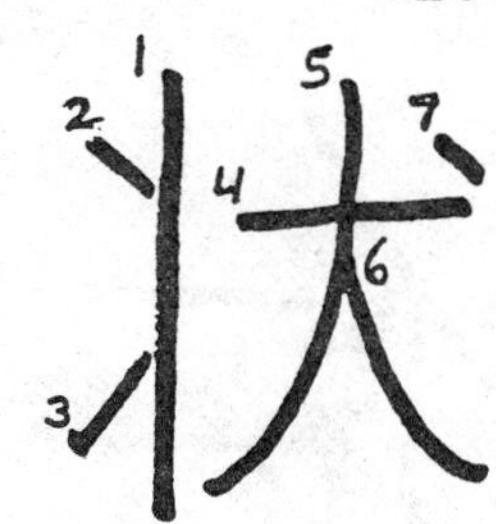

N839
chuang4
M1452
zhuàng
form
appear-ance
shape

片	爿	丬	状	犬	尨
RT. SIDE R 91	LEFT SIDE R 90	LEFT SIDE R 90 ABBRE. (OF TREE)	CONDITION, CIRCUMSTANCES, LETTER	DOG R 94 (RT. REAR LEGGED)	POODLE

A right-footed dog
A left-sided tree
A bow to you
Curtsy to me.

She flirts her skirt
He lifts a knee
And jets a squirt
Of yellow pee

A tree for you
A dog for me
Oh, we are a per-
Fect company.

LEFT-SIDED TREE IS ALSO A BED

JME 819 STROKE 18 RAD 128

SHOKU, EMPLOYMENT, WORK, DUTIES.

IN THE PROCESS OF WEAVING 織 WITH THE SOUND 音 OF THE WEAVER'S BEAM 戈, THE ONE WHO KNOWS, WRITES DOWN, DISTINGUISHES 識 SPEAKS 言 TO THE EMPLOYED 職 WITH WORK, DUTIES 職.

職

N3718
chih2
M990
zhí
govern
oversee
manage
direct

織	識	耳	職	音	戈
TO WEAVE, TEXTILE J 644	TO KNOW, TO WRITE DOWN, TO DISTINGUISH J 627	EAR J 26	EMPLOYMENT, WORK, DUTIES	SOUND J 50 (OF SHUTTLE)	SPEAR R 62 (WEAVER'S BEAM)

Leaves of Grass Walt Whitman
Out of the cradle endlessly rocking,
Out of the mocking-bird's throat, the musical shuttle,
Out of the Ninth-month midnight.

JME 820 STROKE 4 RAD 9

JIN, VIRTUE, BENEVOLENCE, HUMANITY.

PEOPLE, MAN 亻 BETWEEN THE DUALITY 二 (OF HEAVEN AND EARTH 二) HAVE VIRTUE, BENEVOLENCE, HUMANITY 仁. HEAVEN REFLECTED BY EARTH.

仁

Konjaku. Trans. by Yoshiko Dykstra
Confucius....began to preach, "Living through this life, one should have one's own moral principles which will determine one's appearance and mind. Today one has the heaven over one's head and the earth under one's feet. One should firmly uphold affairs in every direction while respecting superiors and showing mercy to inferiors....

N349
jen2
M3099
rén
benevo-
lence
charity
humanity
love

	亻	仁	二
PICTURE	PERSON, MAN R 9	VIRTUE, BENEVOLENCE, HUMANITY	TWO, HEAVEN & EARTH R 7

The Analects: The Master said: I am able to learn even when walking in the company of two other men. I copy the good points of the one and correct in myself the bad points of the other.

SUI, INFER, CONCLUDE, GUESS, RECOMMEND.

RAD 64 STROKE 11 JME 821

THE SHORT-TAILED BIRD 隹 (LIKE A CLIPPED GAME COCK) IS IN THE HAND 扌 (OF THE OWNER) WHO INFERS, CONCLUDES, GUESSES, RECOMMENDS 推

Gamecocks are constantly handled, spurs fastened, wings trimmed, tails cut down, and hackles and rump feathers shortened. Cockfighting has been popular in China, India, Persia, and Egypt for thousands of years as has hawking and falconry.

推

N1950
t'ui 1
M6564
tuì
to push
expel
decline
yield

PICTURED ARM

OLD KANJI

推 INFER, GUESS, CONCLUDE, RECOMMEND

隹 SHORT-TAILED BIRD R 172

PICTOGRAPH OF SHORT-TAILED BIRD

進 TO ADVANCE J 259

A thick glove or gauntlet is worn on the hand for the hawk. She is carried as much as possible and fed by hand. She is constantly caressed or stroked by a feather, and has a padded perch.

CHINESE BRONZE WINE JUG

ZE, (RIGHT, JUSTICE).

RAD 72 STROKE 9 JME 822

RIGHT, JUSTICE 是 IS THE RUNNING 走 LEG 足 OF THE SUN 日 (ON THE SUNDIAL).

Song Barton Booth
True as the needle to the pole,
Or as the dial to the sun.

Romeo and Juliet W.S.
NURSE. Is it good den?
MERCUTIO. 'Tis no less,
I tell you; for the
bawdy hand of the dial
is now upon the prick
of noon.

是

N2120
shih4
M5794
shì
yes
right
is (to be)

日 SUN R 72

是 RIGHT, JUSTICE

𧾷 FOOT IN MOTION R 103

定 TO BE DECIDED, SETTLED J 474

足 FOOT, LEG R 157

正 CORRECT, RIGHT J 46

Ah, Sun-flower Wm. Blake
Ah, Sun-flower! weary of time,
Who countest the steps of the Sun;
Seeking after that sweet golden clime,
Where the traveler's journey is done;

And Isaiah the prophet cried unto the Lord: and He brought the shadow ten degrees backward by which it had gone down in the dial of King Ahab. II Kings

JME 823 STROKE 8 RAD 18

SEI, (ORGANIZATION, LAWS).

SEI SURU, TO CONTROL, TO SUPPRESS, RESTRAIN.

THE (POLLING) KNIFE 刂 FOR THE BULL'S, COW'S 牛(HORNS) CONTROLS, SUPPRESSES, RESTRAINS 制 LIKE ORGANIZATION AND LAWS 制. THE KNIFE 刂 ALSO (CUTS) THE CLOTH 巾 (FOR CLOTHING) IN A CONTROLLED, SUPPRESSED, RESTRAINED 制 (WAY) AS WITH ORGANIZATION, LAWS 制.

N683
chih4
M986
zhì
regulate
govern
restrain

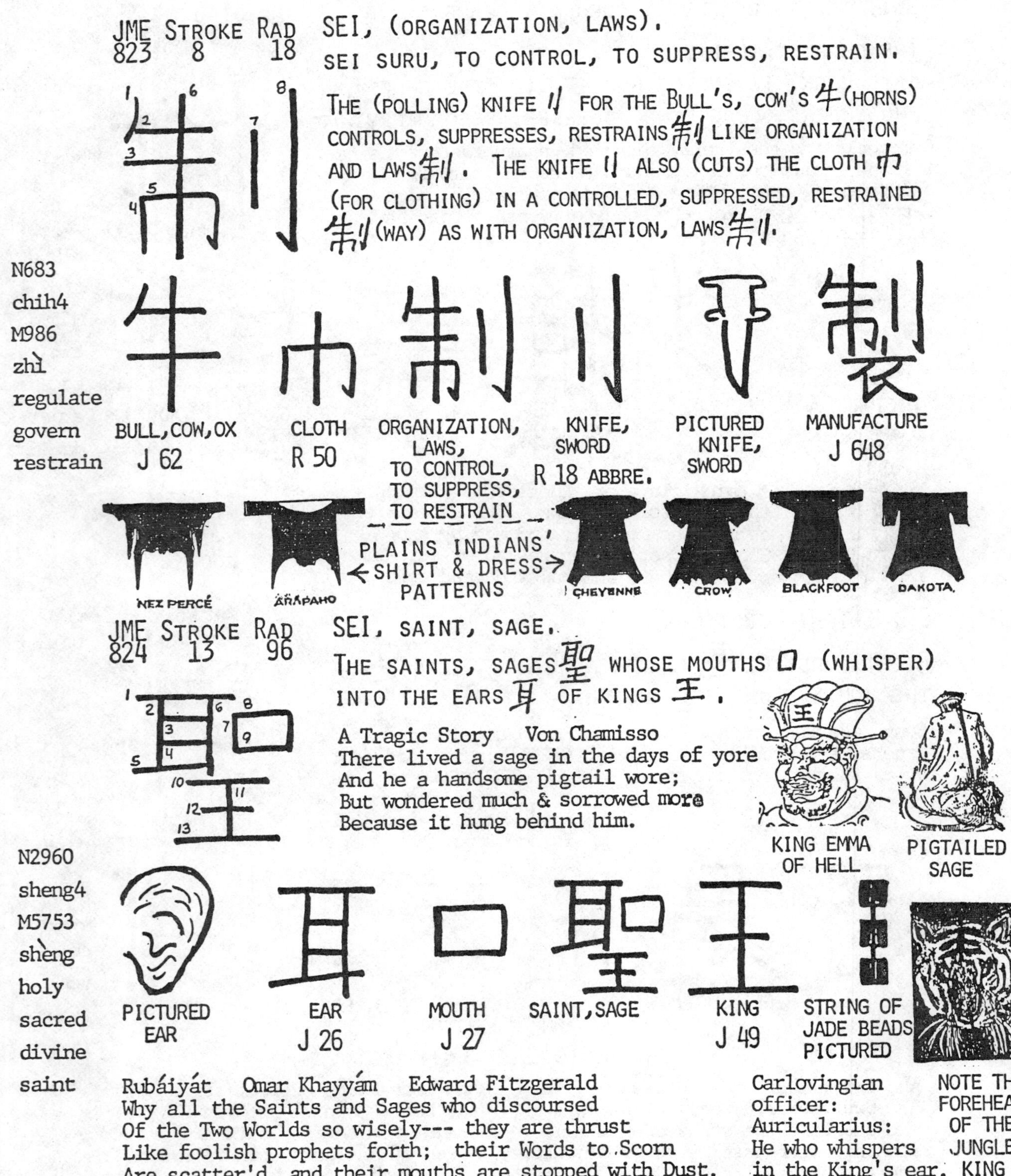

JME 824 STROKE 13 RAD 96

SEI, SAINT, SAGE.

THE SAINTS, SAGES 聖 WHOSE MOUTHS 口 (WHISPER) INTO THE EARS 耳 OF KINGS 王.

A Tragic Story Von Chamisso
There lived a sage in the days of yore
And he a handsome pigtail wore;
But wondered much & sorrowed more
Because it hung behind him.

N2960
sheng4
M5753
shèng
holy
sacred
divine
saint

Rubáiyát Omar Khayyám Edward Fitzgerald
Why all the Saints and Sages who discoursed
Of the Two Worlds so wisely--- they are thrust
Like foolish prophets forth; their Words to Scorn
Are scatter'd, and their mouths are stopped with Dust.

Carlovingian officer:
Auricularius:
He who whispers in the King's ear.

NOTE THE FOREHEAD OF THE JUNGLE KING

SEI; MAKOTO, TRUE, SINCERE.

RAD 149 STROKE 13 JME 825

THE WORDS 言 OF THE BECOME, COMPLETED 成 NAIL, SPIKE 丁 (SOLDIER) WITH HIS SPEAR 戈 ON THE CLIFF 厂 ARE TRUE, SINCERE 誠.

The Art of War Sun Tze
There is no joking in time of war.

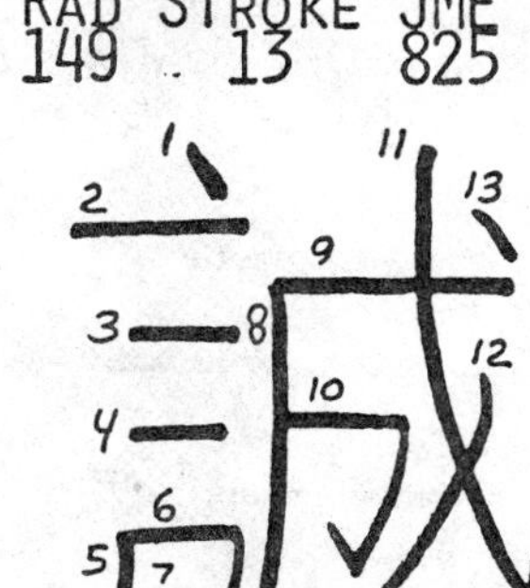

N4352
ch'eng2
M381
cheng
sincere
true
honest

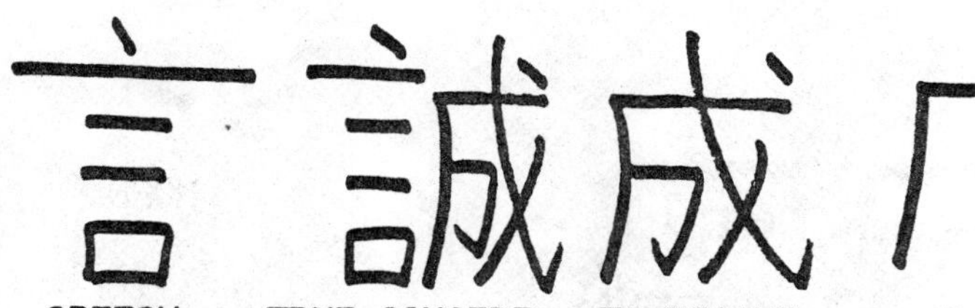

言 SPEECH, WORDS R 149 | 誠 TRUE, SINCERE | 成 TO BECOME, TO BE COMPLETED J 439 | 厂 CLIFF R 27 | 丁 ARCHAIC KANJI FOR NAIL, SPIKE (SOLDIER) 120 YDS. DIVISION OF A WARD OR TOWN J 473 | 戈 SPEAR R 62

ZEI, TAX.

RAD 115 STROKE 12 JME 826

THE TAX 税 FOR THE ELDER BROTHER 兄 MEANS EXCHANGING (CURRENCY) 兑 AND GRAIN 禾.

The Grain Tax Po Chü-i
The officer knocked on my gate at night.
His loud voice demanded the grain tax.
He wanted thirty bushels of grain, a cart load,
And still they shout that I have not paid in full.

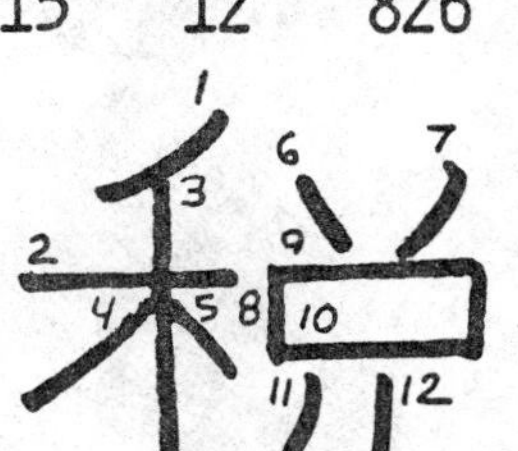

N3287
sui4
M5927
shùi
taxes
revenue

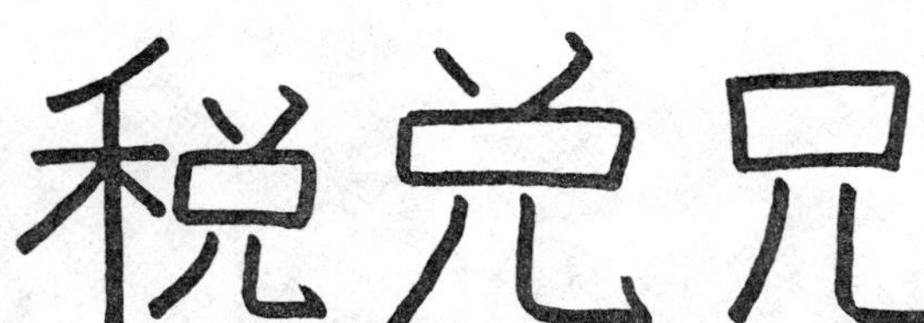

PICTURED GRAIN, RICE | 禾 GRAIN, RICE R 115 | 税 TAX | 兑 TO EXCHANGE (CURRENCY) N 582 | 兄 ELDER BROTHER J 199 | 丷 HORNS (COIFFURE)

JME 827 STROKE 6 RAD 135

ZETSU, SHITA, TONGUE.

THE TONGUE 舌 HAS A HORN- ノ LIKE TIP, A SHAFT | , MOTION 一, AND THE MOUTH 口 (FOR WITHDRAWAL).

Against whom make ye a wide mouth and draw out the tongue? Isaiah

The tongue is like a hand. The dog's tongue laps; the giraffe's tongue grasps; the toad's attacks.

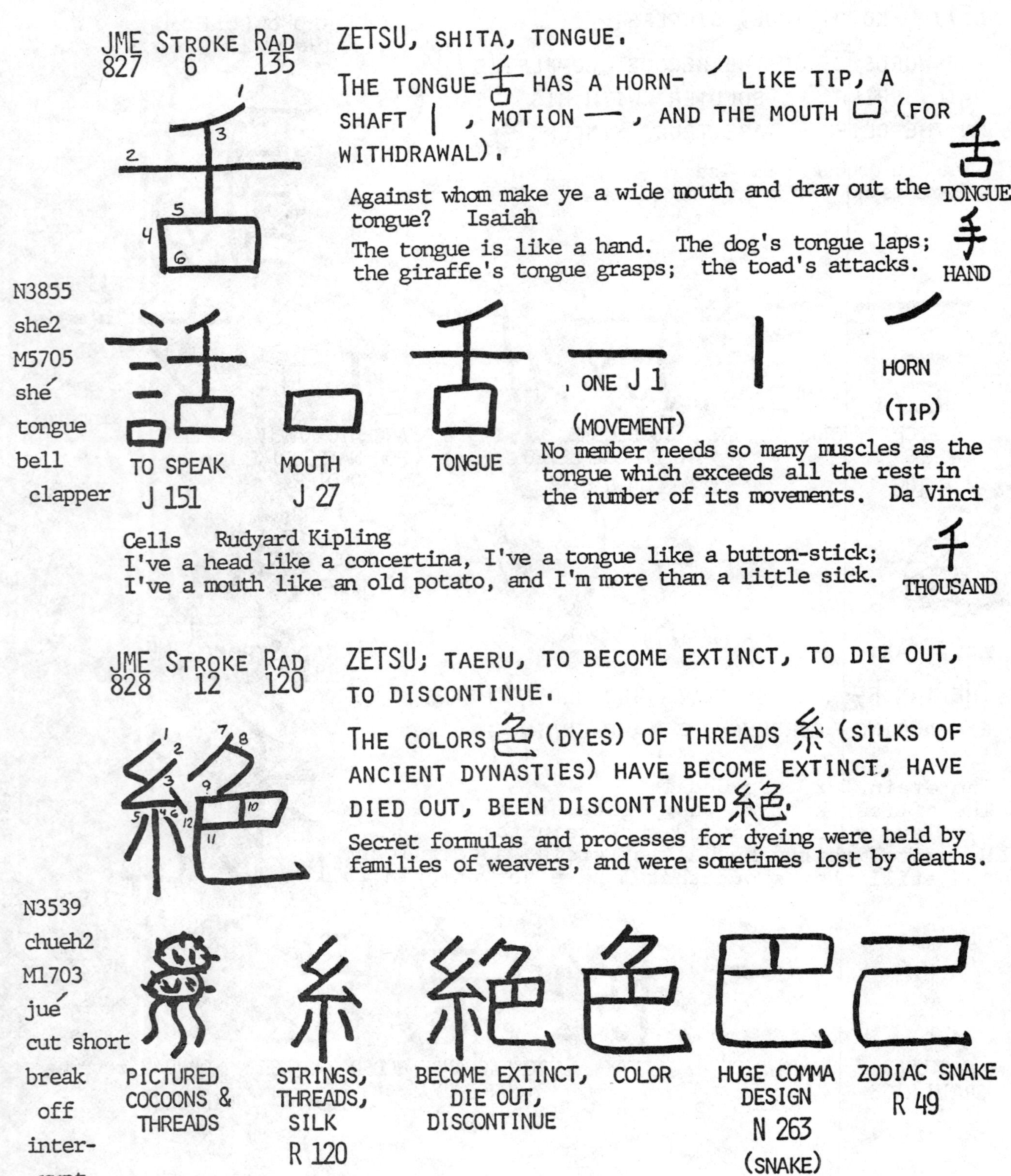

No member needs so many muscles as the tongue which exceeds all the rest in the number of its movements. Da Vinci

Cells Rudyard Kipling
I've a head like a concertina, I've a tongue like a button-stick;
I've a mouth like an old potato, and I'm more than a little sick.

JME 828 STROKE 12 RAD 120

ZETSU; TAERU, TO BECOME EXTINCT, TO DIE OUT, TO DISCONTINUE.

THE COLORS 色 (DYES) OF THREADS 糸 (SILKS OF ANCIENT DYNASTIES) HAVE BECOME EXTINCT, HAVE DIED OUT, BEEN DISCONTINUED 絶.

Secret formulas and processes for dyeing were held by families of weavers, and were sometimes lost by deaths.

SEN, TO SAY, TO STATE.

RAD 40 STROKE 9 JME 829

THE MOUTH 曰 SAYS, STATES 宣 UNDER THE ROOF 宀 AS DOES THE SUN 日 BETWEEN THE DUALITY 二 OF HEAVEN AND EARTH 二.

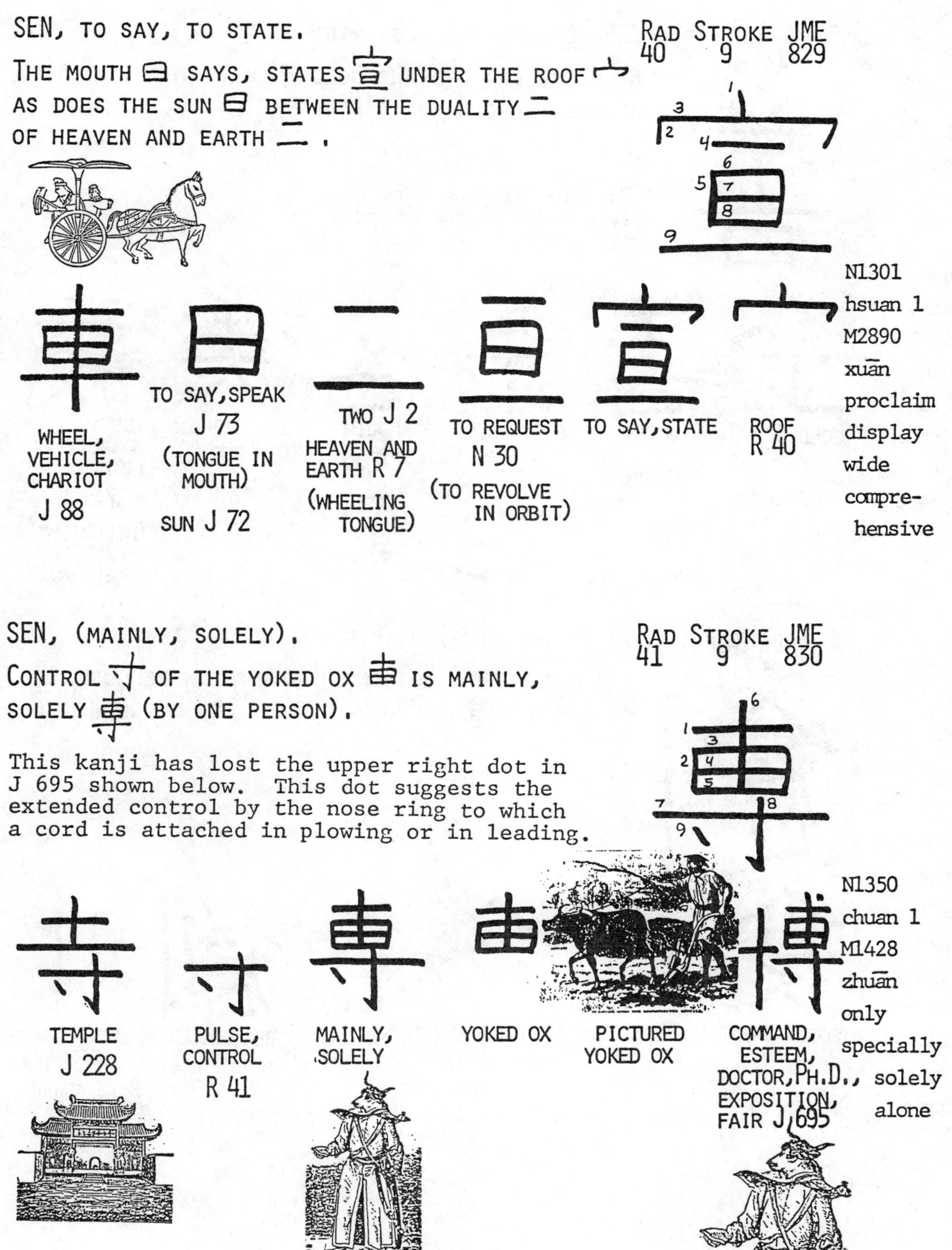

N1301
hsuan 1
M2890
xuān
proclaim
display
wide
compre-hensive

SEN, (MAINLY, SOLELY).

RAD 41 STROKE 9 JME 830

CONTROL 寸 OF THE YOKED OX 叀 IS MAINLY, SOLELY 専 (BY ONE PERSON).

This kanji has lost the upper right dot in J 695 shown below. This dot suggests the extended control by the nose ring to which a cord is attached in plowing or in leading.

N1350
chuan 1
M1428
zhuān
only
specially
solely
alone

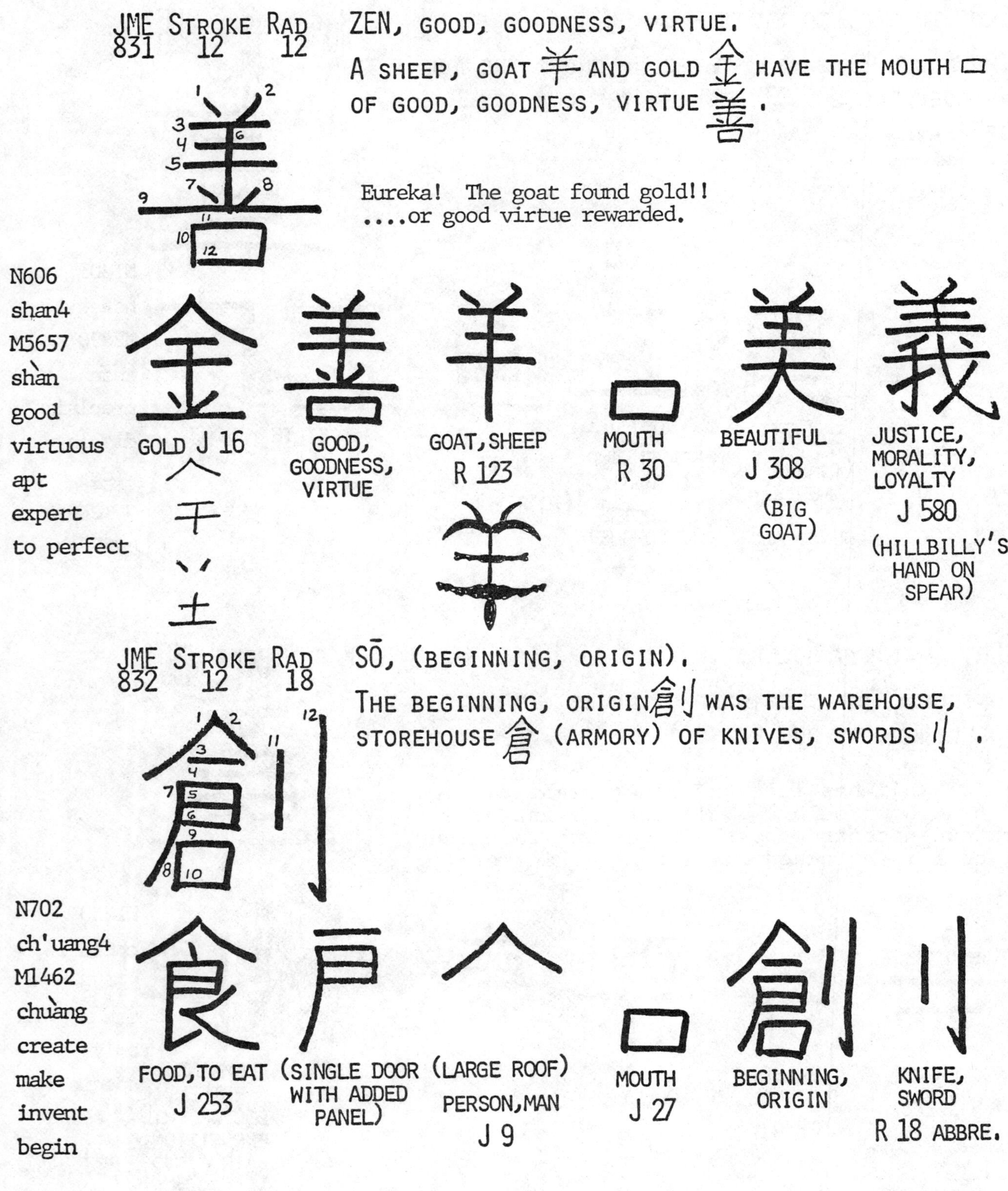

JME 831 | STROKE 12 | RAD 12

ZEN, GOOD, GOODNESS, VIRTUE.

A SHEEP, GOAT 羊 AND GOLD 金 HAVE THE MOUTH 口 OF GOOD, GOODNESS, VIRTUE 善.

Eureka! The goat found gold!!
....or good virtue rewarded.

N606
shan4
M5657
shàn
good
virtuous
apt
expert
to perfect

金 GOLD J 16

善 GOOD, GOODNESS, VIRTUE

羊 GOAT, SHEEP R 123

口 MOUTH R 30

美 BEAUTIFUL J 308 (BIG GOAT)

義 JUSTICE, MORALITY, LOYALTY J 580 (HILLBILLY'S HAND ON SPEAR)

JME 832 | STROKE 12 | RAD 18

SŌ, (BEGINNING, ORIGIN).

THE BEGINNING, ORIGIN 創 WAS THE WAREHOUSE, STOREHOUSE 倉 (ARMORY) OF KNIVES, SWORDS 刂.

N702
ch'uang4
M1462
chuàng
create
make
invent
begin

食 FOOD, TO EAT J 253

戸 (SINGLE DOOR WITH ADDED PANEL)

人 (LARGE ROOF) PERSON, MAN J 9

口 MOUTH J 27

創 BEGINNING, ORIGIN

刂 KNIFE, SWORD R 18 ABBRE.

833

ZŌ, KURA, STOREHOUSE, WAREHOUSE;
ZŌ SURU, TO HIDE, TO HAVE, TO OWN, TO KEEP.

RAD 140 STROKE 15 JME 833

FODDER 艹 IS IN 蔵 THE STOREHOUSE, WAREHOUSE 蔵 LIKE THE CLIFF 厂 WHERE THE RETAINER, SUBJECT 臣 HOLDS 蔵 THE SPEARS 戈.

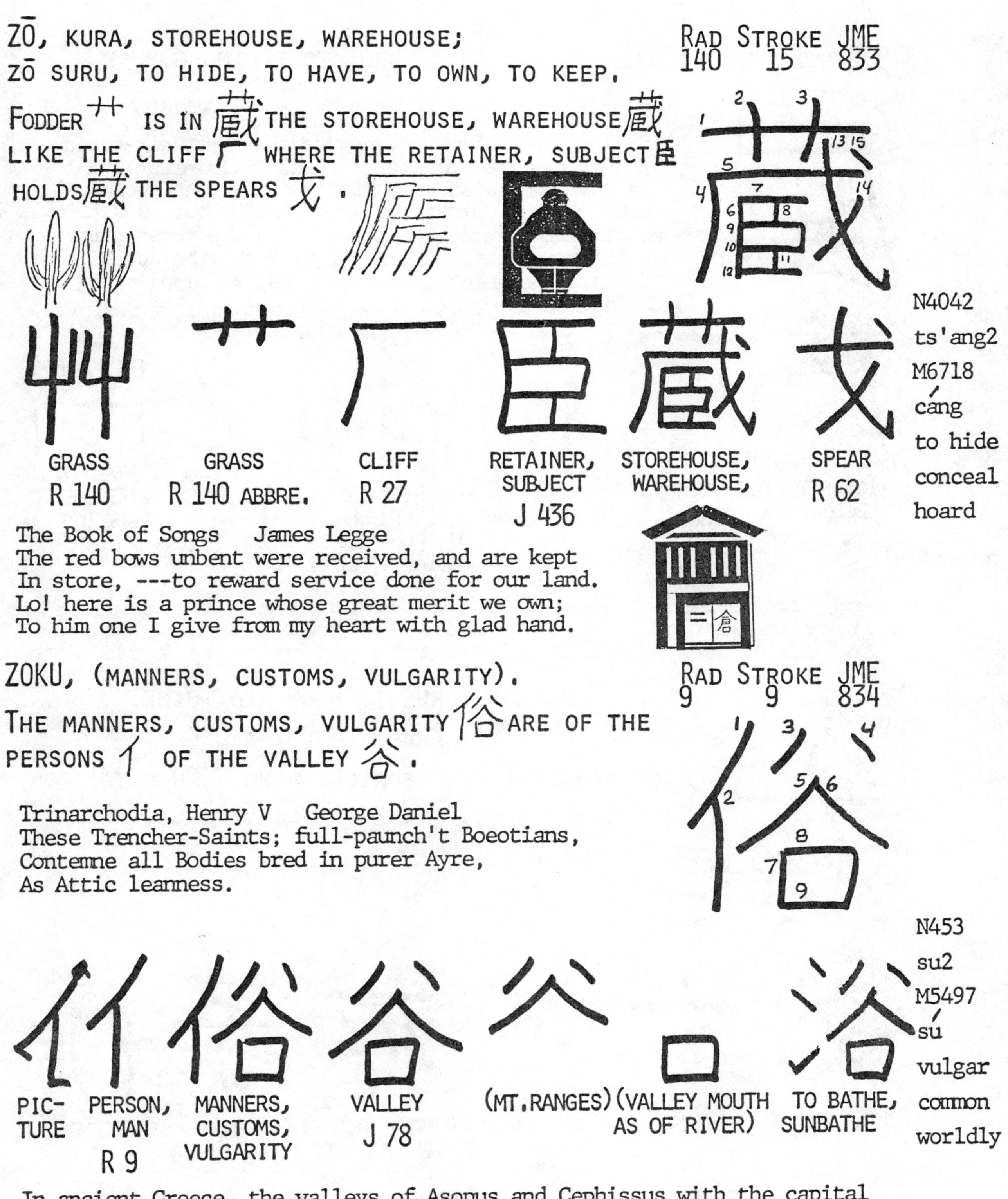

The Book of Songs James Legge
The red bows unbent were received, and are kept
In store, ---to reward service done for our land.
Lo! here is a prince whose great merit we own;
To him one I give from my heart with glad hand.

ZOKU, (MANNERS, CUSTOMS, VULGARITY).

RAD 9 STROKE 9 JME 834

THE MANNERS, CUSTOMS, VULGARITY 俗 ARE OF THE PERSONS 亻 OF THE VALLEY 谷.

Trinarchodia, Henry V George Daniel
These Trencher-Saints; full-paunch't Boeotians,
Contemne all Bodies bred in purer Ayre,
As Attic leanness.

In ancient Greece, the valleys of Asopus and Cephissus with the capital of Thebes constituted the country of Boeotia. Among the Greeks, the people had a reputation for boorishness and dullness in the same way as we speak of Polish jokes.

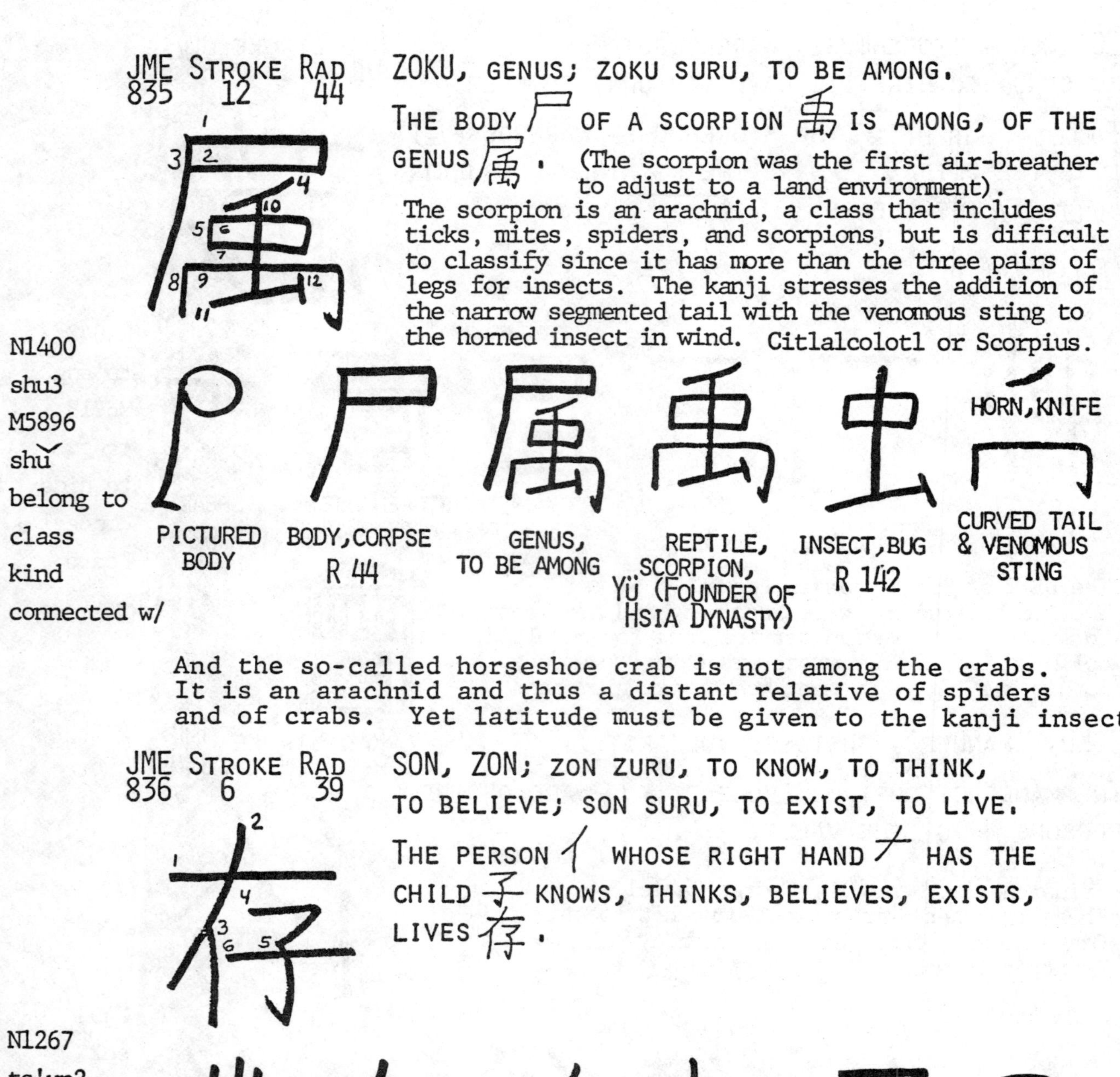

JME	STROKE	RAD
835	12	44

屬

ZOKU, GENUS; ZOKU SURU, TO BE AMONG.

THE BODY 尸 OF A SCORPION 禹 IS AMONG, OF THE GENUS 属. (The scorpion was the first air-breather to adjust to a land environment). The scorpion is an arachnid, a class that includes ticks, mites, spiders, and scorpions, but is difficult to classify since it has more than the three pairs of legs for insects. The kanji stresses the addition of the narrow segmented tail with the venomous sting to the horned insect in wind. Citlalcolotl or Scorpius.

N1400
shu3
M5896
shǔ
belong to
class
kind
connected w/

PICTURED BODY — BODY, CORPSE R 44 — GENUS, TO BE AMONG — REPTILE, SCORPION, YÜ (FOUNDER OF HSIA DYNASTY) — INSECT, BUG R 142 — HORN, KNIFE — CURVED TAIL & VENOMOUS STING

And the so-called horseshoe crab is not among the crabs. It is an arachnid and thus a distant relative of spiders and of crabs. Yet latitude must be given to the kanji insect.

JME	STROKE	RAD
836	6	39

存

SON, ZON; ZON ZURU, TO KNOW, TO THINK, TO BELIEVE; SON SURU, TO EXIST, TO LIVE.

THE PERSON 亻 WHOSE RIGHT HAND ナ HAS THE CHILD 子 KNOWS, THINKS, BELIEVES, EXISTS, LIVES 存.

N1267
ts'un2
M6891
cún
keep
file
exist

ARCHAIC KANJI FOR HAND — RT. HAND — PERSON, MAN J 30 — TO KNOW, THINK, BELIEVE, EXIST, TO LIVE — CHILD J 31 — PICTURED CHILD

SON, LOSS, HANDICAP, DISADVANTAGE;
SON SURU, TO SUFFER A LOSS.

RAD 64 STROKE 13 JME 837

THE LOSS, HANDICAP, DISADVANTAGE SUFFERED 損 FROM THE MEMBER, OFFICIAL, ONE IN CHARGE 員 WITH A HAND 扌 IN THE COWRIES 貝 (TILL).

損

扌 損 員 口 貝

PICTURED HAND, ARM

HAND R 64 ABBRE.

LOSS, HANDICAP, DISADVANTAGE,

MEMBER, OFFICIAL, ONE IN CHARGE

MOUTH J 27

SEA SHELL R 154

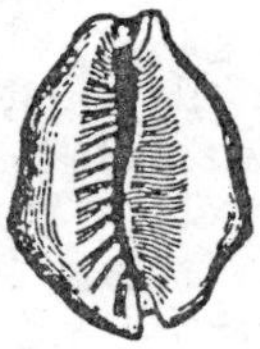

N1979
sun3
M5548
sǔn
injure
destroy
spoil
injury
disad-
vantage

SON, ZON; TATTOI, PRECIOUS, VALUABLE, NOBLE;
TATTOBU, TO VALUE, TO ESTEEM 尊

RAD 12 STROKE 12 JME 838

THE CHIEF, HEADMAN 酋 CONTROLS 寸 THE PRECIOUS, VALUABLE, NOBLE, ESTEEMED 尊 SAKE 酒 AS WELL AS THE FERMENTING LIQUOR 酉 AND (SACRIFICIAL) ZODIAC COCK 酉.

尊

(TEMPLE IS THE PULSE OF THE LAND)

(BODY CONTROLLING PULSE IS ONE INCH FROM THE HAND)

(HORNED CHIEF CONTROLS THE VALUED SAKE)

(HORNED CHIEF FERMENTS THE LIQUOR, SAKE)

(COCK CONTROLS HATCHING EGGS)

寺 寸 尊 酋 酉 酒

TEMPLE J 228

PULSE, TO CONTROL R 41

PRECIOUS, VALUABLE, NOBLE, TO VALUE, TO ESTEEM

CHIEF, HEADMAN N 593

ZODIAC COCK, FERMENTING LIQUOR, R 164

SAKE, SAKA J 422 (SAKE JUG SPLASHES)

N607
tsun 1
M6884
zūn
honorable
to honor
venerate

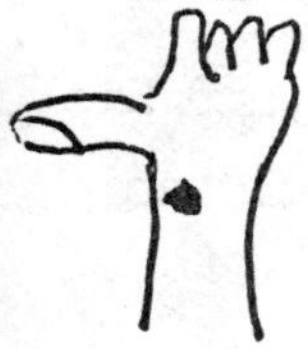

JME STROKE RAD
839 9 162

TAI, SHIRIZOKU., TO RETREAT, TO WITHDRAW, TO RECEDE, TO RETIRE IV; SHIRIZOKERU, TO REPEL, TO EXPEL, TO DRIVE AWAY, REJECT TV.

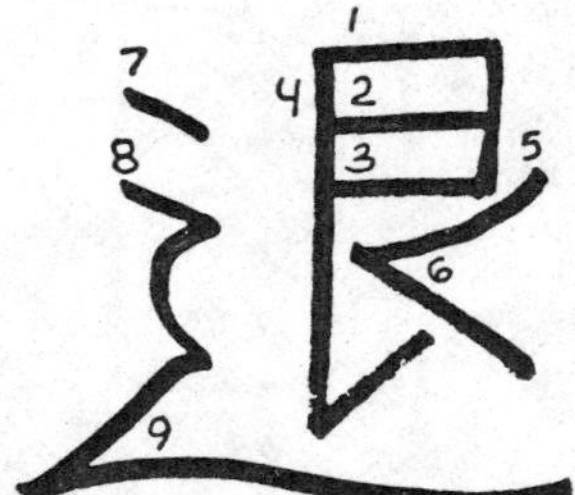

ONE STOPS AND GOES 辶 WITH WHAT IS GOOD 艮 IN RETREATING, WITHDRAWING, RECEDING, RETIRING, REPELLING, EXPELLING, DRIVING AWAY, REJECTING 退. (RETREATING OR DRIVEN BACK TO ONE'S ROOTS).

N4684
t'ui4
M6568
tuì
withdraw
retire
recede
decline
yield
send away

辵 TO STOP & GO R 162

辶 TO STOP & GO R 162 ABBRE.

退 TO RETREAT, TO WITHDRAW, TO RECEDE, TO REPEL, EXPEL

艮 GOOD R 138 (WHITE ROOTS ARE GOOD EATING, AS DAIKON)

根 ROOTS J 216 (WHITE ROOTS OF THE TREE)

進 TO ADVANCE, TO PROGRESS, TO PROCEED J 259

The Retreat Vaughan
Some men a forward motion love,
But I by backward steps would move,
And when the dust falls in the urn,
In that state I came, return.

JME STROKE RAD
840 14 61

TAI, APPEARANCE, CONDITION, FIGURE.

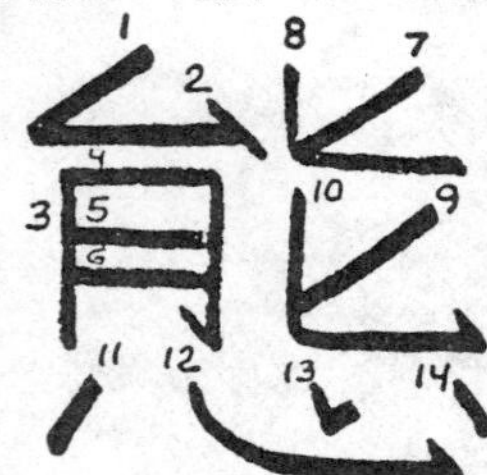

THE APPEARANCE, CONDITION, FIGURE 態 OF THE ONE WITH THE HEART, MIND, SPIRIT 心 WHO IS ABLE, CAN 能 AS IN THE NOH 能 DRAMA.

Macbeth Wm. Shakespear
Approach thou like the rugged Russian bear,
The arm'd rhinoceros, or the Hyrcan tiger,
Take any shape but that, and my firm nerves
Shall never tremble.

GRIZZLY PRINT

N1743
t'ai4
M6024
tài
manner
bearing
behavior
policy
attitude

心 HEART, MIND, SPIRIT J 95

態 APPEARANCE, CONDITION, FIGURE

能 HEAD CLAW BODY CLAW

能 ABILITY, THE NOH J 691

熊 BEAR N 2791

The Truce of the Bear
Horrible, hairy, human, with paws like hands in prayer,
Making his supplication rose Adam-zad the bear. Rudyard Kipling

Like man, the bear can walk on his hind legs with heel, sole, and five digits on the earth in planigrade fashion.

DAN; KOTOWARU, TO REFUSE, TO DECLINE, TO GIVE NOTICE, TO DISMISS, TO WARN; TATSU, TO SEVER, CUT OFF, INTERRUPT.

RAD	STROKE	JME
69	11	841

断

TO REFUSE, DECLINE, GIVE NOTICE, DISMISS, WARN, 断 IS TO SEVER, CUT OFF, INTERRUPT AS BY AN AXE 斤 THE RICE 米 (FOOD, INCOME) OF RECTITUDE L.

直 — TO CORRECT, TO CURE, TO SET RIGHT J 472

L — (RT.ANGLE, RECTITUDE)

米 — RICE J 135

断 — TO REFUSE, TO DECLINE, GIVE NOTICE, DISMISS, WARN, SEVER, CUT OFF, INTERRUPT

斤 — AXE R 69

PICTURED AXE

N078
tuan4
M6547
duàn
stop
cut off
sever
interrupt

CHŪ, LOYALTY, FIDELITY, FAITHFULNESS.

RAD	STROKE	JME
61	8	842

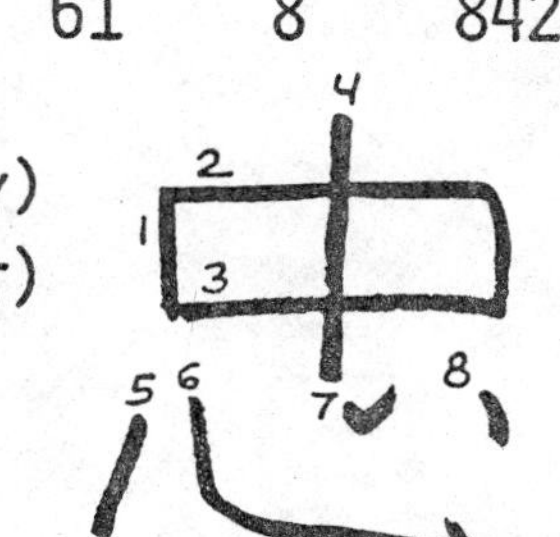

THE LOYALTY, FIDELITY, FAITHFULNESS 忠 OF THE HEART, MIND, SPIRIT 心 (IS EVEN TO DEATH AS BY) A SPIKE, ARROW | THROUGH THE SKULL 口 (TARGET)

Life's Mirror   Mary de Vere

There are loyal hearts, there are spirits brave,
There are souls that are pure and true;
Then give to the world the best you have,
And the best will come back to you.

OLD KANJI FOR HEART

HEART, MIND, SPIRIT J 95

忠 — LOYALTY, FAITHFULNESS

中 — MIDDLE, INSIDE, WITHIN J 23

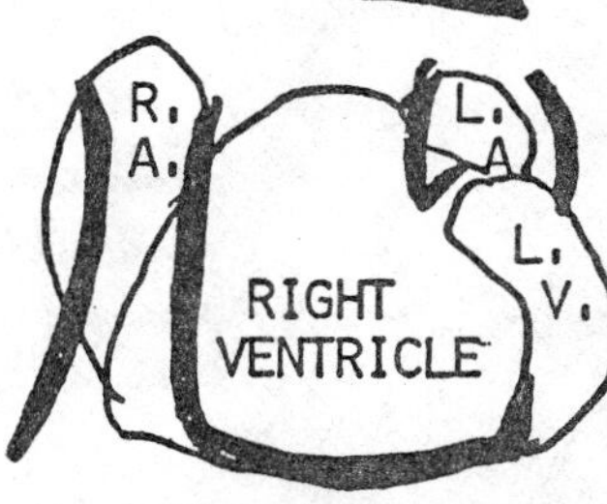

KANJI FOR HEART SUPERIMPOSED ON AURICLES AND VENTRICLES

N1653
chung 1
M1506
zhōng
loyal
patriotic
faithful
devoted

Marmion   Walter Scott

So faithful in love, and so dauntless in war,
There never was Knight like the young Lochinvar.

MARINE MOTTO
Semper fidelis!

JME 843 Stroke 11 Rad 140

CHO; ICHIJIRUSHII, PHENOMENAL, REMARKABLE, NOTABLE; ARAWASU, TO WRITE, TO PUBLISH.

THE PERSON 者 WHO WRITES, PUBLISHES 著 IN THE GRASS 艹 WRITING, (SOSHO 草書) IS PHENOMENAL, REMARKABLE, NOTABLE 著.

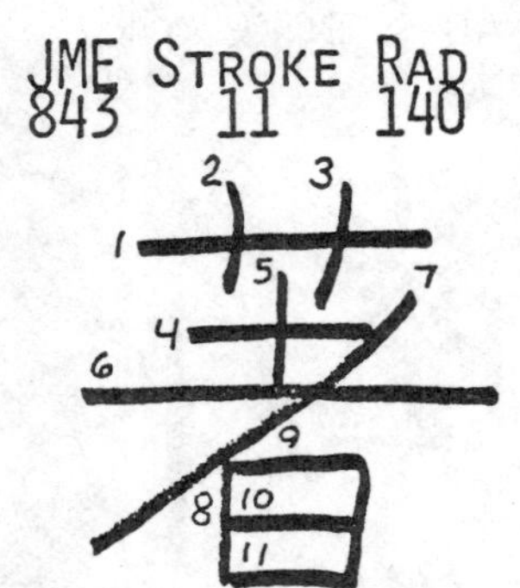

N3983
chu4
M1361
zhù
set forth
manifest
make known
write
(a book)

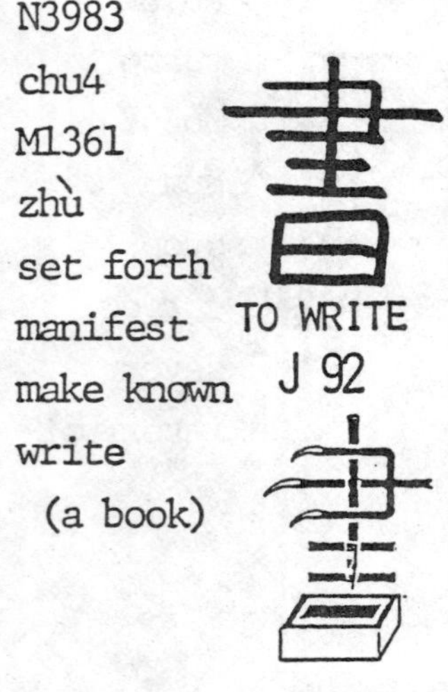

書 TO WRITE J 92

老 OLD MAN J 541 (LIKE A MUMMY CARRYING LOADS OF EARTH WITH A TUMPLINE)

者 PERSON J 235 (MOUTH CHANTS BEARS EARTH WITH TUMPLINE)

著 PHENOMENAL, REMARKABLE, NOTABLE, TO WRITE, PUBLISH ("GRASS WRITING" EQUALS THE ORAL DICTATION SPEED)

艹 GRASS R 140

草 GRASS J 106 (CURSIVE STYLE OF WRITING) (GRASS FLOURISHES IN TEN DAYS)

JME 844 Stroke 13 Rad 96

CHIN, WAGES, RENT, CHARGE, FEE.

THE STANDING MAN 亻 ENTRUSTS 任 A PERSON 壬 WITH DUTY 任 FOR WAGES, RENT, CHARGE, FEE 賃 IN COWRIE 貝.

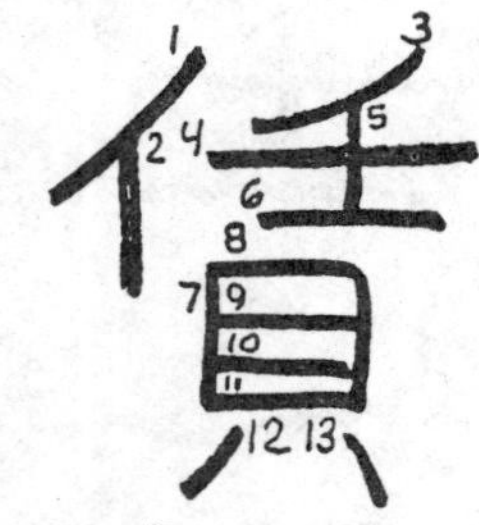

N4509
lin4
M3107
lìn
to rent
to lease

PICTURED SHELL

貝 SEA SHELL R 154

賃 WAGES, RENT, CHARGE, FEE

任 DUTY, TO ENTRUST J 688

壬 (BURDENED MAN, WAGE EARNER) R 96 VARIANT — BURDEN, POLE, MAN, POLE, BURDEN

CARRYING LOADS AT POLE'S ENDS

TEI, TO CARRY IN ONE'S HAND, TO TAKE ALONG.

RAD 64 STROKE 12 JME 845

To carry in one's hand, take along 提 right, justice 是 like a sundial 是 in one's hand 扌.

A Lecture Upon the Shadow John Donne
Walking here, two shadows went
Along with us, which we ourselves produced;
But, now the sun is just above our head
We do these shadows tread.

提

定 TO DECIDE, BE DECIDED J 474

扌 HAND, ARM J 64 ABBRE.

提 CARRY IN HAND, TAKE ALONG

是 RIGHT, JUSTICE J 822 (SUNDIAL)

走 TO RUN

日 SUN J 11

N1967
t'i2
M6233
tí
left in one's hand
raise
pull up
pick up

SUNDIAL

My Shadow R.L. Stevenson
I have a little shadow that goes in and out with me,
And what can be the use of him is more than I can see;
He is very, very like me from the heels up to the head;
And I see him jump before me when I jump into my bed.

TEI, (DEGREE, LAW, RULE).

RAD 115 STROKE 12 JME 846

The degree, law, rule 程 of the king 王 offers, presents 呈 peace, harmony 和 (grain to the mouths of the people).

程

N3285
ch'eng2
M375
chéng
journey
road
career

和 PEACE, HARMONY J 338

禾 GRAIN R 115

程 DEGREE, LAW, RULE

呈 TO OFFER, TO PRESENT N 895

王 KING J 49

口 MOUTH J 27 (CASKET)

JME 847 | STROKE 10 | RAD 44

TEN, TO EXPAND, TO OPEN, TO UNROLL.

展

HANDS 廾 EXPAND, OPEN, UNROLL 展 CLOTH, CLOTHING 衣 AGAINST THE BODY 尸 (IN FITTING OR MEASURING).

Anthropological Papers of the American Museum of Natural History
The concept of tailoring or cutting a garment to follow the lines of the shoulder and trunk is found in America only among the coat-wearing tribes such as the Eskimo and the Algonkin. The idea tends to spread by increasing contact with Europeans.

N1396
chan3
M139
zhàn
to open
unroll
spread
out

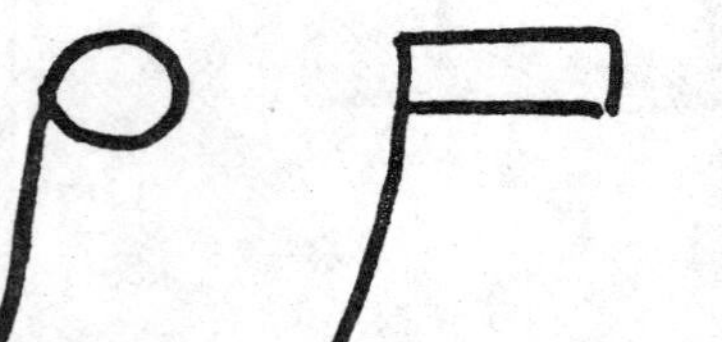

PICTURED BODY | BODY, CORPSE J 44 | TO EXPAND, TO OPEN, TO UNROLL | (HANDS) GRASS | (CLOTHES) | CLOTHES R 145

In the Old World tailoring appears again among the more primitive peoples of the north, but in historic peoples first among the Chinese. Its appearance in Western Europe is relatively recent. Use of the toga and the poncho were due to the limitations of the weaving process and to the unavoidable rectangular textiles. The Chinese escaped by tailoring.

JME 848 | STROKE 10 | RAD 42

TŌ, PARTY, FACTION.

党

THE PARTY, FACTION 党 IS OF ELDER BROTHERS 兄 IN A HALL, TEMPLE 堂.

N1363
tang3
M6094/5
dǎng
clique
party
faction
assn.

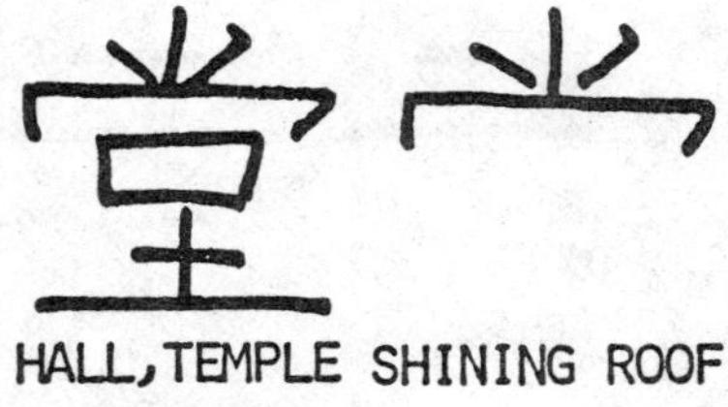

HALL, TEMPLE J 486 | SHINING ROOF | PARTY, FACTION | ELDER BROTHER J 199

TŌ; UTSU, ATTACK, DEFEAT, CONQUER.

RAD 149 STROKE 10 JME 849

TO ATTACK, DEFEAT, CONQUER 討 IS TO CONTROL 寸 WITH WORDS 言.

Attack, defeat, and conquest by the Astecs and their contemporary neighbors were largely to secure victims in a controlled or regulated way for blood sacrifices.

SOUND VIBRATIONS

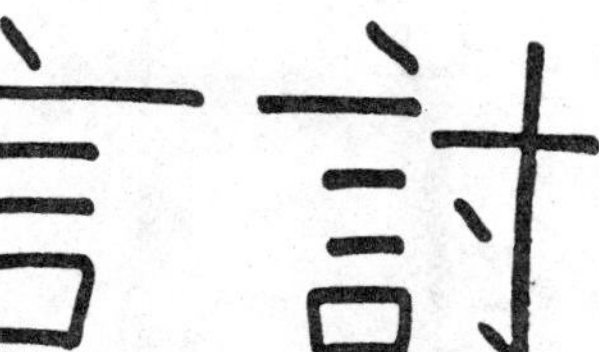
SPEECH, WORDS R 149

TO ATTACK, TO DEFEAT, TO CONQUER

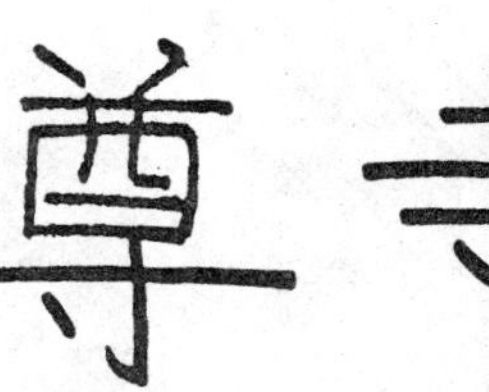
PULSE, TO CONTROL R 41

NOBLE, VALUABLE, TO RESPECT J 838

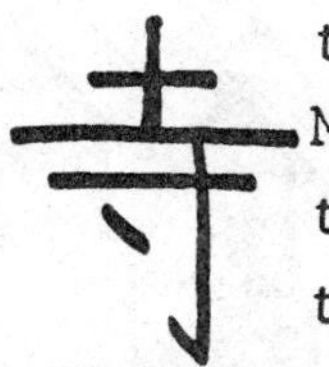
TEMPLE J 228

N4316 t'ao3 M6157 tǎo to beg demand to dun punish exter-minate

MAYAN SOUND VIBRATIONS SHOWN BY THE CURVED NOTES

CONTROLLED DEATH OF DEFEATED VICTIM

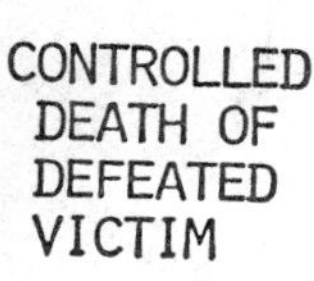
TEMPLE OF CHU KO LIANG (LI)

TOKU, BENEFIT, PROFIT, ADVANTAGE.

RAD 60 STROKE 11 JME 850

THE BENEFIT, PROFIT, ADVANTAGE 得 IS TO THE STEPPING, FOLLOWING 彳 (ONES WHO HAVE THE) CONTROL, MEASURE 寸 IN THE DAWN, MORNING 旦.

Early to bed and early to rise
Makes a man healthy, wealthy, and wise.

Morgenstunde hat Geld im Munde.

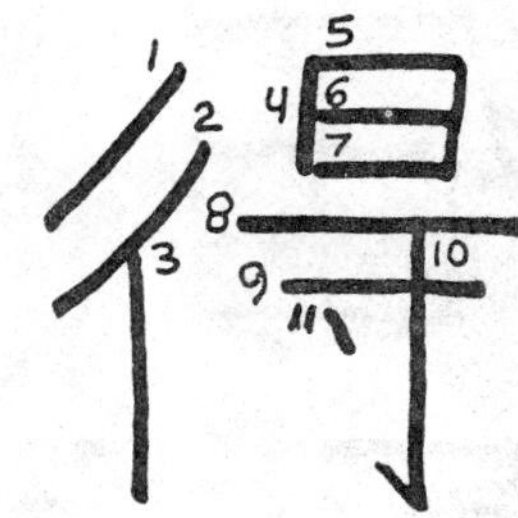

PIC-TURE

PERSON, MAN R 9

BENEFIT, PROFIT, ADVANTAGE

DAWN, MORNING N 2098 (SUN OVER HORIZON)

SUN R 72

ONE J 1 (HORIZON)

CONTROL, MEASURE R 41

N1622 te2 M6161 dé virtue goodness

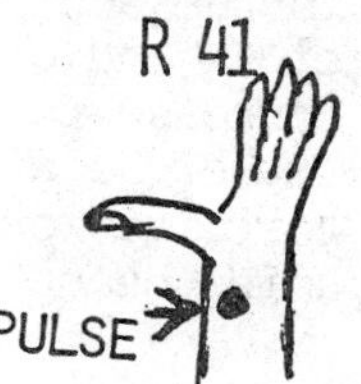

JME 851 | STROKE 14 | RAD 60

TOKU, VIRTUE, GOODNESS.

A HEART, MIND, SPIRIT 心 OF VIRTUE, GOODNESS 德 (VERIFIED BY) TEN 十 PAIRS OF EYES 目 AS MEN FOLLOW 彳.

德

N1633
te2
M6162
dé
virtue
goodness

彳 PICTURE — 彳 TO STEP, FOLLOW — 德 VIRTUE, GOODNESS — 心 HEART, MIND, SPIRIT J 95 — 目 EYES — 十 TEN J 10 — 直 TRUTH, REALITY, UPRIGHT J 438

R.A. VLA R.V. L.V.

JME 852 | STROKE 8 | RAD 44

TODOKU, TO REACH, TO ARRIVE;
TODOKERU, TO FORWARD, TO REPORT.

TO FORWARD, TO REPORT 届 THAT THE BODY 尸 OF REASON, SIGNIFICANCE 由 (A TORTOISE FOR DIVINATION) REACHED, ARRIVED 届.

届

N1385
chieh4
chiai4
M636
jiè
arrive
to reach
a limit
a term

尸 BODY, CORPSE R 44 — 届 TO REACH, TO ARRIVE, TO FORWARD, TO REPORT — 由 SIGNIFICANCE, REASON J 325 (TORTOISE IS ALIVE) — 油 OIL J 522 (AS OF THE TURTLE) — 界 WORLD J 170 (TORTOISE'S TECTONIC PLATES) — 甲 PLASTRON, ARMOR N 92 (DEAD TORTOISE IS INVERTED)

Chuang Tzu was fishing in the P'u River when two officials arrived from the King of Ch'u. The message reaching Chuang Tzu asked him to administer the Kingdom of Ch'u. Chuang Tzu continued to hold his fishing pole and did not turn his head. He said, "I have heard that in the ancestral temple of Ch'u there is a dead tortoise wrapped in cloth and placed in a casket for three thousand years. Would this tortoise rather be dead and have its shell honored thus or would it rather be alive, wagging its tail in the mud?" They answered, "The tortoise would rather wag its tail in the mud." "Forward the report," said Chuang Tzu, "That I also will wag my tail in the mud."

NAN, TROUBLE, DIFFICULTY, DISASTER; KATAI, DIFFICULT, IMPOSSIBLE.

RAD 172 STROKE 18 JME 853

SHORT-TAILED BIRDS 隹 ARE IN IMPOSSIBLE DIFFICULTY, DISASTER 難 IN SUNDRIED LOESS 堇 (WITHOUT WATER).

Cymbeline Wm. Shakespear
Golden lads and girls all must,
As chimney-sweepers, come to dust.

漢 勤 堇 難 隹

CHINA, MALE SUFFIX J 572 — SERVICE, DUTY, TO SERVE, FILL A POST — SUN-DRIED LOESS, CLAY, YELLOW LOAM M 1065 — TROUBLE, DIFFICULTY, DISASTER, IMPOSSIBLE, DIFFICULT — SHORT-TAILED BIRD R 172 — OLD KANJI FOR SHORT-TAILED BIRD

N5038
nan2
M4625
nán
difficult
grievous
troublesome

The Ballad of Endless Woe Po Chu-i trans. by W.J.B. Fletcher
The yellow dust is scattered wide,
And desolate the wind,
As up a spiral bridge of cloud
She leaves the earth behind.

NI, TWO (LEGAL USE), SECOND.

RAD 1 STROKE 6 JME 854

SECOND, TWO 弐 (FOR LEGAL USE) IS TWO 二 SPEARS 戈. ONE STROKE HAS BEEN MOVED TO THE UPPER LEFT AS WITH THE SPEAR IN JME 798 弋.

I or eye or ein is me;
Tu or du or you is ni;
He or she is three or C:
Draust bist du
Und hier sind we! A.D. Counting Rhymes.

武 二 弐 弋 戈

MILITARY ART, " POWER — TWO J 2 — TWO (LEGALESE), SECOND — SPEAR R 62 (STROKE MOVED) — SPEAR R 62 — PICTURED SPEAR

N32
erh4
M1752
èr
two (legal or acctng)

Eine, meine, meena, mu;
We are three, but you are two;
I and erh, and san, shih, wu! A.D. Counting Rhymes.

JME 855 STROKE 14 RAD 149

認

NIN; MITOMERU, TO WITNESS, TO SIGHT, TO DISCERN, TO APPROVE, TO JUDGE.

WORDS 言 OF THE HEART, MIND, SPIRIT 心 LIKE LIKE THE BLADE, EDGE, SWORD 刃 WITNESS, SIGHT, DISCERN, APPROVE, JUDGE 認

CUTTING EDGE IS EXT. OF SWORD

R.A. L.A. R.V. L.V.

N4370
jen4
M3113
rèn
recognize
know
confess
acknow-
ledge

言	認	忍	刃	丶 DOT R 4 / 刀	心
WORDS, SPEECH R 149	TO WITNESS, TO SIGHT, TO DISCERN, TO APPROVE, TO JUDGE	TO BEAR, TO ENDURE, TO HIDE (SELF) N 1648	BLADE, EDGE, SWORD N 152 (BLADE IS DOTTED EXT. OF SWORD)	KNIFE, SWORD R 18	HEART, MIND, SPIRIT J 95

JME 856 STROKE 10 RAD 120

納

NA, NŌ, TŌ; OSAMERU, TO OBTAIN, TO PAY, TO SUPPLY, TO DEDICATE, TO ACCEPT

TO OBTAIN, TO PAY, TO SUPPLY, TO DEDICATE, TO ACCEPT 納 STRINGS 糸 (OF CASH, COWRIES) FOR OR FROM WITHIN, INSIDE, THE HOME 内.

N2547
na4
M4607
nà
give
receive
enter
insert

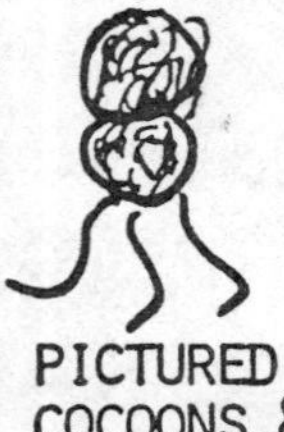
PICTURED COCOONS & STRINGS

糸	納	内	肉
THREADS, STRINGS, SILK R 120	TO OBTAIN, PAY, TO SUPPLY, TO DEDICATE, TO ACCEPT	WITHIN, INSIDE, HOME J 489	MEAT J 297 R 130

PICTURED MEAT HANGS IN FREEZER

HA, (PA), GROUP, PARTY, SECT, FACTION, SCHOOL.

RAD 85 STROKE 9 JME 857

LIKE THE WATER 氵 (SPLASHING AND FLOWING) FROM THE CLIFF 厂 AND DIVIDING INTO RIVULETS (RESEMBLING GARMENT FOLDS, BLOOD VESSELS, VEINS OF ORE), THE GROUP, PARTY, FACTION, SECT, SCHOOL 派 ALSO SPLITS.

派

N2547
p'ai4
M4873
pài
to dispute
to send

DROPS — GROUP, PARTY, SECT, FACTION, SCHOOL — CLIFF R 27 — "RIPPLES" — ORE VEIN, PULSE, BLOOD VESSELS, HOPE J 517 — WATER R 85

HAI, (PAI); AGAMU, TO WORSHIP, TO PRAY, TO REVERENCE.

RAD 64 STROKE 8 JME 858

THE HAND 扌 WITH STRUNG 手 BEADS 三 WORSHIPS, PRAYS, REVERENCES 拝.

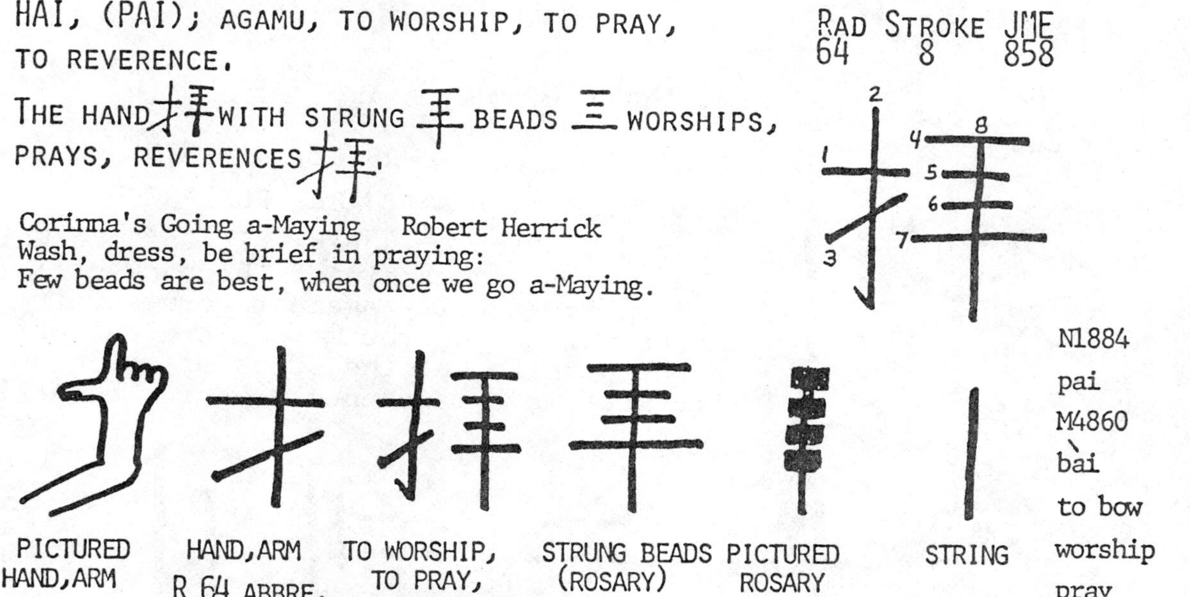

Corinna's Going a-Maying Robert Herrick
Wash, dress, be brief in praying:
Few beads are best, when once we go a-Maying.

N1884
pai
M4860
bài
to bow
worship
pray

PICTURED HAND, ARM — HAND, ARM R 64 ABBRE. — TO WORSHIP, TO PRAY, TO REVERENCE — STRUNG BEADS (ROSARY) — PICTURED ROSARY — STRING

The Eve of St. Agnes John Keats
Numb were the Beadsman's fingers, while he told
His rosary, and while his frosted breath,
Like pious incense from a censer old,
Seemed taking flight for heaven, without a death,
Past the sweet Virgin's picture, while his prayer he saith.

Buddhist priests wear a string of one-hundred-and-eight beads used in counting read chapters of a sutra, etc.

JME 859 STROKE 5 RAD 94

HAN, (PAN), TO COMMIT, TO VIOLATE, TO ASSAULT, TO RAPE.

TO COMMIT, TO VIOLATE, TO ASSAULT, TO RAPE IS THE SEAL, MARK 㔾 OF A DOG 犭.

And yet note the human stance of the dog below.

Romeo and Juliet William Shakespear
NURSE. Ah mocker! that's the dog's name;
R is for the ---

犯

N2869
fan4
M1779
fàn
transgress
offend
violate

犬 DOG R 94 J 66

PICTURED DOG, ANIMAL

犭 DOG, ANIMAL R 94 (TO LEFT)

犯 TO COMMIT, VIOLATE, TO ASSAULT, TO RAPE

㔾 SEAL R 26

PICTURED SEAL (CYLINDER)

R

Rrrrr! and Grrrr! are the growl of the dog.

JME 860 STROKE 7 RAD 18

HAN, (BAN), STAMP, SEAL.

THE STAMP, SEAL 判 WAS CUT 刂 INTO HALVES 半 (AS COUNTERPARTS MATCHABLE FOR PROOF).

Justus Doolittle Social Life of the Chinese
The wide right margin of the bank bill furnishes security against counterfeiting. Words written on the margin are cut off by a sharp knife and the stubs of the bank bill are kept in a reference book for comparison.

判

N673
p'an4
M4893
pàn
to judge
divide
to split
(in two)

牛 BULL, COW, OX J 62

PICTURED OX

半 HALF J 129

判 STAMP, SEAL

刂 KNIFE, SWORD R 18

PICTURED KNIFE, SWORD

East Asia: The Great Tradition Reischauer & Fairbank
Ming commercial arrangements with Japan followed the fashion for tributaries. A series of numbered paper passport tallies were torn from stub books, and sent to the vassal ruler. The stubs were retained and verified at the port of entry against the numbered tallies. Thus a trade monopoly was maintained.

HAN, (PAN, BAN), PRINTING BLOCK OR PLATE, EDITION, PRINTING.

RAD 91 STROKE 8 JME 861

THE PRINTING BLOCK OR PLATE 片反 AND THE EDITION, PRINTING 版 WERE OPPOSITE 反 SIDES 片

版

板
WOODEN BOARD
J 305

The first edition of the classics engraved on wooden boards is dated in the year 952 A.D.
Huc & Gabet Travels in Tartary...

爿 LEFT SIDE R 90

片 RT.SIDE R 91

版 PRINTING BLOCK, " PLATE, EDITION, PRINTING

反 OPPOSITE, AGAINST, ANTI- J 492

厂 CLIFF R 27

又 HAND R 29

N2843
pan3
M4886
bǎn
printing block
type
edition

Inflation-caused satiric parody of Stephen Foster's Civil War song
We are coming, Father Abram: One hundred thousand more;
Five hundred presses printing us From morn till night is o'er.

HI, (PI), NO, NOES; INAMU, TO REFUSE, DECLINE.

RAD 1 STROKE 7 JME 862

THE MOUTH 口 IN NEGATION 不 (SAYS) NO, NOES REFUSES, DECLINES 否. JUST AS THE SCATTERING OF BIRDS IS BAD, NEGATION 不 FOR THE HUNTER.

否

PICTURED MOUTH

口 MOUTH

否 NO, NOES, TO REFUSE, TO DECLINE

不 NEGATION, BAD J 500

一 ONE J 1 (BIRDS IN LINE OF FLIGHT OR LEVEL MARSH)

(BIRDS SCATTERING)

N40
fou3
M1902
fǒu
not
if not
on contrary
to deny

Antigone Sophocles
TEIRESIAS: Upon my ancient seat of augury,
Where every bird has access, lo! I hear
Strange cry of winged creatures, shouting shrill
In clamor sharp and savage, and I knew...
The Gods no longer hear our solemn prayers...

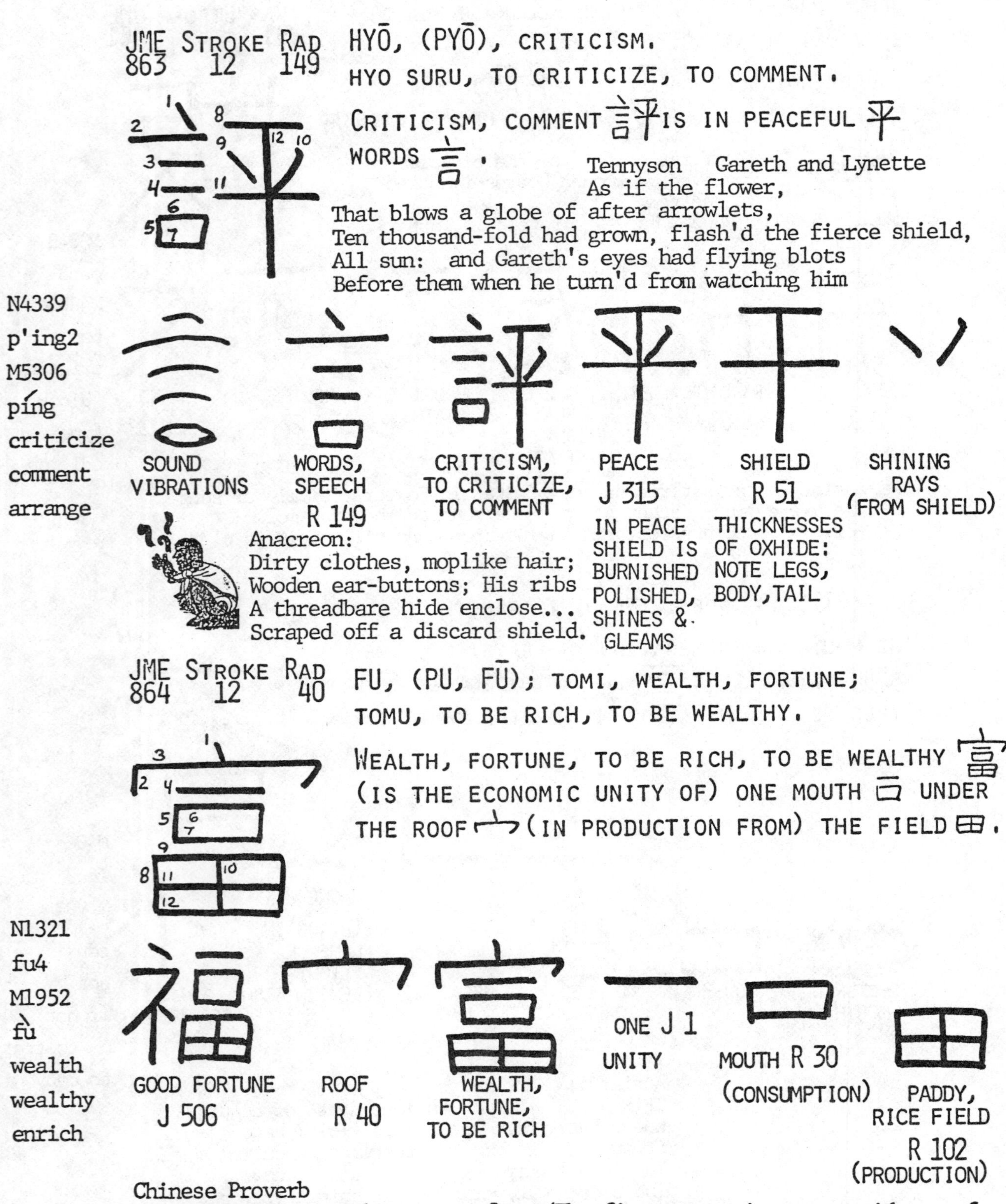

JME	STROKE	RAD
863	12	149

HYŌ, (PYŌ), CRITICISM.
HYO SURU, TO CRITICIZE, TO COMMENT.

CRITICISM, COMMENT 評 IS IN PEACEFUL 平 WORDS 言.

Tennyson Gareth and Lynette
As if the flower,
That blows a globe of after arrowlets,
Ten thousand-fold had grown, flash'd the fierce shield,
All sun: and Gareth's eyes had flying blots
Before them when he turn'd from watching him

N4339
p'ing2
M5306
píng
criticize
comment
arrange

SOUND VIBRATIONS — WORDS, SPEECH R 149 — CRITICISM, TO CRITICIZE, TO COMMENT — PEACE J 315 — SHIELD R 51 — SHINING RAYS (FROM SHIELD)

IN PEACE SHIELD IS BURNISHED POLISHED, SHINES & GLEAMS

THICKNESSES OF OXHIDE: NOTE LEGS, BODY, TAIL

Anacreon:
Dirty clothes, moplike hair;
Wooden ear-buttons; His ribs
A threadbare hide enclose...
Scraped off a discard shield.

JME	STROKE	RAD
864	12	40

FU, (PU, FŪ); TOMI, WEALTH, FORTUNE;
TOMU, TO BE RICH, TO BE WEALTHY.

WEALTH, FORTUNE, TO BE RICH, TO BE WEALTHY 富 (IS THE ECONOMIC UNITY OF) ONE MOUTH 口 UNDER THE ROOF 宀 (IN PRODUCTION FROM) THE FIELD 田.

N1321
fu4
M1952
fù
wealth
wealthy
enrich

GOOD FORTUNE J 506 — ROOF R 40 — WEALTH, FORTUNE, TO BE RICH — ONE J 1 UNITY — MOUTH R 30 (CONSUMPTION) — PADDY, RICE FIELD R 102 (PRODUCTION)

Chinese Proverb
Five Generations under one roof. (The five generations are evidence of sustained economic unity and prosperity).

FUKU, DOUBLE, TO REPEAT, MULTIPLE.

RAD	STROKE	JME
145	14	865

CLOTHING 衤 (IN NORTH CHINA) IS DOUBLE, REPEATED, MULTIPLE 複 (LAYERS). THE PERSON 𠂉 IS WALKING 夂 WITH HIS STICK ノ DOUBLY, REPEATEDLY, MULTIPLE 複 TIMES UNDER THE SUN 日.

Crow Indians took an entire elkskin for the front and another for the back of a woman's dress. Thus the skins are double, repeated. Clothing of cloth or hides may be worn in multiple layers. Cloth may be cut thus.

複

N4255
fu4
M1996
fù
to double
repeat
reiterate

復 RE-, REPEAT, TO RETURN TO, BE RESTORED TO J 710

衣 CLOTHING R 145

衤 CLOTHING R 145 ABBRE.

複 DOUBLE, TO REPEAT, MULTIPLE

𠂉 PERSON / 日 SUN — SUN R 72

夂 STICK IN HAND R 34

FINISHED ELKSKIN DRESS WITH SEWN YOKE & HANGINGS

FRONT A & BACK A' ELKSKINS YOKE B & B' HANGINGS C & D

FUN, FURUU, TO ROUSE, TO BE SPIRITED, TO BE ENERGETIC.

RAD	STROKE	JME
37	16	866

THE SHORT-TAILED BIRD 隹 IS SPIRITED, ROUSES (ITSELF), IS ENERGETIC 奮 FROM THE PADDY 田 INTO THE GREAT 大 (EXPANSE).

奮

N1184
fen4
M1874
fèn
to rouse
to spread wings
impetuous
determined

PICTURED GREAT

大 GREAT, BIG, LARGE R 37

奮 TO ROUSE, BE SPIRITED, BE ENERGETIC

田 PADDY, RICE FIELD

隹 SHORT-TAILED BIRD R 172

OLD KANJI OF SHORT-TAILED BIRD

One asked of Regret,
 And I made reply:
To have held the Bird,
 And let it fly.
Regret. Richard Le Gallienne

HEAVENLY FIELD CONSTELLATION

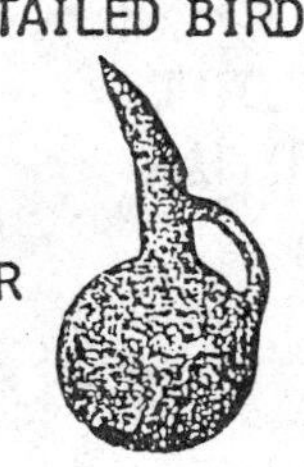

TROY SITE WATER JUG

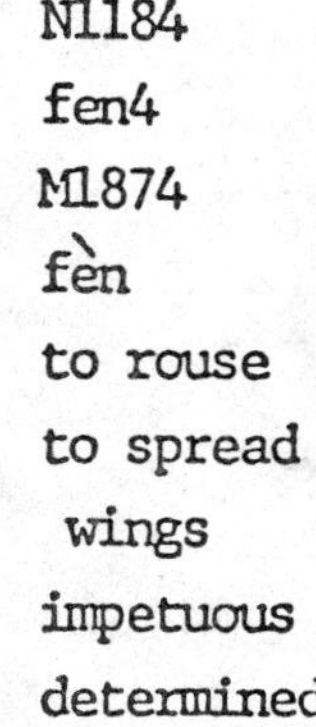

JME 867 STROKE 10 RAD 170

陛

HEI, STEPS (TO THE THRONE).

THE EARTH 土 STEPS 陛 (TO THE THRONE) ON THE MOUND 阝 ARE COMPARABLE 比.

N4988
pi4
M5081
bì
throne
steps
emperor

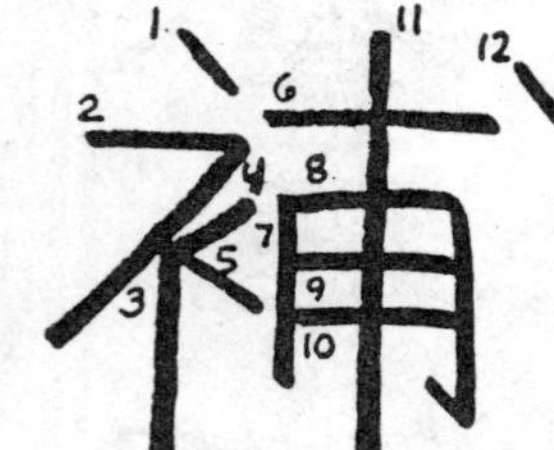

阝 陛 比 土 階

MOUND(S) PICTURED — MOUND R 170 — STEPS (TO THE THRONE) — TO COMPARE, RATIO, COMPARISON J 697 — EARTH, SOIL R 32 — STOREY (BLDG), FLOOR, GRADE J 361

JME 868 STROKE 12 RAD 145

補

HO, OGINAU, TO SUPPLY, TO COMPENSATE, TO SUPPLEMENT.

CLOTHES 衤 (WORN) FOR THE FIRST TIME 甫 SUPPLY, COMPENSATE, SUPPLEMENT 補.

European trade brought American Indian tribes the finest cloth. A special quality known as strouding was from the very first substituted for skins in making garments. The new material had a shape of its own and presented a new problem to the Plains dressmaker accustomed to the two-skin concept. (See J 847). A common solution was to take a rectangular piece of cloth, cut a hole in the middle, join the sides by triangular inserts, and add shoulder extensions. Often the skirt bottom was cut to conform to the old style. Thus the two-skin concept prevailed. Anthropological Papers of the American Museum of Natural History

N4242
pu3
M5372
bǔ
repair
patch
mend
help

衣 衤 補 甫 通 用

CLOTHES R 145 — CLOTHES R 145 ABBRE. — TO SUPPLY, COMPENSATE, SUPPLEMENT — FOR THE FIRST TIME, NOT UNTIL N 135 — TO GO ALONG, PASS THRU J 281 — TO USE, BUSINESS J 146

BO; HAKA, GRAVE, TOMB.

RAD 140 STROKE 13 JME 869

THE GRAVE, TOMB 墓 IS A PICTOGRAPH (OF THE DECEASED) WITH GRASS 艹 FOR HAIR, THE SUN 日 FOR A FACE, GREAT 大 FOR HIS FORM, AND THE EARTH 土 AT HIS FEET.

He is dead and gone, lady,
He is dead and gone,
At his head a grass-green turf;
At his heels a stone.
Hamlet Wm. Shakespear

墓

PICTURED DECEASED

艹 GRASS R 140

日 SUN R 72

墓 GRAVE, TOMB

大 GREAT, BIG, LARGE R 37

土 EARTH, SOIL R 32

N4027
mu
M4586
mù
tomb
a grave

Choric Song of the Lotos-Eaters Tennyson
To muse and brood and live again in memory.
With those old faces of infancy
Heaped over with a mound of grass,
Two handfuls of white dust,
shut in an urn of brass!

Massa's in de Cold Ground
Where de ivy am a creeping
O'er de grassy mound,
Dare old massa am a sleeping
Sleeping in de cold, cold ground.
Stephen C. Foster

HŌ, YUTAKA, ABUNDANT, FRUITFUL, RICH.

RAD 151 STROKE 13 JME 870

A VASE 豆 PICTOGRAPH FILLED WITH A BENDING, TWISTING 曲 MELODY 曲 OF ABUNDANT, FRUITFUL RICHNESS 豊 (A CORNUCOPIA).

A Prayer for My Daughter W.B. Yeats
It's certain that fine women eat
A crazy salad with their meat
Whereby the Horn of Plenty is undone.

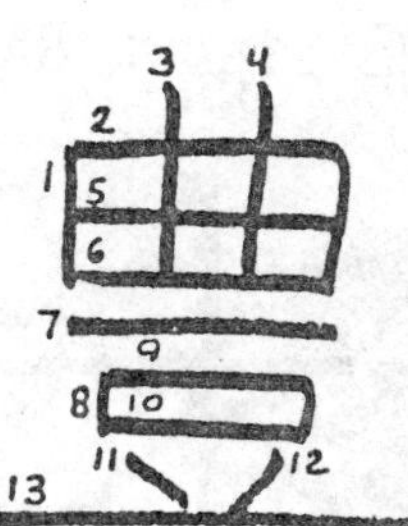

VASE

豆 VASE R 151 BEANS, PEAS N 4465

豊 ABUNDANT, FRUITFUL RICH

曲 MELODY, TO TWIST, BEND, TO TURN J 381

RICH, ABUNDANT, FRUITFUL

農 AGRICULTURE, FARMERS N 4658

N4466
feng1
M1897
fēng
abundant
fruitful
luxuriant

Die schonsten Früchte, frisch gepflückt
Trägt er zum grünen Festaltar
Und bringt, mit Blumen reich geschmückt,
Sie fromm als Morgen opfer dar.

Adams Opfer
Friedrich Hebbel

JME 871 STROKE 15 RAD 72

BAKU, BŌ, VIOLENCE, FORCE, CRUELTY, OUTRAGE.

UNDER THE SUN 日 THE WATER 氺 BRINGS UP THE DOUBLE 共 (SWOLLEN PICTOGRAPHIC CORPSE VICTIM OF) VIOLENCE, FORCE, CRUELTY, OUTRAGE 暴.

暴

John Barleycorn   Robert Burns

They filled up a darksome pit
With water to the brim;
They heaved in John Barleycorn,
There let him sink or swim.

N2157
pao4
M4957
bào
cruel
passionate
sudden
abrupt

日 SUN R 72

暴 VIOLENCE, FORCE, CRUELTY, OUTRAGE

共 BOTH, TOGETHER J 376

氺 WATER R 85

水 WATER R 85

散 TO FALL, SCATTER BE DISPERSED, BE SCATTERED, TO DISPERSE, MEDICINAL POWDER J 407

They laid him out upon the floor,
To work him further woe,
And still, as signs of life appeared,
They tossed him to and fro.

They wasted, o'er a scorching flame,
The marrow of his bones;
But a miller used him worst of all,
For he crushed him between two stones.

JME 872 STROKE 5 RAD 75

MI, (NOT YET, UNTIL NOW); MI, UN-, NOT YET.

A PICTOGRAPH OF THE ZODIAC SHEEP 未 WITH HEAD, FOUR LIMBS, BODY, TAIL, AND BILATERAL TEATS WHO IS NOT YET, UNTIL NOW 未 BRED.

未

The existence of a pair of mammae is a generic character in the genus Ovis as well as in several allied forms; nevertheless, "this character is not absolutely constant even among the true and proper sheep..."
Animals and Plants Under Domestication   Charles Darwin
with quote from Journal of the Asiatic Society of Bengal

N179
wei4
M7114
wèi
not yet
not
not being

養 TO BRING UP, ADOPT, REAR, NOURISH J 731

羊 SHEEP R 123

未 HEAD, FORELEG, BODY, HINDLEG, TEAT, TAIL — ZODIAC SHEEP, NOT YET, STILL, UN-

TEATS AS LEGS ON BOWLS ARE WORLD-WIDE

味 TASTE, RELISH, EXPERIENCE J 516

妹 YNGR. SISTER J 319

A young thing an' canna leave her mither.

A certain operation peculiar to this country is likewise performed upon the woman, namely the artificial lengthening of the labia until they are very like the teats of a she-goat...men are said to enjoy handling the long projections...It is properly said, "There can be no pleasurable Venus without 'Tu' (those parts).   The History of Dahomey   A. Dalzel

MEI, ALLIANCE, TO PLEDGE.

RAD 108 STROKE 13 JME 873

THE SUN 日 AND THE MOON 月 GODS WITNESS THE ALLIANCE, PLEDGE 盟 MADE OVER THE BOWL 皿 (OF LIQUOR OR BLOOD).

To swear by the sun and by the moon over the sacrifice of wine or blood to be allies, or to be allies as long as the sun and moon shall endure. The sun and moon are strange or unlikely allies. In China, the sun represented the Ming and the moon the Manchus who founded the Ch'ing Dynasty.

盟

N3119
meng2
M4426
méng
oath
alliance
contract
to swear

血	皿	日	盟	月
BLOOD J 389	BOWL, DISH R 108	SUN J 72	ALLIANCE, TO PLEDGE	MOON J 74

Somewhat like Pachy and Jenny bundling vertically in the Washington YMCA restroom after a visit to a local bar.

True it is that politics makes strange bedfellows.
My Summer in a Garden Charles Dudley Warner

YAKU, TRANSLATION; WAKE, MEANING, REASON, CIRCUMSTANCES; YAKU SURU, TO TRANSLATE.

RAD 149 STROKE 11 JME 874

TRANSLATION, MEANING, REASON, CIRCUMSTANCES, TO TRANSLATE 訳 IS THE MEASURE 尺 OF WORDS 言.

The Aran Islands John Millington Synge
A translation is no translation unless it will give you the music (measure) of a poem along with the words...

訳

N4327
i4
M3064
yì
explain
interpret
translate

言	言	訳	尺	尺	釈
SOUND VIBRATIONS	SPEECH, WORDS R 149	TRANSLATION, MEANING, REASON, CIRCUMSTANCES TO TRANSLATE	JPN. FOOT, UNIT OF LENGTH MEASURE N 1377	PICTURED JPN. FOOT	TO INTERPRET, TO EXPLAIN J 802

JME 875 STROKE 13 RAD 181

預

YO, AZUKARU, TO TAKE CHARGE OF, TO RECEIVE ON DEPOSIT, TO REFRAIN FROM, TO ENJOY IV; AZUKERU, TO DEPOSIT, TO ENTRUST WITH, TO LEAVE WITH TV.

THE PREVIOUS 予 (WEAPON, HALBERD 矛 ARCHETYPE) WAS DEPOSITED, ENTRUSTED WITH, LEFT WITH 預 THE CHIEF, HEAD 頁 WHO TOOK CHARGE, RECEIVED ON DEPOSIT & REFRAINED FROM ENGAGING THESE PREVIOUS 予 (WEAPONS, HALBERD 矛 ARCHETYPES).

N5123
yu4
M7603
yù
beforehand
prepare
make
ready

予 PREVIOUS J 525 (HALBERD STOCK: BEFORE USE HEADS SHAFTS SEPARATE)

矛 HALBERD N 3164

預 TAKE CHARGE OF, RECEIVE ON DEPOSIT, REFRAIN FROM, TO ENJOY,

頁 HEAD, PAGE OF BOOK R 181

頭 HEAD, BRAIN J 294

TERRACOTTA CONTAINER TROY SITE

JME 876 STROKE 11 RAD 150

欲

YOKU, GREED, AVARICE, DESIRE.

TO BREATH IN, GASP 欠 WITH GREED, AVARICE, DESIRE 欲 FOR A VALLEY 谷.

The Misfortunes of Elphin. Thomas Love Peacock
The mountain sheep are sweeter,
But the valley sheep are fatter;
We therefore deemed it meeter
To carry off the latter.

N4461
yu4
M7671
yù
to desire
wish
long
for
about to

口 MOUTH R 30 (AS OF VALLEY RIVER)

(MT. RANGES)

谷 VALLEY J 78

欲 GREED, AVARICE, DESIRE

欠 LACK, GAP, TO LACK, BREAK J 597

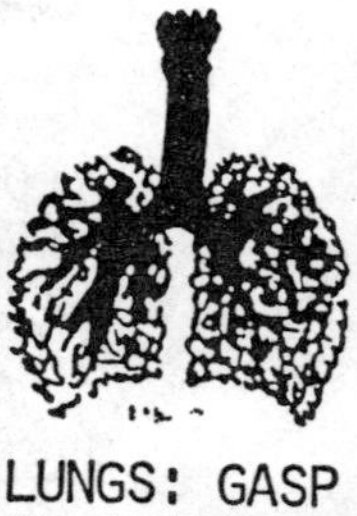

LUNGS: GASP OR INTAKE OF BREATH WITH GREED, AVARICE, DESIRE

Irish Melodies. The Meeting of the Waters. Thomas Moore
There is not in the wide world a valley so sweet
As that vale in whose bosom the bright waters meet.

RITSU, LAW, REGULATION.

THE LAW, REGULATION 律 BY THE PEN 聿 IS FOLLOWED BY PERSONS 亻.

But in these nice sharp quillets of the law,
Good faith, I am no wiser than a daw.
Hamlet Wm. Shakespear

RAD 60 STROKE 9 JME 877

律

N1608
lu4
M4297
lǜ
law
statute
rule

彳 PICTURE, TO STEP, FOLLOW R 60

律 LAW, REGULATION

聿 BRUSH PEN R 129

筆 BRUSH PEN, PEN J 701

FINGERNAILS CLAWLIKE FOR PAINTING AND CALLIGRAPHY

書 BOOK, TO WRITE J 92

The law is the true embodiment
of everything that's excellent;
It has no kind of fault or flaw,
And I, my lords, embody the law.
Iolanthe Wm. S. Gilbert

SOTSU, RITSU, RATE, PERCENTAGE, PROPORTION; HIKI IRU, TO LEAD, TO COMMAND (SOLDIERS).

IN SILK COCOON 幺 PRODUCTION 冫𠂉 UNDER DIRECTION 亠 THERE IS A RATE, PERCENTAGE, PROPORTION 率 (OF YIELD). IN LEADING, COMMANDING (TROOPS) 率 UNDER DIRECTION SENT BY HAND 十 (AS THE HAWK) THERE IS A (MORTALITY) RATE, PROPORTION, PERCENTAGE (AS WITH DYING SILKWORMS).

RAD 8/95 STROKE 11 JME 878

率

N319
lu4 shuai4
M5910
lǜ
to lead
follow
obey
all
generally

卒 SOLDIER, A PRIVATE, TO DIE J 457

亠 HEAD, COVER, AUTHORITY R 8

幺 SMALL, COCOONS R 52

冫𠂉 PRODUCTION

準 WATER LEVEL, RULE J 637

率 RATE, PERCENTAGE, PROPORTION, TO LEAD, TO COMMAND

十 HAND, PERCH

JME 879 | STROKE 11 | RAD 102

RYAKU, ABBREVIATION, OMISSION, ABRIDGEMENT, OUTLINE; RYAKU SURU, TO ABBREVIATE, TO OMIT, TO ABRIDGE.

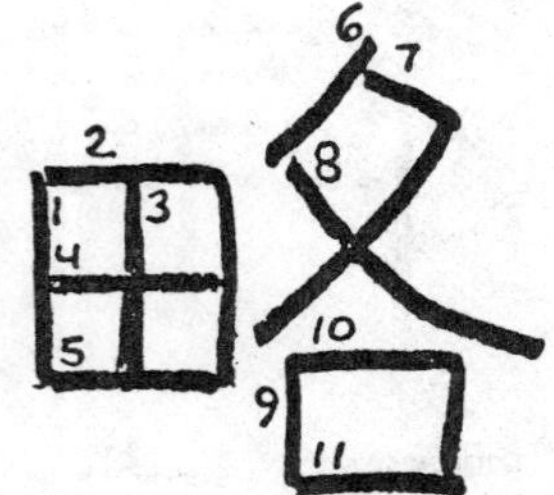

THE PERSON 夂 WITH A TOOL ノ ON THE STOOL 口 IN THE (DISTANT) FIELD 田 IS (SEEN) AS AN OUTLINE 略 (WHOSE DETAILS ARE) ABBREVIATED, OMITTED, ABRIDGED 略.

N3007
lioh4
M4075
lüè
slightly
a little
summary
outline
sketch

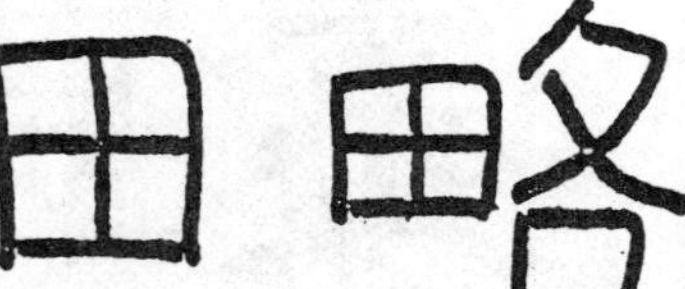

各 夂

PADDY, RICE FIELD — HEAVENLY FIELD CONSTELLATION

ABBREVIATION, OMISSION, ABRIDGEMENT, OUTLINE, TO ABBREVIATE, TO OMIT, ABRIDGE

EACH, EVERY J 568

STICK IN HAND R 34

(STOOL) MOUTH J 30

STATUS J 569

The old ladies of China use footstools only a few inches in height for greater comfort when weeding or otherwise working near ground level in the fields.

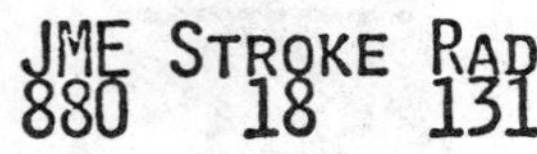

JME 880 | STROKE 18 | RAD 131

RIN; NOZOMU, TO FACE, TO MEET, TO FRONT ON, TO CONFRONT, TO RULE OVER.

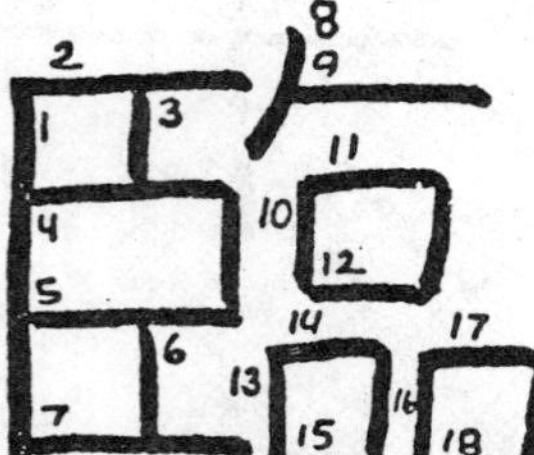

THE PERSON 𠂉 WITH GOODS, DIGNITY, ELEGANCE 品 FACES, MEETS, FRONTS ON, CONFRONTS, RULES OVER 臨 THE RETAINERS, SUBJECTS 臣.

The buttocks of the kowtowing, bowing, cringing, and fawning subject or retainer in the palace enclosure are naturally exaggerated as presented to the camera.

N3840
lin2
M4027
lín
descend
come in
near to
on the
pt. of

GRAPHIC BOWING RETAINER "fatass"

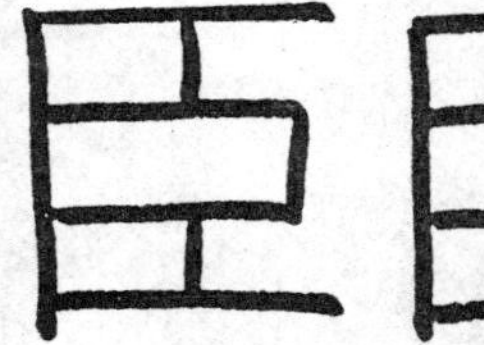

RETAINER, SUBJECT J 436

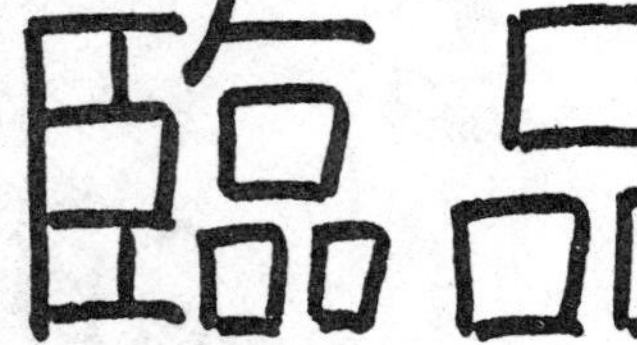

TO FACE, MEET, TO FRONT ON, TO CONFRONT, TO RULE OVER

GOODS, DIGNITY, ELEGANCE J 311

PERSON, MAN R 9

PICTURED PERSON, MAN

Subjects and retainers customarily brought goods of dignity and elegance as gifts when granted an audience with the superior who faced, met, fronted, confronted, or ruled over them.

RON, ARGUMENT, DISCOURSE, OPINION, ESSAY.

RAD 149 STROKE 15 JME 881

ARGUMENT, DISCOURSE, OPINION, ESSAY 論 ARE WORDS 言 AS IN TIGHTLY BOUND 亼 BOOKS, VOLUMES 冊.

Essays Francis Bacon
Men's discourse and speeches are according to their learning and infused opinions.

N4391
lun4
M4253
lùn
discuss
reason
argue
speak

SOUND VIBRATIONS

言 WORDS, SPEECH R 149

論 ARGUMENT, DISCOURSE, OPINION, ESSAY

亼 TIGHT, JOINED

冊 VOLUME, BOOK, BOOK COUNTER N 88

PICTURED TIED VOLUMES

龠 FLUTE, MUSICAL PIPES R 214

輪 RING, CIRCLE, WHEEL J 533

典 CEREMONY, CELEBRATION J 680

曲 MELODY, TO TURN, TO BEND, TO TWIST J 381

豊 ABUNDANT, FRUITFUL, RICH J 870

農 AGRICULTURE, FARMERS N 4658 J 491

HERALDRY AND THE EQUINOCTIAL PRECESSION

THERE IS AN APPARENT RELATIONSHIP BETWEEN THE MOVEMENT OF THE EARTH'S POLAR AXIS REVEALING THE EQUINOCTIAL PRECESSION AND THE LEGENDARY KILLING OF THE DRAGONS BY HEROES SUCH AS SIGURD, BEOWULF, ST. GEORGE, AND HERACLES. THE POLAR SHIFT FROM THE EYE OF DRACO, THUBAN, INDICATED SUCH A DEATH. THE EPIC OR FOLK HERO WHO USUALLY BECOMES THE RULER MOVES TO THE FULCRUM OF MILLENIA-OLD COATS-OF-ARMS ON WHICH HE IS FLANKED BY LIONS, DRAGONS, AND OTHER HERALDIC BEASTS OR MONSTERS. THE HERO IS OFTEN THE FOUNDER OF A DYNASTY. IN CHINA THE EMPEROR WAS THE DRAGON IN SYMBOLIC REALITY, AND THE PRECESSION CAN BE CAUSED BY THE STRUGGLE OF THE CELESTIAL PAIRED DRAGONS FOR THE PEARL OR MAGIC BALL CONTAINING THE MYSTERY OF SHIFTING POLAR AXES.

	0	10	20	30	40	50	
0	THE 214 RADICALS	10 儿 man, legs	20 勹 wrap, wrapping	3 STROKE 30 口 mouth, seat, aperture	40 宀 roof, crown	50 巾 cloth, width kerchief	0
1	1 STROKE 1 一 one, unity	11 入 to enter	21 ⼔ 匕 spoon, pointer corpse	31 囗 enclosure, boundaries	41 寸 inch, rule, pulse, standard	51 干 shield, dry, weapon	1
2	2 丨 up or down movement	12 八 eight, to divide	22 匚 basket, vessel, enclosure	32 土 土 earth, soil	42 小 small, little	52 幺 cocoons, tiny thread (top) young (left)	2
3	3 丶 locus, point ext of time & space	13 冂 borders, empty space	23 匸 cover, conceal	33 士 gentleman, scholar, samurai	43 兀 尢 crooked leg reasonable, weak	53 广 shelter, shed, lean-to	3
4	4 丿 support, horn, scyth	14 冖 cover, a cap	24 十 ten, perfect complete	34 夂 follow, end, walk, to go, hand &stick	44 尸 corpse, body	54 廴 long stride, stretch, lengthen	4
5	5 乙 tail of snake or dragon	15 ; 冫 ice	25 ト 卜 to divine, (plastron cracks)	35 夊 to walk, go	45 屮 sprout, plant, grass	55 廾 twenty legs, joined hands	5
6	6 亅 barb, hook, nail body	16 几 table, stool	26 卩 seal, joint	36 夕 evening, moon	46 山 mountain	56 弋 dart, ceremony	6
7	2 STROKE 7 二 two, duality heaven & earth	17 凵 open vessel	27 丆 厂 cliff	37 大 large, big, man	47 川 巛 river, stream	57 弓 a bow	7
8	8 亠 head, cover, directional	18 刂 刀 sword, knife	28 厶 cocoon, held, private	38 女 woman, girl, female	48 工 work, worker the square	58 彑 ⺕ 彐 boarhead, pighead	8
9	9 亻 𠆢 人 person, man, human	19 力 strength, power, energy	29 又 again, also rt. hand	39 子 child, son, seed, mouse	49 己 self, snake, personal	59 彡 hair, hairshape	9
	0	10	20	30	40	50	

	60	70	80	90	100	110	
0	60 彳 going men, to follow, short step	70 方 direction, side, square, person, way	80 毋 Do not! mother	90 爿 (as of tree) left side, left half	100 生 birth, life, grow	110 矛 spear, lance	0
1	4 STROKE 61 心 ⺗ 忄 heart, mind	71 旡 无 nothing, no, crooked heaven	81 比 比 to compare	91 片 (as of tree) left side, left half	101 用 to use, business	111 矢 arrow	1
2	62 戈 tasseled spear	72 日 sun, day	82 毛 hair, wool, fur, feather	92 牙 tusk, tooth	102 田 paddy, field	112 石 stone	2
3	63 戸 door, house, family	73 曰 say, speak	83 氏 clan, family	93 牛 cow, ox, bull	103 ⻊ 疋 animal ctr. cloth bolt,	113 礻 示 to show, inform	3
4	64 扌 手 hand, arm	74 月 moon, month	84 气 vapor, steam air	94 犭 犬 dog, animal	104 疒 sickness, disease	114 禸 内 track, footprint, pawprint	4
5	65 支 branch, hold	75 木 tree, wood	85 氵 水 water	5 STROKE 95 玄 dark, black, mysterious	105 癶 to shin, move legs	115 禾 grain (growing)	5
6	66 攴 strike, rap	76 欠 exhale, lack, owe, yawn	86 灬 火 fire	96 王 玉 jewel, jade	106 白 white, clear	116 穴 hole, cave, (loess) pit	6
7	67 文 literature, writing, pattern	77 止 stop, halt	87 爫 爪 claw, hand hoof, talon	97 瓜 melon	107 皮 skin, hide, leather	117 立 to stand	7
8	68 斗 capacity unit, Big Dipper	78 歺 歹 death, bad, evil, dried bones	88 父 father	98 瓦 瓦 tile, pottery	108 皿 dish, vessel	6 STROKE 118 ⺮ 竹 bamboo	8
9	69 斤 ax, wt. unit or unit of value	79 殳 to strike, hit, lance	89 爻 to mix	99 甘 sweet	109 目 eye	119 米 rice (polished but uncooked)	9

60 70 80 90 100 110

883

	120	130	140	150	160	170	
0	120 糸 long thread silk,string	130 肉 ⺼ 月 flesh,meat	140 艸 艹 ++ grass	150 谷 valley	160 辛 bitter	170 阜 阝 mound,hill (to left)	0
1	121 缶 water jar, earthenware	131 臣 retainer, subject, minister	141 虍 tiger	151 豆 bean,pea, vase	161 辰 dragon	171 隶 隶 to reach, (servant)	1
2	122 网 罒 ⺲ net	132 自 oneself, nose,from	142 虫 insect,bug worm	152 豕 pig,hog	162 辵 辶 ⻍ go fast & stop sudden	172 隹 short-taild bird	2
3	123 羊 sheep,goat	133 至 arrive	143 血 blood	153 豸 beast	163 邑 阝 city, village (to rt.)	173 雨 ⻗ rain	3
4	124 羽 羽 wings, feathers	134 臼 mortar	144 行 go,going	154 貝 shell, cowrie	164 酉 bird,sake	174 青 靑 blue,green, unripe,in-experienced	4
5	125 老 耂 old,aged	135 舌 tongue	145 衣 衤 clothing	155 赤 red	165 釆 distinguish beast claws	175 非 not,is not, negative	5
6	126 而 whiskers, and,but	136 舛 oppose, dancing legs	146 襾 西 west, a cover	156 走 to run	166 里 village,ri	176 面 face, front,mask, surface	6
7	127 耒 plow	137 舟 boat,ship	147 見 see, show	157 足 ⻊ leg,foot	167 金 gold,metal, money	177 革 tanned hide leather, skin,flay	7
8	128 耳 ear	138 艮 obstinate, hard,good	148 角 horn, corner	158 身 body	168 長 镸 long, headman, senior	178 韋 leather, to rebel	8
9	129 聿 brush pen	139 色 color	149 言 words, speaking	159 車 car, vehicle, carriage, chariot	169 門 gate,door	179 韭 leek,garlic onions	9
	120	130	140	150	160	170	

	180	190	200	210
0	180 音 sound, noise voice, tone	190 髟 髟 long hair	200 麻 麻 hemp	210 齊 level, even, Mr. Saito
1	181 頁 head, page	191 鬥 to fight	12 STROKE 201 黃 黄 yellow	15 STROKE 211 齒 tooth
2	182 風 wind, custom fashion, style	192 鬯 fragrant herbs, sacrificial wine	202 黍 millet	16 STROKE 212 龍 dragon
3	183 飛 to fly	193 鬲 tripod, cauldron	203 黑 黒 black	213 龜 tortoise
4	184 食 food, to eat	194 鬼 demon, devil, ogre, spirit	204 黹 needlework, embroidery, sewing	17 STROKE 214 龠 flute, fife
5	185 首 neck, head	11-STROKE 195 魚 fish	13 STROKE 205 黽 frog, toad	
6	186 香 fragrance, perfume, incense	196 鳥 long-tailed bird	206 鼎 tripod, 3-leg kettle	
7	10 STROKE 187 馬 horse	197 鹵 salt, salt earth	207 鼓 drum	
8	188 骨 bone	198 鹿 deer	208 鼠 rat, mouse	
9	189 髙 高 high, tall	199 麥 wheat	14 STROKE 209 鼻 nose	
	180	190	200	210

885

THE 214 RADICALS

The 214 radicals are used to construct kanji or characters much as words are formed from letters of the alphabet or chemical compounds from elements and radicals. Some of the radicals are complicated, some are seldom used, some have more than one form. Sometimes those on the right affect the sound of the kanji, and those on the left have more to do with meaning. Learn the kanji as separate building blocks, and try to understand how and why they belong in the character or kanji. The radicals are the keys to the kanji. The radical may have different meanings, but the meanings may be related or belong to a single concept. Often the radical will give you the clue to the meaning of a new kanji. The radical for tree may be on the left in kanji for various kinds of trees. This is also true for the radical on the left meaning gold or money and the kanji for different kinds of metals. Just as the study of kanji will explain much of Chinese and Japanese culture, so will the study of Japanese and Chinese history, social life, furniture, and archeology explain the forming of the kanji.

KANJI STROKE INDEX: LOOK UP THE KANJI IN THIS BOOK BY THE NUMBER OF STROKES TO FIND THE J-NUMBER GIVING THE LOCATION.

1	十 10	女 32	五 5	午 207	支 621	火 13	付 502	半 129	失 418	正 46	皮 307
一 1	**3**	子 31	仁 820	友 145	収 631	父 131	代 463	去 189	写 419	母 137	目 25
2	三 3	小 24	今 81	反 492	文 134	牛 62	令 736	古 70	左 18	民 518	石 44
丁 473	上 20	山 38	仏 711	円 48	方 138	犬 66	以 342	句 592	市 222	氷 498	示 622
七 7	下 21	川 39	元 68	天 119	日 11	王 49	兄 199	可 744	布 706	永 550	礼 337
九 9	久 582	工 71	内 489	太 269	月 12	欠 597	冬 120	史 411	平 315	玉 64	立 149
二 2	千 101	己 777	公 210	夫 501	木 15	予 525	出 90	右 19	広 211	生 34	台 272
人 30	口 27	才 217	六 6	少 93	止 220	**5**	刊 750	司 412	必 497	用 146	旧 759
入 125	土 17	万 320	分 133	引 156	比 697	世 263	功 605	四 4	打 460	田 40	処 811
八 8	士 410	**4**	切 99	心 95	毛 142	主 237	加 356	圧 544	未 872	由 325	号 215
刀 289	夕 98	不 500	化 163	戸 69	氏 620	仕 221	包 511	外 56	末 515	申 254	弁 715
力 148	大 22	中 23	区 591	手 28	水 14	他 459	北 139	央 554	本 45	白 37	辺 713

KANJI STROKE INDEX: LOOK UP THE KANJI IN THIS BOOK BY THE NUMBER OF STROKES TO FIND THE J-NUMBER GIVING THE LOCATION.

	6	再 788	在 613	曲 381	米 135	行 73	来 147	否 862	序 638	改 359	究 185	貝 169
灯 485	交 212	列 537	地 111	会 54	糸 83	衣 341	児 801	告 398	延 743	材 403	系 765	売 301
↓	件 598	印 348	多 108	有 523	老 541	西 96	兵 712	囲 343	弟 282	条 817	声 97	赤 35
	任 688	各 568	字 86	次 227	考 74	弐 854	冷 535	図 261	形 200	求 583	臣 436	走 105
	休 61	合 77	守 421	死 223	耳 26	**7**	初 428	坂 304	役 324	決 202	良 530	足 29
	仮 559	同 295	安 153	毎 318	肉 297	似 625	判 860	均 590	志 623	汽 60	花 43	身
	伝 681	名 140	寺 228	気 59	自 229	位 344	別 508	壱 740	快 566	災 789	芽 358	車 88
	先 33	后 780	州 424	池 110	至 796	低 677	利 528	孝 781	応 556	状 818	芸 388	近 195
	光 72	向 213	年 126	争 451	舌 827	住 244	助 248	完 571	我 745	男 109	見 67	返 316
	全 267	回 168	式 417	当 290	色 94	何 51	努 481	対 461	技 579	町 115	角 173	医 345
	両 336	因 548	成 439	百 130	虫 114	作 82	労 542	局 194	投 291	社 234	言 392	里 332
	共 376	団 672	早 104	竹 113	血 389	体 270	君 198	希 575	折 651	私 797	谷 78	防 718

KANJI STROKE INDEX: LOOK UP THE KANJI IN THIS BOOK BY THE NUMBER OF STROKES TO FIND THE J-NUMBER GIVING THE LOCATION.

7 CONT.	制 823	和 338	官 364	忠 842	東 121	注 277	育 347	**9**	品 311	思 84	昼 279
余 728	刷 405	固 393	定 474	念 689	板 305	泳 352	舎 629	乗 251	単 671	急 186	査 611
麦 128	券 768	国 79	実 233	性 645	林 150	版 861	苦 197	係 385	型 595	拾 425	柱 278
8	効 782	夜 144	居 586	所 246	果 560	牧 720	英 353	便 510	客 184	持 231	栄 549
事 230	卒 457	妹 319	届 852	承 639	歩 136	物 313	表 309	俗 834	宣 829	指 226	洋 526
京 63	協 377	妻 790	岩 178	招 814	武 708	画 167	述 809	保 716	室 232	政 646	活 174
使 224	参 616	姉 413	岸 177	拝 858	毒 686	的 478	金 16	信 437	専 830	故 778	派 857
例 737	取 238	始 225	幸 395	拡 747	河 561	直 472	長 116	則 666	屋 161	星 264	海 55
供 760	受 240	委 346	底 475	放 512	油 522	知 112	門 143	前 102	度 288	春 91	浅 655
価 563	周 632	季	店 284	明 141	治 468	空 65	雨 42	勇 524	建 391	昨 404	炭 274
具 383	味 516	学 57	府 503	易 545	法 513	者 235	青 36	南 124	後 208	昭 249	独 687
典 680	命 519	完 805	往 555	服 505	波 298	肥 699	非 698	厚 606	待 271	是 822	界 170

KANJI STROKE INDEX: LOOK UP THE KANJI IN THIS BOOK BY THE NUMBER OF STROKES TO FIND THE J-NUMBER GIVING THE LOCATION.

9 CONT	秒 499	軍 593	飛 493	兼 769	差 399	料 531	流 334	純 810	財 793	馬 127	問 520
発 303	紀 578	迷 724	食 253	勉 317	師 624	旅 335	浴 732	紙 85	起 181	高 76	基 755
皇 783	約 726	追 280	首 239	原 205	席 444	時 87	消 429	素 658	通 281	党 848	堂 486
県 203	級 187	退 839	点 285	員 349	帯 669	書 92	特 685	耕 784	速 453	11	婦 707
相 452	美 308	送 268	10	夏 52	庫 206	校 75	留 733	能 691	造 662	停 476	宿 634
省 640	胃 546	逆 758	修 633	孫 458	庭 477	株 749	病 310	脈 517	連 538	健 599	寄 576
研 204	茶 275	重 245	儀 702	宮 374	弱 236	根 216	益 742	航 396	郡 384	側 667	帳 470
祖 657	草 106	限 601	倉 659	害 362	徒 480	格 569	真 438	荷 165	配 299	副 709	常 642
祝 635	要 729	面 322	個 603	家 53	従 808	案 340	破 692	蚕 817	酒 422	動 296	康 608
神 257	計 201	革 746	倍 694	容 730	恩 558	帰 182	称 815	討 849	陛 867	務 722	張 675
秋 89	変 509	音 50	候 607	展 847	息 454	残 409	粉 507	訓 764	院 350	唱 430	強 192
科 164	負 312	風 132	借 420	島 292	挙 375	殺 614	納 856	記 180	除 813	商 431	得 850

890

KANJI STROKE INDEX: LOOK UP THE KANJI IN THIS BOOK BY THE NUMBER OF STROKES TO FIND THE J-NUMBER GIVING THE LOCATION.

11 CONT	望 514	産 408	経 596	貨 357	魚 190	報 717	景 386	港 397	税 826	着 276	買 300
情 643	械 360	略 879	習 426	責 649	鳥 117	場 252	晴 265	湖 394	程 846	落 330	貸 670
悪 152	欲 876	異 738	船 266	転 479	黄 214	富 864	暑 247	湯 482	童 487	葉 327	費 495
授 803	液 552	眼 754	菜 401	週 242	黒 80	寒 175	最 402	温 162	筆 701	衆 806	貿 719
採 791	深 258	票 703	著 843	進 259	**12**	尊 838	朝 118	満 721	等 484	補 868	賀 565
接 652	混 787	祭 400	術 636	部 504	備 700	就 807	期 183	無 723	答 293	覚 363	軽 387
推 821	清 440	移 547	規 577	都 287	創 832	属 835	森 41	然 450	策 795	評 863	遊 326
教 191	済 792	章 432	視 798	釈 802	勝 250	復 710	植 435	焼 434	結 390	詞 799	運 157
救 584	率 878	第 273	設 653	野 323	勤 762	悲 494	極 382	営 741	絶 828	証 816	過 562
敗 693	現 602	細 218	許 587	陸 529	博 695	提 845	検 771	番 306	給 585	象 663	道 122
断 841	球 188	終 241	訳 874	険 770	善 831	散 407	減 775	登 483	統 682	貯 674	達 465
族 455	理 333	組 103	貧 705	雪 100	喜 370	敬 766	測 668	短 466	絵 172	貴 756	量 734

KANJI STROKE INDEX: LOOK UP THE KANJI IN THIS BOOK BY THE NUMBER OF STROKES TO FIND THE J-NUMBER GIVING THE LOCATION.

12 CONT.	13	損 837	節 446	話 151	預 875	様 328	綿 725	酸 618	鼻 496	熱 490	賛 619
開 171	働 488	数 262	絹 772	誠 825	塩 354	歌 166	練 539	銀 196	15	確 570	輪 533
間 58	勢 441	新 256	続 456	豊 870	14	歴 536	総 661	銅 683	億 557	線 447	選 449
陽 527	勧 752	暗 154	罪 794	賃 844	像 664	漁 588	聞 314	銭 656	器 372	編 714	遺 739
隊 462	園 159	業 380	置 469	資 800	境 761	演 553	製 648	関 365	導 684	蔵 833	養 731
階 361	墓 869	楽 331	群 594	路 540	増 665	疑 757	複 865	際 612	敵 678	課 564	16
集 243	幹 751	準 637	義 580	辞 626	察 406	種 423	認 855	雑 615	暴 871	調 471	奮 866
雲 47	想 660	漢 572	聖 824	農 491	徳 851	穀 786	語 209	需 804	標 704	談 467	憲 773
順 427	意 155	照 433	腸 676	遠 160	態 840	算 219	誤 779	静 442	横 355	論 881	整 443
飲 351	愛 339	盟 873	解 567	鉄 283	慣 574	管 573	説 654	領 735	権 774	諸 812	橋 193
飯 696	感 176	禁 763	試 416	鉱 610	旗 371	精 647	読 123	駅 158	歓 753	賞 641	機 373
歯 414	戦 448	福 506	詩 415	電 286	構 785	緑 532	適 679	鳴 321	潔 767	質 628	燃 690

KANJI STROKE INDEX: LOOK UP THE KANJI IN THIS BOOK BY THE NUMBER OF STROKES TO FIND THE J-NUMBER GIVING THE LOCATION.

16 CONT.												
	積 445	薬 521	輸 727	館 366	厳 776	謝 630	織 644	観 367	額 748	験 600	鏡 378	競 379
	築 673	衛 551	録 543	燈 485	績 650	18	職 819	難 853	顔 179	19	願 368	議 581
	興 589	親 260	頭 294	17	講 609	曜 329	臨 880	題 464	類 534	識 627	20	護 604

CHINESE TIGER POSES LIKE A MAYAN JAGUAR

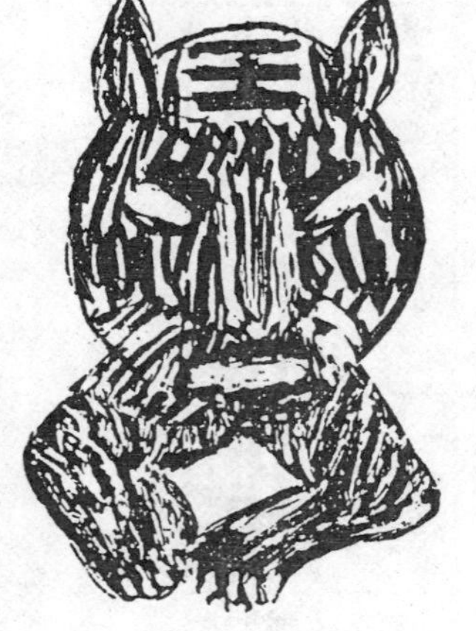

王

KING

J 49

MAYAN JAGUAR IN GREEN TILE

M.W.STERLING, LA VENTA'S GREEN STONE TIGERS

黄

YELLOW

J 214

ZODIAC KANJI TIGER UNDER THE CAVE ROOF

MAYAN GOD ITZAMNA CENTRAL TO SPLIT REP. OF BIRD OF HEAVEN

ADAPTED FROM COLOR PAINTING BY NGS ARTIST CHRISTOPHER A KLEIN, COPAN R.A.FASQUELLE,W.L.FASH,JR,PHOTOS BY K GARRETT;MAYA ARTISTRY UNEARTHED ©NATIONAL GEOGRAPHIC OF SEPTEMBER 1991, KIND PERMISSION GRANTED AUTHOR

abiru-CHŌ 893

ALPHABETICAL JAPANESE WORD INDEX FOR JME NUMBERS

(On readings are in capitals; kun readings in small letters).

CHŌ-gyakuni 894

ie-KAKU 896

KAKU-kisou 897

kita-KYŪ 898

899 ma-narau

SHIKI-SŌ 902

903 SŌ-TEI

TEI-uji 904

uke-yurushi 905

yurusu 許 587
yutaka 豊 870
yuu 結 390

ZAI 材 403
ZAI 在 613
ZAI 財 793
ZAI 罪 794
ZAN 残 409
ZATSU 雑 615

ZE 是 822
ZEI 説 654
ZEI 税 826
ZEN 前 102
ZEN 全 267
ZEN 然 450
ZEN 善 831
zeni 銭 656
ZETSU 舌 827

ZETSU 絶 828
ZŌ 雑 615
ZŌ 造 662
ZŌ 象 663
ZŌ 像 664
ZŌ 増 665
ZŌ 蔵 833
zosuru 蔵 833
ZOKU 族 455
ZOKU 続 456

ZOKU 属 835
zokusuru 属 833
zon 存 836
zonzuru 存 836
ZU 図 261
ZU 頭 294
zukuri 造 662
-zure 連 538
zuri 刷 405

DUAL FORCES CONTESTING SYMBOL OF SUPREMACY/ HEGEMONY: DUAL FORCES SUBSERVIENT TO CENTRAL HEGEMON.

TWIN CELESTIAL DRAGONS CIRCLING A HAN MIRROR CONTROL HEAVEN & EARTH NOTE AX/AXIS

VICTORIAN COAT-OF-ARMS: THE LION & THE UNICORN FOUGHT FOR THE CROWN IN THE ROYAL CIRCLE

FOOTPRINT OF BUDDHA

PEKING OBSERVATORY DRAGONS GRASPING CELESTIAL GLOBE (LI UNG BING)

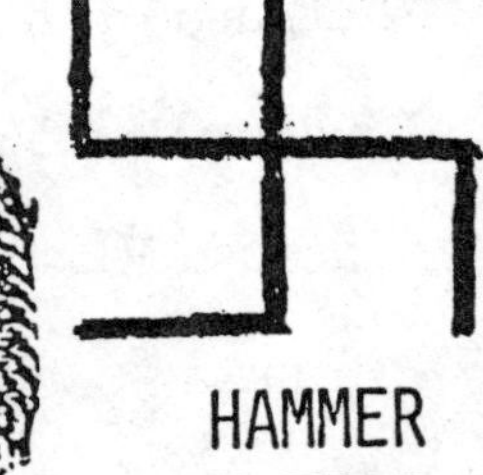

HAMMER OF THOR

KATAKANA						HIRAGANA				
ア a	サ sa	ナ na	マ ma	ル ru		あ a	さ sa	な na	ま ma	る ru
イ i	シ shi	ニ ni	ミ mi	レ re		い i	し shi	に ni	み mi	れ re
ウ u	ス su	ヌ nu	ム mu	ロ ro		う u	す su	ぬ nu	む mu	ろ ro
エ e	セ se	ネ ne	メ me	ワ wa		え e	せ se	ね ne	め me	わ wa
オ o	ソ so	ノ no	モ mo	ヲ o		お o	そ so	の no	も mo	を o
カ ka	タ ta	ハ ha	ヤ ya	ン n		か ka	た ta	は ha	や ya	ん n
キ ki	チ chi	ヒ hi	ユ yu			き ki	ち chi	ひ hi	ゆ yu	
ク ku	ツ tsu	フ fu	ヨ yo			く ku	つ tsu	ふ fu	よ yo	
ケ ke	テ te	ヘ he	ラ ra			け ke	て te	へ he	ら ra	
コ ko	ト to	ホ ho	リ ri			こ ko	と to	ほ ho	り ri	

Katakana and hiragana are used in Japanese writing to supplement the kanji. Katakana are used to represent sounds in foreign languages. Hiragana are used with the kanji to conclude verbs, when the meaning is clear, for postpositions, or when no word in kanji exists.

Katakana and hiragana are used in Japanese writing to supplement the kanji. Katakana are used to represent sounds in foreign languages. Hiragana are used with the kanji to conclude verbs, when the meaning is clear, for postpositions, or when no word in kanji exists.

907

JAPAN AN ATTEMPT AT INTERPRETATION LAFCADIO HEARN (1904)

OTHER FACTS IN MODERN EDUCATION SUGGEST EVEN MORE FORCIBLY HOW MUCH OF THE OLD LIFE REMAINS HIDDEN UNDER THE NEW CONDITIONS, AND HOW RIGIDLY RACE-CHARACTER HAS BECOME FIXED IN THE HIGHER TYPES OF MIND. I REFER CHIEFLY TO THE RESULTS OF JAPANESE EDUCATION ABROAD, A SPECIAL HIGHER TRAINING IN GERMAN, ENGLISH, FRENCH, OR AMERICAN UNIVERSITIES. IN SOME DIRECTIONS THESE RESULTS, TO FOREIGN OBSERVATION AT LEAST, APPEAR TO BE ALMOST NEGATIVE. CONSIDERING THE IMMENSE PSYCHOLOGICAL DIFFERENTIATION, --- THE TOTAL OPPOSITENESS OF MENTAL STRUCTURE AND HABIT, --- IT IS ASTONISHING THAT JAPANESE STUDENTS HAVE BEEN ABLE TO DO WHAT THEY ACTUALLY HAVE DONE AT FOREIGN UNIVERSITIES.

TO GRADUATE AT ANY EUROPEAN OR AMERICAN UNIVERSITY OF MARK, --- WITH A MIND SHAPED BY JAPANESE CULTURE, FILLED WITH CHINESE LEARNING, CRAMMED WITH IDEOGRAPHS, --- IS A PRODIGIOUS FEAT: SCARCELY LESS OF A FEAT THAN IT WOULD BE FOR AN AMERICAN STUDENT TO GRADUATE AT A CHINESE UNIVERSITY. CERTAINLY THE MEN SENT ABROAD TO STUDY ARE CAREFULLY SELECTED FOR ABILITY; AND ONE INDISPENSABLE REQUISITE FOR THE MISSION IS A POWER OF MEMORY INCOMPARABLY SUPERIOR TO THE AVERAGE OCCIDENTAL MEMORY, AND DIFFERENT ALTOGETHER AS TO QUALITY, --- A MEMORY FOR DETAILS; --- NEVERTHELESS, THE FEAT IS AMAZING. BUT WITH THE RETURN TO JAPAN OF THESE YOUNG SCHOLARS, THERE IS COMMONLY AN END OF EFFORT IN THE DIRECTION OF THE SPECIALITY STUDIED, --- UNLESS IT HAPPENS TO HAVE BEEN A PURELY PRACTICAL SUBJECT. DOES THIS SIGNIFY INCAPACITY FOR INDEPENDENT WORK UPON OCCIDENTAL LINES? INCAPACITY FOR CREATIVE THOUGHT? LACK OF CONSTRUCTIVE IMAGINATION? DISINCLINATION OR INDIFFERENCE? THE HISTORY OF THAT TERRIBLE MENTAL AND MORAL DISCIPLINE TO WHICH THE RACE WAS SO LONG SUBJECTED WOULD CERTAINLY SUGGEST SUCH LIMITATIONS IN THE MODERN JAPANESE MIND.

THE UNPARALLELED INVASION JACK LONDON (1910)

THE WESTERN NATIONS HAD FAILED TO TAKE INTO ACCOUNT THAT BETWEEN THEM AND CHINA WAS NO COMMON PSYCHOLOGICAL SPEECH. THEIR THOUGHT PROCESSES WERE RADICALLY DISSIMILAR. THERE WAS NO INTIMATE VOCABULARY. THE WESTERN MIND PENETRATED THE CHINESE MIND BUT A SHORT DISTANCE WHEN IT FOUND ITSELF IN A FATHOMLESS MAZE. THE CHINESE MIND PENETRATED THE WESTERN MIND AN EQUALLY SHORT DISTANCE WHEN IT STRUCK A BLANK INCOMPREHENSIBLE WALL. IT WAS ALL A MATTER OF LANGUAGE. THERE WAS NO WAY TO COMMUNICATE WESTERN IDEAS TO THE CHINESE MIND. CHINA REMAINED ASLEEP. THE MATERIAL ACHIEVEMENT AND PROGRESS OF THE WEST WAS A CLOSED BOOK TO HER; NOR COULD THE WEST OPEN THE BOOK. BACK AND DEEP DOWN ON THE TIE RIBS OF CONSCIOUSNESS, IN THE MIND, SAY, OF THE ENGLISH-SPEAKING RACE, WAS A CAPACITY TO THRILL TO SHORT SAXON WORDS. BACK AND DEEP DOWN ON THE TIE RIBS OF CONSCIOUSNESS OF THE CHINESE MIND WAS A CAPACITY TO THRILL TO ITS OWN HIEROGLYPHICS, BUT THE CHINESE MIND COULD NOT THRILL TO SHORT SAXON WORDS; NOR COULD THE ENGLISH-SPEAKING MIND THRILL TO HIEROGLYPHICS. THE FABRICS OF THEIR MINDS WERE WOVEN FROM TOTALLY DIFFERENT STUFFS. THEY WERE MENTAL ALIENS. AND SO IT WAS THAT WESTERN MENTAL ACHIEVEMENT AND PROGRESS MADE NO DENT ON THE ROUNDED SLEEP OF CHINA.

CAME JAPAN AND HER VICTORY OVER RUSSIA IN 1904. NOW THE JAPANESE RACE WAS THE PARADOX AMONG EASTERN PEOPLES. IN SOME STRANGE WAY JAPAN WAS RECEPTIVE TO ALL THE WEST HAD TO OFFER. JAPAN SWIFTLY ASSIMILATED THE WESTERN IDEAS, AND DIGESTED THEM, AND SO CAPABLY APPLIED THEM THAT SHE SUDDENLY BURST FORTH, FULL PANOPLIED, A WORLD POWER. THERE IS NO EXPLAINING THIS PECULIAR OPENNESS OF JAPAN TO THE ALIEN CULTURE OF THE WEST. AS WELL MIGHT BE EXPLAINED ANY BIOLOGICAL SPORT IN THE ANIMAL KINGDOM.

THE UNPARALLELED UNVASION Jack London (1910)

Best of all, from the standpoint of Japan, the Chinese were a kindred race. The baffling enigma of the Chinese character to the West was no baffling enigma to the Japanese. The Japanese understood as we could never school ourselves or hope to understand. Their mental processes were the same. The Japanese thought with the same thought symbols as did the Chinese, and they thought in the same peculiar grooves. Into the Chinese mind the Japanese went on where we were balked by the obstacle of incomprehension. They took the turning which we could not perceive, twisted around the obstacle, and were out of sight in the ramifications of the Chinese mind where we could not follow. They were brothers. Long ago one had borrowed the other's written language and, untold generations before that, they had diverged from the common Mongol stock. There had been changes, differentiations brought about by diverse conditions and infusions of other blood; but down at the bottom of their beings, twisted into the fibers of them, was a heritage in common, a sameness in kind that time had not obliterated.

ISBN 0-017880-03-X

Distributed by the University of Hawaii Press
Honolulu, Hawaii 96822

COUNT HERMANN KEYSERLING

....THE JAPANESE, OR RATHER, THOSE SOCIAL LAYERS OF THEM WHO COUNT POLITICALLY, ARE NOT ORIENTALS, IF THE CONCEPT OF THE ORIENTAL IS UNDERSTOOD TO INCLUDE SIMULTANEOUSLY THE ESSENTIAL QUALITIES OF THE CHINESE AND THE INDIANS; THE JAPANESE ARE NEARER TO US THAN THEY ARE TO THE CHINESE, AND TO THIS EXTENT THEY HAVE A DIVINE RIGHT TO EMULATE US. THEIR SIMILARITY TO THE CHINESE DEPENDS, FOR THE MOST PART, ON THE CULTURE IMPORTED FROM CHINA; ACCORDING TO THEIR TEMPERAMENT THEY ARE, LIKE OURSELVES, A PROGRESSIVE PEOPLE, WHICH, MOREOVER, THEIR HISTORY DEMONSTRATES FROM THE BEGINNING UP TO THE PRESENT DAY; THEY WENT TO SCHOOL, AS IT WERE, IN KOREA AND CHINA IN FORMER DAYS IN EXACTLY THE SAME SENSE AS THEY EMULATE US TODAY.

FOR THIS REASON, THE WESTERNISATION OF JAPAN CANNOT BE REGARDED IN THE SAME LIGHT AS THAT OF INDIA OR CHINA. WHEN I SAILED THROUGH THE INLAND SEA, I WAS NOT A LITTLE SURPRISED BY THE IMPRESSION OF ENTERING A WORLD ENTIRELY NEW TO ME, WHICH WAS DIVIDED BY A PROFUND CHASM FROM THAT OF CHINA; IT SEEMED TO ME AS IF I WAS BREATHING THE SAME ATMOSPHERE AS IN THE GREEK ARCHIPELAGO, THE ATMOSPHERE OF A DARING AND ADVENTUROUS SEAFARING LIFE. I FELT NOTHING OF THAT COSMIC CALM, THE MAJESTIC PEACE OF CHINA, NOTHING EVEN OF THE JAPAN WHICH LAFCADIO HEARN HAS DESCRIBED. THIS JAPAN, OF COURSE, EXISTS. BUT I MAY SAY TODAY THAT MY FIRST GENERAL IMPRESSION WAS CORRECT: THE ESSENTIAL QUALITY OF THE JAPANESE PEOPLE IS THEIR ENTERPRISING, EXPLOITING QUALITY, THEIR PLIANT, PRACTICAL ADAPTABILITY, NOT THEIR JAPONERIE.

THE JAPANESE IS TYPICALLY NOT A CREATOR, NOR IS HE AN IMITATOR, AS HAS BEEN ASSERTED GENERALLY --- HE IS ESSENTIALLY AN EXPLOITER IN THE SENSE OF THE JIUJITSU

912

FIGHTER: JIUJITSU IS THE VERY SYMBOL OF THE JAPANESE. WHAT ARE THE QUALITIES WHICH ARE REQUIRED TO BE A MASTER OF THIS ART? NOT CREATIVE INITIATIVE, BUT AN EXTRAORDINARY POWER OF OBSERVATION, AN INSTANTANEOUS UNDERSTANDING FOR THE EMPIRICAL SIGNIFICANCE OF EVERY EXPRESSION, AND THE ABILITY TO DRAW THE GREATEST POSSIBLE PRACTICAL ADVANTAGE FROM IT. IT REQUIRES TO THE UTMOST THAT PARTICULAR COOPERATION OF HEAD AND HAND WHERE ALL RECOGNITION LEADS INSTANTLY TO THE MOST APPROPRIATE REACTION OF MOVEMENT, IN WHICH ALL MEMORY EXPRESSES ITSELF AS AUTOMATIC ACTION.

ALL SPECIFICALLY JAPANESE CIVILISATION DEPENDS UPON THIS ABILITY, AND JAPANESE "IMITATION" IN PARTICULAR HAS THIS SIGNIFICANCE. THE JAPANESE DOES NOT REALLY IMITATE --- HE DERIVES AN ADVANTAGE, JUST AS THE WRESTLER DOES FROM THE MOVEMENTS OF HIS OPPONENT; HE DOES NOT COPY, BUT HE CHANGES HIS ATTITUDE; IT IS GIVEN TO HIM TO ENTER WITH INCOMPARABLE EASE INTO ALL ALIEN APPEARANCE, SO AS TO UNDERSTAND FROM WITHIN ITS PECULIARITY (NOT ITS ESSENTIAL NATURE!); HAVING THUS ENTERED INTO ORGANIC RELATION WITH IT, HE THEN EXPLOITS IT AS FAR AS IT CAN BE EXPLOITED.

THE FALLACY OF JAPAN BASHING NEWSWEEK: JANUARY 11, 1988

THE JAPANESE, IN FACT, HAVE BECOME EXPERTS IN THE ART OF JUDO ECONOMICS. BECAUSE OF THEIR HUGE PRESENCE IN THE UNITED STATES MARKET, JAPANESE COMPANIES CAN OFTEN DEFLECT PROTECTIONIST PRESSURE. INDEED, THEY CAN USUALLY RELY ON CUSTOMERS TO SCREAM WHENEVER SPECIFIC PROPOSALS ARE ENACTED THAT HURT JAPANESE SUPPLIERS. TWICE IN THE LAST NINE MONTHS, THE UNITED STATES HAS SOUGHT RETRIBUTION AGAINST JAPANESE FOR VIOLATIONS OF INTERNATIONAL TRADE. EACH TIME, THE ORIGINAL RETALIATORY RESPONSE WAS TONED DOWN WHEN IT BECAME CLEAR THAT IT WAS HURTING THE UNITED STATES AS WELL AS JAPAN.